PHYSICIANS AND MANAGEMENT IN HEALTH CARE

Edited by
Montague Brown, MBA, DrPH, JD
Editor, *Health Care Management Review*
and
Chairman
Strategic Management Services, Inc.
Washington, D.C. and
Shawnee Mission, Kansas

HEALTH CARE MANAGEMENT REVIEW

AN ASPEN PUBLICATION®
Aspen Publishers, Inc.
Gaithersburg, Maryland
1992

Library of Congress Cataloging-in-Publication Data

Physicians and management in health care / edited by Montague Brown.

p. cm.
Reprints of articles originally published in Health care management review.
Includes bibliographical references and index.
ISBN: 0-8342-0300-6
1. Hospital—physician relations. 2. Health services administration. I. Brown, Montague.
II. Health care management review.
[DNLM: 1. Health Facilities—organization & administration—collected works. 2. Health Facility Administrators—collected works. 3. Leadership—collected works. 4. Physicians—collected works.
WX 150 P5773]
RA971.9.P59 1992
362.1'1'068—dc20
DNLM/DLC
for Library of Congress
92-7147
CIP

Editorial Services: Ruth Bloom

Library of Congress Catalog Card Number: 92-7147
ISBN: 0-8342—0300-6

Printed in the United States of America

1 2 3 4 5

Contents

vii Preface
MONTAGUE BROWN

xi Acknowledgments

I Physician-Hospital Relations

3 **Hospital-Physician Relations: A Marketing Approach**
ROBIN SCOTT MACSTRAVIC
New developments are increasing the importance of hospital-physician relations. A marketing approach suggests ways to improve these relations.

15 **Managing Hospital-Physician Relations: A Strategy Scorecard**
HOWARD L. SMITH, RICHARD A. REID, AND NEILL F. PILAND
This article reviews several popular strategies designed to achieve mutually satisfying hospital-physician relations.

27 **Physician Goals: Impact on Hospital Performance**
SAMUEL C. WEBB
Three variations of two basic theoretical models contrast performance of for-profit and not-for-profit hospitals.

37 **HCA's Acquisition Process: The Physician's Role and Perspective**
STEPHANIE L. McFALL, STEPHEN M. SHORTELL, AND LARRY M. MANHEIM
Physicians play an active role in the acquisition process. A study showed that acquisitions improved the quality of the medical staff and their working conditions.

49 **Physicians' Ranking of Hospital Attributes: A Comparison by Use Group**
ANDREAS MULLER AND PATRICIA BLEDSOE
Because physicians play a central role in supplying hospitals with patients, it is important for hospital managers to learn more about physicians' preferences.

57 **The Valuation of a Medical Practice**
ROBERT F. REILLY
The valuation of a medical practice is important to the practice owners, employees, bankers, and others for many reasons, including taxation, transaction pricing, financing, litigation, and management planning. This article presents the three most common approaches to practice valuation.

II Organizational Issues

69 **The New Hospital Challenge: Organizing and Managing Physician Organizations**
STEVE McDERMOTT
Hospitals must develop close working relationships with physicians organized to effectively support managed care.

75 **The Uniqueness of a Professionally Dominated Organization**
DANIEL S. FOGEL
Twelve key points to help executives manage professional bureaucracies.

85 **The Secret of Medical Management**
JAMES E. ROHRER
A review of the research on group practices punctures the myth of physician autonomy.

93 **Building Physician Alliances for Cost Containment**
ROBERT B. GREIFINGER AND MAURA S. BLUESTONE
Physician alliances can help efforts to contain costs without hurting quality.

103 **The End of Autonomy? Reflections on the Postprofessional Physician**
STEPHEN J. O'CONNOR AND JOYCE A. LANNING
This article describes a reduction in autonomy in the medical profession and reviews potential impacts of this reduction on the profession, patients, payors, health care organizations, and managers.

III Practice Issues

115 **Physician Practice Profiles: A Case Study of the Use of Audit and Feedback in an Ambulatory Care Group Practice**
ROBERT L. BRAHAM AND HIRSCH S. RUCHLIN
A computerized audit and feedback program can be used to allocate costs to the provider generating the costs. This program has been shown to save money.

121 **Using Data Describing Physician Inpatient Practice Patterns: Issues and Opportunities**
ROBERT G. HUGHES AND DOUGLAS E. LEE
This article describes the kind of information on physician inpatient practice patterns that is becoming increasingly available, provides illustrations of how these data can be used, and discusses issues and potential problems with using the data.

129 Physician Satisfaction in a Major Chain of Investor-Owned Walk-In Centers
SUZANNE B. CASHMAN, CINDY LOU PARKS, ARLENE ASH, DAVID HEMENWAY, AND WILLIAM J. BICKNELL
This article describes physicians at a major chain of investor-owned free-standing walk-in centers and reports on their job satisfaction.

IV Team Building

143 Justice As a Prelude to Teamwork in Medical Centers
ANDRE L. DELBECQ AND SANDRA L. GILL
Based on data concerning personality propensities and values of physician leaders, it appears that due process is a more realistic leadership aspiration than cohesion.

151 Clinic Management Teams: Integrators of Professional Service and Environmental Change
SUSAN HOEFFLINGER TAFT AND JAMES A. PELIKAN
The clinic management team is an optimum management structure that can help a health care organization to maintain both flexibility and stability.

165 An Integrated Inpatient Management Model
FREDERICK A. CREIGHTON, ANNETTE M. BERNARD, AND LAURENCE F. McMAHON, JR.
The Integrated Inpatient Management Model attempts to address the issue of competition in clinical activity, while at the same time enhancing the academic health center's education and research roles.

175 Building a Team on a Medical Floor
BERNARD J. HORAK, JOAN H. GUARINO, CAROLYN C. KNIGHT, AND SANDRA L. KWEDER
This article describes a case in which trained facilitators used team-building techniques to address dysfunctional teamwork that was threatening patient care on medical units.

V Physician Executive Leadership

185 Physician Managers: Personal Characteristics versus Institutional Demands
HAVA TABENKIN, STEPHEN J. ZYZANSKI, AND SONIA A. ALEMAGNO
The issue today is how to make physicians more effective as partners in management.

191 **High-Performing Managers: Leadership Attributes for the 1990s**
MONTAGUE BROWN AND BARBARA P. McCOOL
Successful leaders work on a variety of challenging projects and are able to play multiple roles. Aspects of effective leadership are explored.

199 **Lessons Learned Hiring HMO Medical Directors**
DAVID J. OTTENSMEYER AND M.K. KEY
The survey discussed in this article sought to examine the attributes of effective HMO medical directors from the perspective of 30 experts who are employers of medical directors.

209 **Commitment and Discipline in Hospitals: Leadership Protocols and Legal Precedents**
SANDRA L. GILL, ERIC W. SPRINGER, AND ANDRE L. DELBECQ
Leadership protocols may be used to develop commitment to organizational goals and norms.

217 **The Entrepreneurial Physician**
RICHARD L. JOHNSON
Physicians at mid-career have growing concerns about what lies ahead for them. Drawing on the experience of hundreds of interviews, the author has created a character, Dr. Charles Evans, to describe some of the major possibilities being explored by physicians.

225 **Index**

231 **About the Editor**

Preface

OVERVIEW

Health Care Management Review seeks articles with insight into management issues dealing especially with the health care sector. Articles deal with management issues that span many sectors. For example, when *Health Care Management Review* began, hardly any articles on the use of the management discipline of marketing had been published in any health care journal. Over the years, articles on that subject have spanned the range of major marketing issues and their application to various subsectors of health care. Since the journal seeks a health care audience, all of our articles couple management theory and practice with some aspect of health care.

Not surprisingly, articles dealing with physicians show up in nearly every issue of *Health Care Management Review*. More articles on physicians can be anticipated as reimbursement control systems, managed care companies, group practices, networks and other managed arrangements involve physicians. As control structures, organizational arrangements, and direct employment of physicians grow, so, too, can we anticipate that physicians will increasingly become executives, subject to but controlling the structures that influence the practice of the profession. In a classic sense, we expect that as the "foreign" discipline of management seeks control over physicians, physicians will master the discipline of management in order to return ultimate control of medicine to its own practitioners—albeit, practitioners who are also masters of management!

The articles in this volume illustrate the many ways in which management disciplines can be brought to bear on issues related to physicians working in, with and for large-scale organizations.

PHYSICIAN-HOSPITAL RELATIONS

Hospital relations with physicians is a frequently discussed topic, so the few articles in this section by no means exhaust the subject in this volume. One marketing expert, Robin Scott MacStravic ("Hospital-Physician Relations: A Marketing Approach") lays out how his discipline can be used in hospital-physician relations. A group management academic and a group practice researcher outline the strategies used in improving such relations in "Managing Hospital-Physician Relations: A Strategy Scorecard" (Smith, Reid, and Piland). Webb, an economist, considers the profit and not-for-profit goals among physicians and hospital performance ("Physician Goals: Impact on Hospital Performance"), while an organizational theorist and other management disciplinarians consider the role of physicians in the hospital acquisition process of HCA ("HCA's Acquisition Process: The Physician's Role and Perspective" by McFall, Shortell, and Manheim). Muller and Bledsoe outline many of the attributes that attract physicians to hospitals in "Physicians' Ranking of Hospital Attributes: A Comparison by Use Group." All in all, there are many insights to be gained by executives and physicians about the bonding issues between hospitals and physicians.

The final article in this section, "The Valuation of a Medical Practice" (Reilly) deals with the issues of valuation of a medical practice. While this subject is not, strictly speaking, a hospital relations issue, it is our impression that the buying, selling, merging, and building of group and institutional practices does and will continue to be on the minds of most of our management executive and physician executive readers throughout the rest of this decade and beyond. The industry is consolidating and issues of valuation will grow, not lessen over time.

ORGANIZATIONAL ISSUES

This section deals more with organizational issues when physicians are at the core of the operation. Article titles often reach the core issue. McDermott writes about "...Organizing and Managing Physician Organizations." That challenge is clearly outlined and complemented by Fogel in "The Uniqueness of a Professionally Dominated Organization." Rohrer ("The Secret of Medical Management") explodes some myths of physician autonomy in hospitals while Greifinger and Bluestone ("Building Physician Alliances for Cost Containment") point out ways to build alliances with physicians that can hold cost down. Finally, O'Connor and Lanning ("The End of Autonomy? Reflections on the Post-Professional Physician") question whether or not physician autonomy in their professional duties is being undermined and whether and what we might want to do about the situation. All are thoughtful articles and all address the core issue of whether or not more or less control over practice can or should be exerted. Management tool availability notwithstanding, these issues require more than hard thinking by managers. Patients, physicians and society will get what they deserve and whether that should be a more or less controlled physician is a question being asked more and more.

PRACTICE ISSUES

Practice issues deals with profiles of practice in multiple settings. Braham and Ruchlin ("Physician Practice Profiles: A Case Study of the Use of Audit and Feedback in an Ambulatory Care Group Practice") deal with the use of audit data in ambulatory group practice. Hughes and Lee show how data systems make it easier to use data in managing physician inpatient practice. Cashman, Parks, Ash, Hemenway, and Bicknell ("Physician Satisfaction in a Major Chain of Investor-Owned Walk-In Centers") document physician satisfaction in a chain of investor-owned walk-in treatment centers. Each of the articles improves our understanding of how different kinds of data can be used for monitoring care systems to improve performance. Management tools can be applied much more widely in this arena.

TEAM BUILDING

Multidisciplinary teams in a variety of settings are discussed in team building. Starting out this section, Delbecq and Gill ("Justice As a Prelude to Team Work in Medical Centers") remind us that most of the traditional approaches to team building probably miss a critical component essential for physician team building—justice! Due process has been elevated to a very high degree in hospital relations with physicians, in law and in practice, as this article forcefully reminds us.

Team building takes many forms and follows multiple paths as seen in articles such as "Clinic Management Teams: Integrators of Professional Service and Environmental Change" (Hoefflinger Taft and Pelikan), "An Integrated Inpatient Management Model" (Creighton, Bernard, and McMahon) and "Building a Team on a Medical Floor" (Horak, Guarino, Knight, and Kweder). All of these efforts look at complex settings in tertiary institutions, situations which undoubtedly need greater assistance in coordinating the efforts of the multiple care givers and administrators involved. As managed care settings become larger, more and different kinds of care givers become involved, and the intensity of care available in hospitals escalates, this subject will become increasingly important.

PHYSICIAN EXECUTIVE LEADERSHIP

The final section deals with physician executive leadership. Tabenkin, Zyzanski, and Alemagno ("Physician Managers: Personal Characteristics versus Institutional Demands") addresses issues of personal characteristics and organizational demands to set when dealing with issues of task performance. Brown and McCool ("High-Performing Managers: Leadership Attributes for the 1990s") look at a wide range of high performing executives including physicians and set out some of the characteristics needed for health care enterprises in the coming decade. Ottensmeyer and Key ("Lessons Learned Hiring HMO Medical Directors") use a mailed questionnaire to help probe the attributes and characteristics of medical directors. Gill, Springer, and Delbecq ("Commitment and Discipline in Hospitals: Leadership Protocols and Legal Precedents") present an interesting case for focusing on medical leadership to gain the necessary commitment and discipline to enable hospitals to have sufficient control to carry out their legal and organizational responsibilities for medical practice. Finally, Johnson's delightful essay ("The Entrepreneurial Physician") on the pressures on the profession presents a compelling case for how and why even physicians wishing only to practice medicine will need to become more and more entrepreneurial as managed care and related payment systems eat away at the practice of medicine.

CONCLUSION

More physician-oriented articles are in the pipeline for publication. Having reviewed these articles again for use in this series, gaps appear in what we know about the development and career tracking for physicians who move into executive leadership. How do they interact with physicians after having crossed or straddled the line between management and profession? How do they relate to and compete with those trained exclusively in management? What kinds of roles are they playing in managed care, university settings and traditional hospitals?

We look forward to seeing more papers on such subjects and others of interest to our authors and readers.

—Montague Brown

Acknowledgments

Editors of volumes such as this get principal billing on the cover although as the readers quickly discover, the real feast is in the articles themselves. The real authors are those whose names appear on each article.

But it takes many people to make such articles possible. Before submission, authors typically have many others read and comment on their writings. When it arrives on the editor's desk, two or more outside reviewers are assigned to read and critique the article using criteria established by *Health Care Management Review*. These anonymous readers spend countless hours to provide insights and suggestions that often greatly strengthen the authors' initial efforts. Frequently, authors revise their articles. Once accepted at this level, Aspen editors copyedit the article to fit *HCMR* style requirements.

Thus, each article here represents the work of the named authors and the work of countless others who make substantial contributions to the final product.

This book is dedicated to the unpaid editorial board members and other reviewers who served *HCMR* during the period when these papers were originally published.

Dedicated to

In addition, *HCMR* wishes to thank the many ad hoc reviewers for their exemplary service in bringing out the best in the articles presented here.

PART I

PHYSICIAN–HOSPITAL RELATIONS

Hospital–physician relations: a marketing approach

Robin Scott MacStravic

Hospital–physician relations have traditionally been an important foundation to the mission and survival of hospitals. New developments are increasing the importance of this relationship. A marketing approach asks some simple questions and suggests specific proposals about how to strengthen and improve these critical relationships.

HCMR, 1986, 11(3), 69–79

Hospitals have always depended on physicians as the only licensed and appropriate source of medical diagnoses, prognoses, and therapy. Without them, the hospital would be simply a hotel for the sick, as it was in the middle ages. The physician is the chief marketing agent for the hospital. By and large, people first select a physician, and the physician then decides whether, when, and where the patient will go for hospital care.[1] Although the roles of consumers and third parties in hospital selection are no doubt increasing in importance, the physician is still the primary source of patients[2] and the determinant of what services will be used by each patient who comes to the hospital.[3]

TRADITIONAL REALITIES

The prosperous hospital has typically been the institution with the large, active, and loyal medical staff. Hospital administrators have long recognized this market dependence and incorporated it in their management approach. Legend has it that one administrator went so far as to volunteer to personally wave a fan for a high-admitter surgeon who was upset when the hospital's air-conditioning system broke down. While not all administrators automatically adopt such an obsequious approach to physician relations, they generally are fully cognizant of the importance of such relationships. Those who forget tend to lose their jobs.[4]

In addition to the marketing importance of physicians, the hospital shares an enormous malpractice risk with its medical staff. Recently, courts have held that the hospital may be responsible for what the physician does or does not tell the patient in the process of securing consent for treatment.[5] A case in Washington state actually included the hospital as codefendant in a suit over actions that took place entirely in the physician's office. The argument was that by according the physician medical staff privileges, the hospital was vouching to the community that the physician was qualified, and hence could be liable if the physician proved negligent.[6] While the court in

Robin Scott MacStravic, *Ph.D., is Vice President of Planning and Marketing at Health and Hospital Services in Bellevue, Washington. He is also a Clinical Associate Professor in the Graduate Program in Health Services Administration at the University of Washington, Seattle. He is the author of five books and over 100 published papers on planning and marketing health services.*

this case discharged the hospital as a codefendant, the argument may well recur.

If medical staff fail to act properly, the hospital can risk its accreditation status or lose out on its right to police its own clinical performance.[7] The morale of hospital employees, especially nursing staff, is greatly influenced by the quality of their relations with medical staff.[8] As nurses gain technical knowledge and skills and aspire to greater authority and responsibility in patient care, relations with physicians tend to become more strained. Since physicians enjoy virtually complete authority for patient care,[9] nurses can gain authority primarily at the expense of the physicians.

In the past, physicians have made life-and-death decisions such as who receives kidney dialysis treatment. Now Medicare coverage makes it possible for almost everyone to benefit. With the available life-preserving technology, both ethical and financial conflicts arise with increasing frequency when similar decisions have to be made. The solution to such dilemmas is dependent on the medical staff in whole or in part.

When the hospital needs the community for political support in a zoning or certificate-of-need decision, or for financial support in a fund drive, the institution often turns to the medical staff. The physicians' active support in talking to their patients, serving as public speakers in support of fund drives, and contributing their own funds to such efforts is yet another critical role that physicians play in the affairs of the hospital.[10]

A host of developments, some well under way, others barely beginning, will significantly affect hospital–physician relations in the future.

IMPORTANT DEVELOPMENTS

A host of developments, some well under way, others barely beginning, will significantly affect hospital–physician relations in the future. These can be examined under four categories: (1) market developments, (2) changing approaches to paying hospitals and physicians, (3) changes in the nature and extent of competition in medical care, and (4) ethical issues regarding what hospital and physicians do. Each individual development, as well as the combined effect of all, presents new challenges to hospitals and physicians in terms of maintaining good and preferably symbiotic working relationships.

Changing market conditions

Market developments include substantial changes in the people who need and use medical care as well as in the types and amounts of care they need and use. Significant demographic changes in the age and residences of the U.S. population brings significant impact on the hospital–physician market. As people age they tend to need and use more of most services. At the same time, efforts by government, insurance, and business groups[11] aim at reducing use of services, or shifting use toward the least costly alternatives.

Changing attitudes toward health include heightened interest in wellness or positive health with increasing skepticism about medical care and lowered respect for health care providers.[12] Interest in self-care is growing though its effect on use of medical care is unclear.[13] In any case, it is likely that insurance coverage changes that place more responsibility on the consumer for deductibles and copayment will significantly reduce demand for hospital and medical services.[14]

Another feature of the market, in addition to demand changes, is the supply side. Here the major developments involve significant increases in the number of physicians[15] coupled with foreseen decreases in the number of hospitals.[16] Both regulatory efforts and financial constraints threaten the viability of hospitals, especially in states such as New York and New Jersey. Business coalitions like those in Arizona[17] are pushing for reduction in the supply of providers or provision of services, apart from insurance efforts aimed at curtailing demand. The combination is certainly aimed at reducing the total market for medical care, coupling lower demand with fewer hospitals. Physicians would have to fend for themselves since their numbers cannot be reduced the way the number of hospitals can.

Another inevitable and observable consequence of increasing physician supply is the proliferation and distribution of specialists. Hospitals that once enjoyed franchises for specific services and markets by having the only qualified specialists in such services are finding that more and more of their competitors have the same specialists. Urban hospitals are competing more with each other in specialized services. Suburban institutions and even rural hospitals are striving to keep more inpatient and outpatient demand at home. With declining populations in large cities and expected declines in utilization, such proliferation represents a significant threat to the viability of referral center hospitals.

Changing payment programs

Changing approaches to payment represent a special and crucial factor in the market for medical care that affects both hospitals and physicians. Prospective payment for hospitals, whether based on diagnosis related group (DRG) structures or not, substantially changes the incentives that apply for hospitals while momentarily ignoring those that apply to physicians. When costs exceed prospective payments, hospitals tend to blame their medical staffs for overproviding care; physicians see the problem as one of inefficient management.[18] Hospital-applied pressures on physicians to reduce length of stay and use of ancillary services can threaten the physician's traditional prerogatives but also increase risk of malpractice liability for both.[19]

How hospitals evaluate each physician will shift from merely counting how many admissions and patient days each medical staff member contributes, to examining whether each keeps patient care costs within prospective payment limits. Physicians who appear to overorder may be denied staff privileges. No mechanism exists in most medical staff bylaws, however, for removing a physician who consistently produces financial losses for the hospital.[20]

The relationships between hospitals and their contract physicians are under significant pressure from the Tax Equity and Fiscal Responsibility Act of 1982 (TEFRA). This legislation seems bent on removing such physicians from hospital costs and in the process breaking some longstanding contract relationships.[21] Countering this trend is growing interest in salaried positions rather than traditional fee-for-service practice.[22] How many physicians will be tied to hospitals by contract or employee status in future is a factor that will greatly influence hospital–physician relationships.

The growth of health maintenance organizations (HMOs), individual practice associations (IPAs), preferred provider organizations (PPOs), exclusive provider organizations (EPOs), and other arrangements for financing health care is sure to create new pressures for physicians and hospitals.[23] Depending on the specifics of contracts, physicians are likely to reduce hospital use *and* the costs of hospital care. This may make them prudent buyers for their patients rather than agents in the traditional active, loyal medical staff mode.[24]

Growing competition

Growth in the number of physicians is creating significant competitive battles among physicians.[25] Physicians on the medical staff of one hospital compete with medical staffs of other institutions. If physicians on the same medical staff compete with each other and fight court battles over which specialists are qualified to treat which cases, the hospital can only be the loser, whatever the outcome.[26]

Physicians, and particularly physician-owned and operated businesses such as freestanding "emergency" centers, are increasingly competing with both hospitals and traditional private-practice physicians.[27] Should hospitals sponsor or otherwise support or even develop working relationships with such centers in light of their potential impact on hospital–physician relations?[28] Such centers can be sources of inpatient and ancillary referrals as well as competitors.

One dramatic change that has taken place in hospital–physician relationships as a consequence of competition is reflected in hospital-sponsored medical care programs such as primary care centers. Just ten years ago, these centers were being touted as significant innovations in extending hospital markets and responding to unmet needs.[29] At the time some doubts were voiced about the appropriateness of such developments,[30] but recently disaster stories regarding such programs have become common. The St. Francis Hospital, San Francisco, case is probably the best known,[31] but hospital efforts to be providers of care have produced negative reactions by local physicians in a number of states.[32]

Physicians have expressed concern that hospitals enjoy an unfair advantage in marketing health care services.[33] Longstanding traditional and professional attitudes tend to make physicians extremely reluctant to engage in advertising, for example.[34] Hospitals are adopting this marketing tool more and more.[35] Hospitals can afford to hire professional marketing staff, as they have done increasingly over the past ten years. Individual physicians and even most physician groups would be hard pressed to afford the kinds of marketing personnel that hospitals have access to.

Whether hospitals enjoy advantages in light of their high fixed-cost overhead and bureaucratic inflexibility is certainly open to question. A more critical concern, however, is whether hospitals can afford to compete with physicians. If the institution competes with its own medical staff, can it expect them to remain active and loyal? If the hospital competes with other physicians in the community, will not its medical staff end up losing referrals as a result? Although it is certainly in the hospital's best interests to persuade its medical staff not to develop programs that compete with hospital services (ambulatory surgery, imaging centers, radiation therapy, etc.), it is not clear what the hospital can or should do when physicians actually do set up competitive activities. In any case, being in competition with each other would certainly have an impact on hospital–physician relations.

Although many hospitals and physicians may view competition as inappropriate and undesirable,[36] the federal government is avidly promoting it. Federal Trade Commission efforts are increasingly focused on the medical care industry, and eliminating barriers to competition.[37] Lawsuits seem to come up daily over hospital activities that restrict the number of physicians it has on its medical staff.[38] Any cooperation among hospitals and physicians is likely to be subject to antitrust scrutiny.[39]

Ethical issues

One of the thorniest aspects of hospital–physician relations is the set of incentives present in prospective payment, whether based on government dictate or competitive bids. Such an approach to payment forces the hospital to protect and further its financial health by attempting to reduce the use of its services by each patient admitted.[40] Aside from the schizophrenic implications this has for the hospital itself, it means that physicians will be asked to minimize what they do for their patients. If physicians are to be informed about cost implications of their decisions through "economic grand rounds" or similar approaches, it might be argued that they are merely being asked to be prudent advocates for their patients. When physicians share an economic risk as in a PPO, EPO, HMO, IPA, or medical staff hospital partnership (MeSH) arrangement,[41] or are offered economic incentives to keep expenditures below prospective payment levels in specific cases, their role as patient advocates means conflicting interests.[42]

Physicians are inefficient managers of their patients' inpatient care if they schedule tests, surgery, or therapy in ways that extend stays or use truly unnecessary services. Improving their efficiency is a legitimate aspiration for the hospital and the public.[43] When incentives are applied in individual cases to reduce the use of services per se, however, patients have cause to question who is on whose side. On the other hand, if physicians have enormous capital investment in such businesses as ambulatory surgery centers, both patients and hospitals might question how physicians decide between an inpatient or outpatient approach to surgery, and between the hospital or the physician-owned center.[44]

We can hope that both hospitals and physicians are immune to economic incentives and will always place patient welfare above financial considerations.[45] But if this is true, DRG and other prospective payment systems, even if applied to physicians' services, would have little effect on the quality of care. Prospective payment systems would merely threaten the financial viability of hospitals and the economic status of physicians. To the extent that economic forces push both hospitals and physicians into more entrepreneurial roles as compared with service obligations, the public may wonder whether they are likely to be exchanging past overuse of health care for future underuse, and exchanging present cost cutting for serious future financial consequences.

One of the most disturbing aspects of prospective payment, especially as it begins to produce lower and lower payment levels in the interest of government and business cost savings, is the extent to which it puts hospitals and physicians at odds. In the past, the hospital has frequently asked physicians to do tasks that were not in their personal interests, such as attend committee meetings, complete paperwork, and participate in peer review programs. Quality of care and professional standards were always behind such requests, however. Prospective payment requires that hospitals ask physicians to reduce the use of services in the interest of preserving the hospital's financial health. No clear justification in terms of quality and probably some reduction in physician income underlie such requests.

Overall, the combination of demand and supply shifts, together with payment system changes, and increased competition presents a significant challenge to hospital–physician relations. Hospitals have always depended on physicians for patients, medical expertise, employee relations, risk management, quality control, and critical decisions on life and death, as well as community and financial support. Now they also depend on physicians to be prudent managers of patient care[46] and hope that physicians will act like colleagues rather than competitors. In light of this even greater dependence, it becomes even more necessary for hospitals to maintain systematic physician relations programs.

Given the already vital and growing importance of good hospital–physician relations, it makes sense for hospitals to explore all avenues in their search for the best ways of managing these relations.

MANAGING HOSPITAL–PHYSICIAN RELATIONS

Given the already vital and growing importance of good hospital–physician relations, it makes sense for hospitals to explore all avenues in their search for the best ways of managing these relations. Marketing offers a simple but potentially effective set of insights into this challenge, both in what it knows and what it does. The first contribution it can make is in using the exchange model to understand, predict, and influence relationships. This simple but basic concept asks that the parties to a relationship be described and analyzed in terms of what each wants from the relationship and can contribute to that relationship. In other words, what can each give to and get from the other as a basis for establishing and maintaining a good relationship.

What do hospitals want?

Clearly, every hospital will have its own idiosyncratic set of needs, expectations, and wishes relative to its medical staff. There are also likely to be a number of traditional and new expectations common to most situations. In addition to their traditional contributions as sources of patients, quality control, etc., the hospital will be turning to physicians for help in at least four new areas that result from a changing environment: acceptance of program reductions, admissions scheduling, efficient use of care, and noncompetition.

In the past, program reductions were usually dictated by the medical staff. If the hospital lost all or most of its obstetricians to a competing facility, it might lose its obstetrics program. If it attracted all the pediatricians in town, it could become the sole source of pediatrics. With prospective payment systems, hospitals will increasingly be forced to take long, hard looks at their programs. If a portfolio analysis[47] shows that one or more programs just cannot be self-supporting and would seriously drain resources away from other programs, the hospital will have to consider deleting the unsuccessful programs. Medical staff acceptance and support of such decisions will be needed to keep the side-effects of dropped programs to a minimum. Otherwise, hospitals may lose all their gynecology if they drop obstetrics or may suffer similar serious consequences.

Admissions scheduling has long been available to hospitals as a means of coping with reduced capacity.[48] It is also a potentially significant device for increasing productivity and efficiency by evening out workloads and increasing use of capital, facilities, and equipment.[49] With prospective payment, the ability to increase efficiency and reduce unit costs can mean the difference between survival and bankruptcy. Since admissions scheduling significantly reduces the choices and power of attending physicians and surgeons, the medical staff must accept it before it is implemented.[50] Here too, the medical staff will be asked to modify clinical behavior in the interest of hospital financial health with no advantages to them or their patients.

Asking physicians to be more efficient managers of care involves three areas: admission, care, and discharge management.[51] Wherever possible physicians should arrange for testing to be done prior to admission so as to minimize both length of stay and inpatient ancillary service use. Each inpatient stay should be closely managed to ensure that testing is ordered, completed, and reported quickly, that care is rendered promptly, and that the need for continued stay is evaluated regularly. Discharge planning should aim to ensure that patients are discharged as promptly as possible to whatever alternative form of care is appropriate to their needs.

Noncompetition will surely be the touchiest but potentially most significant area in which physician cooperation can help the hospital. If the institution already has significant investment in outpatient services such as diagnostic imaging, ambulatory surgery, and radiation therapy, it is bound to be hurt by physicians who develop competing freestanding alternatives. If the hospital is considering such programs, perhaps joint ventures with the medical staff can preclude competition.[52] Hospitals should be clear about the purpose of any joint venture, of course, and be prepared to yield as much as necessary to physicians.

What do physicians want?

Individual physician or medical staff desires are also bound to be idiosyncratic. Nevertheless, there appear to be a number of needs and wants that are common to many physicians and may apply in most situations. The hospital should regularly assess its own medical staff attitudes plus heighten its sensitivity to the expectations of individual physicians. Systematic market research and organizational accountability for hospital–physician relations are basic efforts in this direction.[53]

Physician expectations may generally be characterized as falling into three categories: professional, economic, and personal. These often overlap, but at least they provide a way of examining what physicians may be looking for in their relations with hospitals. Each hospital must consider how well it can afford to meet these expectations given the cost to the hospital of doing so. The ability to meet or even exceed existing expectations represents what the hospital has to offer its medical staff, that is, the degree to which it can promise satisfaction.[54]

Professional interests

Professional interests cover the motivations and expectations that characterize the physician as a uniquely trained provider of services. Perhaps foremost among these is physicians' wishes to have access to the facilities, equipment, supplies, and trained personnel to do all that each is trained and equipped to do. This includes having access to the latest technology and information, a fully equipped workshop capable of completely offering what each patient needs. The hospital should assist its physicians in fulfilling their professional obligations to their patients.[55]

In addition to the essential workshop opportunities the hospital can offer, it should be prepared to fulfill physician needs for continued learning and professional development, for networking with their peers, and for some basic freedom to manage their patients as they see fit.[56] This latter desire may obviously run counter to the hospital's responsibility toward quality of care and risk management as well as its financial interests under prospective payment.

Physicians wish to have confidence in hospital care, in the nursing and technical support services provided by the institution. This enables physicians to concentrate on their clinical and personal roles in patient care. It may translate into a desire for separate designated units offering specialized facilities and personnel unique to their specialty. If so, it can threaten the hospital's ability to maintain high occupancy, productivity, and efficiency. Given prospective payment, the cost to the hospital of providing separately operated units for many specialties may prove too expensive.

Increasingly, physicians are asking for and getting a more significant role in decision making by the hospital.[57] Such power sharing may be essential to protecting and furthering their professional interest.[58] It may also be used to protect their economic interests, presenting possibilities of antitrust legal action if other physicians consider themselves damaged by hospital decisions. The hospital must be careful to focus on the professional reasons for medical staff membership and privilege decisions[59] lest it become embroiled in economically motivated turf battles in which the only question will be how much it loses.

Economic interests

Physicians' economic interests are equally subject to protection, enhancement or damage by the hospital. Physicians wish to use their time efficiently, for personal and professional as well as economic reasons, and any help the hospital gives them in this regard is likely to be appreciated.[60] Medical office buildings on the hospital campus and efforts to reduce physician paperwork are likely to be welcomed.

On the other hand, physicians may not take as kindly to efficiencies that reduce their own incomes.

Another important contribution that hospitals make to their medical staff physicians lies in satisfying patients. Patient representatives may serve to enhance physician efficiency by intercepting and taking care of patient concerns. To the extent that patients are satisfied, physicians avoid having to deal with specific dissatisfactions, and run reduced risk of losing the patient to the competition or even of being sued for malpractice.[61] To the extent that outcomes meet patients' expectations and hospital services adhere to quality standards, the physician is similarly protected from litigation.

The reputation of the hospital and its ability to gain preferential status among patients and prospects can help the physician's own marketing efforts. The physician's perceived link to the hospital has been cited as at least one of the factors that people use in selecting a physician.[62] When the hospital offers a physician referral service and generates a number of requests by newcomers or people seeking a physician, it can directly increase the number of patients in each physician's practice.

The hospital also serves to enhance physician referral networking.[63] To the extent that the institution can further the quality of interphysician relations and increase the satisfaction of referral and referring physicians on its medical staff, it will benefit directly from the consequences of as well as improve its physician relations. Further research is needed into what physicians expect from each other as well as from the hospital.

Physicians, like most people, are interested in security for their families and in enjoying their retirement. In some cases, they are willing to become hospital employees in the interest of greater security,[64] although salaried status appears to be a minority aspiration especially among physicians who have built successful practices. On the other hand, the hospital would be well advised to employ more physicians in administrative positions, including such functions as director of medical education, medical director, director of physician relations, and chief of services.[65]

Personal interests

On the personal side, physicians, like most people, prefer warm, friendly working relationships with each other as well as with nurses, technicians, administrators, and hospital employees generally. The more time physicians spend in the hospital interacting with hospital personnel, the more critical such relationships become. It has always been important for hospitals to train, evaluate, and reward employees for the quality of their patient relations. The same applies equally well to physician relations. While the hospital may assign someone the responsibility for physician relations, it must be everybody's job if it is to be done well.

Physicians expect rather more than the ordinary degree of respect and are used to getting it. While public respect for physicians has remained high, compared with that for lawyers or politicians, for example, it has declined in recent years. As nurses and technicians gain increasing expertise in their own fields and acceptance of social hierarchies diminishes, affording physicians as much respect and deference as they expect is likely to be a problem for the hospital. The hospital should encourage both hospital employees and physicians to work on better and closer working relationships rather than devoting all its attention to encouraging employees to be more deferential to physicians.

The hospital should encourage both hospital employees and physicians to work on better and closer working relationships rather than devoting all its attention to encouraging employees to be more deferential to physicians.

Efforts to develop separate units or programs will add to physician's personal enjoyment of hospital relationships as well as conform more closely to their professional wishes. Freeing the physician from excessive paperwork can make hospital relations more enjoyable as well as efficient and professionally rewarding. Physicians, like most people, wish to enjoy a sense of control over their own time and obligations, and unlike most people, they are used to getting it. If the hospital asks physicians to surrender some control, as in admissions scheduling and case management, it should be prepared to offer something significant in return.

What hospitals are asking physicians to do in many cases is to alter their perception of a good physician.

In the past, physicians have been expected to do everything possible for the patients, applying all technology that might be beneficial, constrained only by the obligation to do no harm. In the new payment structures, they are asked to examine the cost-benefit and cost-effectiveness relationships of procedures, to become prudent shoppers, champions of cost containment and hospital financial health. This is clearly more than any one professional can do.

It can certainly be hoped that physicians will become comfortable with conservative use of expensive services[66] rather than force hospitals to cut expenses in the few areas subject to administrative control.[67] It is also hoped that physicians and hospitals will find an accommodation that enables both to carry out their obligations to patients while surviving new payment realities.

SUGGESTED MARKETING APPROACHES

Considering what hospitals and physicians want from their relations, and given the environmental context in which both function, some specific marketing approaches can be suggested. These include both traditional approaches to enhancing physician relations and some relatively innovative ideas that may be unfamiliar to many. It is likely that most of the traditional efforts will be continued, though some modifications may be necessary. Because the newer approaches have little if any history behind them, they are recommended chiefly to the more adventurous and innovative institutions.

Traditional perquisites and amenities

Hospitals have long provided their medical staff members with concrete demonstrations of their importance and value to the institution. Reserved parking, physicians' lounges, and deferential treatment are common examples. Showing favoritism toward the most active, loyal, and profitable members of the medical staff may not always occur but is certainly common.[68] When budget decisions, especially on capital purchases, are made, physicians have a strong voice in the matter, even when they occupy no formal position in the decision-making process.

In the interest of recruiting new physicians and retaining those already on staff, hospitals have developed medical office buildings, provided subsidies for practice development, financed vacations, offered preferential admitting power, and otherwise manifestly expressed their dependence on physicians. In the future, both tax exemption and cost considerations may reduce some of this activity, but physicians will probably enjoy "most-favored-person" status in hospitals for some time. Positions of power, including significant numbers on the governing board, will become more typical of hospital–physician relations.

Communication

One of the most important steps hospitals can take to improve physician relations is to develop more systematic communication networks between the medical staff and the medical community. Hospitals need regular, thorough inputs about and from physicians to keep track of their needs and attitudes, their management of patients in the hospital, and their satisfaction with the hospital experience. The institution can use physician communications to keep them informed about plans and developments, problems, and strategies that will affect both the physicians and the hospital.

Each hospital should include a systematic communications program as part of its physician relations effort.[69] Regular medical staff newsletters, meetings on an individual and collective basis, and special phone and mail communications are appropriate components of such a program.[70] Administrators and others involved in physician relations should schedule time to accompany physicians on rounds, demonstrating their commitment to enhancing physician relations as well as fostering closer communications.

Joint ventures

The term *joint venture* in regard to hospitals is becoming the same sort of instantaneous but indistinct watchword that "corporate restructuring" was a few years ago. The possibility of specific, cooperative joint physician efforts is not a new idea although its widespread popularity is recent.[71] Whether this should or even can include joint ventures in the sense of full financial partnership is another question, at least for nonprofit hospitals. Questions of private inurement under the Internal Revenue Service's 501(c)3 exemptions would necessarily arise in a conventional joint venture.

Cooperative efforts, on the other hand, are both more general and potentially less problematic. Cooperation is still accorded a certain respect, at least rhetorically, in health care. Hospitals, physicians, and the public can benefit from cooperation in many areas, even while public policy seems to favor competition. By working together on more endeavors, and especially by succeeding, hospitals can forge closer working relations with physicians.

Economic joint ventures such as PPOs, EPOs, or MeSHs[72] represent ways of sharing risks and benefits between hospitals and their medical staffs. Care must be taken, of course, to avoid designing the arrangement solely to meet the wishes of physicians and hospitals only to discover that it does not meet the expectations of the market.[73] All three joint ventures create new corporate organizations in which physicians and hospitals share decision making. The arrangements will provide different incentives depending on whether contracts are based on per-case or per-capita payments.[74] The MeSH approach is intended to be broader in scope and to include the possibility of similar contracts. It is intended also to develop new programs and enter new markets.[75]

It is difficult to predict the sorts of pitfalls and triumphs such joint or cooperative ventures might encounter. Traditionally, the distance between hospitals and physicians has been carefully preserved. Giving both identical financial incentives will certainly affect this distance; but it will also threaten the traditional physician–patient and even hospital–patient relationship. There is certainly some question as to whether a full hospital–physician partnership based on mutual financial risk and benefit is in the best interests of patients. Since both hospitals and physicians are committed to patient care as their reasons for existence, ethical and professional commitments will temper financial considerations.

Marketing assistance

Increasingly, hospitals are taking notice of what physicians do outside the walls of the institution and how well they do it. To be successful, to enjoy a strong niche in an increasingly competitive market, the hospital must ensure that its medical staff is successful. This may be accomplished through the traditional approach of carefully selecting staff members and cultivating good relations with them. It can also be accomplished by aiding physicians in their own practices.

For-profit hospital chains frequently if not universally offered practice development, management, and marketing assistance. National Medical Enterprises, for example, has a practice management division devoted to helping the medical staff members in all its hospitals become more successful.[76] Practice support services can include traditional start-up support but also extend to ongoing management assistance in such areas as billing and collections, and equipment financing. The hospital can also provide marketing assistance to physicians whenever they feel in need of support.

The simplest type of marketing support a hospital can provide involves market assessment: keeping track of changes in population characteristics (demographics), in people's beliefs and attitudes about health, the use of services and specific providers (psychographics), and in people's health-related behavior. Such information is worth gathering for the hospital's own strategic planning, program planning, and marketing but would also serve its physicians. Individual physicians and groups looking to locate or relocate a practice as well as physicians concerned about meeting their own patients' expectations can benefit from such marketing intelligence.

Hospitals can also support their medical staff through marketing communications. Where specialists are interested in strengthening or increasing their referrals, the hospital can aid in developing educational programs, visual aids, and other materials that will assist the specialists.[77] Publicizing a physician referral service should promote the practices of the medical staff. Gaining attention to the hospital's services through publicity or advertising should benefit the physicians responsible for those services. Generally, physicians feel more comfortable about the hospital promoting their practices than they do about promoting it themselves.[78]

In addition to promotional marketing designed to increase the practices of their medical staff, hospitals can assist physicians in retaining their current patients. Attitudes toward patients' personal physicians can be monitored along with patient satisfaction with hospital services. Identifying potential and operative satisfiers and dissatisfiers relative to physician care can benefit physicians directly and the hospital indirectly. Information may be gathered by monitoring published studies on the subject of patient satisfaction as well as through surveys of the local market.

The hospital may also offer educational training programs to physicians and their employees. In addition to covering the business side of operating a practice or clinic, the hospital can offer tips on marketing. A hospital that conducts periodic patient relations programs for its employees could easily include physician employees. This could augment the marketing success of physicians as well as strengthen the hospital's relations with the staff.

For the hospital to serve as a source of support and assistance to its medical staff, it must achieve and maintain high levels of trust among staff members. This is likely to be impossible if the hospital is competing with physicians to any significant degree. Each hospital faces a pivotal choice between competing through and competing with its medical staff. In light of the hospital's increasing dependence on physicians, the former seems by far the more appropriate choice.

REFERENCES

1. Goldsmith, J. *Can Hospitals Survive?* Homewood, Ill.: Dow Jones-Irwin, 1981.
2. Relman, A. "The New Medical-Industrial Complex." *New England Journal of Medicine* 303 (October 23, 1980): 966.
3. Young, D., and Saltman, R. "Prospective Reimbursement and the Hospital Power Equilibrium." *Inquiry* 20, no. 2 (1983): 20.
4. Holoweiko, M. "How Doctors Kicked Out a Hospital Board." *Medical Economics* 60, no. 14 (1983): 92.
5. Horty, J. "Informed Consent—M.D. or Hospital Duty?" *Modern Healthcare* 14, no. 2 (1984): 1.
6. Pedroza v. Bryant, 677 P.2d 166 (Wash. 1984).
7. "Medical Staff Chief Ousted." *Modern Healthcare* 13, no. 4 (1983): 10.
8. Hughes, G.D. "Can Marketing Help Recruit and Retain Nurses?" *Health Care Management Review* 4, no. 3 (1979): 61.
9. Cunningham, R. "What Are We Doing Here?" *Trustee* 33 (February 1979): 32.
10. Koger, D., and Perry, F. "Physician-Centered Marketing." *Hospital and Health Services Administration* 28, no. 3 (1983): 43.
11. "Paying Employees Not to Go to the Doctor." *Business Week* (March 21, 1983): 38.
12. "A Report Card from Your Patients." *Medical Economics* 60 (May 30, 1983): 8.
13. "Patient Education Seen as Cost Cutting Mechanism." *Hospitals* 58 (January 16, 1984): 64.
14. Newhouse, J., et al. "Some Interim Results from a Controlled Trial of Cost Sharing in Health Insurance." *New England Journal of Medicine* 305 (1981): 1501.
15. Ginzberg, E., et al. "The Expanding Physician Supply and Health Policy." *Milbank Memorial Fund Quarterly* 59 (Fall 1981): 508.
16. Holoweiko, M. "What a Crackdown on Surplus Beds Can Do to Doctors." *Medical Economics* 56 (March 3, 1980): 25.
17. "Arizona Firms Seek Hospital Regulation." *American Medical News* (November 25, 1983): 1.
18. McMahon, S. "Prospective Pricing Ushers in New Era in Hospital/MD Relations." *Hospital Medical Staff* 12, no. 8 (1983): 2.
19. Punch, L. "Pressures to Pare Length of Stay May Pose Liability Pitfalls for Hospitals." *Modern Healthcare* 13, no. 10 (1983): 70.
20. Palmisano, D., and Conrad, R. "DRG's, Bylaws and Staff Privileges: Is Confrontation Inevitable?" *Hospital Medical Staff* 12, no. 12 (1983): 10.
21. Robinson, M. "TEFRA Forces Hospitals to Rethink Contract Arrangements with Doctors." *Modern Healthcare* 13, no. 2 (1983): 48.
22. Friedman, E. "Salaried Doctors." *Hospital Medical Staff* 12, no. 8 (1983): 10.
23. O'Connor, M. "Preferred Provider Organizations." *Hospital Forum* 25, no. 6 (1982): 16.
24. Kodner, K. "Competition: Getting a Fix on PPO's." *Hospitals* 56 (November 16, 1982): 59.
25. Kaiser, L. "Survival Strategies for Not-for-Profit Hospitals." *Hospital Progress* 64 (December 1983): 40.
26. Hershey, N. "Medical Staff Appointment Decisions: When the Anti-Competitive Spirit Surfaces." *Hospital Forum* 26, no. 2 (1983): 49.
27. Punch, L. "Payment Changes Pit M.D.s vs. Hospitals." *Modern Healthcare* 13, no. 5 (1983): 38.
28. Brown, B. "Post Mortem on a Classic Battle: Doctors versus Hospital." *Hospital and Health Services Administration* 28, no. 5 (1983): 58.
29. Simpson, J. "The Ashland Plan: An Ambulatory Care Outreach Alternative for a Community Hospital." *Hospital Administration* 20, no. 3 (1975): 33.
30. MacStravic, R.S. "Hospital-Sponsored Primary Care—The Wave of the Future?" *Hospital and Health Services Administration* 21, no. 1 (1976): 60.
31. "Physicians Control Majority on Board: President Resigns." *Modern Healthcare* 13, no. 4 (1983): 10.
32. Rosenberg, M. "Your Hospital May Be Your Toughest Competitor." *Medical Economics* 59 (December 6, 1982): 164.
33. "Hospitals Edge over Doctors Isn't Fair: AMA." *Modern Healthcare* 13, no. 7 (1983): 41.
34. Starr, P. *The Social Transformation of American Medicine.* New York: Basic Books, 1982.
35. Lee, J. "Marketing Ensures Success of Maternity Care Programs." *Hospitals* 54 (December 16, 1980): 91.
36. Cunningham, R. "Not All Physicians Are Embracing a

New 'Corporate Sector' in Healthcare." *Hospital Medical Staff* 12, no. 9 (September 1983): 24.
37. Tabor, W. "The Battle for Hospital Privileges." *JAMA* 249 (1983): 526.
38. "Denial of Medical Staff Privileges Not Antitrust Issue." *Hospital News* 20, no. 2 (1984): 3.
39. Hyde v. Jefferson Parrish Hospital District, 686 F.2d 286 (1982).
40. Pellegrino, E. "Competition: New Moral Dilemmas for Physicians, Hospitals." *Hospital Progress* 64, no. 2 (1983): 8.
41. Ellwood, P. "When MDs Meet DRGs." *Hospital Medical Staff* 12, no. 12 (1983): 2.
42. Capron, A., and Gray, B. "Between You and Your Doctor." *Wall Street Journal* (February 6, 1984): 20.
43. Beyer, J. "Physician Involvement in Hospital Cost Control." *Hospital Forum* 26, no. 2 (1983): 17.
44. Wallace, C. "Alternative Healthcare Firms' Stock Is Hot." *Modern Healthcare* 13, no. 6 (1983): 60.
45. Kahn, L. "Meeting of the Minds." *Hospitals* 57 (March 16, 1983): 84.
46. Hoffman, P. "Physician–Administrator Collaboration Slows Hospital Cost Increases." *Hospital Progress* 64, no. 7 (1983): 59.
47. MacStravic, R.S., et al. "Portfolio Analysis for Hospitals." *Health Care Management Review* 8, no. 4 (1983): 69.
48. Student, K. "The Success of Admission Scheduling at Baker Hospital." In *Cost Control in Hospitals,* edited by Griffith et al. Ann Arbor, Health Administration Press, 1976, p. 342.
49. Griffith, J., and Chernow, R. "Cost Effective Acute Care Facilities Planning in Michigan." *Inquiry* 13, no. 3 (1977): 58.
50. Student, K. "The Failure of Admission Scheduling at Able Hospital." *Cost Control in Hospitals,* p. 327.
51. Young and Saltman, "Prospective Reimbursement."
52. "Partnership Allows High-Tech Purchase." *Hospitals* 57 (October 1, 1983): 33.
53. Tucker, S. "Introducing Marketing as a Planning and Management Tool." *Hospital and Health Services Administration* 22, no. 1 (1977): 44.
54. Levitt, T. "Marketing Intangible Products and Product Intangibles." In *The Marketing Imagination,* edited by T. Levitt. New York: Free Press, 1983, p. 95.
55. Wolinskay, F. "Why Physicians Choose Different Types of Practice Settings." *Health Services Research* 17, no. 4 (1980): 399.
56. Nathanson, C., and Becher, M. "Work Satisfaction and Performance of Physicians in Pediatric Outpatient Clinics." *Health Services Research* 10, no. 1 (1973): 17.
57. Noie, N., et al. "Survey of Hospital Medical Staffs—Part 1." *Hospital Medical Staff* 12, no. 12 (1983): 18.
58. Angermeier, I., and Booth, R. "Establishing an Appropriate Role for Physician Involvement in Hospital Departmental Operations." *Hospital and Health Services Administration* 28, no. 6 (1983): 59.
59. Hunt, K. "DRG—What It Is; How It Will Work and Why It Will Hurt." *Medical Economics* 60 (September 5, 1983): 265.
60. Koger and Perry, *Hospital and Health Services Administration.*
61. Sommers, P., and Thompson, M. "The Best Malpractice Insurance of Them All: Consumer Satisfaction." *Health Marketing Quarterly* 1, no. 1 (1983): 83.
62. Nathanson and Becher, "Work Satisfaction and Performance."
63. Ludke, R. "An Examination of the Factors that Influence Patient Referral Decisions." *Medical Care* 20, no. 8 (1982): 782.
64. Friedman, E. "Declaration of Independence." *Hospitals* 57 (July 1, 1983): 73.
65. Angermeier and Booth, "Establishing an Appropriate Role for Physician Involvement."
66. McClure, W. "Toward Development and Application of a Qualitative Theory of Hospital Utilization." *Inquiry* 19, no. 2 (1982): 117.
67. Young and Saltman, "Prospective Reimbursement."
68. Holoweiko, M. "Why Hospitals May Be Giving Your Colleagues an Edge." *Medical Economics* 56 (January 21, 1980): 85.
69. Galvin, J.M. "There's Lots of Talk about DRGs, But the Key Word Is 'Communicate.'" *Modern Healthcare* 13, no. 10 (1983): 148.
70. Koger and Perry, "Physician Centered Marketing."
71. Mullahey, R., and Glavas, J. "Want a DSA Facility? Try a Limited Partnership." *Hospital Medical Staff* 12, no. 10 (1983): 20.
72. "Aim PPOs at Businesses, Not Providers." *Modern Healthcare* 13, no. 4 (1983): 38.
73. LaViolette, S. "New Corporations Might Help Dispel Doctors', Hospitals' Mutual Suspicions." *Modern Healthcare* 13, no. 4 (1983): 36.
74. Kuntz, E. "Hospitals That Start Their Own PPOs Are Sharing Discounts, Survey Finds." *Modern Healthcare* 13, no. 10 (1983): 26.
75. "Medicine and Management: An Evolving Partnership." *Hospital Medical Staff* 13, no. 8 (1983): 21.
76. Turner, C. "The NME Practice Management Program." *Practice Perspectives* 1, no. 1 (1983): 1.
77. Sussman, G., and Gonzales, C. "Healthcare Marketing and the Regional Model." *Hospital and Health Services Administration* 28, no. 3 (1983): 62.
78. Shonyo, J. "Advertise Your Physicians." *Profiles in Hospital Marketing* (July 1982): 48.

Managing hospital–physician relations: A strategy scorecard

Howard L. Smith,
Richard A. Reid,
and
Neill F. Piland

Since the initiation of prospective payment, hospitals have been struggling to develop strategies that improve their prospects for long-run viability. Foremost among these strategy formulations have been efforts to build hospital–physician relations. This article reviews several popular strategies designed to achieve mutually satisfying hospital–physician relations.

Health Care Manage Rev, 1990, 15(4), 23–33

Hospitals face numerous challenges directly affecting their survival in the next decade.[1,2] Foremost is the need to formulate and implement distinctive strategies responding to prospective payment, managed care, and competitive pressures.[3,4] As many hospitals have discovered during the 1980s, physician relationships are extremely important in addressing these forces and maintaining organizational viability.[5,6] Not only do physicians serve as gatekeepers in delivering medical care, they also play a prominent role in deciding when and where patients receive hospital care. Although physician control of these decisions is diminishing due to factors such as alternative delivery models, multiple entry points into the patient care system, and rising consumer awareness, physicians still significantly influence hospital occupancy levels.

A hospital without a steady flow of inpatients faces fiscal crisis unless it has skillfully diversified its services, obtained a subsidy (e.g., a tax levy), or invoked some similar strategic advantage.[7] However, in the experience of many hospitals, a promising strategy is to attract and retain competent medical staff members while simultaneously eliciting their cooperation in making cost-effective service delivery decisions.[8] For most acute care providers, decisions on service utilization, length of stay, and discharge plans reside with the responsible medical practitioner. These decision-making privileges remain part of the unique purview of physicians.

Developing mutually productive and satisfying relationships between hospitals and medical staff members has become more difficult for and more critical to each party.[9] Hospital executives have less flexibility for cultivating these relationships due to constrained organizational resources.[10,11] As managed care plans proliferate, competition intensifies, and prospective payment expands, the challenge will become even more difficult.[12] Hospital executives and medical staff members remain seriously concerned about the implications of these trends.[13] When Medicare's prospective payment

---

Howard L. Smith, *Ph.D., is a Professor of Strategic Management at the Anderson School of Management of the University of New Mexico, Albuquerque.*

Richard A. Reid, *Ph.D., is Professor of Management Science at the Anderson School of Management of the University of New Mexico, Albuquerque.*

Neill F. Piland, *Dr.P.H., is Director of the Division of Health Services Research and Education at Lovelace Medical Foundation in Albuquerque, New Mexico.*

system was introduced, an optimistic atmosphere prevailed, implying that prospective payment could be constructively managed. Hospitals had many avenues for addressing prospective payment as well as competition.[14] Today, however, the future is less promising.[15] Some of the strategies that appeared to have merit are successful while others are ineffective.

At this point, it is worthwhile to revisit recent hospital responses to prospective payment and competition; especially the management of hospital–physician relations. The purposes of this article are to review the evolution of hospital responses to major environmental pressures and their implications for physician relations, assess which strategies have lived up to their promise of creating mutually beneficial linkages between hospitals and physicians, determine how strategies can be improved to generate better hospital–physician relations, and explore potential directions for hospital–physician relationships in the future.

EVOLVING HOSPITAL RESPONSES TO PROSPECTIVE PAYMENT

For the most part, changes in the health care environment have occurred gradually, allowing providers ample opportunities to develop workable responses.[16] Consequently, hospitals have been able to successfully plan for and manage their operations without being unduly affected by transitions in reimbursement, regulation, or the marketplace.[17] In recent years, the complexity and uncertainty of the hospital environment has increased significantly.[18] Initiated by major policy changes in third party reimbursement and the growth of investor-owned health care corporations, competition intensified throughout health care markets. These forces accentuated the importance of viable hospital–physician relations.

Figure 1 depicts the evolution of strategic hospital responses to prospective payment. Medicare's adoption of prospective payment in 1983 sent a clear message throughout the health care sector. Governmental and private third party insurers would reorchestrate their payment policies. This policy shift implied the following changes in hospital operations: decreased average length of stay, fewer inpatient diagnostic tests, service specialization to achieve economies of scale, procurement of advanced medical technology as a means to achieve cost savings and capture market share, reduction of excess capacity, adoption of sophisticated management control systems, and vertical integration among services.[19,20] Each of these changes in hospital operations affected physicians and their traditional practice patterns. Moreover, these changes produced growing tension between physicians and hospitals about several patient care issues including ad-

FIGURE 1.

THE EVOLUTION OF STRATEGIC HOSPITAL RESPONSES TO PROSPECTIVE PAYMENT

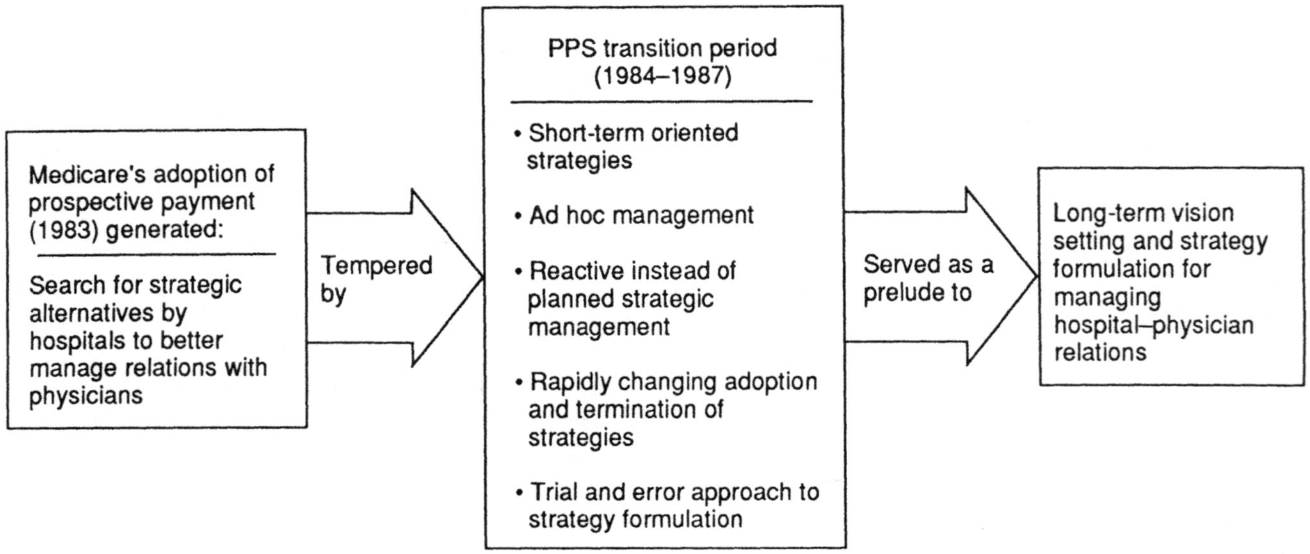

mission practices, preferred diagnostic and treatment regimens, and discharge policies.[21]

Hospitals recognized that physicians were the common denominator in controlling costs and enhancing revenues. As Figure 1 suggests, hospitals began to experiment with alternative strategies capable of helping them better manage physician relationships. Experimentation was tempered by the gradual introduction of prospective payment over a transition period. In theory, the transition period would allow new strategies to be slowly phased in, thereby minimizing disruption in the continuity and integrity of medical services. Conceptually, the transition strategy would attenuate disruptions in the delivery of patient care. In reality, it coincided with rising competition, which severely agitated hospital operations. Hospitals confronted two major challenges; not only did they need to control costs, but they also faced mounting pressures to fill beds and otherwise enhance revenues.

The end result of the prospective payment transition period was expanded strategy experimentation among hospitals. Countervailing prospective payment pressures such as the necessity to raise occupancy levels culminated in the usage of short-term–oriented strategies, ad hoc management, reactive instead of planned strategic management, rapidly changing adoption and termination of strategies, and a trial-and-error approach to strategy formulation.[22-24] During this dynamic transition period, prospective payment dramatically influenced the interactions between hospitals and physicians. In general, relationships migrated from harmonious associations toward a more competitive stance where each viewed the other more or less as a rival.[25-27] This legacy prevails at a time when hospitals must develop long-run plans that counteract prospective payment pressures and that promote viability.

THE HOSPITAL STRATEGY SCORECARD

A summary of hospital strategies predicted to improve hospital–physician relations under prospective payment is presented in Table 1. Beginning in 1983 and continuing throughout Medicare's transition phase, the hospital literature depicted a growing interest in strategy formulation. The strategies described in Table 1 are representative of the wide variety reported in the literature.[28,29] Hospital executives have focused primarily on these alternatives for developing more fruitful relationships with physicians.

Now that the Medicare transition period is history, it is useful to assess the success of various strategies in improving hospital–physician relations. To facilitate this evaluation, Table 1 presents a postprospective payment scorecard. The hospital strategy scorecard specifies the perceived effectiveness of each strategy (based on reports, discussions, analyses, and evaluations in the literature) and recommends revisions that could improve the strategies. Attention focuses on ascertaining how well the strategy recommendations in the preprospective payment and early transition phases ultimately performed in solidifying hospital–physician relations.

Emphasize quality medical care

From a hospital's perspective, the best-qualified medical staff must be attracted and retained. A high-quality staff contributes positively to quality medical care and enhances the hospital's image in both the community and the medical profession. There is no substitute for quality. An emphasis on quality medical care is widely acknowledged among a hospital's constituency even though tangible proof of this quality may be difficult to provide. An inpatient facility's reputation for quality is frequently associated with higher occupancy rates and lower financial risk from malpractice litigation.[30] These attributes serve to further enhance the hospital's reputation. Philanthropic contributions and endowments are thereby easier to acquire. These funds can be used to augment current operations or to serve special needs. In general, quality medical care attracts physicians of greater competence who enhance the institution's reputation.

A high-quality staff contributes positively to quality medical care and enhances the hospital's image in both the community and the medical profession.

From a strategy perspective, promoting high-quality medical care may produce an advantage for cultivating high service demand. Hospitals seeking fiscal viability by reducing the quality of patient care only increase their financial risk in the long run. Cutting costs by lowering quality standards may attract medical staff members who possess a similar perspective or who are unwilling to make sacrifices to ensure quality. Hence, hospitals, like any other business organization, must capture the best and the brightest of available medical

TABLE 1

A STRATEGY SCORECARD FOR MANAGING HOSPITAL–PHYSICIAN RELATIONS

Early predictions of strategies that may improve hospital–physician relations under prospective payment	Perceived effectiveness	Recommended revisions after prospective payment transition
1. Emphasize quality medical care	High	Identify and support distinctive services.
2. Initiate joint ventures with physician groups	Low	Joint ventures are not a panacea; therefore, it is necessary to develop solid business propositions based on well-researched and realistic market opportunities before pursuing joint ventures.
3. Expand hospital amenities to medical staff members	High	Promote attention to operational details that facilitate physicians' delivery of services; marginal increases generate high payoffs in cooperation and commitment.
4. Reassess medical staff privileges; selective elimination of high-cost providers	Low	Medical staff members producing high costs or poor quality of care are not necessarily difficult to identify (especially if a hospital has been consistently monitoring its medical staff). However, termination is a negative last resort. Hospitals can enlighten and educate abusers rather than terminating medical staff privileges.
5. Enhance hospital's image in the community	High	Stress quality of care, reputable medical staff, availability of medical technology, patient access, and guest relations. Incorporate these factors into a comprehensive marketing plan rather than just advertise desired image.
6. Develop organization cultures that promote a collegial atmosphere among physicians and hospital staff	Unclear	Physicians continue to view themselves as relatively autonomous practitioners and have resisted attempts to incorporate them into organization cultures. Stress opportunities for physician involvement and leadership.
7. Expand physician participation in hospital benefit programs and establish incentive compensation	Low	Tax and legal considerations have removed hospitals' flexibility to create innovative payment and commission arrangements; more flexibility exists when medical staff are on contract.
8. Include physicians in hospital governance and policy making	High	Physicians should share in the governance of hospitals. They need more access to board and management positions. Representation should underscore their contribution rather than offer a token appeasement.
9. Procure special equipment to support care delivery	High	Equipment leasing or purchase should be incorporated into the strategy of emphasizing quality care. Support physicians by providing tools and an environment that enhances their effectiveness.

practitioners if they are to prosper in a dynamic and competitive marketplace.

At the onset of prospective payment, significant amounts of rhetoric associated with high-quality medical care were expressed by hospitals. There is a big difference between espousing commitment to quality and implementing the appropriate tactics to guarantee its attainment.[31] The accuracy of predictions that hospitals would pursue quality-enhancing strategies was very high. However, many hospitals were unable to provide sufficient resources for or create programs capable of transforming their services into ones universally associated with unquestioned quality.

During the prospective payment transition, some hospitals adopted a realistic perspective of their situation.[32,33] Rather than thinking that quality medical care could be attained across the board in all service areas, reflective thinking by hospital executives encouraged them to pursue distinctive competencies in key service areas.[34] By setting realistic and attainable objectives for high quality in selective areas, there is a better prognosis that quality medical care will evolve no matter how difficult it may be to measure this concept. Service emphasis sets a foundation from which quality can be transferred or generalized to other service areas. This approach is consistent with prospective payment constraints. Not all services can reach a desired level of quality simultaneously; however, this does not mean that the quest should be abandoned.

Initiate joint ventures

Joint ventures represent a formal relationship between physicians and hospitals that unites the objectives of both parties while sharing risks and benefits.[35] During the evolution of prospective payment, considerable variation in these cooperative alliances surfaced, reflecting an era of innovation and experimentation.[36] Joint ventures can be either relatively simple in structure or very complex. For example, a group of obstetricians may contractually agree to lease an office building wing in a hospital to develop an on-site clinic. Alternatively, a corporation may be created between a hospital and a group of surgeons to provide patient diagnostic services utilizing a magnetic resonance imager. Each party would contribute a prescribed portion of the necessary capital for facility operation and equipment purchase while sharing proportionately in any surpluses generated.

There were many reasons underlying the growth of joint ventures between physicians and hospitals. The benefits include that

- diversification plans and practice patterns can be readily expanded or adapted to marketplace demands,
- the mix of third party payers can be more directly controlled,
- risks and rewards are shared,
- investment capital is accessed at reasonable cost, and
- patient care services can be readily expanded.

The major advantage in formalizing collaborative arrangements is the opportunity to design a less adversarial relationship (i.e., one in which cooperation is obviously a mutually beneficial proposition).[37]

Joint ventures were held in high esteem at the onset of prospective payment. However, as Table 1 suggests, a posttransition view provides an entirely different assessment. Hospitals and physicians have learned that joint ventures are not a panacea.[38] There is no substitute for seeking solid business propositions—not every good joint business proposal will perform positively in a given health care market.[39] Particularly critical is thorough implementation planning. Successful joint ventures do not happen spontaneously, but are built on insightful vision, judicious design, and prudent implementation. Therefore, neither hospitals nor physicians should view joint ventures as a fail-safe strategy for building a closer relationship. Admittedly, many joint ventures offer the distinct benefit of reinforcing hospital–physician relations. However, there are also more exceptions than were initially apparent. The end result is greater caution by both groups in proposing and sanctioning joint ventures.

Successful joint ventures do not happen spontaneously, but are built on insightful vision, judicious design, and prudent implementation.

Expand hospital amenities

Some hospitals have attempted to expand the level of amenities offered to physicians as a mechanism for improving relations.[40] As the strategy scorecard in Table 1 suggests, hospitals are continuing to benefit by accentuating the small-operating-level details that facilitate medical practice. The scope and nature of amenities is limited primarily by the creativity and imagination of hospital executives. The following are illustrative tactics for expanding physician-oriented amenities:

- implementation support for physician-initiated patient care innovations,
- highly trained clinical support staff for new therapeutic activities,
- specialized patient diagnostic and treatment equipment,
- special reserved parking spaces,
- comfortable physician lounge and locker room,
- private physician dining area or separate dining room,
- complimentary athletic or social club memberships,
- social events,
- seminars and retreats,
- practice management workshops, and
- professional financial investment consultation services.

Before dismissing these ideas as too simple to enlist cooperation from sophisticated professionals, it is relevant to realize that the scope and nature of these programs are open to definition.

For example, consider hospital sponsorship of an annual retreat for selected members of the medical staff and their spouses at a glamorous location. The purpose of the retreat might be to develop mutual understanding and respect on timely issues such as cost control or competition. Morning sessions might be allocated to information exchange and consensus-generating activities, with the remaining time devoted to social and recreational activities. By including a cross-section of the administrative staff, the hospital pursues mutual accord among administration and medical staff. An appreciation for alternative perspectives could emerge as differing viewpoints are communicated in an informal atmosphere.

Managing amenities provides a visible indication of a hospital's concern for physicians. These supportive efforts demonstrate a tangible willingness to treat physicians with dignity and respect and reinforce the partnership needed to achieve hospital productivity and patient census goals. The primary problem that hospitals encounter in providing the amenities is not a philosophical issue but rather, a pragmatic constraint. Fiscal austerity is limiting the ability of some hospitals to develop this strategy.

Reassess medical staff privileges

When prospective payment was initiated, it appeared that hospitals would reassess medical staff privileges. Physicians providing high-cost or low-quality medical care could have their staff privileges revoked. Hospitals had little choice but to respond to the economic incentives they faced. Consequently, some instituted a policy of denying staff privileges to physicians having excessive patient care costs relative to hospital revenues. For most hospitals, there was limited precedence for such action. Most medical staff bylaws did not address the new prospective payment and competitive environments. Membership policies were open to redefinition. Furthermore, it was often difficult to agree on measures indicating that a medical practitioner had violated cost or quality norms. Thus, valid and reliable standards for evaluating medical staff members were often missing, causing contention between physicians and executives.[41]

The problem of assessing medical staff and subsequent hospital-physician conflict have been partially resolved by reflecting on the specific missions of hospitals. For example, a medical staff credentials committee may not fulfill its fiduciary responsibilities in a particular community if a staff member is dismissed solely for incurring cost overruns. The physician in question may be a specialist and the only provider available in the hospital's catchment area. Under these circumstances, an alternative to dismissal would be to initiate a cost-containment education program for the physician rather than lose a scarce community resource.

Various support systems are needed to help physicians achieve cost-containment and patient-referral goals. At the very least, a three-phase strategy can be considered:

1. Provide physicians with direct assistance in incorporating hospital goals into their patient case decision-making framework. This can be achieved by continuing education, individual consultation, or peer mentoring.
2. Periodically review physicians' performance levels and provide personalized feedback.
3. Reassess admitting privileges when a physician fails to improve despite supportive efforts to correct inappropriate behavior.

By adopting a constructive approach that enlightens rather than reprimands physicians who fall outside normal practice patterns, hospitals can institute corrective action without threatening overall hospital-physician relations. Naturally, there are limits to the extent of flexibility that is proper in any given situation. Hospitals may discover that there is no option other than to sever relations with habitual policy abusers.

Enhance community image

A hospital establishes its reputation both informally and formally. The image projected in a community is partially formed by experiences that patients, employees, and medical staff share with one another and other community residents. Image is also formed by developing marketing strategies that react to various environmental pressures. In recent years, hospitals have turned to more formal approaches in promoting a desired image. It is widely recognized that a hospital's image is a valuable asset in managing the challenges of prospective payment and competition. Nonetheless, the state-of-the-art in hospital marketing has repeatedly been questioned.[42,43]

Patients communicate inpatient experiences to their physicians as well as to other patients and friends. Hospital employees may share their workplace perceptions with friends, professional colleagues, and physicians with whom they interact. Physicians determine their impressions of a hospital by actual experiences and through informal discussions and fraternizing with medical colleagues. Due to word-of-mouth communication and firsthand experiences, physicians' opinions of hospitals are highly respected and valued. As Table 1 suggests, during the earlier stages of prospective payment, a good public image within the medical community was identified as a promising hospital strategy. However, the primary question was how to implement this idea.

Hospital executives are increasingly recognizing that they should attempt to regard facilities, services, and patient care policies from the viewpoint of admitting physicians. By failing to understand the physician's perception, service delivery changes leading to a positive image may be difficult to envision or implement. Referring physicians are responsible for admissions, which aid in the attainment of other hospital goals. Unless key medical practice issues have been addressed, physicians may not refer patients or may consider joining another medical staff. Programs that can enhance a hospital's image in the medical community include:

- active teaching and inservice education programs,
- ability to support a variety of clinical specializations,
- links to academic and research centers,
- programs to monitor and maintain patient care quality, and
- demonstrated concern for physicians by the administrative staff.

The presence of these attributes reflect positively on a hospital's reputation and may outweigh major expenditures on hospital advertising.[44] A postprospective-payment perspective suggests that health care executives have learned to emphasize substantive program resources rather than broad forms of advertising.

Promote collegial organization culture

Some hospitals perceived the need to develop a collegial organization culture as a strategy for addressing prospective payment.[45] Confronted by a growing hostile environment, many health care executives turned to strategies already in vogue among other business sectors. Books such as *Theory Z*,[46] *In Search of Excellence*,[47] *The Art of Japanese Management*,[48] and *A Passion for Excellence*[49] were prototypes reinforcing the role of corporate cultures for improving organizational performance. Enticed by the acclaim these concepts received, hospitals began to mimic their corporate counterparts. They adopted family- or clan-oriented organization cultures to increase staff cohesiveness, raise productivity, instill pride in service delivery, and achieve quality of care. The benchmark of shared values among all providers in the delivery setting became a desired goal of hospital organization cultures.[50–52] Adopting excellence as a target, whether in cost control, revenue enhancement, or quality services, was consistent with the new health care environment. As a byproduct, staff may manifest an improved client orientation, thereby enhancing guest relations. Some hospitals contemplated wholesale adoption of Japanese management philosophies wherein a dominant organizational culture promotes service delivery.[53,54] In sum, a common belief system was viewed as a promising strategy for turning hospitals around.

As Table 1 indicates, the accuracy of this forecast is somewhat uncertain. Hospitals continue to rely on ideas of excellence and participative management as strategies for coping with prospective payment. However, there is little empirical evidence in either business or health care that these strategies actually help organizations to perform better.[55] While the ideas have strong intuitive and conceptual appeal, their implementation has not been uniformly effective. Consequently, organizations may not be exercising these strategies in the same manner as firms described by advocates of the *Excellence* or *Theory* Z cultures.

It is clear that collegial organization cultures are not universally accepted by physicians.[56] This presents a paradox that hospitals must overcome. Physicians presumably are motivated to provide leadership in the

Many physicians retain a value system supporting autonomy in medical practice. These values and beliefs are contrary to hospital strategies aimed at solidifying patient care networks and team approaches.

delivery of patient care. Collaborative organization cultures imply a willingness of providers to support collaborative patient care plans. This presents a conflict. Many physicians retain a value system supporting autonomy in medical practice.[57] These values and beliefs are contrary to hospital strategies aimed at solidifying patient care networks and team approaches. This raises numerous questions about the strategical wisdom of creating collegial organization cultures. Physicians may not immediately support such efforts at team building due to traditional professional values.

Extend hospital benefit programs

Like other professionals, physicians are motivated by a wide variety of factors including remuneration for services rendered. As prospective payment policies began to proliferate, the possibility of integrating medical staff members into the overall compensation system provided to regular hospital employees was considered. Arguments against such a policy stemmed from the fact that medical staff members traditionally do not receive direct compensation from hospitals. Although incentive compensation programs for salaried physician staff members such as pathology, radiology, anesthesiology, or clinical department heads are widely prevalent, including admitting physicians in these programs as the next step in expanding incentives raised considerable controversy.

While attractive theoretical benefits may be obtained from utilizing economic incentives in physician compensation, serious ethical, legal, and tax constraints also exist. Strategies such as incentive compensation and commissions appeared promising because they were consistent with prospective payment incentives and philosophy. However, in time, legal and tax regulations effectively removed these innovative options from consideration. Hospitals' ability to create incentive payments and commission arrangements remains constrained for the foreseeable future.

Facilitate involvement in hospital governance

Inviting physician membership on the board of directors (or in other policy-making positions) represents another strategy for resolving prospective payment problems.[58] This strategy includes physicians directly in the fiduciary responsibilities of trustees and exposes them to the tough decisions hospitals are being forced to make.[59] Additionally, physician board members provide a unique perspective relative to evaluating alternative policies being considered by the board. They are also able to communicate the board's perspective to medical colleagues.[60,61]

Although hospital governing boards are shrinking in size (i.e., in number of board members), there is some indication that more are including medical staff members as representatives.[62,63] Incorporating physicians on the board has the potential to assure that medical staff concerns are considered during policy formulation. However, it is questionable whether this participation is effective in presenting physicians' perspectives due to the diversity of the medical staff. Nonetheless, hospitals are concerned about eliciting physician commitment to cost-containment and patient-referral goals.[64] Including physicians on the board or in policy-making positions represents an important step toward forming a cooperative association and building commitment.

Procure special equipment

Hospital executives and governing boards normally control the budgets for replacing obsolete equipment and purchasing new equipment. Prospective payment has provided added incentive to use medical technology as a strategic organizational advantage in capturing market share. However, there are also incentives to reduce diagnostic testing associated with medical technology.[65] These countervailing incentives place hospitals in a difficult position. Equipment-acquisition decisions can encourage productive physicians to join a hospital because of the diagnostic and treatment capacities of the technology. Yet, the very technology raises capital costs while threatening operating margin if overutilization occurs. On balance, it appears that selective purchases of medical technology are most prudent in developing service delivery strategies. Laser angioplasty, tissue plasminogen activators, fertility technologies, mammography, biotechnology in oncology, and orthopedics technologies are promising equipment-acquisition decisions for the future.[66]

Purchase of specialized equipment can clearly be an effective method for attracting physicians and offering new services if controls are implemented to ensure the equipment's proper use. Consequently, capital equipment decisions should reflect criteria that provide hospitals with a distinct competitive advantage to draw patients and to deliver cost-effective care. As reimbursement guidelines for capital equipment are adjusted by third party payers, decision criteria for capital expenditures will need to be updated accordingly. Traditional concerns with effectively managing working capital and avoiding long-term debt continue to be prime considerations when making medical-equipment-procurement decisions.

MANAGERIAL IMPLICATIONS

The management of physician relations presents a significant and continuing challenge for hospital executives. Obtaining physician cooperation and commitment toward achieving hospital goals remains a strategic concern of virtually every executive. Analyses of many management strategies predicted to facilitate hospital–physician relations show mixed results. The strategy scorecard indicates that as prospective payment policies and competitors' responses evolve, hospitals must remain flexible in formulating and implementing adaptive strategies. Experience suggests that there is no one best way to promote a cooperative relationship among medical staff members. However, the presence of significant differences among hospitals, medical staffs, and hospital-medical service markets dictate that an effective plan, uniquely designed for a specific marketplace, will incorporate a variety of the strategies reviewed in this scorecard.

Hospital executives must determine the costs and benefits associated both with implementing a multiplicity of strategies and with each type of cooperation-building program before a comprehensive plan can be formulated. While costs are usually readily identifiable, the effectiveness of a particular venture or motivational program is much more difficult to determine. Only subjective estimates of effectiveness can be considered because there are no guarantees that physician cooperation and participation will be secured through implementation of any particular component of a strategic plan.

REFERENCES

1. Goldsmith, J.C. "Competition's Impact: A Report From the Front." *Health Affairs* 7, no. 3 (1988): 162–73.
2. Fuchs, V.R. "The Competition Revolution in Health Care." *Health Affairs* 7, no. 3 (1988): 5–24.
3. Desai, H.B., and Margenthaler, C.R. "A Framework for Developing Hospital Strategies." *Hospital and Health Services Administration* 32 (May 1987): 235–48.
4. Autrey, P., and Thomas, D. "Competitive Strategy in the Hospital Industry." *Health Care Management Review* 11, no. 1 (1986): 7–14.
5. Bettner, M., and Collins, F. "Physicians and Administrators: Inducing Collaboration." *Hospital and Health Services Administration* 32 (May 1987): 151–60.
6. Grayson, M.A. "Survey Spots the Tight Turns in MD–CEO Relations." *Hospitals* 62, no. 3 (1988): 48–53.
7. Des Harnais, S., et al. "The Early Effects of the Prospective Payment System on Inpatient Utilization and the Quality of Care." *Inquiry* 24 (Spring 1987): 7–16.
8. Georgopoulos, B.S., D'Aunno, T.A., and Saavedra, R. "Hospital–Physician Relations Under Hospital Prepayment." *Medical Care* 25, no. 8 (1987): 781–95.
9. Bloomfield, R.D. "Hospital–Physician Relationships: A Changing Dynamic." *New York State Journal of Medicine* 88, no. 1 (1988): 5–6.
10. Smith, H.L., and Reid, R.A. *Competitive Hospitals.* Rockville, Md.: Aspen Publishers, 1986.
11. Van Sumeren, M.A. "Organizational Downsizing: Streamlining the Healthcare Organization." *Healthcare Financial Management* 40, no. 1 (1986): 35–39.
12. Burda, D. "DRGs: Five Years of PPS Have Fostered Division and Fierce Competition." *Modern Healthcare* 18, no. 45 (1988): 26–28, 30.
13. McDermott, S. "The New Hospital Challenge: Organizing and Managing Physician Organizations." *Health Care Management Review* 3, no. 1 (1988): 57–61.
14. Shortell, S.M., Morrison, E., and Robbins, S. "Strategy Making in Health Care Organizations: A Framework and Agenda for Research." *Medical Care Review* 42 (1985): 219–66.
15. Guterman, S., and Dobson, A. "Impact of the Medicare Prospective Payment System for Hospitals." *Health Care Financing Review* 7 (1986): 97–114.
16. Harrell, G.D., and Fors, M.F. "Planning Evolution in Hospital Management." *Health Care Management Review* 12, no. 1 (1987): 9–22.
17. Files, L.A. "Strategy Formulation and Strategic Planning in Hospitals: Application of an Industrial Model." *Hospital and Health Services Administration* 28, no. 6 (1983): 9–20.
18. Files, L.A. "Strategy Formulation in Hospitals." *Health Care Management Review* 13, no. 1 (1988): 9–16.
19. Farley, D. *Trends in Hospital Average Lengths of Stay, Casemix, and Discharge Rates, 1980-1985.* Research Note 11. DHHS Pub. No. (PHS) 88-3420. Washington, D.C.: Government Printing Office, 1988.
20. Guterman, S., and Dobson, A. "Impact of the Medicare Prospective Payment System for Hospitals." *Health Care Financing Review* 7 (1986): 97–114.
21. Glandon, G.L., and Morrisey, M.A. "Redefining the Hospital-Physician Relationship Under Prospective Payment." *Inquiry* 23 (Summer 1986): 166–75.

22. Weiner, S.L., et al. "Economic Incentives and Organizational Realities: Managing Hospitals Under DRGs." *Milbank Quarterly* 65 (1987): 463–87.
23. Smith, D.B., and Pickard, R. "Evaluation of the Impact of Medicare and Medicaid Prospective Payment on Utilization of Philadelphia Area Hospitals." *Health Services Research* 21 (1986): 529–46.
24. Rosko, M.D., and Broyles, R.W. "Short-Term Responses of Hospitals to the DRG Prospective Pricing Mechanism in New Jersey." *Medical Care* 25, no. 2 (1987): 88–99.
25. Fuchs, V.R. "The Battle for Control of Health Care." *Health Affairs* 2, no. 2 (1982): 5–13.
26. Kralewski, J.E., et al. "The Physician Rebellion." *New England Journal of Medicine* 316 (1987): 339–42.
27. Ottensmeyer, D.E., and Smith, H.L. "A New Agenda for the Practice of Medicine." *Frontiers of Health Services Management* 3, no. 1 (1986): 3–29.
28. Spivey, B.E. "The Relation Between Hospital Management and Medical Staff Under a Prospective Payment System." *New England Journal of Medicine* 310 (1984): 984–86.
29. Shortell, S.M. "The Medical Staff of the Future: Replanting the Garden." *Frontiers of Health Services Management* 1, no. 3 (1986): 3–48.
30. May, J.J., and Wasserman, J. "Selected Results From an Evaluation of the New Jersey Diagnosis-Related Group System." *Health Services Research* 19 (December 1984): 547–59.
31. Lohr, K.N., et al. *Impact of Medicare Prospective Payment on the Quality of Medical Care.* Santa Monica, Calif.: Rand Corporation, 1985.
32. Perry, L. "The Quality Process: Hospitals Begin To Emphasize Quality in Devising Strategic Plans." *Modern Healthcare* 18, no. 14 (April 1, 1988): 30–34.
33. Tresnowski, B.R. "Quality Can Be Saved in a Price-Based System—But It Isn't Easy." *Inquiry* 24 (1987): 3–4.
34. Wyszewianski, L., Thomas, J.W., and Friedman, B. "Case-Based Payment and the Control of Quality and Efficiency in Hospitals." *Inquiry* 24 (Spring 1987): 17–25.
35. Glusman, D.H., and Kepner, J.C.S. "Strategic Issues in Joint Ventures." *Medical Group Management Journal* 35, no. 5 (1988): 18–25.
36. Frederick, L. "Joint Ventures: The Hottest Game in Medicine." *Medical Economics* 64, no. 7 (1987): 38–39.
37. Gleason, S.C., and Sullivan, P.C. "Physician–Hospital Joint Venture Addresses Mutual Needs." *Health Progress* 67, no. 10 (1986): 55–57.
38. Koska, M.T. "Easing Physician Resistance to New Ventures." *Hospitals* 62, no. 15 (1988): 62.
39. Richards, G. "How Do Joint Ventures Affect Relations With Physicians?" *Hospitals* 58 (December 1, 1984): 68–72.
40. Glandon, G.L., and Morrisey, M.A. "Redefining the Hospital–Physician Relationship Under Prospective Payment." *Inquiry* 23 (Summer 1986): 166–75.
41. McDermott, S. "The New Hospital Challenge: Organizing and Managing Physician Organizations." *Health Care Management Review* 13, no. 1 (1988): 57–61.
42. McDevitt, P. "Learning by Doing: Strategic Marketing Management in Hospitals." *Health Care Management Review* 12, no. 1 (1987): 23–30.
43. Clarke, R.N., and Shyavitz, L. "Health Care Marketing: Lots of Talk, Any Action?" *Health Care Management Review* 12, no. 1 (1987): 31–36.
44. McCarthy, E.J. "How Much Should Hospitals Spend on Advertising?" *Health Care Management Review* 12, no. 1 (1987): 47–54.
45. Bice, M.O. "Corporate Culture and Business Strategy: A Health Management Company Perspective." *Hospital and Health Services Administration* 29, no. 4 (1984): 64–78.
46. Ouchi, W.G. *Theory Z.* Reading Mass.: Addison-Wesley, 1981.
47. Peters, T.J., and Waterman, R.H. *In Search of Excellence.* New York, N.Y.: Harper & Row, 1982.
48. Pascale, R.T., and Athos, A.G. *The Art of Japanese Management.* New York, N.Y.: Warner Books, 1981.
49. Peters, T.J., and Austin, N. *A Passion for Excellence.* New York, N.Y.: Harper & Row, 1985.
50. Deal, T., and Kennedy, A.E. *Corporate Cultures.* Reading, Mass. Addison-Wesley, 1982.
51. Sathe, V. *Culture and Related Corporate Realities.* Homewood, Ill.: Irwin, 1985.
52. Wiener, Y. "Forms of Value Systems: A Focus on Organizational Effectiveness and Cultural Change and Maintenance." *Academy of Management Review* 13 (October 1988): 534–45.
53. Ikegami, N., and Goldsmith, S.B. "Quality Circles: The Myth and Reality of Hospital Management." *Health Care Management Review* 10, no. 3 (1985): 45–33.
54. Shortell, S.M. "Theory Z: Implications and Relevance for Health Care Management." *Health Care Management Review* 7, no. 2 (1982): 7–21.
55. Barney, J.B. "Organizational Culture: Can It Be a Source of Sustained Competitive Advantage?" *Academy of Management Review* 11 (July 1988): 656–65.
56. Burchell, R.C., et al. "Physicians and the Organizational Evolution of Medicine." *Journal of the American Medical Association* 260, no. 6 (1988): 826–31.
57. Starr, P. *The Social Transformation of American Medicine.* New York, N.Y.: Basic Books, 1982.
58. Quintana, J.B., Duncan, W.J., and Houser, H.W. "Hospital Governance and the Corporate Revolution." *Health Care Management Review* 10, no. 3 (1985): 63–71.
59. Griffith, J.R. "Voluntary Hospitals: Are Trustees the Solution?" *Hospital and Health Services Administration* 33, no. 3 (1988): 295–310.
60. McGowan, R.A. "An Integrated Approach to Board Development." *Health Care Management Review* 12, no. 3 (1987): 29–33.

61. Blair, J.D., and Whitehead, C.J. "Too Many on the Seesaw: Stakeholder Diagnosis and Management for Hospitals." *Hospital and Health Services Administration* 33, no. 2 (1988): 153–66.
62. Alexander, J.A., Morlock, L.L., and Gifford, B.D. "The Effects of Corporate Restructuring on Hospital Policymaking." *Health Services Research* 23, no. 2 (1988): 311–37.
63. Greene, J. "Harsh Climate May Test Hospital Governing Boards." *Modern Healthcare* 18, no. 30 (1988): 32–33.
64. Greifinger, R.B., and Bluestone, M.S. "Building Physician Alliances for Cost Containment." *Health Care Management Review* 11, no. 4 (1986): 63–72.
65. Sloan, F.A., Morrisey, M.A., and Valvona, J. "Medicare Prospective Payment and the Use of Medical Technologies in Hospitals." *Medical Care* 26, no. 9 (1988): 837–53.
66. Wilkinson, R. "New Technology That Will Change Key Services." *Hospitals* 62, no. 10 (May 20, 1988): 56–61.

Physician goals: Impact on hospital performance

Samuel C. Webb

Controversy prevails concerning the relative superiority of for-profit versus not-for-profit hospitals. Presented here are three variations to each of two basic theoretical models that contrast performance of for-profit and not-for-profit hospitals.

Health Care Manage Rev, 1989, 14(1), 81–89

Just as agribusiness is replacing the family farm, the investor-owned hospital is replacing the old "doctor's hospital."[1,2] Hospitals have merged with horizontally and vertically integrated corporate organizations to create what Wohl refers to as the "medical industrial complex."[3] Centralized control and corporatization in the health care industry is a growing concern among managers of not-for-profit organizations, among legislators, and among the general public. All groups fear that the result will be higher health care costs, dilution of the quality of care, compromise of physicians' selfless devotion to their patients' welfare, reduction of care for the indigent, and diversion of resources from education and research.

The alleged superiority of the for-profit structural form was asserted in the recent empirical work of Harvard's Herzlinger and Krasker.[4] This study has been severely criticized by Fitzgerald and Jacobson and numerous other health care analysts who have written critical letters to the editor of the *Harvard Business Review*.[5]

A much larger and more authoritative study than that of Herzlinger-Krasker was made by the Institute of Medicine (IOM). The IOM report cast serious doubt on the assertion that the for-profit hospital organizational form is best for society.[6] Results of the IOM study committee are summarized briefly in the next section. Several very basic economic models of the hospital are presented that are consistent with the IOM report—models that could be built upon in future empirical studies and help guide managers of health care facilities to achieve their goals.

IOM STUDY COMMITTEE RESULTS

In 1983, the IOM initiated a major two-year study of for-profit and not-for-profit health care organizations. The study committee reviewed all current literature on the subject and commissioned additional studies to help fill some of the information gaps. Because of the comprehensiveness of the study and the expertise of the participants who included both theoreticians and prac-

Samuel C. Webb, *Ph.D., M.S., B.S., is Professor of Economics, Barton School of Business at The Wichita State University, Wichita, Kansas. His teaching and research interests are in the fields of managerial, health care, and monetary economics.*

The author acknowledges comments by Gerard F. Carvalho, Ph.D., M.B.A., B.S.E., Associate Professor of Management Systems, Ohio University, and Philip L. Hersch, Ph.D., M.A., B.A., Assistant Professor of Economics, Wichita State University.

titioners, the conclusions reached are probably the best information currently available on the characteristics of for-profit and not-for-profit organizations in the complex and rapidly changing health care industry.

The major findings of the IOM study committee with regard to for-profit enterprise in health care are:

1. Health care cost
   ". . .the rise in investor ownership of hospitals has increased health care costs."[7]

   > In sum, although standard economic theory predicts greater efficiency in for-profit than in not-for-profit organizations, the expected ability of investor-owned for-profit organizations to produce the same services at lower cost than their not-for-profit counterparts has not been demonstrated. Large organizations theoretically benefit from economies of scale and reduced transaction costs, but such savings may be offset by central office costs, higher capital costs resulting from a growth orientation, and the payment of taxes and dividends.[8]

2. Access to care
   ". . .for-profit hospitals proportionately provide less uncompensated care than do not-for-profit hospitals."[9] "Comparatively low levels of uncompensated care in for-profit hospitals in such states [where for-profit hospitals are numerous] is strong evidence that the presence of these hospitals contributes to the problem of access to care for people who lack the means to pay [and] can threaten the financial well-being of nearby hospitals that serve larger numbers of people who are unable to pay."[10]
3. Quality of care
   "The limited indicators of hospital quality that are now available—primarily hospital accreditation, board certification of staff physicians, and amount of nursing personnel—show no overall pattern of either inferior or superior quality in investor-owned chain hospitals when compared with not- for-profit hospitals."[11]
4. Education and research
   In the past, investor-owned health care companies have had little involvement in professional education and unsponsored research, benefiting from the unprofitable efforts of others and drawing away the revenues of well-insured patients whose payments helped subsidize education and research. However, most of the hospitals acquired by investors have been small non-teaching hospitals and the practice of cross-subsidization to finance education and research is questionable. Recently there have been examples of participation in medical education and research by investor-owned companies.[12]
5. Relative social value of for-profit versus not-for-profit health care organizations
   The committee found insufficient evidence on which to recommend opposition to, or support for, the investor-owned type of organization. Disadvantages include the higher costs to payers and less service to non-paying patients. "No clear differences in quality have been demonstrated. The cost and quality of care, access to care, and the support of health professional education and academic health centers are all major public policy issues that must be addressed on their own terms, rather than primarily as an issue of for-profit health care."[13] Advantages of having for-profit organizations include (1) their ability to raise needed capital independently of government subsidy, (2) acquisition and construction activities provided more and probably more-improved services than would have been available otherwise, and (3) contribution to a more dynamic industry which seeks to serve patients more efficiently in innovative and diverse ways.[14]

A THEORETICAL ANALYSIS OF FOR-PROFIT AND NOT-FOR-PROFIT ORGANIZATIONS

An economic analysis of for-profit and not-for-profit health care organizations is presented with reference to quantity, quality, and price of health care services based upon several alternative assumptions about organizational goals and profit functions. First is a description of the nonprofit hospital under several alternative assumptions about corporate goals. In each of the models considered, it is assumed that the hospital's *product* market is somewhat monopolistic while its *resource* market is somewhat monopsonistic. That is, the hospital supplier of medical services has some degree of monopolistic hold over its local or regional market due to locational convenience, urgency of treatment, and loyalty or trust of known closer-to-home physicians

The committee found insufficient evidence on which to recommend opposition to, or support for, the investor-owned type of organization.

and hospitals. Also, the hospital as a buyer of resources is assumed to exert some control over its resource markets (e.g., markets for the services of physicians, nurses, clerks, and medical supplies).

Monopoly on the supply side is evident from the highly concentrated nature of the hospital industry.[15] Barriers to entry of new competing hospitals are attributable to three categories of controls: (1) regulatory constraints, (2) professional control, and (3) third party payment for services.[16] Regulatory constraints include accreditation and licensure requirements, and certificate of need (CON) controls on capital expansion.[17] Professional control may be exerted by physicians who make hospital selection and treatment decisions for their minimally informed patients, by local hospitals that can limit the number of physicians on their medical staffs, and by hospital professional associations. The latter act to (1) increase the demand for hospital services, (2) expand the types of services offered, (3) acquire government subsidies, (4) limit substitutes for hospital care, and (5) restrict entry of more hospitals where there are member hospitals in the area.[18] Third party payment for services insulates the consumer from price negotiations for services, while cost-based reimbursement methods create no incentives for hospitals to control costs. More recent use of DRGs and prepaid contracts has created cost-control incentives.

Other possible barriers to entry include economies of scale, economies of scope, the limited size of the local market, and a transportation cost advantage over hospitals located outside the region.[19,20]

MODEL 1. NOT-FOR-PROFIT HOSPITAL

By definition, not-for-profit hospitals provide an output level (Q) of health care services where total revenues (TR) are matched by total costs (TC). Surplus revenues over costs (S), or profits, are set equal to zero, that is,

$$S = TR - TC = 0 \tag{1}$$

Revenues are derived from both fees and gifts. Fees are paid variously and collectively from the patient's pocketbook, indirectly from prepaid private insurance benefits, from government welfare benefits, and sometimes from the hospital's fund of surplus revenues and gifts. Fees are set at the highest price that will be paid in the competitive market. The demand function is

$$P = f(Q) \tag{2}$$

where P is the price of hospital output.

Gifts include governmental subsidies, charitable contributions, and personal services of volunteer workers. Total costs are the sum of expenditures for management (administrators and physicians) (M), the labor of nurses and other nonmanagement employees (L), and capital expenditures for building, equipment, and supplies (K), that is,

$$TC = r_1M + r_2L + r_3K \tag{3}$$

where M, L, and K are each dependent upon the level of output:

$$M = f(Q) \tag{4}$$

$$L = f(Q) \tag{5}$$

$$K = f(Q) \tag{6}$$

and where r_1 are the monopsonistically determined wage rates and prices of inputs.[21,22]

Model 1 is shown graphically in Figure 1. In Figure 1(a), the revenue and cost functions are such that a minimum level of output at Q_5 is required for the hospital to break-even. All output levels below Q_5 have total costs in excess of total revenues including gifts. This condition forces management to strive to maintain the equilibrium level to ensure the hospital's survival. In the Figure 1(b) configuration, there is a surplus that gives more flexibility for management decisions. Survival of the hospital is assured within the range of output between the two break-even levels Q_1 and Q_5 over which the hospital could show a profit if the management chose to do so. At some intermediate level of output, management can spend surplus income for purposes it considers appropriate and can adjust the curves to the Figure 1(a) configuration.

At this juncture in the development of Model 1, some different assumptions must be made about the hospital's goals. Hospital Type 1A, for example, is a predominantly public service oriented hospital that devotes its attention to providing a maximum amount of basic medical services to as many patient/customers as possible. Hospital Type 1B, with a discretionary surplus, tends to cater to the desires of a smaller number of patients than the Type 1A hospital, that is, patients who desire and can afford higher quality services. Of course, patients of the Type 1B hospital type consume more staff time and other resources of a less essential "Cadillac" nature similar to those provided in luxury hotels and expensive retirement homes. Some support for this assumption is provided by Coelen's study, which found large differences in ancillary charges per case: ". . .compared to nonprofit independents, proprietary

FIGURE 1

OPTIMUM OUTPUT LEVEL FOR MODEL #1 TYPE HOSPITAL IS AT Q_5

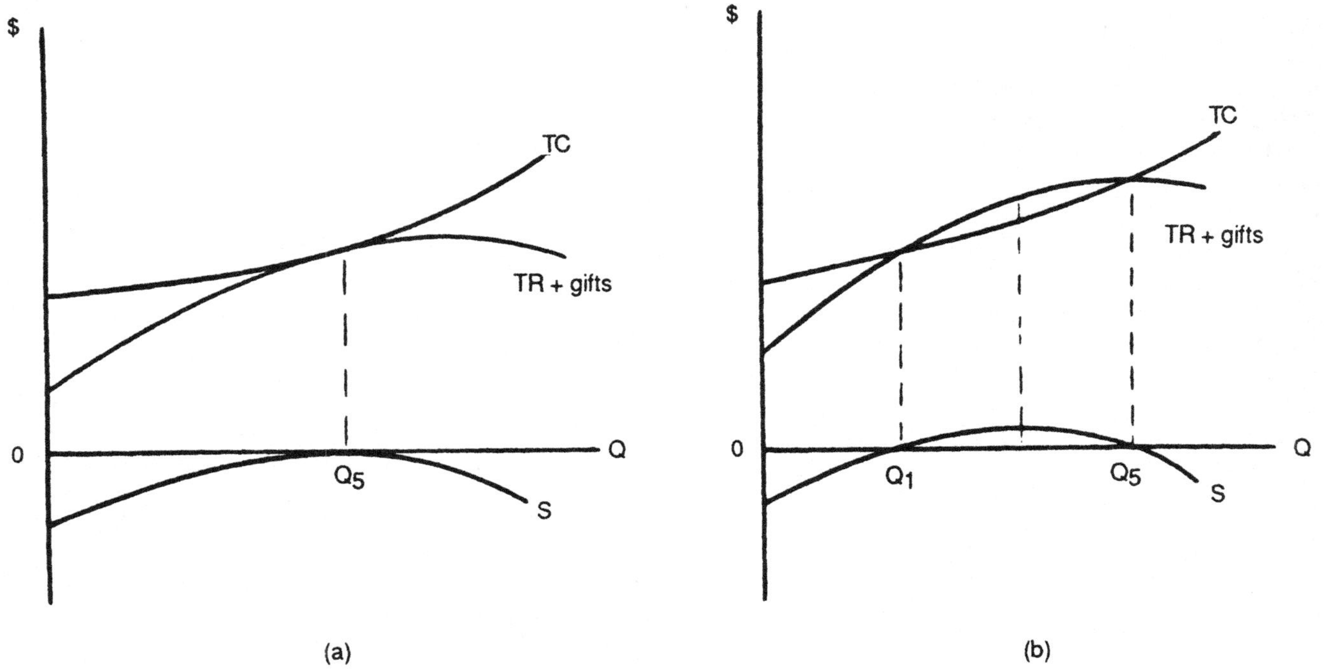

chains bill 34 percent more per patient for ancillary services on average; proprietary independents bill 15 percent more; and non-profit chains bill 5 percent more."[23] Of course, ancillary charges cover essential services as well as some that might be considered nonessential.

In contrast to hospital types 1A and 1B that are wholly public service or patient oriented, Hospital Type 1C is assumed to operate additionally to maximize the utility of management and staff employees. Thus, the not-for-profit hospital's character and image are hypothesized to depend upon the policy decision as to which type of not-for-profit hospital is chosen. The policy decision could be made explicitly or implicitly, but in practice the decision is probably made implicitly because the hospital's public image could be harmed if the public was informed that the hospital was being operated for any purpose that was not obviously beneficial to patients.

In reality, the board of trustees or corporate board of directors sets the policy, but the managers (administrators, physicians, nurses, and other employees having some discretionary decision-making abilities) implement the policy with day-to-day decisions using their own judgments and in manners consistent with the managers' and employees' individual utility functions, that is, within the limits allowed by the trustees' ability to monitor and enforce stated policies. Inevitably, there is some slack in the implementation of hospital policy.

The Type 1A hospital devotes itself to human service of the no-frills kind needed to get people back on their feet and on the job. Less concern is given to whether the patient can pay for the treatment. Donors often support this type of hospital with a vision of "helping the needy."[24] The earliest hospitals for ethnic groups and the general public were of this type; help was given with no expectation that fees would cover expenditures. Benevolence was the guiding principle. Ideally, output would gravitate to Q_5 in Figure 1.

The Type 1B hospital caters more to affluent patients who can afford much of what the latest developments in technology can offer. The physician spares no expense in treating patients and takes time to apply a more congenial and empathetic bedside manner. The staff adds a more prompt and personal touch. Amenities such as a private room, color television, and attractive ambience are considered part of the treatment. This sort of treatment is probably quite representative of that provided by many hospitals in the United States. According to Pauly, "The great bulk of medical care in the United States is purchased by people who are not poor. A majority of medical care costs are paid for in the private sector by upper- and middle-income people, either via insurance or out-of-pocket payments. Virtually all of the tax subsidy goes to the nonpoor."[25]

The higher cost of treatment in Type 1B hospitals compared to Type 1A can be reflected in Figure 1(b) by an upward shift in the TC curve and a concomitant downward shift in the S curve, as shown in Figure 2. A consequence of the upward shift in the TC curve is that the break-even output level moves to the left of Q_5. Some quantity of service is given up to provide higher quality.

However, if the TR curve can be shifted upward by an equal or greater amount than the TC curve is shifted, the break-even output level need not diminish and the output level Q_5 can be maintained or even increased. Higher revenues and profits could result if the increased quality is reflected in increased prices and if the more technologically advanced services and amenities have greater unit profitability (which they generally do) than basic services. As a marketing ploy, policymakers and managers might decide to concentrate on providing better service to a segment of the market that is willing and able to pay for higher quality and greater comfort. As a business decision, this makes a lot of sense, but, as a public policy decision, an important social problem is ignored: how to serve the poor. The poor would have to be served by other organizations or with outside support.

FIGURE 2

TYPE 1B HOSPITAL SHIFTS TC CURVE UPWARD*

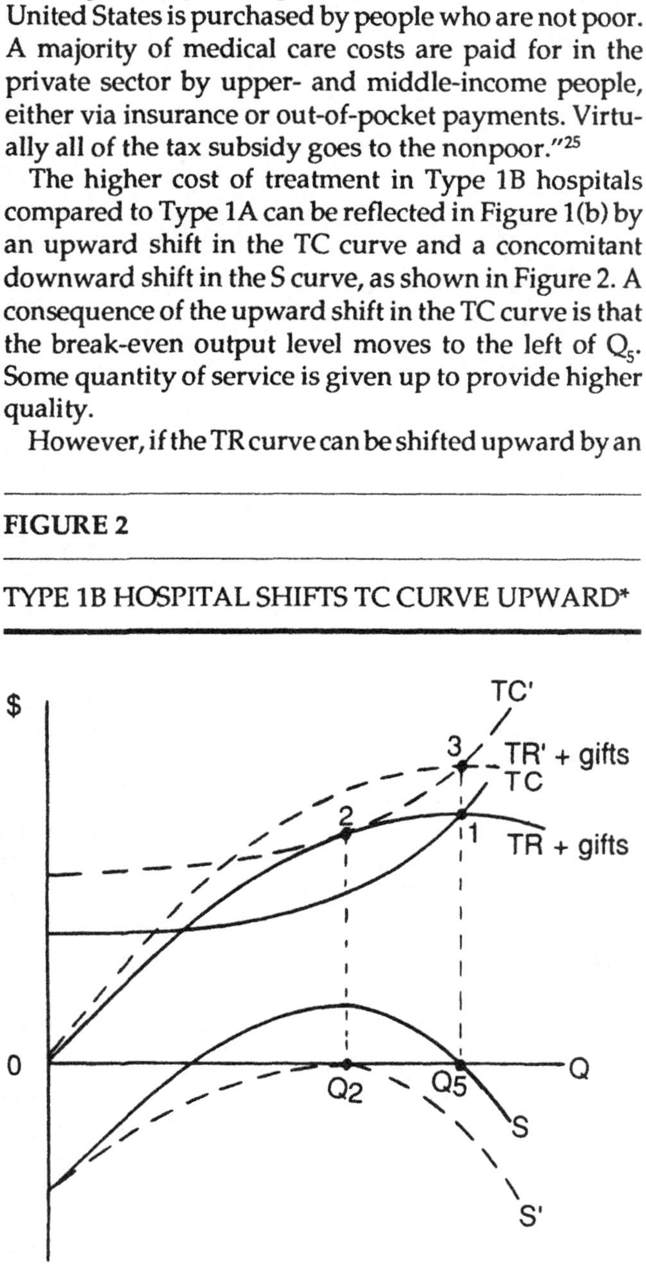

*Output level may fall from Q_5 to Q_2 unless TR curve can be shifted upward also.

The great bulk of medical care in the United States is purchased by people who are not poor.

The Type 1C hospital differs from Types 1A and 1B in that it is operated as much as possible to maximize the utility of the managers (administrators and physicians) rather than the utility of the patients. Higher utility of managers takes the form of higher salaries and less demanding work schedules. Higher costs and less efficient operations shift the TC curve upward and S curve downward (as shown in Figure 2 for the Type 1B hospital), without increased revenues, causing the break-even output level to be left of the Q_5 equilibrium level associated with optimality from a patient/consumer's point of view. Because the quality of treatment is no higher than before, the possibility of increasing TR to maintain the output level is less likely than for the Type 1B hospital, except when the hospital resorts to exploitation of its monopoly powers (where they exist) to raise prices.

Model 2. For-profit hospital

While many variations of the for-profit hospital model are possible depending upon the extent of profit maximization desired and how operating profits are used, the focus is on three variants. Type 2A hospitals attempt to maximize profits in the manner of the classical pure monopolist who exploits the market to the fullest extent. Profits are maximized by equating marginal revenues and marginal costs, which occur at the output level where the first derivative of the profit function (equation 1) is set equal to zero and where the second derivative for that output level is negative, that is, where

$$dS/dQ = d(TR)/dQ - d(TC)/dQ = 0 \quad (6)$$

and/or $$d(TR)/dQ = d(TC)/dQ \quad (7)$$

where $$d^2S/dQ^2 < 0 \quad (8)$$

Output is restricted to Q_2 in Figure 3 where surplus revenues (or profits) are maximized and where marginal cost (MC) equals marginal revenue (MR) so that the price charged to all patient/customers may be raised from P_5 to P_2 on the demand curve (D). It is assumed here that all profits are paid out as dividends to stockholders rather than used for the benefit of patients, managers, or employees.

FIGURE 3

TYPE B1 FOR-PROFIT HOSPITAL MAXIMIZES PROFITS BY RESTRICTING OUTPUT TO Q_2 AND CHARGING A PRICE P_2

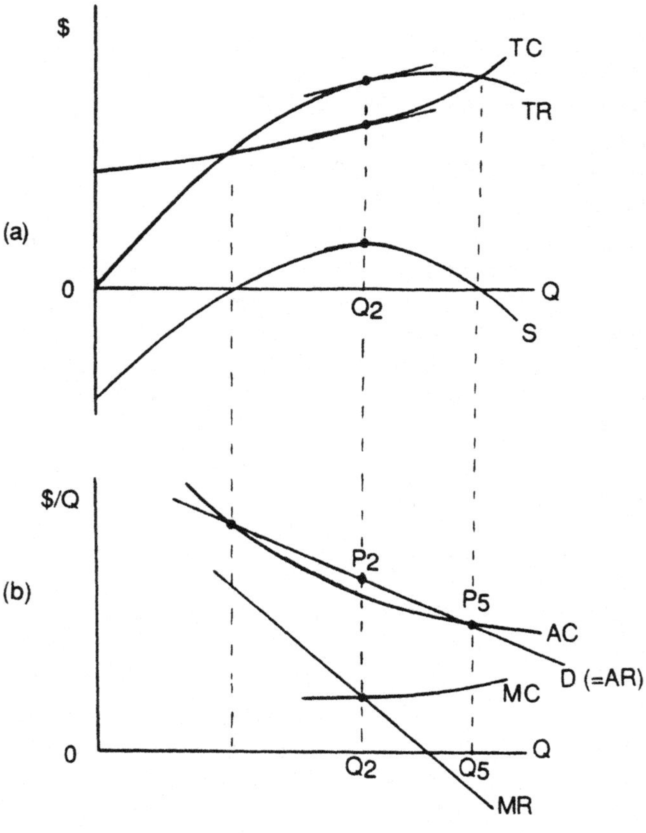

FIGURE 4

TYPE 2B FOR-PROFIT HOSPITAL CHOOSES MAXIMUM OUTPUT SUBJECT TO A MINIMUM PROFIT CONSTRAINT AT Q_4; TYPE 2C MAXIMIZES MANAGEMENT'S UTILITY AT Q_3

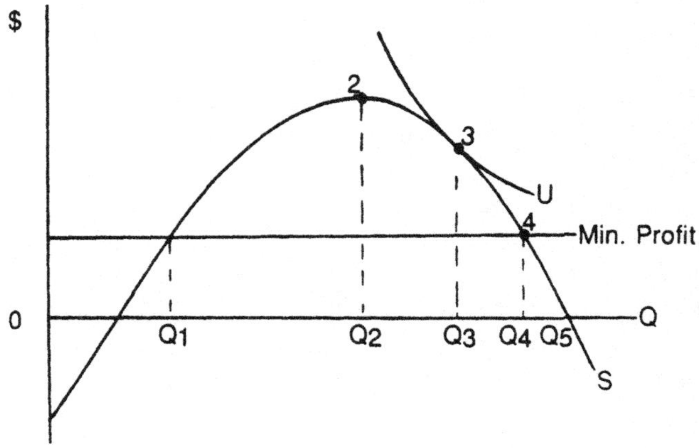

Model 2B is of the Baumol type which maximizes sales subject to a minimum profit constraint. According to this model, the managers of large hospital corporations attempt to increase their sales as much as possible because their salaries and bonuses are tied to increased sales. From the standpoint of personal gain, managers would like to maximize the hospital's total revenues, but first they must achieve the targeted minimum level of profits required to ensure their continued tenure. Targeted profits are needed to please stockholders, bankers, and other potential investors. The hospital that is managed in accordance with Baumol's hypothesis operates at output level Q_4 in Figure 4 which is intermediate to the socially optimal nonprofit level Q_5 and the profit maximization level Q_2.[26]

Reder observes that hospitals are impelled to expand and improve their facilities to attract physicians of the highest qualifications.

> These [prestige] motives operate with special force in the case of hospitals partly because of the predominance of prestige considerations in the minds of sponsors and partly because of the opportunities and incentives that bear upon hospital managements. A hospital administrator can gain

no kudos from paying large dividends; if he succeeds in earning a "profit"—and for him this is not a very important measure of success—all he can do is plow it back. Moreover, his prestige and salary are related to the size, completeness, and modernity (from the medical point of view) of his establishment rather than to any measure of profitability. Hence, the desire to retain "good management" would prompt hospital boards toward expansion if nothing else did. In short, hospitals of the kind under discussion tend to be run as though their objective was to maximize the weighted number of patients treated (per time period), the "weights" being the professional prestige of the doctors attending them.[27]

Boulding observes in his microeconomics text that the managers of a firm are given a good deal of slack over the range of output between Q_1 and Q_4 in which to make decisions because of the high costs of searching for information and of enforcing changes that would raise profits above the satisfactory level.[28]

Managers tend to associate their progress with larger-sized and expanding operations.

Model 2C recognizes the discretion of managers to use limited amounts of profits as they see fit, perhaps for improving the income, prestige,[29] security, power, professional satisfaction[30] and working conditions of managers and employees; and/or perhaps to improve the quality of treatment of patient/customers; perhaps to invest in expansion, research, training, public image and status of the hospital, share of the market, and enhanced profits over a longer time horizon. The utility indifference curve (U) which reflects the composite of management's goals is most likely to be downward sloping as drawn in Figure 4, because managers tend to associate their progress with larger-sized and expanding operations.

Boulding explains that a manager who is willing to go beyond maximum profits (that is, sacrifice profits) to get more of anything, such as size of enterprise, "uncertainty, liquidity, security of control, public reputation, or quality of labor relations,"[31] will have downward sloping indifference curves similar to the management utility indifference curve. The selected point of tangency of the U and S curves will be at some output level Q_3 between Q_2 and Q_4.

While Newhouse concludes that hospital administrators use the surplus to raise both the quality and quantity of output, Lin adopts a broader range in use of profits.[32] Lin defines the portion of the hospital's surplus above the "minimum profit tolerable" as the hospital administrator's "discretionary profit"; such profits can be used for a range of utility producing expenses that include "output, quality, staff, salary, perquisites of office, budget or value of medical services, assets, survival, and (negatively) the level of efforts."[33]

SUMMARY AND CONCLUSIONS

Controversy prevails in the literature of health economics concerning the relative performance and social desirability of not-for-profit versus for-profit hospitals. Application of static models of service maximization and profit maximization to not-for-profit and for-profit hospital organizations, respectively, leads to the theoretical conclusion that patients will be given more basic treatment by a not- for-profit system than by a for-profit system. On the other hand, such comparison overlooks the dynamic workings of profit incentives that motivate hospital managers and decision makers to do their jobs more or less efficiently from a hospital organization viewpoint, depending upon their opportunities to advance their personal ambitions and interests.

The output level decisions of not-for-profit and for-profit hospital organizations were examined theoretically under three different assumed goals (see Box). A general conclusion derived from the models is that hospital output levels will be lower in hospitals where

Outline of Hospital Types Based on Organizational Goals

Not-for-profit hospitals maximize

- Basic service to a maximum number of patients
- Patient satisfaction for those served (higher quality service to fewer patients)
- Managerial utility (operated more to satisfy managers)

For-profit hospitals maximize

- Profits
- Sales subject to profit satisfying
- Managerial discretion subject to profit satisfying

decision makers have goals other than the provision of basic services to a maximum number of patients.

The output level of not-for-profit hospitals will be lower under a goal of providing high quality to fewer patients than under a goal of basic service to a maximum number of patients. Most people would agree that higher quality service to fewer patients is a worthy goal if "higher quality" means that the hospital is devoted to serving patients with the most complex and difficult ailments to treat. In either case—higher quality or not—the number of patients served is reduced where hospital resources are diverted to enhancing the utility of managers.

The output level for the financially successful for-profit hospitals will range from the lower level where profits are maximized (Q_2 in Figure 4) to the highest level, which provides the minimum acceptable level of profit (at Q_4). The level picked within the acceptable range (Q_2 to Q_4) gives the greatest enhancement of managers' utility.

To the extent that the proceeding models have their counterparts in the real world, it is understandable why different people who study the performance of for-profit and not-or-profit hospitals reach different conclusions. Once it is admitted that not-for-profit hospitals can pursue goals other than simply the provision of basic service to a maximum number of patients, then it is unclear what level of services will be produced by a given hospital of either the not-for-profit or for-profit type. Thus it is unclear which organizational form is superior for serving society. What is needed in hospital research is a more clearly defined performance index that takes into account managerial goals.

• • •

The message of this study to managers of health care organizations, whether profit-seeking or non-profit, is that managers should have clearly in mind what their specific goals are, should state them explicitly, and should seek support of those goals by all members of the organization. Managers must be sensitive to the individual goals of all members of the health care team and devise incentives to encourage members to advance organizational goals in their own best interest. Such effort should promote a smoother operation and improve the chances of success of the health care organization in today's increasingly competitive environment.

REFERENCES

1. Gray, B.H., ed. *The New Health Care For-Profit.* Washington, D.C.: National Academy Press, 1983.
2. Gray, B.H., and McNerney, W.J. *The New England Journal of Medicine Special Report* 314 (June 1986): 1523–28.
3. Wohl, S. *The Medical Industrial Complex.* New York: Harmony Books, 1984.
4. Herzlinger, R.E., and Krasker, W.S. "Who Profits from Nonprofits?" *Harvard Business Review* 65 (January/February 1987): 93–106.
5. Fitzgerald, J., and Jacobson, B. "Study Fails to Prove For-Profits' Superiority." *Health Progress* 68, no. 3 (April 1987): 32–37.
6. Gray, B.H., ed. *For-Profit Enterprise in Health Care.* Washington, D.C.: National Academy Press, 1986.
7. Ibid., 185.
8. Ibid., 186–87.
9. Ibid., 187.
10. Ibid., 188.
11. Ibid., 189.
12. Ibid., 190–91.
13. Ibid., 191.
14. Ibid., 191–92.
15. Salkever, D.S. "Competition Among Hospitals." *Competition in the Health Care Sector: Past, Present, and Future.* Washington, D.C.: Federal Trade Commission, 1978, pp. 149–61
16. Langwell, K.H., and Moore, S.F. *A Synthesis of Research on Competition in the Financing and Delivery of Health Services.* U.S. Department of Human Services, National Center for Health Services. Research Report Series No. (PHS) 83 3327, (October 1982): 19–23.
17. Hospitals are required to have a state license and generally must be accredited by the Joint Commission on the Accreditation of Healthcare Organizations (Joint Commission) to be eligible to participate in the Medicare program, to receive payment and funds from other government programs, to gain Blue Cross contracts, and to participate in medical research and education programs.
18. Feldstein, P.J. *Health Associations and the Demand for Legislation: The Political Economy of Health.* Cambridge, Mass.: Ballinger, 1977.
19. Cowing and Holtman believe that, in regard to economies of scope (efficiencies from joint production), more attention is required in health care studies: "Our results indicate. . .that more attention should be paid to the concept of economies of scope since it may be at least as important as scale effects in designing more efficient hospital service delivery systems."
    Cowing, T.G., and Holtmann, A.G. "Multiproduct Short-Run Hospital Cost Functions: Empirical Evidence

and Policy Implication from Cross-Section Data." *Southern Economic Journal* 49 (January 1983): 652.

20. . . .adding a new product expands sales of all products. This results because hospitals with a broad product scope attract more physicians. In turn, these physicians admit their patients to the hospital for the full variety of treatments offered by the hospital. . . . The competition for physicians leads to a proliferation of expensive, high technology equipment, often used at low volume levels. At the same time, hospitals merely maintain a status quo, and do not benefit by their product scope expansion.

    (Finkler, S. A. "The Hospital as a Sales Maximizing Entity." *Health Services Research* 18, no. 2 (Summer 1983): 132.) Reprinted with permission from Health Services Research, Chicago, Illinois, copyright 1983.
21. Pauly, M.V., and Redisch, M. "The Not-For-Profit Hospital as a Physicians Cooperative." *American Economic Review* 63, no. 1 (March 1973): 88.
22. Kwon, J.K. "On the Relative Efficiency of Health Care Systems." *Kyklos* 27 (1974): 830.
23. Coelen, C.G. "Hospital Ownership and Comparative Hospital Costs." In *For-Profit Enterprise in Health Care,* edited by B.H. Gray. Washington, D.C.: National Academy Press, p. 328.
24. Bruce C. Vladeck, President of the United Hospital Fund of New York, October 1984 speech to the California Hospital Association. "Most of the older hospitals in this country were originally created as facilities for poor people who had nowhere else to go, whether they were very sick or not." (Vladeck, B.C. "The Dilemma between Competition and Community Service." *Inquiry* 22 (Summer 1985): 116).
25. Pauly, M.V. "Taxation, Health Insurance, and Market Failure in the Medical Economy." *Journal of Economic Literature* 24 (June 1986): 632.
26. W.J. Baumol's book (1959) explains his famous sales maximization model for the large corporation. (Baumol, W.J. *Business Behavior, Value and Growth,* rev. ed. New York: Harcourt, Brace & World, 1967.) Several other authors have extended Baumol's model to the health care industry: Rice, R.S. "Analysis of the Hospital as an Economic Organism," *Modern Hospital* 106, no. 4 (April 1966): 87–91; Davis, K. "Economic Theories of Behavior in Nonprofit, Private Hospitals." *Economic and Business Bulletin* 24, no. 2 (Winter 1972): 1–13; Finkler, S.A. "The Hospital as a Sales Maximizing Entity," 117–33; and Paroush, J. "Sales-Optimization under an Unstable Profit-Constraint." *Managerial and Decision Economics* 72 (June 1986): 145–46.
27. Reder, M.W. "Some Problems in the Economics of Hospitals." *American Economic Review—Papers and Proceedings* 55 (May 1965): 479–80.
28. Boulding, K.E. *Economic Analysis—Volume I—Microeconomics.* 4th ed. New York: Harper & Row, 1966, p. 600.
29. Newhouse, J.P., "Toward a Theory of Nonprofit Institutions: An Economic Model of a Hospital." *American Economic Review* 60 (March 1970): 64–74. Newhouse believes that the performance of the administrator of a nonprofit hospital is a function of the prestige of the institution which, in turn, depends upon the quality and quantity of the product produced subject to a budget constraint.

    A more recent study assumes that all legally not-for-profit hospitals are prestige maximizers and that "prestige is a function of the hospital's attributes and medical staff size." (Custer, W.S. "Hospital Attributes and Physician Prices." *Southern Economic Journal* 52 (April 1986): 1011.)
30. Lee, M.L. "A Conspicuous Production Theory of Hospital Behavior." *Southern Economic Journal* 38 (July 1971): 49.
31. Boulding, *Economic Analysis,* 608–9.
32. Lin, S.A.Y. "A Managerial Discretion Theory of Hospital Behavior." *Journal of Economics—Selected Papers and Notes* 5 (1979): 88.
33. Ibid.

HCA's acquisition process: The physician's role and perspective

Stephanie L. McFall,
Stephen M. Shortell,
and
Larry M. Manheim

Physicians play an active role in the acquisition process. A study of acquisition impact showed that postacquisition, medical staffs grew and became more specialized and board certified. Greatest physician satisfaction was with the overall facility, medical equipment, and administrative responsiveness.

Health Care Manage Rev, 1988, 13(2), 23–34

One of the most dramatic structural changes in the American hospital industry has been the growth of multihospital systems. Growth of investor-owned systems has been particularly rapid, with the bulk of the growth coming through acquisition.[1] Since 1976, investor-owned systems have bought or leased three times as many hospitals as secular not-for-profit systems and twice as many as religious systems.[2] Growth of investor-owned systems has been largely through acquisition of hospital chains and independent proprietary hospitals, but has also come through the acquisition of not-for-profit and government hospitals.[3]

This article examines the acquisition process, focusing on the physician's role in the process, using detailed comparative case studies of seven hospitals acquired by Hospital Corporation of America (HCA) in 1980. It also compares medical staff characteristics of all hospitals acquired by HCA between 1977 and 1984 to HCA's market area competitors. Issues addressed include the physicians's role in the acquisition decision; changes in medical staff size, composition, board certification status, and turnover; physician satisfaction with the acquisition; and ongoing management of hospital-physician relationships after acquisition.

While the sample of acquired hospitals in this study is limited to acquisitions by a single investor-owned corporation, it does reflect acquisitions by the largest corporation. Furthermore, selection of a single chain avoids differences due to variation in acquisition and operational strategies. In addition, HCA was more likely than other investor-owned companies to acquire not-for-profit or public hospitals.[4]

When a hospital is acquired by a multihospital system, physicians on the medical staff face a number of issues. How will decisions about medical staff member-

Stephanie L. McFall, *Ph.D., is Project Director at the Center for Health Services and Policy Research, Northwestern University, Evanston, Illinois.*

Stephen M. Shortell, *Ph.D., is the A.C. Buehler Distinguished Professor of Hospital and Health Services Management and Professor of Organizational Behavior, J.L. Kellogg Graduate School of Management, Northwestern University.*

Larry M. Manheim, *Ph.D., is Associate Director of the Center for Health Services and Policy Research, Northwestern University.*

The project on which this article is based was funded by HCA Foundation, Nashville, Tennessee. In addition, the authors acknowledge assistance from the Center for Health Studies, Hospital Corporation of America.

ship and hospital privileges be made? To what extent and in what areas will local hospitals be autonomous? Will physicians have less input into hospital decision making? What will be their relationship with the corporate office? How much, if any, input will physicians have into corporate policy? How intrusive will the new administration be with regard to practice patterns of physicians?

A growing body of literature addresses such questions from the corporate or system standpoint.[5,6] Studies from hospital administration or physician perspectives have been rare, consisting of case studies of single hospitals[7-10] One theme in these studies is the importance of involving the medical staff in planning for such mergers and acquisitions to gain physician support and facilitate the transition. The importance and difficulty of involving physicians in the acquisition decision was also noted by corporate spokespersons.[11] The case studies of mergers do not compare physician involvement in acquisition across types of hospitals, nor do they assess the impact of acquisition on medical staff size and composition, participation in decision making, or satisfaction with the change in ownership.

Physician reactions to hospital acquisition should be viewed in light of the major shifts taking place in hospital-medical staff relationships in general.[12] Increasingly, hospitals and physicians have developed interdependent relationships. Traditionally, many factors emphasized the independence of physicians. Few physicians were direct hospital employees and formal control over physician behavior was exerted indirectly via the organized medical staff. Physicians were influential because they admitted patients and through their orders generated much of the costs of patient care. Hospitals were often seen as being organized around these physician functions. The growing importance of sophisticated technology and increased competitiveness among physicians have made physicians more dependent on hospitals. Furthermore, hospitals' legal responsibility for quality of care has also encouraged more complex webs of interdependency and control. The acquisition process must be considered within this context.

OVERVIEW OF THE ACQUISITION PROCESS

Acquisition is a sequence of events involving three stages: (1) the decision on the part of the local hospital to sell; (2) the decision on the part of the corporation to buy; and (3) the final agreement.

Stage 1: Deciding to sell the hospital

In this stage the hospital considers sale as an option. Factors considered by the case study hospitals included pressure from regulatory and licensing agencies, problems with financial management, conflict over hospital leadership, and problems with access to capital. In the hospitals the authors studied, lack of access to capital often triggered the decision to sell but was rarely the sole motivating factor. The hospital's decision to sell was influenced by the owners' goals and their beliefs that these goals could be better achieved through sale than through continued operation. Besides financial gain, goals included continued service, indigent care, improved quality, and maintenance of the hospital's reputation. Typically, the hospital initiated contact with the corporation about the possibility of the sale.

Stage 2: Deciding to bid on the hospital

The hospital system's decision to bid on the hospital was based on an analysis of the expected rate of return. Elements to be considered in the determination of a bid included projected revenues from the hospital, based on history of earnings, changes in the market (economic growth, mix of payers, population characteristics), and ability to make improvements in hospital management; costs associated with the acquisition, such as capital improvements, professional fees, and payment of outstanding debt; and expectations of local hospital stakeholders regarding constellation of services to be offered, capital investments, and desired profits on the hospital investment. The presence of aggressive competitors in the bidding can greatly alter the price and other terms of the proposal. While formal analysis of these factors typically awaited the approach from the hospital, it is important to realize that the hospital system had more industry experience than the local hospital on which to base calculations. The hospital system could thus quickly perform sophisticated evaluations of the hospital's management and market potential.

Stage 3: Reaching an agreement

During the period studied, 1977-1984, most acquisitions involved competitive bidding; however, for simplification negotiation is seen as taking place between a single buyer and seller. Informal negotiation begins with gathering data for the bid, a process that permits exploration of the expectations of the various hospital stakeholders. The openness of such explorations depends on type of hospital ownership. Public hospitals had the greatest public accountability, resulting in wider and more formal consultation with stakeholders. Subject to approval of regulatory agencies, the decision for investor-owned hospitals belonged to the owners and few others were consulted. The not-for-profit hospitals were intermediate in the number and breadth of stakeholders consulted. After presentation of a formal proposal, additional negotiations occurred, in effect fine tuning the deal. This typically involved a smaller circle of participants. With an agreement reached, preparation began for the transition of ownership.

METHOD OF STUDY

The seven case study hospitals were selected to satisfy the following criteria: The acquisitions were independent, that is, hospitals were not purchased as part of a group of hospitals; the acquisitions took place prior to 1982, with several years to evaluate the outcomes; the hospitals were not contract managed by HCA prior to acquisition; and the hospitals reflect, as a group, a range of characteristics (type of prior ownership, size, and presence of competitors). All seven hospitals studied were acquired in 1980 and met the selected criteria (See Table 1). Table 1 also indicates bed size, percentage of the population that is urban, and construction of a replacement facility. The construction of Hospital E was not initiated by HCA, but was completed shortly before the acquisition.

To assess the generalizability of these seven acquired hospitals to other acquisitions, the authors compared them on several dimensions with other freestanding acquisitions made by HCA between 1977 and 1984. In 1979, the year prior to acquisition of the case study hospitals, the case study hospitals were equally likely as the other HCA acquisitions to be accredited by the Joint Commission on Accreditation of Hospitals (about 83%). They also were similar in bed size. Both groups were concentrated in the Southeast and Southwest, and had similar demographic profiles with respect to urban population, white population, and median family income. The case study communities had a higher percentage of their population over age 65 and consequently had higher Medicare utilization. The case study hospitals differed from the other freestanding acquisitions in type of preacquisition control, being more likely to be investor owned (43% versus 18%) and less likely to be a county or hospital district facility (29% versus 51%). Hospitals acquired through the purchase of another hospital management company (chain ac-

TABLE 1

DESCRIPTION OF CASE STUDY HOSPITALS: INDIVIDUAL ACQUISITIONS, 1980

Hospital	Bed size at acquisition	Previous control	Replacement facility	Single-hospital county	Urban population (%)
A	Fewer than 100	Not for profit	No	No	18
B	Greater than 200	Investor owned	No	No	89
C	150–200	Government	Yes	Yes	91
D	Fewer than 100	Not for profit	Yes	Yes	0
E	100	Investor owned	New building	Yes	26
F	150–200	Investor owned	No	No	81
G	150–200	Government	No	Yes	59

quisitions) were less concentrated in the Southeast and were located in more urban and more competitive areas than the case study hospitals.

The case studies included interviews with physicians, members of the hospital management team, board members, and community leaders. Physician respondents were selected to represent particular positions on the medical staff. At each site, interviews were conducted with the chief of staff, a physician governing board member, and a young physician (less than 40 years old). The younger physicians were interviewed to get their perspectives on new health care developments. In addition, former owners of the physician-owned hospitals were interviewed to provide background information about the acquisition process. Altogether, 25 physicians were interviewed. The interviews were semistructured with some standardized questions rating hospital characteristics before and after the acquisition. The physician interviews averaged 45 minutes and were taped. Information was also collected about the size and composition of the medical staff, committee organization, and physician participation in hospital decision making in 1979 and 1985. The minutes of the medical staff and its executive committee meetings for those periods were also reviewed.

The 1983 American Hospital Association (AHA) Annual Survey was used to provide data on HCA acquired hospitals and their market area competitors. The competitor hospitals are located within 15 miles of the focal HCA acquisitions.[13] When the acquired hospital had no nearby competitors, a matching hospital of similar size from the same state was used.

RESULTS

Data presented here relate to the following questions: (1) What role did physicians play in acquisition? (2) What changes took place in medical staff structure following acquisition? and (3) How did physicians evaluate the acquisitions?

Physician input into the acquisition process

Looking at the seven acquisitions as a whole, physicians had input into the acquisition in all three stages, as direct decision makers, or more frequently, as indirect influential participants. The type and extent of physician involvement in acquisition varied by type of hospital.

Decision to sell

Physicians often had a role in the hospital's decision to sell. The physicians interviewed often expressed dissatisfaction with the existing level and quality of medical technology, the availability of diagnostic services, and the overall condition of the facility. The hospitals all faced difficulty in obtaining capital (although this shortage was not a crisis in all sites), which contributed to difficulties in satisfying the desires of the medical staff for improved equipment and technology. This dissatisfaction led to perception of the administrator as nonresponsive to physician needs. The major complaints of the physicians interviewed related first to the hospitals' financial troubles and second to management. Physicians saw fewer problems related to direct patient care, that is, the quality of care, the nursing staff, and patient satisfaction. The likelihood of future problems in maintaining the competitive position of the hospital increased physician support for sale although this support was not universal.

Physicians had input into hospital acquisitions as direct decision makers, or more frequently, as indirect influential participants.

Physicians' concerns were interrelated. Hospital D is an example of how financial problems and perceptions of management interact. The hospital was led by two physicians, one of whom had been the administrator for many years. The younger physicians wanted the hospital to purchase equipment and amenities for the patients' rooms that would modernize the old building. The administrator and governing board often resisted their requests, giving in only when convinced that the equipment was absolutely necessary.

To put this conflict into context, it should be noted that the desired improvements ranged from basics such as adding a toilet to each patient room to developing more sophisticated diagnostic services. The physician community of general practitioners and general surgeons was slow to grow and the hospital provided few specialized services. The conflict stemmed from differing values. The young physicians were committed to providing the best care possible, using modern equipment and methods, while the administrator wished to keep costs low for patients while providing basic services. This longstanding conflict was put aside only when the facility no longer met structural licensure requirements. This crisis united the physicians, the administrator, and the governing board, and they decided that the transition to HCA control was the only way to keep the hospital in the community.

Input into the corporate decision to bid

Medical staff members were interviewed by prospective purchasers about needed improvements in medical technology and service areas that the physicians wanted to develop. These discussions provided data for the preparation of the proposals by the bidding hospital systems. However, these discussions were more than the elicitation of physician "shopping lists." They were opportunities to win influential members of the medical staff over to the idea of an acquisition. Convincing physician leaders that the acquisition would permit a standard of facility, equipment, and technology not possible given the current hospital ownership was a potent argument. The interviews also helped the prospective purchaser appraise the quality of the medical staff.

Formal and informal negotiations

HCA had additional opportunities to win over the physicians. One method was to encourage physicians to tour nearby HCA hospitals. Physicians from five of the case study hospitals toured other HCA hospitals or corporate offices. Talking with their physician counterparts in HCA-owned facilities allayed many concerns about HCA's management approach and administrative interference with medical practice. Most visits were scheduled by HCA, but one physician at Hospital D reported conducting his own informal tour so that he could reach his own conclusions about HCA.

Physician courtship was more ardent in publicly made decisions. In communities C and G, which had government-owned hospitals, physicians were expected to provide expert endorsement of the anticipated quality of the facility and its services under the new management. For example, physicians at Hospital C were asked by the competing bidders to speak in favor of their proposals at meetings of the county commissioners. With multiple companies bidding, each trying to enlist the aid of members of the medical staff, conflict and turmoil resulted. For example, the negotiations for the sale of Hospital A involved such complications. The hospital governing board had made a preliminary decision in favor of a regional not-for-profit system and was in the process of fine tuning the agreement. But the hospital governing board complained that two of the companies that had been rejected (including HCA) were "still trying to stir the pot" by continuing to press their case with members of the board and medical staff. The board directed that communication with the hospital management companies cease by anyone other than the board negotiation committee.

Physicians also had input with respect to the decision to sell to a particular bidder. The major concern physicians had with a sale to HCA, as opposed to other buyers, was the possibility of corporate control of conditions of practice, which includes concern about the impact of profit orientation and fear of losing local control. Both, it was thought, would have an adverse impact on professional autonomy.

Variation by hospital type

The role of physicians in the acquisition process varied by type of hospital control. The investor-owned hospitals present an interesting paradox. The physician-owners had greater than usual physician input, since the final authority for the decision was theirs. The privileges of ownership made certain factors important in the sale agreement. They were concerned that HCA might exert undue control over physician behavior. One physician from Hospital B was quoted in the press: "The control of the hospital will remain in our hands. It's got to. Believe me, I spent a lot of blood, sweat and tears over it. We're not going to give it away and I'm not going to watch it go down the drain." This exaggerated emotional outburst illustrates the depth of concern felt by the investors. The physician-owners took great care to preserve physician influence. For example, the acquisition agreement for Hospital F contains clauses calling for physician board representation and the ability of the local board (physician dominated) to remove administrators by petition to the regional vice-president.

Physicians at not-for-profit and government hospitals had significant input into the decision to sell and in the negotiations. However, their reported concerns were more likely to be about congruence of past and future operating goals under the new ownership. One concern involved care of the indigent and possible price increases. Physicians in the not-for-profit and government hospitals were also more likely than their counterparts in for-profit hospitals to worry about the scope of services to be offered under the changed ownership. For example, physicians at Hospital A did not want to become a satellite facility for a nearby larger HCA hospital. These concerns were addressed in discussions with physicians and in the structure of the proposed acquisition agreement. For example, the proposals to acquire Hospital C included the range of services that would be offered, the policy for continuation of indigent care, and an estimate of the amount of uncompensated care to be given.

The fear that HCA might interfere with medical practice as a result of the loss of local control was hard to counter in advance of experience with HCA. This concern was found to some extent in all sites studied and was usually not completely dispelled before the acquisition. Discussion of this issue largely hinged on HCA management philosophy and was shaped by the tours of other HCA facilities. Some physicians felt they shared values with the corporate founders, who were physicians. They were also reassured by the HCA position at that time of not competing with its medical staffs. HCA was viewed more favorably than other management companies by the physicians interviewed. It must be recognized, however, that the hospitals studied chose HCA. Physicians in hospitals acquired by other hospital systems might have different opinions.

Changes in medical staff structure

Changes in the size and composition of the medical staff could reflect the level of acceptability of HCA ownership. While data are not available to compare changes over time in the medical staffs of competitor hospitals, it is possible to compare the size and composition of HCA acquired hospitals with their competitors using data on medical staff organization from the 1983 AHA survey.

Change in staff size and rate of turnover

Table 2 shows the change in the size of the active medical staff and the rate of turnover from 1979-1984 for the seven case study hospitals. Substantial increases in the relative size of the active staff occurred in all hospitals following the acquisition, with the exception of Hospitals A and F, which also had relatively high turnover. The rate of turnover was, in general, relatively low. Hospital A, with relatively high turnover, continues to pursue representatives of some of the basic specialties, such as obstetrics. It is difficult to determine the forces in Hospital F that may have resulted in higher than average turnover. Most prominently, the closing of the pediatric department just before the acquisition prompted some departures. Indeed, one-third of physicians leaving the staff between 1979 and 1984 were pediatricians or family or general practitioners.

TABLE 2

SIZE OF ACTIVE STAFF AND RATE OF TURNOVER PRE- AND POSTACQUISITION

Hospital	Preacquisition	Postacquisition	Turnover rate 1979–1984*
A	14	14	.222
B	115	165	.098
C	39	61	.047
D	12	16	.158
E	8	17	.150
F	124	121	.239
G	24	33	.108
Mean	48	61	.146

*Includes retirees as well as those leaving for other reasons.

It is not easy to assess the optimum level of turnover. Some attrition clearly can be beneficial. Studies cited by Luft[14] suggest annual turnover rates of 5 percent to 13 percent in the staffs of prepaid group practices and 10 percent among the Veterans Administration full-time physician staff. Turnover was higher among probationary members and lower among partners or those with a financial stake in the organization.[15] However, the average yearly turnover in the seven case study hospitals was estimated at 3 percent, so by all indications, acquisition did not lead to an exodus among physicians.

As part of planning, administrators analyze characteristics of the medical staff to determine whether additions are needed in particular specialty areas. This includes determining whether older physicians who may soon want to begin limiting their workloads predominate. For several of the smaller hospitals studied, recruitment of additional physicians was seen as an important marketing strategy. The difficulties of recruiting in small rural hospitals are well known.[16,17] In the rural hospitals studied, like Hospitals A and E, many of the young physicians interviewed said that they would not have come to practice in the community given the conditions of the old hospital. Thus HCA's investment in equipment and facility renovation enhanced the hospital's ability to recruit physicians.

Nevertheless, despite the renovation and replacement of hospital facilities, some of the sites studied still had recruitment problems. For example, Hospital D was located in an area of high unemployment, and like many farming communities, had been hurt by the downturn in the agricultural economy. However, HCA administrators were slow to initiate recruiting in the face of opposition from physicians in the town.

Composition of medical staff

In addition to changes in size, medical staff changes in level of specialization and certification were examined. Table 3 summarizes two aspects of change in the composition of the active medical staff: the primary care ratio and the percentage of board-certified physicians. The primary care ratio represents the number of general and family practitioners, pediatricians, general internists, and obstetricians on the staff relative to the other members of the staff. Values under 1 indicate more specialists than generalists. This ratio shifted downward over the period, indicating the addition of more specialists than generalists (as did a more restrictive ratio of general and family practitioners to other medical staff members). There is still substantial variation in the case study sites with respect to change in the primary care ratio. While the overall shift is toward greater specialization, primary care practitioners continue to dominate Hospitals A and G.

Table 3 also summarizes the board certification of the active medical staff members in 1979 and 1984. With the exception of Hospitals A and G, the postacquisition medical staffs were more likely to be board certified, with an overall increase from 55 percent to 61 percent. This is in comparison to a national figure of 68.9 percent.[18] Overall, 49 percent of the 73 physicians who resigned from the active staffs of the case study hospitals were board certified, in contrast to 68 percent of the 164 active staff additions. This offers some support to the view of gradual improvement in medical staff qualifications after acquisition.

The change in medical staff structure and composition was largely in the direction of larger and somewhat more specialized staffs. Active staff members were also more likely to be board certified following the acquisition. Comparative longitudinal data with which to compare changes over time for acquired hospitals and their competitors are unavailable, but it is possible to compare hospitals at a single point in time.

TABLE 3

COMPOSITION OF ACTIVE MEDICAL STAFF PRE- AND POSTACQUISITION

Hospital	Primary care ratio		Board certified (%)	
	Pre-acquisition	Post-acquisition	Pre-acquisition	Post-acquisition
A	1.80	1.80	50	50
B	.47	.50	64	74
C	1.43	.79	59	70
D	1.00	.46	8	38
E	.60	.54	NA*	47
F	.63	.34	75	83
G	1.40	1.67	75	64
Mean	1.04	.87	55	61

*Data not available.

Medical staff size and composition compared to competitors

Table 4 compares the staff size, composition, and board certification status of the active and associate medical staff of HCA acquired hospitals and their market area competitors. The table cells indicate the subgroup mean, standard deviation (in parentheses), and range. In testing the difference in means in medical staff size and specialty category size, a natural log transformation was used to stabilize the variation. In addition, the difference in means was tested after adjusting for bed size.

As shown, the acquired hospitals consistently had smaller medical staffs than their competitors, for all specialty groups. However, after adjusting for bed size, the differences are not statistically significant, nor is the

TABLE 4

MEDICAL STAFF SIZE AND COMPOSITION: ACQUIRED HOSPITALS AND COMPETITORS, 1983

Specialty	HCA acquired hospitals (N=71)	Competitor hospitals (N=146)	*t* value* (probability)
General/family practice	12.14 (8.59) 0–42	17.71 (14.37) 0–77	.21 (.834)
Pediatrics	3.82 (6.65) 0–48	11.61 (19.01) 0–143	-.56 (5.79)
Internal medicine	12.37 (16.86) 0–98	24.57 (42.05) 0–407	.18 (.860)
Other medical specialty	9.86 (11.68) 0–66	21.48 (24.55) 0–129	-1.26 (.208)
General surgery	6.99 (6.55) 1–39	12.53 (12.54) 0–81	-.36 (.717)
Obstetrics	6.44 (7.74) 0–39	12.83 (16.54) 0–132	-1.18 (.239)
Other surgical specialty	18.51 (18.73) 0–87	34.18 (35.75) 0–229	.35 (.726)
Other specialties†	12.89 (10.43) 0–49	23.03 (31.48) 0–266	.36 (.716)
Total staff	86.80 (70.50) 5–327	165.18 (169.20) 3–1326	1.24 (.218)
Generalist ratio	.35 (.46)	.33 (.60)	.22 (.822)
Primary care ratio	1.08 (1.22)	.85 (1.66)	1.85 (.065)
Percentage board certified	63.37 (17.33)	63.76 (16.87)	-.16 (.875)

*Test for differences in means in staff size (natural log transformation), adjusted for bed size.
†Includes pathology, radiology, anesthesiology, and psychiatry.

direction of the adjusted difference consistent across the various specialty categories.

A number of indicators of staff composition were examined, but the acquired hospitals differed little from their competitors on these measures. While acquired hospitals showed a slight trend toward primary care specialties, this difference was not statistically significant ($p > .05$). Overall, members of the staffs of acquired hospitals were as likely to be board certified as members in competing hospitals.

Given the availability of data from 1983 only, it is not possible to assess whether the difference in medical staff composition between HCA acquired hospitals and their competitors has changed over time, that, that is, whether a hospital becomes more competitive in terms of medical staff characteristics once it has been acquired. If such improvements in medical staff composition were taking place, the hospitals acquired earlier would have more board-certified members than those acquired more recently, since HCA had more time to affect the staff. In a regression analysis that controlled for bed size, urban population, and region, no support was found for this hypothesis. In fact, more recently acquired hospitals had a somewhat higher percentage of board-certified specialists although this difference was not statistically significant ($p > .05$). Possible explanations are that the continued presence of HCA in the early acquisition induced the board-certified members to leave or less highly trained physicians to join the medical staffs, or that the more recent acquisitions had a higher percentage of board-certified specialists than the earlier hospitals at acquisition. This second explanation is far more plausible and consistent with both the case study findings and the observation that HCA selection criteria for acquisitions have become more stringent over time.

Physician satisfaction

One way of framing the question of whether the physicians got what they wanted from the acquisition is to compare their pre- and postacquisition ratings of hospital attributes. Table 5 summarizes the mean ratings for the two time periods. The overall trend is positive as indicated by paired *t* tests of the differences in pre- and postacquisition ratings. Positive values indicate characteristics rated higher after acquisition than before. The greatest increases, and typically also the highest postacquisition scores, are seen with respect to the quality of medical equipment and technology, the

TABLE 5

PHYSICIAN RATINGS OF HOSPITAL CHARACTERISTICS PRE- AND POSTACQUISITION*

Characteristic	Preacquisition mean	Postacquisition mean	Mean difference	*t*	Degrees of freedom	Probability
Technology and equipment	2.53	4.65	2.06	10.87	17	.001
Scope of services	2.47	4.47	1.78	8.57	22	.001
Administrative responsiveness to physicians	2.71	4.29	1.59	5.12	16	.001
Financial health	2.71	3.82	1.17	3.08	22	.005
Quality of facility	2.65	4.47	1.65	7.12	22	.001
Reputation in community	2.71	3.94	.87	3.54	22	.002
Staffing levels	3.12	3.35	.24	.85	16	.410
Diagnostic services	3.18	4.18	1.00	4.12	17	.001
Meeting community needs	3.12	4.24	.96	4.70	22	.001
Quality of nursing	3.12	3.59	.44	2.87	22	.009
Patient satisfaction	3.12	4.00	.61	2.71	22	.013
Quality of care	3.29	3.76	.44	2.47	22	.022

*Characteristics rated on a scale from 1 = unacceptable to 5 = excellent.

quality of the facility, the scope of services provided, and responsiveness of the administration to physician concerns, and the hospital's financial health.

Physician satisfaction with the quality of the facility and medical equipment was low prior to the acquisition. The substantial increase in these ratings supports interview data suggesting that physicians received a large measure of what they wanted. Two of seven case study hospitals were replaced, one completed a lagging building program, and the remaining hospitals had major renovations and expansions, with particular emphasis on improving the ancillary departments.

The physicians interviewed repeatedly praised the local administrators for their competence, their professionalism, and their open communication with the medical staffs. Several of the administrators interviewed said they had an open door policy, in which physicians were welcome to drop by and state their concerns. One chief executive officer (CEO) said that he tried to go to the hospital everyday and speak with as many physicians as he could. Thus a common thread in the administrators' philosophies was to encourage communication with the physicians on an informal basis.

With respect to physician participation in formalized decision making, HCA policy calls for a mixture of physician and lay community representation on the local hospital advisory board. Most financial decisions are not within the province of the boards, but they do have important functions in approving medical staff privileges, monitoring quality of care, and providing a forum for voicing local professional and community concerns. Physician membership at the case study sites ranged from 29 percent to 80 percent in 1985, heaviest in the two formerly physician-owned hospitals. In several hospitals, this represented an increase in physician participation in decision making. For example, in 1979, Hospital C had no physician representative; the board was appointed by the state governor, resulting in a board better connected to party politics than to local community, business, or professional interests. The sole physician board member at Hospital A was elected from among the other financial contributors to the not-for-profit corporation, not for his professional position. Physician representation was most extensive in physician-owned hospitals B and F. The remaining facilities were not dominated by physicians nor did they exclude them, so the physician-to-layperson balance was about 1:4. Within the confines of the reduced functions of the hospital boards, physicians have increased representation on a body with local authority for several issues of concern to them.

The physicians interviewed repeatedly praised the local administrators for their competence, their professionalism, and their open communication with the medical staffs.

A related issue is physician input into corporate policy. The majority of the physicians interviewed appeared not to have given much thought to the question of how much input physicians should have into corporate decisions. HCA's philosophy of decentralized management resulted in little physician contact with the division vice-presidents. HCA has established a 19-member Physician Board of Governors made up of members of medical staffs of HCA hospitals, but few physicians interviewed knew of the activities or functions of the board, or even knew of its existence.

Improvement in facility, improvement in management, and growth of the medical staff contributed to perceived improvements in the scope of services. Improvement in ancillary areas led to the expansion of services. Before acquisition, some of the hospitals had only routine radiology and laboratory tests. After acquisition, one CEO stated, "All major ancillary areas have been totally renovated, enlarged, or relocated." A number of the hospitals have tried to develop or encourage the use of outpatient services such as ambulatory surgery. Services to absorb excess bed capacity are being introduced in several of the sites. A number of administrators spoke of making rooms available to patients' families. Hospital D was beginning to develop a new substance abuse program that could be marketed beyond the immediate service area. The larger, more diverse medical staffs and the ability of the hospital to provide the needed specialized equipment also contributed to the greater range of services.

It was difficult for the physicians rating the financial health of the hospital to distinguish the financial status of the hospital from that of the corporation. The physicians were quite aware of the general declines in occupancy levels and inpatient days. Each site that was visited had implemented many measures to control costs. Many physicians did not feel that the cost-control measures were adversely affecting their practice, with the exception of capital purchases, but concerns about future limitations or restrictions were expressed. Their comments about their hospital's financial status were also shaped by their awareness of the difficulties of other area hospitals. They found it a great strength to be associated with a large system like HCA, speaking of it as a source of security. The majority of the physicians thought they had benefited from the investment HCA made in their hospitals. However, they remain uncertain about the financial future of their hospitals.

The smallest increases were seen in physicians' ratings of the levels of support staff and the overall quality of care and quality of nursing. These ratings may indicate areas of residual concern to physicians. There are, of course, limitations to the validity and precision of such ratings. They are perceptual and partially retrospective. Yet the physicians did not appear to view the preacquisition hospitals with nostalgia. Given the importance of these dimensions and the unique perspective of physicians in these areas, the relatively small improvements in these ratings can be viewed as significant, given that a "ceiling effect" is not operating.

In the preacquisition period, the overall quality of care and the quality of nursing were among the highest rated attributes. Changes other than the acquisition may be affecting physician confidence in the quality of care; for instance, the advent of prospective reimbursement raised quality concerns for many physicians. There is also the possibility that as efforts to review quality become more organized, the awareness of remaining problems increases. While the cause cannot be determined, there are signs of physician concern about the quality of care.

Ratings of quality of nursing care are associated with the level of support staff. Both issues were a matter of some concern to some physicians interviewed. The hospitals had instituted several measures to control salary costs—measures that, at some level, could potentially impinge on patient care. Whether or not the quality of nursing care, for example, was actually affected, physicians feared that staff cutbacks could lower the level of care provided, possibly cutting back on the "caring and the smiles."

HOSPITAL-PHYSICIAN RELATIONSHIPS IN ACQUIRED HOSPITALS

Physicians played an important role in acquisition. Financial problems, leading to a vicious circle of declining facility, service, and prestige, made physicians more receptive to options that included the sale of the hospital. In the course of discussions and negotiations, physicians sought to ensure minimal encroachment in professional prerogatives and improvement in their workplace. HCA attempted in this phase to win over physician opinion leaders. Most major changes that would disturb the medical staff were introduced gradually and were preceded by extensive communication with the medical staff organization and individual physicians. Physicians were key decision makers in the acquisition only in the case of physician-owned hospitals. But widespread opposition to a particular bidder would discourage corporate enthusiasm for the purchase, if not steer the hospital toward other potential buyers.

Changes in medical staff size and composition offer some hints about physician reaction to acquisition. The size of the active medical staffs generally increased, medical staff turnover in the five years following the acquisition was reasonable, and staffs became more heavily weighted toward subspecialists and board certification. In general, the findings indicate some degree of medical staff development.

One objective of the physician interviews was to assess their perceptions of the strengths and limitations of the association with HCA, now and in the future. From this analysis HCA has devoted extensive attention to developing good relationships with the majority of physicians in the hospitals it has acquired. Compared with preacquisition experiences, physicians give particularly high marks to improvements in medical technology and equipment, scope of services offered, administrative responsiveness to physician concerns, quality of facilities, and improvements in diagnostic services. There has also been improvement in the extent to which physicians are actively involved at the individual hospital board level. Physicians positively evaluated HCA's potential power as a lobbyist and its resources for helping local hospitals and practitioners deal with third party policies and regulations. The strength and expertise provided by the corporation was expected to help the local hospitals make the best of their position in the marketplace.

This is not to say that the physicians had no reservations about the acquisition. The acquired hospitals, along with other multisystem hospitals, face a number of challenges to maintaining a favorable hospital-physician relationship. These challenges will take three primary forms: the need to be more cost competitive, the need to diversify services, and the need to provide for meaningful physician input at the corporate level.

The need to become more cost competitive will mean continued attention to staffing composition and levels, productivity improvement programs, and departmental and program consolidation. HCA physicians may see these as putting undue emphasis on cost containment to the exclusion of quality and service objectives. This will be particularly true to the extent that these changes are seen as being made primarily by the corporate office rather than by the individual hospitals.

Service diversification may take many forms. Examples include alternative delivery system involvement such as preferred provider organizations and health maintenance organizations, insurance-service linkages (e.g., Equitable Insurance joint venture), hospital-physician joint ventures such as diagnostic imaging and ambulatory surgery, buying of physician practices, and involvement with multispecialty group practice clinics. Each of these poses threats to physicians because they involve activities that are new and different from the way medicine has been practiced in the past. In particular, they involve a much closer merging of economic managerial interests and activities with clinical issues and activities. Some shifts will inevitably be seen by the physicians as competition from the hospitals. Again, to the extent that these new strategies and program developments are perceived to be made by the corporate office, with little input from individual hospitals and their medical staffs, unproductive conflict may be expected.

However, to the extent that these strategies are seen as responses to market changes threatening their hospital and their own practices, physicians are likely to be far more receptive to such changes. Providing physicians greater access to hospital and corporate governance activities will help physicians understand the underlying corporate strategy's relevance to local economic conditions. This is likely to reduce unnecessary antagonisms during a period of dramatic change in the health care environment.

REFERENCES

1. Hoy, E.W., and Gray, B.H. "Trends in the Growth of the Major Investor-Owned Hospital Companies." In *For-Profit Enterprise in Healthcare*, edited by the Institute of Medicine, Washington, D.C.: National Academy Press, 1986, pp. 250-59.
2. Alexander, J.A., Lewis, B.L., and Morrissey, M.A. "Acquisition Strategies of Multihospital Systems." *Health Affairs* 4 (1985): 49-66.
3. Hoy and Gray, "Trends in the Growth of the Major Investor-Owned Hospital Companies."
4. Ibid.
5. Morlock, L.L., Alexander, J.A., and Hunter, H. "Formal Relationships Among Governing Boards, CEO's and Medical Staffs in Independent and System Hospitals." *Medical Care* 23 (1985): 1193-1213.
6. Alexander, J.A., Morrissey, M.A., and Shortell, S.M. "The Effects of Competition, Regulation and Corporatization on Hospital-Physician Relationships." *Journal of Health and Social Behavior* 27 (1986): 220-35.
7. Brown, M. "Multihospital Systems: Implications for Physicians." *Hospital Medical Staff* 8 (1979): 2-11.
8. Tremonti, L., and Manning, M.R. "Merging Hospitals and Physician Support." *Journal of the American Medical Association* 250 (1983): 2628-32.
9. Shirley, R.C. "Analysis of Employee and Physician Attitudes Toward Hospital Merger." *Academy of Management Review* 16 (1973): 465-80.
10. Williams, A.H. "Medical Staff Merger Is No Easy Task." *Hospitals* 54 (1980): 55-62.
11. Alexander, Lewis, and Morrissey, "Acquisition Strategies."
12. Shortell, S.M. "The Medical Staff of the Future: Replanting the Garden." *Frontiers of Health Services Management* 1 (1985): 3-48.
13. Luft, H.S., and Maerki, S.C. "Competitive Potential of Hospitals and Their Neighbors." *Contemporary Policy Issues* 3 (1984): 89-102.
14. Luft, H.S. *Health Maintenance Organizations: Dimensions of Performance*. New York: Wiley, 1981.
15. Ibid.
16. Clark, J.W. "Recruiting for the Rural Hospital." In *Persuading Physicians*, edited by R. Rubright. Rockville, Md.: Aspen Publishers, 1984, pp. 21-23.
17. Lawley, J.B., and Copelan, H.N. "Physician Recruitment." In *Management Issues for Rural Hospitals*, edited by S.L. Weiss, D.F. Phillips, and J.G. Schuman. Chicago: American Hospital Publishing, 1986, pp. 143-55.
18. Morrissey, M.A., Shortell, S.M., and Noie, N.E. "A Survey of Hospital Medical Staffs—Part 2." *Hospitals* 57 (1983): 91-94.

Physicians' ranking of hospital attributes: A comparison by use group

Andreas Muller
and
Patricia Bledsoe

Because physicians play a central role in supplying hospitals with patients, it is important for hospital managers to learn more about physicians' preferences. A review of the literature and a new survey help to pinpoint what physicians value in hospitals.

Health Care Manage Rev, 1989, 14(3), 77–84

In the last decade, hospitals have made deliberate efforts to become more consumer-oriented. Billboards, television commercials, and newspaper advertisements promoting hospital services have become commonplace, especially in urban areas where competition for patients exists.

So far, most market research for hospitals has focused on consumers,[1-4] while physicians have received much less attention. This is somewhat surprising, as physicians are influential intermediaries between patients and hospitals. According to a national study, only about one quarter of the consumers surveyed said that they selected hospitals without consulting physicians.[5]

Because physicians play a central role in supplying hospitals with patients, it is important for hospital managers to learn more about physicians' preferences. With such knowledge, they may be able to present the hospital in a more appealing way to physicians, or to guide the setting of priorities in an effort to satisfy physicians' needs more fully. Presumably such a strategy will attract and retain physicians.

OBJECTIVES AND RATIONALE

This article reports on a study conducted to determine which hospital characteristics are of the greatest importance to physicians. The study had two main objectives: (1) to determine how physicians rank various hospital attributes; and (2) to determine whether prime admitters rank hospital attributes differently than nonprime admitters.

Of three previous studies that investigated physicians' rankings of hospital attributes, none organized its analysis according to physicians' admission volume. An analysis by volume of use is important, however, in that it provides the opportunity to focus on the needs of the group of physicians that is most valuable to the hospital. According to Kotler and Clarke,[6] about four fifths of the patients at a given hospital are admitted by one fifth of the physicians who refer to that hospital. Identifying the hospital attributes that influence those physicians who refer most heavily is of special interest

Andreas Muller, *Ph.D., is an Associate Professor in the Graduate Program for Health Services Administration, University of Arkansas at Little Rock.*

Patricia Bledsoe, *R.N., B.S.N., is Chief Executive Officer at the Atoka Memorial Hospital, Atoka, Oklahoma.*

to financially oriented hospital managers, who know that the loss of a prime admitter can represent a revenue loss of $500,000 or more per year.

The comparison of prime and nonprime admitters is also useful from the perspective of marketing strategy. If sizable differences between user groups are found, then hospital marketers can segment the physician market and appeal differently to prime and nonprime admitters. This strategy is referred to as target marketing.[7]

PRIOR RESEARCH

Ambrose and Purdum[8] asked physicians in two Nebraska counties and the city of Omaha to rank in order of importance various hospital selection characteristics. Physicians ranked 16 hospital characteristics that could be grouped into four broad categories: medical factors, convenience factors, patient preferences, and environmental factors. Among the various hospital characteristics, nursing care was ranked highest, followed by medical facilities and hospital reputation. In contrast, a patient's religion and financial status and the hospital's distance from the physician's home were rated least important by the 168 physicians who answered the survey. Significant variations in the rank ordering of hospital characteristics were also associated with physicians' specialty. For example, pathologists ranked nursing care as less important than did other physicians. However, no data were provided that permit assessment of the size of these differences.

Among the various hospital characteristics, nursing care was ranked highest, followed by medical facilities and hospital reputation.

Okorafor's[9] mail survey of active physicians in five Indianapolis hospitals asked physicians to rank a set of 17 hospital attributes that the author classified into three categories: medical, reputation, and convenience factors. Medical factors, which included adequate nursing care, adequate medical equipment and technology, and adequate professional personnel, were ranked highest; parking facilities, food service, hospital ownership, and physician's office and home location were ranked lowest in importance. In the sample of 101 responding physicians, Okorafor could not find any statistically significant differences among clinical specialties in the ranking of attributes. One of Okorafor's most interesting findings was that medical factors, including modern medical technology and good nursing care, were also rated highly by a parallel survey of consumers.

Nordstrom, Horton, and Hatcher[10] used a list of 30 hospital attributes in a recent study of physicians living in a metropolitan area in California. Of the 400 physicians surveyed, 163 responded, one third of whom were surgeons. As in the previous studies, nursing and medical facilities were ranked highest, while hospital appearance and parking were among the lowest-ranked attributes.

These authors also performed a factor analysis on a subset of 25 hospital attributes that determined seven independent dimensions. The ranking of the seven factors indicated that diagnostic and treatment attributes were most important, followed by convenience attributes and admission/discharge procedures. However, physicians rated image and appearance attributes as being least important.

Nordstrom et al. conducted a separate factor analysis for surgeons and found the same seven dimensions that had been identified by the entire sample of physicians. Surgeons, however, ranked surgical attributes first and convenience attributes (e.g., travel time from office or home) much lower than did other physicians.

A recent informal nationwide survey of 100 physicians that was conducted for *Hospitals*[11] also found that the quality of nursing staff was most important to physicians. Over four fifths of the respondents indicated that hospital reputation, accessibility of consulting physicians, and availability of specialized medical equipment were important to them.

METHODOLOGY

The data in this study were derived from a survey of physicians conducted in Oklahoma City during late March and early April of 1987. All physicians in the Oklahoma City telephone directory were included in the study. A one-page questionnaire was mailed to 1,204 physicians. For a variety of reasons, 33 survey forms were not delivered. Of the remaining physicians, 295 responded to the survey, a response rate of 25%.

The questionnaire asked physicians to rate 21 hospital attributes using a four-point scale on which "1" is extremely important, "2" is important, "3" is slightly important, and "4" is not important. The attributes listed in Figure 1 were chosen on the basis of a focus-group discussion with physicians and a consideration

FIGURE 1

SECTION OF PHYSICIAN HOSPITAL ATTRIBUTES SURVEY

Please rate the following 21 hospital characteristics according to their importance to you by circling the following....

1. Extremely important
2. Important
3. Slightly important
4. Not important

1.	Current "state-of-the-art" medical equipment	1	2	3	4
2.	Quality of food service	1	2	3	4
3.	Quality of radiology services	1	2	3	4
4.	Quality of pharmacy services	1	2	3	4
5.	Quality of intensive care unit services	1	2	3	4
6.	Quality of coronary care unit services	1	2	3	4
7.	Quality of operating room services	1	2	3	4
8.	Quality of laboratory services	1	2	3	4
9.	Patient charge rates	1	2	3	4
10.	Quality of nursing care	1	2	3	4
11.	Patient care standards	1	2	3	4
12.	Physician amenities (lounge, parking, etc.)	1	2	3	4
13.	Hospital reputation	1	2	3	4
14.	Evaluation of the hospital by my patients	1	2	3	4
15.	Quality of affiliated medical staff	1	2	3	4
16.	Administration–physician relationship	1	2	3	4
17.	Variety of specialty services offered	1	2	3	4
18.	Quality of specialty services offered	1	2	3	4
19.	Closeness of the hospital to my home	1	2	3	4
20.	Closeness of the hospital to my office	1	2	3	4
21.	Hospital cleanliness	1	2	3	4

of previous studies.[12,13] Hospital attributes were not presented in any deliberate order on the questionnaire with the exception of nursing care, which was placed in the middle of the attribute list, and food service, which was placed in the second position. These placements were intended to test for the possibility of response sets.

To make the findings of this study more comparable with previous research, the rank order was based on comparisons of arithmetic means and independent *t*-tests. The data were analyzed by the Statistical Analysis System (SAS) software.

FINDINGS

Prime admitters are defined here as physicians who reported admitting 200 or more patients per year to hospitals; 31% of the responding physicians belonged in this group. In contrast, nonprime admitters are physicians who reported admitting fewer than 100 patients. We estimate that prime admitters were responsible for more than two thirds of all hospital admissions, while nonprime admitters contributed less than 10% of the total number of hospital admissions for which the physicians in the sample were responsible. Different definitions of prime admitters were tried, without affecting the findings.

Table 1 provides a statistical profile of three physician groups. The data clearly show that three specialties are overrepresented in the prime admitter subgroup: surgeons, orthopedists, and obstetrician–gynecologists. In contrast, family medicine practitioners and psychiatrists send substantially fewer patients to the hospital.

Physicians do not attribute much importance to the quality of hospital food or hospital location.

Physicians who are starting up their practice or planning to retire are less likely to be prime admitters. Prime admitters tend to be disproportionately male physicians, and they are more likely to be associated with alternative delivery systems such as independent practice associations (IPAs) than are nonprime admitters. Prime admitters have clinical privileges with more hospitals than nonprime admitters have.

Table 2 presents the ranking of hospital attributes for three physician groups. The ranking indicates that nursing care is the most important hospital attribute, followed by specialized clinical services such as laboratory, intensive care unit (ICU), radiology, and the operating room. The ranking of these attributes is similar for the three physician groups.

Physicians do not attribute much importance to the quality of hospital food or hospital location; these hospital characteristics were ranked lowest on the list of physician preferences. Patients' evaluations of the hospital, the administration–physician relationship, variety of services, hospital reputation, and patient's expense are more important than the previous set of characteristics, but they do not rank first.

It should be pointed out that the ranking, based on means, is also reflected in the percentage of physicians who rated an attribute to be "extremely important."

TABLE 1

PHYSICIAN CHARACTERISTICS BY ADMITTING GROUP

Characteristic	Prime admitters (N=74)	Nonprime admitters (N=110)	*t*	All admitters (N=238)
Medical specialty (%)				
Surgery	21.6	4.5	3.27†	12.2
Orthopedics	10.8	1.8	2.33*	6.3
Oncology	9.5	4.5	1.24	5.9
Obstetrics–gynecology	21.2	3.6	2.02*	8.0
Internal medicine	17.5	13.6	.71	13.9
Family medicine	4.1	18.1	-3.24†	12.6
Psychiatry	0	8.2	-3.12†	4.2
Age group (%)				
25–35	12.2	21.8	-1.75	16.4
36–45	29.7	28.2	.23	32.4
46–55	31.1	23.6	1.10	23.9
56–64	20.3	11.8	1.50	16.8
65+	4.1	12.6	-2.20*	8.8
Sex (%)				
Male	98.6	87.0	3.30†	92.7
Systems association (%)				
HMO	33.8	24.5	1.34	29.4
PPO	73.0	65.5	1.09	67.2
IPA	43.2	21.8	3.05†	31.1
Practice arrangement (%)				
Solo practice	36.5	27.3	1.30	32.8
Staff physician	14.9	30.9	-2.64*	23.5
Multispecialty group	14.9	12.7	.41	13.0
Clinical privileges				
Number active	1.78	1.20	3.82†	1.42

* Probability of *t* value < .05
† Probability of *t* value < .01

More than seven of ten physicians said that nursing care, laboratory, ICU, radiology, and the operating room were extremely important, while fewer than one fifth of the physicians thought that the quality of hospital food, hospital location, or amenities were extremely important (data not shown).

A comparison of rank orders of the 21 hospital characteristics shows that the three physician groups rank very similarly. The rank-order correlation coefficient between prime and nonprime admitters (p = .996) and that between prime admitters and all physicians (p = .972) is close to unity, indicating nearly identical rankings. In addition, when means for prime and nonprime admitters were compared by independent *t*-tests, none of the 21 comparisons was statistically significant at an alpha error of .05. Therefore, the observed ranking

TABLE 2

HOSPITAL ATTRIBUTES BY ADMITTING GROUPS

Attribute	Prime admitters (N=74)		Nonprime admitters (N=110)		All physicians (N=289)	
	Mean	Rank	Mean	Rank	Mean	Rank
Quality of:						
nursing care	1.16	1	1.19	1	1.22	1
laboratory	1.32	4	1.29	3	1.29	2
ICU	1.38	6	1.34	4	1.33	3.5
patient care	1.34	5	1.26	2	1.33	3.5
radiology	1.31	2.5	1.38	5	1.35	5
operating room	1.31	2.5	1.44	7	1.40	6
affiliated medical staff	1.39	7	1.42	6	1.43	7
State-of-the-art medical equipment	1.43	9	1.48	8	1.45	8
Quality of coronary care unit	1.58	11	1.50	9.5	1.49	9.5
Hospital cleanliness	1.41	8	1.50	9.5	1.49	9.5
Quality of specialty services	1.53	10	1.53	11	1.53	11
Quality of pharmacy	1.61	12	1.56	12	1.59	12
Evaluation of hospital by patients	1.62	13	1.65	13	1.67	13
Administration–physician relationship	1.80	15.5	1.84	15	1.80	14
Variety of specialty services	1.78	14	1.77	14	1.84	15
Hospital reputation	1.80	15.5	1.94	16	1.86	16
Patient charge rates	2.12	17	1.96	17	2.02	17
Quality of food	2.16	19	2.19	18.5	2.17	18
Closeness to office	2.14	18	2.19	18.5	2.28	19
Physician amenities	2.63	20	2.63	21	2.61	20
Closeness to home	2.80	21	2.57	20	2.71	21

differences could be attributed to sampling variation. A visual image of the similarity in rankings is shown in Figure 2, which displays the ranking of attribute means for prime and nonprime admitters.

The close similarity between the rank orders of prime and nonprime admitters is somewhat puzzling. Frequent users of hospitals had been thought to be more technology- and surgery-oriented than infrequent users; if so, they should have ranked relevant services more highly than did infrequent users. It is possible that these presumed differences do not show up when prime admitters comprise an aggregate of physician specialties with distinct ranking profiles.

In order to test this hypothesis, we compared the rankings of physicians in two medical specialties, surgery and family practice, for whom statistically reliable comparisons could be made. These specialties are substantially different in hospital use: Surgeons admitted an average of 199 patients per year, while family practitioners admitted only 103. Table 3 and Figure 3 show the results of this comparison. Surgeons do indeed attribute greater importance to the ICU, operating room, modern medical technology, affiliation with medical staff, and hospital cleanliness than do family practitioners. Surgeons also pay less attention to the quality of hospital food and to the distance between home and hospital. Although the differences between the two specialties confirm our expectations and are statistically significant, Figure 3 clearly shows that the rank orders of attribute means are generally the same ($p = .87$) and comparable to those of other physicians (see Figure 2).

FIGURE 2

ATTRIBUTE MEANS BY ADMITTING GROUP

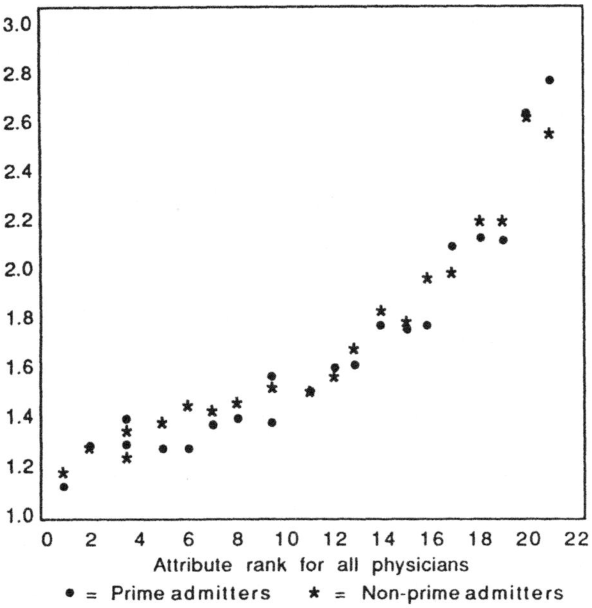

FIGURE 3

ATTRIBUTE MEANS BY MEDICAL SPECIALTY

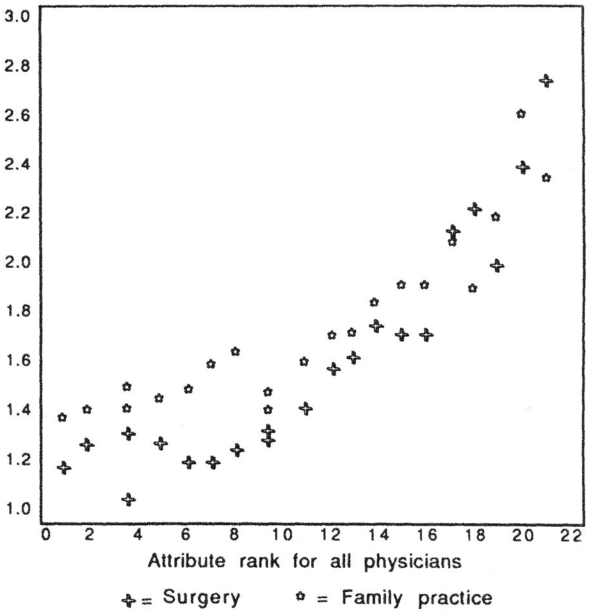

DISCUSSION

The study found that nursing care, up-to-date medical equipment, and advanced technological services are most important to physicians, while convenience concerns such as office location, distance from home, and availability of parking facilities rank much lower. These findings are consistent with those of two prior studies.[14,15] In addition, the physicians' top ranking of nursing care is a finding shared with all prior surveys.[16–19] This is remarkable in that the various surveys covered a 14-year period and canvassed physicians in different urban areas of the United States. Moreover, the surveys used somewhat different wordings of questions and different numbers of hospital attributes. Nevertheless, it must be remembered that the findings of all prior studies as well as the current one are based on low response rates that are typical for mail surveys. There is no way to know whether nonresponding physicians would rank hospital attributes differently.

Assuming that its findings are generalizable, this study provides some indications for hospital managers. First, segmentation of the physician market by admission volume should employ such physician characteristics as specialty, association with alternative delivery systems, and age and sex. For example, surgeons, orthopedists, and obstetrician–gynecologists seem to be prime targets for marketing efforts intended to attract large numbers of patients.

Second, market segmentation according to prime and nonprime admitters on the basis of rankings of hospital attributes does not appear to be useful, since both groups rank the attributes similarly. Although some ranking differences could be observed when surgeons were compared with family practitioners, these differences were fairly small and should not be exaggerated. A larger sample of physicians would be required to determine reliably the preferences of rarer specialists such as neurologists or allergists.

The salient message of the study is that, regardless of

The salient message of the study is that, regardless of specialty, physicians want good nursing care, medical technology, and facilities to support their interventions.

TABLE 3

HOSPITAL ATTRIBUTES BY MEDICAL SPECIALTY

Attribute	Surgery (N=45)		Family practice (N=33)		All physicians (N=289)	
	Mean	Rank	Mean	Rank	Mean	Rank
Quality of:						
nursing care	1.18	2	1.38	1	1.22	1
laboratory	1.29	6	1.42	3	1.29	2
ICU*	1.07	1	1.42	3	1.33	3.5
patient care	1.33	9.5	1.50	7	1.33	3.5
radiology	1.31	8	1.45	5	1.35	5
operating room†	1.20	3.5	1.52	8	1.40	6
affiliated medical staff*	1.20	3.5	1.63	10	1.43	7
State-of-the-art medical equipment†	1.24	5	1.67	11	1.45	8
Quality of coronary care unit	1.30	7	1.42	3	1.49	9.5
Hospital cleanliness*	1.33	9.5	1.48	6	1.49	9.5
Quality of specialty services	1.42	11	1.59	9	1.53	11
Quality of pharmacy	1.58	12	1.70	12	1.59	12
Evaluation of hospital by patients	1.62	13	1.72	13	1.67	13
Administration–physician relationship	1.75	16	1.83	14	1.80	14
Variety of specialty services	1.71	14.5	1.94	16.5	1.84	15
Hospital reputation	1.71	14.5	1.94	16.5	1.86	16
Patient charge rates	2.11	18	2.06	18	2.02	17
Quality of food†	2.22	19	1.88	15	2.17	18
Closeness to office	2.02	17	2.19	19	2.28	19
Physician amenities	2.40	20	2.63	21	2.61	20
Closeness to home†	2.76	21	2.34	20	2.71	21

* Comparison between surgeons and family practitioners significant at .01 level
† Significant at .05 level

specialty, physicians want good nursing care, medical technology, and facilities to support their interventions. Every cardiologist in the sample thought that the coronary care unit was extremely important. Similarly, every radiologist thought that radiological facilities were extremely important. It seems reasonable to conclude that physician recruitment efforts should emphasize both the quality of nursing care and the facility/technology that is of particular interest to the physician. Presumably managers have employed this strategy intuitively when introducing physicians to their hospitals.

• • •

The conclusion of this study is that physicians, regardless of specialty or admission volume, seem to share similar preferences when ranking hospital attributes. Physicians' top priorities are good nursing care and up-to-date medical facilities in support of their areas of specialization.

In competing for doctors and patients, hospitals have traditionally recognized the importance of modern technology and specialized services.[20] This study suggests that hospital managers should pay closer attention to nurses; they are the most critical links among physicians, patients, and the hospital. The quality of the physician–nurse relationship may thus be decisive in hospitals' competition for doctors and patients.

REFERENCES

1. Inguanzo, J., and Harju, M. "How Do Consumers Receive Local Health Care Information?" *Hospitals* 59, no. 7 (1985): 74–76.
2. Inguanzo, J., and Harju, M. "What Makes Consumers Select a Hospital?" *Hospitals* 59, no. 6 (1985): 90–94.
3. Inguanzo, J., and Harju, M. "Consumer Satisfaction with Hospitalization." *Hospitals* 59, no. 9 (1985): 81–83.
4. Jackson, B., and Jensen, J. "Majority of Consumers Support Advertising of Hospital Services." *Modern Healthcare* 14, no. 5 (1984): 93–97.
5. Jackson, B,. and Jensen, J. "Most Consumers Would Accept Lower Quality Health Care to Save Money." *Modern Healthcare* 14, no. 9 (1984): 88–96.
6. Kotler, P., and Clarke, R.N. *Marketing for Health Care Organizations*. Englewood Cliffs, N.J.: Prentice-Hall, 1987.
7. Ibid.
8. Ambrose, D. M., and Purdum, J.J. "Physicians Rank Hospital Characteristics." *Hospitals* 48, no. 12 (1974): 95–100.
9. Okorafor, H. "Hospital Characteristics Attractive to Physicians and the Consumers: Implications for Public General Hospitals." *Hospital and Health Services Administration* 28, no. 1 (1983): 50–65.
10. Nordstrom, R.D., Horton, D.E., and Hatcher, M.E. "How To Create a Marketing Strategy Based on Hospital Characteristics that Attract Physicians." *Journal of Health Care Marketing* 7, no. 1 (1987): 29–36.
11. Powills, S. "Young MDs Seek Special Programs for Patients." *Hospitals* 61 no. 14 (1987): 40.
12. Ambrose and Purdum, "Physicians Rank Hospital Characteristics."
13. Okorafor, "Hospital Characteristics."
14. Ambrose and Purdum, "Physicians Rank Hospital Characteristics."
15. Okorafor, "Hospital Characteristics."
16. Ibid.
17. Ambrose and Purdum, "Physicians Rank Hospital Characteristics."
18. Nordstrom, Horton, and Hatcher, "How To Create a Marketing Strategy."
19. Powills, "Young MDs Seek Special Programs."
20. Feldstein, P.J. *Health Care Economics*. New York: John Wiley & Sons, 1979.

The valuation of a medical practice

Robert F. Reilly

The valuation of a medical practice is important to the practice owners, employees, bankers, and others for many reasons. These reasons include taxation, transaction pricing, financing, litigation, and management planning. This article presents the three most common approaches to practice valuation: discounted net cash flow, market data comparable, and asset accumulation. Comprehensive illustrative examples of all three approaches are presented.

Health Care Manage Rev, 1990, 15(3), 25-34

A current, accurate determination of the value of a medical, dental, or similar professional service practice is important to the practice owners, to nonowner employees, to physicians, to lenders, to associated hospitals, and to other interested parties. There are many taxation-related motivations requiring the valuation of medical, dental, and similar professional practices, including Federal income tax, gift tax, estate tax, and estate planning. Other motivations include transaction pricing and structuring (e.g., sale of a practice, buy-in of a new partner); financing securitization and collateralization (e.g., both cash flow–based and asset-based borrowing); litigation support and dispute resolution (e.g., marital dissolutions); and management information and planning (e.g., creating buy or sell agreements).

The reasons for a practice valuation directly influence the objective of the valuation. The objective of a practice valuation encompasses the following three factors:

1. The definition of value, such as fair market value, acquisition value, insurable value, or collateral value.
2. The premise of value—the differences between the premise of "value in use" (on a going concern basis) and "value in exchange" (on either a forced liquidation or orderly liquidation basis)—will have a material impact on the results of the practice valuation.
3. The definition of the asset, property, or business entity to be appraised—the clear definition of the business unit to be appraised (e.g., total assets versus net assets versus professional corporation stockholders' equity) and the ownership interest to be appraised (e.g., minority fractional interest, majority fractional interest, or total business entity)—are obviously essential to the practice valuation.

Of these three elements of the valuation objective, the importance of the definition of value is most often overlooked. With respect to the appraisal of a typical medical practice, the two most common definitions of value are fair market value and acquisition value. These alternative definitions of value will be explained briefly.

The *fair market value* of a professional practice is the price at which an equity interest would change hands between a willing buyer and willing seller, neither

Robert F. Reilly, *M.B.A., is Managing Director of Valuation Engineering Associates in Chicago, Illinois.*

being under compulsion to buy or to sell, with both fully cognizant of all relevant facts and circumstances and with both seeking their maximum economic self-interests. Fair market value contemplates the value of a professional practice on an "as is, where is" basis. The practice is valued as a stand-alone business entity with current capabilities and limitations of its capital, management, practice services and specialties, practice service delivery hours and areas, hospital and health maintenance organization (HMO) affiliations, physician shareholders, and physician employees.

The *acquisition value* of a medical practice is the price at which an equity interest would change hands between a willing buyer and a willing seller, with the buyer being uniquely motivated to buy and the seller being aware of this unique motivation; with both the buyer and the seller fully aware of the economic impact of the association of the buyer and seller; and with the buyer seeking to maximize and the seller seeking to leverage off of these prospective economic effects of the association.

MEDICAL PRACTICE VALUATION APPROACHES

There are numerous generally accepted medical practice valuation formulas, equations, methodologies, and procedures. All of these specific applications can be generally aggregated into the following three distinct categories of medical practice valuation approaches:

1. the discounted net cash flow or earnings capacity approach,
2. the market data comparable or analysis of transactional data approach, and
3. the asset accumulation or adjusted net worth approach.

The discounted net cash flow approach

This approach requires the quantification of the prospective net economic benefits associated with the medical practice ownership. This quantification requires the projection of the net cash flow generation capacity of the practice. This projection is made for a discrete period of time, usually five years.

The actual number of years in the projection period is determined by how long it would take for a physician to create a comparable competitive practice. For example, assume that the subject practice is a successful internal medicine practice. Assume also that the most likely buyer of the practice would be a new internist, recently graduated from residency. If the new internist could create an economically successful practice in the local competitive environment in five years, then the projection period would be five years. That is, the buying physician will not be willing to pay for the subject practice earnings capacity for a period greater than would be required to recreate that earning capacity.

The buying physician will not be willing to pay for the subject practice earnings capacity for a period greater than would be required to recreate that earning capacity.

The projection of the net cash flow generation of the practice requires that the following analyses be made:

- a revenue forecast, based on an analysis of the professional fee schedule of the subject practice, the mix of office versus hospital revenues, the level of Medicare or Medicaid patients in the practice, the degree of competition among physicians in the local market, and so forth;
- a cost forecast, based on an analysis of fixed versus variable costs and on cash versus noncash costs of operating the practice;
- an investment forecast, based on an analysis of required prospective investments in medical supplies, office furniture and fixtures, and office medical equipment;
- a cost-of-capital forecast, based on an analysis of the capital structure of the practice (i.e., will the buying physician assume any of the practice long-term debt?), the cost-of-equity capital (i.e., the opportunity cost of funds) of the buying physician, and the inherent risk of the subject practice; and
- an incremental benefit forecast, based on an analysis of the earnings capacity of the subject practice incremental to the earnings that could be generated from a competitive start-up practice.

It is important to note that under this approach a buying physician will pay only the value of the practice represented by the incremental economic benefit generated by the established practice, as compared to the earnings available from a start-up practice opportunity. This incremental nature of a professional practice valuation makes such an appraisal quite different from the valuation of manufacturing firms or other service forms. The fair market value of the medical practice is the cumulative present value of all future cash flow projections, incremental to that which would be generated by a hypothetical, competitive start-up practice.

The market data comparable approach

This approach requires the identification and analysis of actual buy or sell transactions of medical practices that are comparable to the subject practice. For purposes of this approach, the principal comparability criterion is the type of medical subspecialty. The database of transactional events should include an adequate number of sales of the same type of medical subspecialty. Clearly, it would be inappropriate to value a pediatrics practice by reference to sale transactions of obstetrics–gynecology, radiology, or psychiatry practices. In addition to medical subspecialty, other practice comparability criteria include the following:

- geographic location of the practice, particularly with respect to the local competitive environment for similar practices;
- the degree of turnover of the subject practice patient population;
- the degree of turnover of the subject practice support (nursing and clerical) work force;
- the number of physicians in the practice;
- the average revenues and profits per physician;
- the average fees charged per procedure and per visit compared to other practices in the same subspecialty;
- the composition of the practice revenues (hospital versus office, insurance versus direct pay, HMO, Medicare, etc.);
- the number and prestige of hospitals to which the practice admits;
- the number and prestige of hospital committee appointments and other comparable professional achievements (e.g., awards or publications) earned by the principal physicians; and
- the degree to which an established patient referral system exists, particularly from general practitioners to subspecialists.

The objective of the market data comparable approach is to set a standardized unit of measure for use between both the actual selling prices of the transactional data analyzed (i.e., the actual sales of comparable specialty practices) and such data as annual revenues, annual profits, and total assets. For the sample transactions analyzed, these market data multiples (price–revenues, price–earnings, price–assets, etc.) are applied to the historical financial data of the subject practice. Of these multiples, the one that is by far the most common is the price–annual professional revenues multiple. When the subject practice revenues are capitalized by this price–revenues multiple, the result is an estimate of the fair market value of the subject practice.

The market data comparable approach requires relatively few discount and premium adjustments for such factors as lack of marketability, illiquidity, or minority or majority ownership interest. That is because this approach analyzes actual completed sales transactions of medical practices that are comparable, in the aggregate, to the subject practice.

The asset accumulation approach

This approach quantifies the fair market value of the subject medical practice as the aggregate value of all of the practice assets minus the aggregate value of all of the practice liabilities. Accordingly, this approach requires a discrete appraisal of each one of the subject practice assets and liabilities.

Typically, medical practice assets may be grouped into four categories: (1) financial assets, (2) real properties, (3) tangible personal properties, and (4) intangible assets. Each of these assets should be appraised for fair market value.

Financial assets typically include cash, patient accounts receivable, prepaid expenses, and an inventory of medical and office materials and supplies. Real property includes owned and leased land, buildings, and building improvements. Tangible personal property includes medical equipment, office furniture and fixtures, and office and computer equipment. Intangible assets typically include patient charts and records (by far, the most important intangible asset for a medical practice), a trained and assembled work force, going concern value, and good will.

Each of these categories of assets should be valued using one or more of the three traditional asset appraisal approaches: (1) the income approach, (2) the market approach, and (3) the cost approach. Significant judgment and experience are required to identify and correctly appraise all of the medical practice assets, particularly the intangible assets. Particular judgment also must be applied to ensure that no asset values are counted twice.

The fair market value of the medical practice liabilities also must be determined. These liabilities include current liabilities and all long-term notes, bonds, mortgages, and debentures. The fair market value of these debt instruments is a function of embedded interest rates, current yields on comparable debt instruments, and term to maturity.

Under the asset accumulation approach, the fair market value of the medical practice is the total value of its assets minus the total value of its liabilities. Typically, very few adjustments need to be made to the recorded practice liabilities, and relatively few adjustments need to be made to the valuation conclusion. This is because the individual formulas required for the appraisal of each individual asset type are adaptable to quantifying majority control premiums, lack of control discounts, illiquidity discounts, and so on.

EXAMPLE OF A MEDICAL PRACTICE VALUATION

The following example can be used to illustrate all three of the medical practice valuation approaches. Young Dr. Jones has just completed a residency in internal medicine and a fellowship in infectious disease medicine. Dr. Jones is contemplating the purchase of the established practice of old Ben Brown, M.D. Ben Brown, also an internist, wishes to sell his practice and retire, having had a distinguished, 30-year medical career.

Quantitatively, Ben Brown's practice is fairly lucrative. On a cash receipts basis, the practice grosses $300,000 per year. Jones estimates that the practice will continue to increase at the compound rate of 10% per year. As a practical matter, the maximum revenues that a general internist can generate in sole practice is $400,000 per year.

The total expenses of operating Dr. Brown's office equal 50% of net revenues. This includes support staff, rent, utilities, office supplies, insurance, and all other expenses except Brown's compensation. Included in this total are $10,000 per year in depreciation expenses.

After inspecting Ben Brown's office, Dr. Jones has concluded that he would have to spend $50,000 in his first year in the practice for new office furniture, fixtures, and medical equipment. Dr. Jones estimates that after the first year, annual capital expenditures would approximate $10,000. These capital expenditures will increase depreciation expenses to $20,000 per year for the next five years. However, even with increased depreciation, Jones believes he can maintain the practice's 50% profit margin.

Most importantly, Dr. Jones has evaluated two career options as alternatives to buying Ben Brown's practice. First, Jones has carefully analyzed the local competitive environment for general internists. Although it would be an arduous task, Jones is convinced that he could develop a reasonably successful practice competitive to the Ben Brown practice—from a start-up position—in five years. Second, Jones could obtain employment from a local primary care clinic at an annual salary of $100,000 per year.

Lastly, it is important to note that the Brown practice is very highly regarded in the local medical community. Ben Brown, a highly published and learned internist, is well liked by his patients and well respected by his colleagues. He uses the most prestigious hospitals in town. In fact, he has had several prestigious committee appointments at these hospitals in recent years. Due to his infectious disease orientation, Brown receives frequent referrals from family practitioners and other internists. He refers his patients to only the most prominent subspecialists in town. The sole significant detriment to the Brown practice is that Dr. Brown has been winding down somewhat over the last few years in anticipation of retirement. Dr. Jones plans to acquire the Ben Brown practice on or about December 31, 1988.

Discounted net cash flow approach

Table 1 presents the results of the discounted net cash flow practice valuation analysis. It is important to reiterate that five years is considered to be the reasonable period required to start up a reasonably successful internal medicine practice. Of course, under the incremental valuation premise, there is no residual value to the subject value after the discrete forecast period. As indicated in Table 1, the discounted net cash flow value of the Brown practice is $270,000.

Market data comparable approach

Table 2 presents the results of a systematic analysis of actual medical practice sale and purchase transactions during the years 1987 and 1988. The table presents the reasonable range of medical practice transaction values by medical practice subspecialty. Previously in this article, a listing was presented of the many quantitative and qualitative factors associated with positioning the subject practice within the reasonable range of subspecialty practice values. As indicated in Table 3, the market data comparable value of the Ben Brown practice is $270,000.

Asset accumulation approach

Financial assets normally include cash, accounts receivable, prepaid expenses, and inventory and supplies. Since the objective of the appraisal is to state the

TABLE 1

MEDICAL PRACTICE OF BEN BROWN, M.D.
FAIR MARKET VALUE: DISCOUNTED NET CASH FLOW ANALYSIS AS OF DECEMBER 31, 1988 (IN THOUSANDS)*

	Account projection	Year 1	Year 2	Year 3	Year 4	Year 5
	Practice cash revenues†	330	363	399	400	400
Less:	Start-up practice revenues‡	−120	−144	−173	−207	−249
Equals:	Incremental practice revenues	210	219	226	193	151
Less:	Incremental operating expenses	−105	−109	−113	−97	−75
Equals:	Incremental before-tax profit	105	110	113	98	76
Times:	Effective tax rate, 40%	× .42	× .44	× .45	× .39	× .30
Equals:	Incremental after-tax profit	63	66	68	59	46
Plus:	Depreciation expense	+20	+20	+20	+20	+20
Less:	Capital expenditures	−50	−10	−10	−10	−10
Plus:	Start-up capital expenditures§	+100				
Equals:	Incremental net cash flow	133	76	78	69	56
Times:	Present value factor, at 20%	× .833	× .694	× .579	× .482	× .402
Equals:	Net present value	111	53	45	33	23
	Total net present value					265
	Practice fair market value (rounded)					270

* This example assumes that there is no acquired practice long-term debt. Also, it assumes a 20% discount rate—i.e., an alternative cost of equity capital rate, risk-adjusted.

† Practice revenues represent last year Brown revenues, compounded at 10% per year, to a maximum of $400,000.

‡ Start-up practice revenues represent the estimate of the net revenues generated by Jones's hypothetical start-up ("opportunity cost") practice.

§ Start-up capital expenditures represent the estimate of the leasehold improvements, office furniture and fixtures, and medical equipment required to create the hypothetical start-up practice; these expenditures will not be incurred if Jones buys the Brown practice.

property in terms of its current cash value, the value of the cash account is already stated at fair market value. The fair market value of accounts receivable is the present value of anticipated collections. Prepaid expenses would include items such as prepaid rent, prepaid insurance, and prepaid utilities. Typically, the historical cost of these assets is indicative of their fair market value. Medical practice inventory includes both office materials and supplies and medical materials and supplies. Materials and supplies that are used in current operations should be valued at current replacement cost.

The tangible real and personal property of most medical practices typically will include office furniture and fixtures, medical equipment, leasehold improvements, and leasehold interests. To appraise the owned real and personal property, estimates are made of the cost of replacing all owned office furniture and medical equipment. Allowance is made for the physical deterioration, functional obsolescence, technological obsolescence, and economic obsolescence associated with each piece of office or medical equipment.

The typical medical practice has the following intangible assets: patient charts and records, a favorable

TABLE 2

MARKET DATA COMPARABLE APPROACH: RANGE OF TRANSACTIONAL ANALYSIS DATA BASED ON MEDICAL PRACTICE SALES AND PURCHASE FOR THE YEARS 1987 AND 1988*

	Fair market value transaction price (as a percentage of annual net revenues)		
Medical practice specialty	**Low value**	**High value**	**Median value**
General or family practice	55	95	75
Internal medicine	70	100	85
Surgery	80	100	90
Pediatrics	55	75	65
Obstetrics–gynecology	80	100	90
Radiology	85	115	100
Psychiatry	65	85	75
Anesthesiology	100	125	110

* All fair market value range observations have been rounded to the nearest 5%, for simplicity of presentation. In order to present relevant reasonable ranges, outlying data points were eliminated from the reasonable range determination; that is, any data point observations in excess of ± two standard deviations around the initial mean were eliminated from the population. The quantity and quality of data would not permit further disaggregation of medical subspecialties (e.g., different surgical subspecialties). No attempt was made to disaggregate the total database by geographical region, although this would be statistically feasible. The data included in this analysis are from transaction prices represented and deemed to be accurate; however, no attempt was made to independently verify these transaction prices.

office lease or office location, a trained and assembled work force, physician and employee employment contracts, a currently hospitalized patient population, patient referrals from general practitioners, going-concern value, and good will. Each of these intangible assets is subject to appraisal. To a greater or lesser extent, each of these intangible assets can represent the most significant portion of the overall value of the medical practice. Several of the most common medical practice intangible assets—i.e., patient charts and records, a trained and assembled work force, going-concern value, and good will—are illustrated in the Appendix, which presents an example of the valuation of the intangible assets associated with the hypothetical practice of Ben Brown, M.D.

The value of the medical practice's total assets is the summation of the fair market values of the practice's financial assets, real property, tangible personal property, and identified intangible assets, including good will.

The value of the medical practice's total assets, then, is the summation of the fair market values of the practice's financial assets, real property, tangible personal property, and identified intangible assets, including good will. This total represents the collective value of the practice's assets as a going-concern business, but not the fair market value of the practice's equity. In order to determine the value of the equity, the current value of the practice's liabilities must be subtracted from the fair market value of the practice's assets.

Medical practice liabilities may be grouped into two categories: current liabilities and long-term liabilities. The first step in the appraisal of liabilities is to remove from the balance sheet all accounts that are not bona fide liabilities of the practice. This adjustment typically involves the reclassification of liability accounts that are, in fact, equity accounts. Liabilities that may be reclassified as equities include notes payable to the physician, owners, or immediate family members of the major physician or shareholders. If these liabilities are

TABLE 3

MEDICAL PRACTICE OF BEN BROWN, M.D.
FAIR MARKET VALUE: MARKET DATA COMPARABLE APPROACH AS OF DECEMBER 31, 1988 (IN THOUSANDS)*

Annual revenues of Ben Brown, M.D. practice, year ended 12/31/88	$300
Range of fair market value transaction prices for general interest subspecialty	70%–100%
Point estimate fair market value selected for Brown practice based on quantitative and qualitative analysis	90%
Estimate of fair market value of the internal medicine practice of Ben Brown, M.D. ($300,000 × 90%)	$270

* The point estimate of the subject practice within the reasonable range of practice values is admittedly subjective. Therefore, this estimation should be made by an appraiser with significant experience in the valuation of medical, dental, and similar professional practices. In the instant case, the point estimate was based on the reputation, size, and profitability of the subject practice, modified by the fact that Brown has been winding down his practice in recent years.

considered to be equity positions by the creditors, and if the practice does not have a plan for the repayment of these obligations, then they may be reclassified as equity.

The fair market value (FMV) of the medical practice's equity interest is, quite simply, the difference between the fair market value of the assets and the current value of the liabilities. Algebraically, this relationship is expressed,

$$\text{FMV business enterprise} = \text{FMV total assets} - \text{FMV total liabilities}$$

If the asset accumulation approach has been properly applied, the fair market value of the business enterprise represents what a willing buyer would pay for a 100% equity interest in the practice.

Table 4 presents an example of the application of the asset accumulation approach to the medical practice valuation of Ben Brown, M.D. This example illustrates

TABLE 4

MEDICAL PRACTICE OF BEN BROWN, M.D.
FAIR MARKET VALUE: ASSET ACCUMULATION APPROACH AS OF DECEMBER 31, 1988 (IN THOUSANDS)

	At historical cost	At fair market value
Assets		
Current assets*:		
Cash	10	10
Accounts receivable	40	40
Prepaid expenses	10	10
Medical and office supplies	10	20
Total current assets	70	80
Plant, property, and equipment*:		
Office furniture and fixtures	100	60
Medical equipment	100	60
Gross plant, property, and equipment	200	120
Less: Accumulated depreciation	-100	
Net plant, property, and equipment	100	120
Intangible assets†:		
Patient charts and records		69
Trained and assembled work force		7
Going-concern value		20
Good will		21
Total intangible assets		117
Total assets	170	317
Liabilities and owner's equity		
Liabilities:		
Accounts payable	10	10
Wages payable	10	10
Taxes payable	20	20
Total liabilities	40	40
Owner's equity:	130	277
Total liabilities and owner's equity	170	317
Fair market value of practice equity ($277 rounded):		$280

* The fair market value of current assets and of property, plant, and equipment is based on depreciated replacement cost appraisals.

† The fair market value calculation regarding intangible assets is presented in the Appendix.

TABLE 5

MEDICAL PRACTICE OF BEN BROWN, M.D.
FAIR MARKET VALUE: VALUATION SYNTHESIS AND CONCLUSION AS OF DECEMBER 31, 1988
(IN THOUSANDS)

Approach	Fair market value ($)
Discounted net cash flow approach	270
Market data comparable approach	270
Asset accumulation approach	280
Total valuation synthesis and conclusion*	270

* The valuation synthesis and conclusion is based on the weighted average of the results of the various valuation procedures employed. The weighted averaging scheme is based on the quantity and quality of available data, the experience and judgment of the professional appraiser, and the degree of confidence placed on each valuation approach by the professional appraiser.

both the revaluation of on–balance sheet assets and liabilities and revaluation (creation through appraisal) of off–balance sheet intangible assets. Based on the asset accumulation approach, the fair market value of the Ben Brown medical practice is $280,000.

FAIR MARKET VALUE OF THE MEDICAL PRACTICE

Table 5 presents the valuation synthesis and conclusion of the Ben Brown, M.D., practice. Based on a synthesis of the three valuation approaches, the estimate of the fair market value of this hypothetical practice is $270,000.

• • •

There are numerous reasons to assess the value of medical, dental, and similar professional practices. These reasons fall into the following categories: taxation (compliance and planning), transaction (pricing), financing (cash-flow based and asset based), litigation (and dispute resolution), and management (i.e., ownership) information purposes.

APPENDIX

MEDICAL PRACTICE OF BEN BROWN, M.D.
FAIR MARKET VALUE: VALUATION OF INTANGIBLE ASSETS AS OF DECEMBER 31, 1988

Patient charts and records

Total number of active-patient charts in the practice	5,000
Average revenue per patient per year (including both office revenue and hospital revenue)	$60
Average before-tax profit margin	50%
Average before-tax profit per patient per year	$30
Effective tax rate	40%
Average after-tax profit per patient per year	$18
Fair return on other practice assets (assume 15% of revenues)	$9
Practice return attributable to patient population	$9
Total practice return attributable to patient population (5,000 patients × $9)	$45,000
Average expected life of patient relationship—4 years	
Average expected remaining life of patient relationship (2 years*)	
Present value discount rate—20%	
Present value of annuity factor, at 20% for 2 years	1.527
Present value of patient charts and records ($45,000 × 1.527)	$69,000

Trained and assembled work force

Dr. Brown has three loyal and competent staff members, all of whom have worked for the practice for several years. The appraisal of this work force follows:

Staff member	Annual salary ($)	Cost to recruit, hire, and train (%)†	Fair market value of work force ($)
Rhonda Receptionist	12,000	10	1,200
Nancy Nurse	20,000	10	2,000
Mary Medtech	24,000	15	3,600
Total (rounded)			7,000

Going-concern value

The prospective buyer estimates that it would take three months to create the nascent medical practice, i.e., to lease an office, hire employees, order and install office and medical equipment, etc. During that three-month period, the Ben Brown practice will generate $20,000 of positive net cash flow, compared to zero cash flow for the start-up practice.‡ Accordingly, the Brown practice going-concern value is $20,000.

Appendix, continues

Good will

The following is a projection of practice net cash associated with good will (in thousands):

		Year 1	Year 2	Year 3	Year 4	Year 5
	Aggregate practice before-tax profit	165	182	200	200	200
Less:	Alternative employment income§	– 100	– 120	– 140	– 140	– 140
Equals:	Incremental practice profit	65	62	60	60	60
Times:	Effective tax rate, 40%	× 26	× 25	× 24	× 24	× 24
Equals:	Incremental after-tax profit	39	37	36	36	36
Less:	Fair return on all other practice assets	– 30	– 30	– 30	– 30	– 30
Equals:	Incremental economic return on practice ownership	9	7	6	6	6
Times:	Present value factor, at 20%	× .833	× .694	× .579	× .482	× .402
Equals:	Present value of economic return	7	5	4	3	2
Sum:	Practice good will value	21				

* The remaining life calculation for patient charts is based on an analysis of historical patient turnover rates.
† The cost to recruit, hire, and train a replacement work force is estimated.
‡ The start-up period used to calculate going-concern value is based on analysis of the subject practice.
§ The alternative employment income is based on the projection of prospective salaried internist wage rates.

Part II

ORGANIZATIONAL ISSUES

The new hospital challenge: Organizing and managing physician organizations

Steve McDermott

A new challenge facing hospital management is the task of developing a close working relationship with physicians organized to effectively support managed care. How this challenge is met may play a pivotal role in the hospital's future.

Health Care Manage Rev, 1988, 13(1), 57–61

The historic relationships between management and medicine have ranged from wariness to antagonism. But under new market conditions, cooperative relationships between hospitals and physicians are the key to provider success. The traditional separation of hospitals and private practice medicine, in many instances reduced to a we-they conflict, is not the basis for mutual cooperation. This separation and internal conflict within hospitals stands in the way of competing effectively. However, in the past two years substantial changes have occurred in health care that can provide new common ground for hospitals and physicians.

- A classic competitive market is developing. Quality, scope of services, product control, delivery capability, and price are increasingly the criteria for success.
- For the first time, business and insurance companies are taking an active buyer role toward health care services. In response, health care delivery will be organized over the next five years into large health care systems and networks.
- The current growth of group practice signals the development of organized medical corporations. Independent physicians outside of such groups will see their prerogatives steadily eroded, options narrowed, and patient bases reduced.

If cooperation is to be achieved, the future of hospitals and their medical staffs must be characterized by mutual efforts, mutual rewards, trust, and a true partnership. The successful health care corporation of the future will not distinguish between the needs and goals of the institution and those of its constituent physicians. Both will have as a common purpose the provision of efficient, effective services to common customers.

This article reviews the changing nature of the medical environment and identifies how it provides a unique opportunity for hospitals to work with their physicians. It is particularly relevant to chief executive officers and those physicians in the hospital who set the tone of the organization and provide leadership and direction. The article is intended only as a beginning, a starting point leading to many choices. Success in the new market will

Steve McDermott *is President of the Hill Health Care Corporation, a hospital-physician joint venture management company he helped organize in Oakland, California. He also serves as President of PriMed, Inc., a management consulting firm.*

require bold new expressions, in many instances complete turnabouts for management-physician relations, recognizing the changes taking place in health care delivery.

THE CHANGING ENVIRONMENT OF PRIVATE PRACTICE

After decades of near total control over medical care, physicians' influence is waning. The effects of competition, of increasing supply against decreasing demand, are evident. There is growing recognition by physicians, however reluctant, that the invisible hand of the marketplace is being felt.

The traditional pyramid of medicine has had the specialists at the top, managers of medicine's technology and beneficiaries of medicine's highest rewards. Much of the talent drain has gone to the specialty services where large fees produce personal net incomes well into six figures. An important change now occurring is the reversal of this pyramid as utilization review systems and cost control programs place the primary care physician as gatekeeper. In the new market, where controlling costs is important, the primary care physician represents less expensive medicine.

Thus far, physicians have been slow to organize. Their historic nature is fiercely protective of their independence. The oft repeated refrain is to "control their destiny." But the new crop of physicians just entering practice have a different view. When they look at the tight market, the costs of starting a practice, and the increasingly high possibility of economic failure, their response is, "I want a job, one with predictable hours, shared call, steady work, collegiality, and an attractive benefits package." Who is hiring these primary care physicians? The answer is group practices and staff model health maintenance organizations (HMOs). Kaiser Permanente, long a beggar in the medical recruitment marketplace, now has waiting lists in every specialty. While not perfect, it is the Kaiser model that most represents the future to young physicians.

MANAGED HEALTH PLANS AND CONTRACT MEDICINE

Managed health plans, in the form of HMOs and preferred provider arrangements, represent a revolution in how health care will be delivered in this country. Managed health plans are a move from passive indemnity insurance plans to active direction and involvement in how the health care system is structured. The common characteristic of these new plans is control: control over utilization, provider participation, and price. Managed health plans, representing millions of consumers, are creating the most radical changes in health care delivery and are dictating the terms of the future.

Managed health plans, representing millions of consumers, are creating the most radical changes in health care delivery and are dictating the terms of the future.

A hospital's future lies in being a contractor with at least several of the successful new health plans. But that alone is not enough. Being selected as a contractor under a managed health plan only provides admission to the game; it does not guarantee a winner. Having low costs and utilization control helps. A crucial component, however, will be the participation and commitment from physicians within the medical staff. Many of the managed health plans already understand this. Increasingly they are holding up hospital contracts while they investigate medical staff support, or are contracting exclusively with fully integrated multispecialty medical groups where they are available.

EXPERIENCE OF MEDICAL STAFF CORPORATIONS

Medical staff corporations have been created in many California hospitals as a mechanism to unite and organize the active medical staff. The objective of these corporations is to act as a bargaining agent for member physicians and to maximize physician influence in the changing environment. Their conceptual framework is to preserve physician independence and the fee-for-service system. Such goals are not in sync with the new environment. The marketplace will not support what is tantamount to a unionizing effort of the most highly paid professionals in the nation. Medical staff corporations have little to show for their efforts, and most are only paper organizations. Key problems of these efforts include

- lack of appreciation of the new market;
- lack of management, or inexperienced administrators;

- lack of physicians at risk; and
- lack of a continuing source of income.

While such medical staff corporations are failing, they can be a learning experience. As an outcome of their efforts to organize, physicians are often left with a greater awareness of the changing realities. Their future dependence on structure, on organization, and on the need for contracting mechanisms often becomes clearer. It is in this learning process that leadership from the hospital can come forward and it is at this point that hospital administration can begin a dialogue with physicians that leads to more meaningful organizing efforts.

DEVELOPING HOSPITAL-AFFILIATED MEDICAL GROUPS

Hospitals need an affiliated and organized primary care base to participate in managed health plans. In turn, physicians need hospitals to help them organize. Capitalizing on this interdependency is the new hospital opportunity. Many administrators, hardened by hospital and medical staff wars, may not succeed in making the radical change in attitude needed to open the dialogue for joint efforts. But this change in attitude is the new leadership challenge for hospital management. Some key ingredients to building the new base are

- *Organizational commitment:* An organized group of physicians must be recognized as an important part of the hospital's overall future and should be a key component of the broader strategy of the hospital.
- *Management leadership:* Organizing physicians requires the best management talent. It requires openness, integrity, innovation, and discipline.
- Education: Both physicians and management need to rethink basic assumptions about each other's roles. The education effort should include a detailed and objective market analysis, recognizing the new reality of a buyer-driven system.
- *Quality:* Organizing to provide medical services in a businesslike fashion does not mean losing quality. Commitment to quality and a set of measurable standards are essential to the success of any business in a competitive environment and should be the cornerstone of any joint effort to provide health care services.
- *Clear purpose and goals:* Both physicians and hospital management need to agree on a common purpose and adopt common goals against which future decisions can be measured.
- *Market orientation:* The end product of the organizing effort should be consistent with marketplace demands, that is, it should be consumer conscious rather than physician oriented or hospital oriented.

If hospitals do not organize their own medical services from within their medical staffs, they should soon expect outside independent medical entities to show up in their service areas. Some hospitals may find it easier to deal with outsiders than to take on the difficult and risky prospect of organizing from within. Organizing physicians can be viewed as a lion-taming act without the whip. A few hospitals are delicately inviting outside medical groups into their flocks. Such groups will be less demanding but also less dependent, looking to use the hospital only as a source of short-term capital rather than establishing a true long-term relationship. Whether home-grown or imported, the closer the alliance the hospital has to an organized medical group, the more likely it is that the hospital will be successful.

MANAGEMENT STRUCTURES FOR THE HOSPITAL-PHYSICIAN JOINT VENTURE

There is tremendous interest in ambulatory care and satellites for market expansion. Hospitals are experimenting in this new field through trial and error. While much time is spent on the financial pro formas, advertising techniques, and building specifications, less attention has been given to the basic organizational structure required to support such efforts. With the marketplace moving toward contracting, what is needed is a single medical corporation that links these ambulatory care efforts, an organizational structure that can merge existing practices and bring established physicians as well as new physicians into an organized practice. Ultimately this will lead to an entirely new health care organization. Some models already exist, such as Kaiser, Lovelace, Virginia Mason, and Scripps Clinic. These organizations all have the physicians, hospital, and management under one structure. Within that structure they have common goals, pooled resources, and coordinated services. Kaiser, for example, is structured as follows:

Kaiser Hospital and Clinics (Facilities)	——	Kaiser Health Plan HMO (Insurance)	——	Permanente Medical Group, Inc. (Medical Services)

The Kaiser Health Plan HMO represents the joint venture. The Health Plan annually meets with the hospitals and the medical group regarding how much per subscriber each will receive in operating revenues. At the end of the year, health plan profits are distributed to the hospitals and medical group according to an established formula.

As hospitals form alliances with medical organizations or develop their own, there is a need to establish a permanent, ongoing linkage. One option is to create a jointly owned medical management corporation. The joint corporation would have a long-term management contract with the medical group to secure the continuation of the relationship. The joint corporation would provide basic management services such as financial services, personnel administration, marketing, facilities management, physician recruitment, and contract negotiations. The key component of this arrangement is the joint hospital-physician decision-making structure leading to joint ventures and sharing of risk and reward. The following diagram illustrates this organizational pattern.

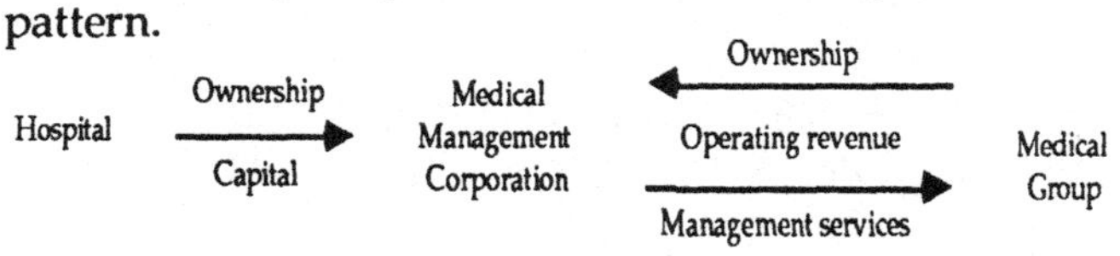

AVOIDING POTENTIAL PITFALLS

Although a positive, mutually supportive relationship between physicians, and between organized physicians and hospitals, is necessary to successfully compete in today's market, there is little evidence that such an approach is workable. If anything, the relationship between physicians and hospital management seems to be at an all-time low as competition squeezes physicians for the first time. As many in the field have noted, the lions are restless. It is this new competitive environment, however, that presents the opportunity for hospital management to move into the disorganized, splintered, and increasingly anxious physician ranks. The following are four problem areas common to hospital-physician organizing efforts:

1. Fifty-fifty deals (half ownership by physicians, half by the hospital) are organically tough environments, building into the organizational decision-making process the historic we-they conflict. If possible, a third independent but interested participant, such as a local employer, union, or insurance company, should be involved.
2. Hospital administrative personnel, for the most part, lack the experience of private practice medicine needed to adequately represent or understand the physician side and are generally viewed as too hospital biased or hospital controlled to be accepted as support staff for the organizing effort. Experienced, independent management is usually needed from a source that is jointly selected and accountable to the hospital and physicians, but finding the right people and convincing them to take on the effort may be quite difficult.
3. Organizing efforts compete with each other. The hospital should make an exclusive commitment to one organizing effort. This will legitimize the process and stave off movements by some physicians to create splinter groups. Commitment to multiple physician organizing efforts might keep the medical staff off balance but will also mire the effort in internal competitive squabbling.
4. Physicians often do not support these efforts financially. Physicians should not be allowed to play for free and should be required to provide financial support. The hospital may be willing and able to pay for the whole organizing effort, but it is more useful to building physician support and commitment to have the physicians invest.

• • •

Special organizational skills are needed to achieve consensus within the hospital environment. Successful planning with physicians will have the following characteristics:

- accurate, organized, and comprehensive knowledge of the market;
- clear purpose and objectives;
- a well-defined joint hospital-physician decision-making process; and
- demonstrated management competence and innovative approaches.

For most hospitals, the long-term strategy must include participation in a larger health care system. While the new operative word is "networks," the ultimate stage will be single, large corporations providing coordinated, comprehensive care to an entire market. What will likely emerge in each major region in the country are three or four such systems that collectively serve the majority of the population. Examples of the future of health care already exist today in banking, the airline industry, and retail food distribution.

The above-structured management corporation is, over the long term, intended to directly embrace the difficult political, governance, and management issues that hospitals face in trying to compete. Joint hospital-physician ownership provides the mechanism for joint planning, decision making, and oversight between physicians and hospitals. It can develop into the hospital-physician model that has helped make Kaiser successful. To do so will require a realignment of present hospital management thinking, in some instances giving up studied (but false) independence of each of the parties for true interdependence between physicians and hospital management.

The uniqueness of a professionally dominated organization

Daniel S. Fogel

Professional bureaucracies are unique organizations whose special characteristics have implications for strategy formulation and implementation and for developing physicians as managers. This article offers 12 key points to help executives manage such organizations.

Health Care Manage Rev, 1989, 14(3), 15–24

Many discussions in the health care literature elucidate recent trends in health care: its new "bottom-line" orientation; its competition; changes in the design of its organizations; and the rise of for-profit chains. Some commentators have challenged the morality, integrity, and efficiency of using these changes to manage health care organizations.[1] Some have complained of the deprofessionalization of medicine.[2] Others have called for more management expertise.[3,4]

Within all of these commentaries lies a plea to understand health care organizations more fully. This article describes the typical organization in which physicians operate, identifies unique aspects of the organization, suggests how it can best be managed by its key executives, and addresses the important problems of working out strategy and developing managerial skills among physicians. It is hoped that this discussion will be particularly helpful to group practices and organizations in which physicians manage other physicians.

KEY CONCEPTS

A professional bureaucracy is an organization that relies on the skills and knowledge of its operating professionals to produce standard products and services. The professional, in the terms of this article, is a physician who belongs to the medical profession. Medicine has members who have highly specialized skills and theoretical knowledge that were acquired through a formal learning process. Entry into the profession is via a state examination. Once accepted into the profession, the physician is given considerable authority to relate independently to patients.

Physicians can practice alone. Many of them prefer this autonomy so that they do not have to serve organizational as well as personal goals. Other physicians, however, choose to affiliate with organizations, for reasons that will become clear. When physicians work together within an organization, that organization is best labelled a professional bureaucracy.

Daniel S. Fogel, *Ph.D., is Dean of the International Management Center in Budapest, Hungary. He has held senior management positions in three other organizations, including a health care system. His second book, entitled* Healthcare Management: Designing and Implementing Successful Strategies *will be published in 1990.*

THE CHARACTERISTICS OF A PROFESSIONAL BUREAUCRACY

Organizations in which the primary or core tasks are performed by physicians can vary along a continuum according to the amount of power members possess to make important organizational decisions.[5] For example, at one extreme the officials delegate to physicians responsibility for defining and implementing goals, setting performance standards, and seeing to it that the standards are maintained. This model is most commonly used in health care clinics or newly formed firms. At the other extreme, physicians' power is subordinated to an administrative function; their authority is circumscribed, and they are subject to routine supervision. This model is common in large university settings and in hospitals with strong administrators. In the middle of the continuum is the type of organization in which physicians and administrators are roughly equal in power and in the importance of their functions. This model is common in well-run hospitals and in organizations with diverse product and service lines. All professional bureaucracies, whether they accentuate the physician's or the administrator's role, share certain characteristics.

Professional bureaucracies present management challenges not usually found in other types of organizations.

The box titled "Characteristics of a Professional Bureaucracy" specifies attributes of this unique type of organization. Professional bureaucracies present management challenges not usually found in other types of organizations. The executive's success is predicated on an ability to understand and respond to this organizational uniqueness and to manage physicians toward productivity. How executives should address the management issues that arise in such organizations is the subject of the next section.

Characteristics of a Professional Bureaucracy

- A standard set of skills is shared by the professionals.
- The organization is decentralized.
- Marketing and functional units operate side by side.
- The bureaucracy serves the professionals and relies on their skills and knowledge.
- The organization produces standardized products and services.
- The keys to success are service and expertise.

TWELVE KEY POINTS TO REMEMBER WHEN MANAGING A PROFESSIONAL BUREAUCRACY

1. The physicians are trained to operate independently.

The professionals are initially trained outside the organization, in universities that transfer a circumscribed body of knowledge and standards to the professionals. The training prepares physicians to work relatively independently of their colleagues, although closely with the patients they serve, and to exercise considerable discretion in applying their learned skills and knowledge. This professional independence is one reason why medical schools try to select students with proven ability to act independently. These students also undergo an extensive socialization process as they are absorbed into the profession.

2. Power rests with the physicians.

Physicians' work is too complex to be supervised by lay managers or analysts; thus physicians enjoy a certain level of power and independence. Their services are typically in demand, as they possess a socially valuable body of knowledge and skills. They usually have considerable mobility within the profession. Physicians' power and independence are at least partly responsible for their tendency to identify more strongly with the medical profession in general than with a specific organization.

3. Physicians join organizations for shared resources and skill enhancement.

Physicians cite many reasons for joining a particular organization. They join in order to profit from the image of the organization, to share resources, to learn from colleagues, or to obtain patients from the organization and other colleagues. In general, an organization is better at serving a patient who needs diverse services than is an autonomous professional.

4. Work is coordinated and enhanced primarily through standard routines, communication, and knowledge shared among professionals.

Professionals have a repertoire of standard programs that predetermine what is to be done when a patient enters the physician's office.

The physician proceeds with two major activities: (1) categorizing the patient's need in terms of the standard programs (diagnosis), and (2) applying or executing the programs. This process allows physicians to accomplish work without making decisions at every moment, as the programs are routine and well known among the professionals.

The goal of a well-coordinated organization is to channel external dissimilarity into uniform categories. The admissions office, physician referral, and diagnosis related group (DRG) designations of a clinic or hospital are critical in meeting this goal. Each performs prescribed functions in a relatively uniform manner across organizations. The physicians' ability to diagnose quickly and prescribe a standard procedure is equally important to the coordination within the organization.

Nonstandard treatments and physicians' inability to conform to the organization's requirements are matters of increasing concern to many health care executives. The non-standard programs used by physicians are often the source of conflict.

5. Control is extremely difficult.

Control within the professional bureaucracy relies extensively on formalizing the professionals' work or on systems for satisfying patients' needs. The most effective controls in a professional bureaucracy are those most closely associated with the standard skills used by the physician, mainly peer review.

Several types of peer control exist in professional bureaucracies. In one type a practitioner observes, corrects, and, if necessary, sanctions a colleague. This method is used often, but its effectiveness is questionable. For example, physicians may not have sufficient opportunity to observe the work of their colleagues, may not possess the particular specialized competence to evaluate the work observed, or may not have a sufficiently varied set of effective sanctions to reinforce their evaluations.

Another type of peer control is the use of seniority, principally in the form of tenure. Tenured professionals exert control over nontenured members of the organization by virtue of their power to admit them as partners or permanent members of the staff. Control may also be exercised through a number of formally defined positions. In hospitals these positions may be the chief of staff, department chair, or director of a clinic. Another control mechanism is the use of an elaborate committee structure.

Finally, external review groups mandated by legislation exert powerful control over physicians. The profession's standards and codes of ethics originate largely outside the organization in self-governing associations of colleagues. Authority to license practitioners belongs to the state, with licensing and admission boards made up chiefly of members of the profession.

These control devices seem to work effectively in many situations. In professional bureaucracies, administrative managers should constantly remember that their control relates only to organizational goals, not professional delivery. Administrative controls are not efficient if they interfere with patient contact and professional discretion.

Geographic separation results in unique problems of control in the professional organization. The more geographically dispersed the locations are, the greater the need to train physicians, indoctrinate new professionals, and rely on "team players" at the branch locations. Thus executives must carefully select the physicians who are to be geographically separated from the main organization. This problem of control has been exacerbated by the increased use of ambulatory care and feeder facilities, as in the case of such large medical facilities as Mayo Alton, Ochsner Medical Clinic, and Cleveland Clinic.

A final control issue is the difficulty of removing incompetent or unconscientious members. Executives face major dilemmas in evaluating and giving feedback to professionals. The primary dilemmas are these: (1) The effort and approach of a professional may be of high quality but fail to prevent negative outcomes; (2) comparison of physicians is difficult; (3) short-term failures may turn into long-term successes; and (4) a performance by the professional may be good only in the eye of the beholder. How a manager solves these dilemmas partially determines the manager's status in the organization and his or her effectiveness in accom-

The most effective controls in a professional bureaucracy are those closely associated with the standard skills used by the physician, mainly peer review.

plishing organizational goals. The discretion that physicians are customarily allowed enables some to ignore the needs of patients and the organization. For this reason, superior professional bureaucracies have excellent peer review systems with power to enforce the profession's standards. However, given the autonomy of physicians, their licensed discretion, and the difficulty of defining performance standards, incompetence is difficult to prove and excise.

6. The patient has certain powers of coordination.

One odd characteristic of the professional bureaucracy is the patient's role in coordinating activities within the organization. The patient's coordinating function includes choosing a physician, scheduling an appointment, and selectively following the physician's advice. The patient may or may not be willing to see certain physicians in the organization. This involvement on the part of the patient provides an excellent opportunity for physicians to cross-sell various services and to assist with some of the patient's purchase decisions. For this reason, clinics offer various services, each of which can serve a different need of the patient.

7. The bureaucracy is set up to serve the physicians' needs.

The organization is a combination of marketing and functional units that work together to produce standard products and services. The functional units contain support staff who are employed to serve the physicians by ensuring that medical resources are available or that tasks necessary to the delivery of medical care are completed.

The managers in the functional units are effective to the extent that they conceive of the organization as a horizontally integrated, loosely woven organization. If they perceive it as a machine to be made to run more efficiently, they will not be successful.

The age and size of the organization are not important. Little start-up time is needed for a professional bureaucracy to become effective. The larger the professional bureaucracy, the more formalized the organization tends to become.

The way work gets done is not complicated, even though the skills and knowledge applied are complicated. Thus the organization's design need not be complex. The more the need exists for coordination among physicians and units within the organization, however, the more complicated will be the organization's design. Physicians in relatively large clinics can be grouped meaningfully to the extent that they serve the same types of markets. Strategic business units are important ways to focus attention on market demands for services and to pool resources for meeting those demands.

8. Key executives are powerful only when they are perceived to be serving the physicians.

The key manager of the professional bureaucracy is most successful when he or she is a physician, preferably elected or hired by physicians. Such managers maintain power as long as they are seen to be serving the physicians.[6,7]

Key executives spend most of their time addressing disturbances in the structure—for example, resolving jurisdictional disputes among powerful physicians. The method by which these disputes are settled is usually negotiation. Administrators in the professional bureaucracy do not ordinarily have the luxury of arguing from a position of authority; they must negotiate.

These executives must also spend time with people outside the organization. They keep outsiders informed and prevent them from interfering with the physicians. Consequently, public relations and "playing politics" are important to the executive's success.

Ironically, the professionals become dependent on the executive, either because the professionals will not do the administrative work or because they cannot meet their professional obligations and also manage the organization. Thus power flows to executives as long as they are perceived to be serving the physicians' needs and are willing to do the work that the physicians do not do.

Administrators in the professional bureaucracy do not ordinarily have the luxury of arguing from a position of authority; they must negotiate.

Some observers have concluded that the physicians' independence should be subordinated to organizational controls in the interest of improved quality and efficiency of medical care. For example, a movement toward appointing full-time medical directors and chiefs of staff reflects the view of some that the doctor's individual entrepreneurial role must be considerably modified in favor of strong management and institutionalized teamwork. While this subordination of physicians may vary from organization to organization, a trend toward placing greater power in the hands of administrators is evident in health care institutions.

9. Marketing is the province of each professional as well as of the organization.

Another unique aspect of the professional bureaucracy is that the marketing of services and products is done jointly by the organization and by individual physicians. The professionals choose their own marketing strategy, which relates to their training and professional styles. For example, the impression that the physician makes on patients will dictate further sales of his or her services. In other words, the sale of a physician's services will usually be within that person's capabilities.

For these reasons centralized goals are difficult to realize; in fact, the paradox that executives often confront is that centralization may be detrimental to the professional's success yet essential to the success of the organization as a whole.

10. Innovation and change are difficult to achieve.

The professional bureaucracy tends to be conservative and to change slowly. The organization is typically inflexible; new problems are forced into old pigeonholes. Physicians tend to use deductive reasoning, while innovation generally requires inductive reasoning. Therefore, the professional usually relies on the key executives to introduce change and innovation into the organization.

When change occurs, it is slow and painful, the result of political intrigue and shrewd maneuvering by the physicians and executives who are seeking the change. The executive quickly realizes that a majority of physicians must agree on a change before it can be implemented. For this reason, the timing of the decision making process is vitally important.

Typical managerial solutions to major problems do not usually facilitate efforts to make changes in professional bureaucracies. Examples of such managerial actions are those intended to (1) increase direct supervision or narrow the span of control, (2) standardize technology, and (3) increase standardization of output. These solutions do not work because the complex functions of physicians cannot be performed effectively unless they are under the control of the physician. Technocratic controls serve only to weaken professional conscientiousness and to cause physicians to become passive (or passive-aggressive).

The key executive should never lose sight of the fact that service to patients and to all physicians must be included in the rationale for any new actions, strategies, or changes in the organization. Any other rationale will thwart the change effort.

11. The successful professional bureaucracy gives preference to professional goals over bureaucratic goals.

Because physicians are typically more committed to the medical profession than to an organization, certain tendencies exist in the professional bureaucracy. Control through reliance on professional expertise supersedes control imposed by bureaucratic discipline. Professional goal emphasis supersedes the profit motive. Professional authority supersedes administrative (bureaucratic) authority.

These tendencies, which are prevalent, can be detrimental to the organization's overall success. For example, when organizational goals are determined, the goals of individual physicians must be taken into account. The reward system places greater emphasis on professional accomplishment than on organizational loyalty and profitability. This bias makes the establishment of organizational goals difficult.

12. Selection of physicians is the most important organizational process.

The process of selecting physicians is critically important for the professional bureaucracy. First, the quality of a professional's performance persists over time. Attempts can be made within the organization to increase the skills and knowledge of the professional who is not adequately trained or skillful on the day of hire; however, these attempts can prove to be futile and costly. Second, a relatively small percentage of physicians are responsible for a disproportionately large percentage of both the best and the worst performance.[8]

Many selection criteria can be used to identify physicians who might function well within the organization, but the most important qualifications are (1) excellent technical skills; (2) the ability to enhance group performance and image; and (3) initiative. These criteria suggest that one strategy for hiring a professional is to select a well-known worker, which would have the effect of decreasing turnover, increasing productivity quickly, or shifting the organization's orientation.

The selection process should command a substantial budget and should involve some of the most qualified professionals in the organization. This process can save

Twelve Points to Remember

1. The professional is trained to operate independently.
2. Power rests with the professionals.
3. Professionals join organizations to obtain shared resources and skill enhancement.
4. Work is coordinated and enhanced primarily through standard routines, communication, and common knowledge.
5. Control is extremely difficult.
6. The patient has certain powers of coordination.
7. The bureaucracy is set up to serve the professionals.
8. Key executives are powerful only when they are perceived to be serving the professionals.
9. Marketing is the province of each professional as well as of the organization.
10. Innovation and change are difficult to achieve.
11. The successful professional bureaucracy gives preference to professional goals over bureaucratic goals.
12. Selection of physicians is the most important organizational process.

the organization much money if it effectively screens out candidates who will not perform well for the organization.

The twelve key aspects of managing professional bureaucracies (see the box titled "Twelve Points to Remember") present a backdrop for making decisions and managing physicians. The next two sections draw on these key points to illustrate how executives can develop and implement strategy in a professional bureaucracy and how the managerial skills of physicians can be developed.

STRATEGY FORMULATION AND IMPLEMENTATION

All of the issues just discussed have unique implications for the development and implementation of strategy in health care environments.

Professional goals should take precedence over bureaucratic goals. Professional desires are the closest to market desires. The executive is obliged to include support of physicians' goals as a strategic issue, since the physicians' goals represent market desires. In the professional organization, no administrator should be completely governed by administrative values, and no practitioner should subscribe exclusively to professional values. In a healthy professional bureaucracy the values of both physicians and administrators mesh to form a strong, unified strategic stance.

More people should get involved in strategy formulation in this type of organization. Thus the executive should maintain that the development of a strategic plan is partially the responsibility of the physicians. This involvement usually demands reeducating the physicians and creating a participative process for decision making.

Physicians are important sources of values and information for strategy formulation. For example, support for research and training, which are important to most physicians, should become a strategic priority of the professional bureaucracy.

Top management should spend its time preventing fiefdoms (powerful groups that disenfranchise themselves from the organization), creating constant coordination among physicians, creating meaningful reward systems, and in general ensuring that the managers manage and the physicians do professional work.

One major weakness of the professional bureaucracy is that peer controls can be ineffective in this context. The efficacy of collegial controls appears to be undermined by the ethics of professional courtesy. Evidence does exist that a highly structured medical staff organization is associated with a high level of care and a loosely structured one with a lower level of care.[9]

In the professional organization, no administrator should be completely governed by administrative values, and no practitioner should subscribe exclusively to professional values.

Some practitioners disagree with this logic, however. McKinlay and Arches discuss the "proletarianization of physicians": "Will the employed physician who does not achieve minimal standards of profitability for the corporation be replaced by under-employed physicians who are satisfied or compelled to act as deprofessionalized labor for the corporate owners?"[10] This question is prominent in some physicians' minds as they experience the changes in the health care system. Executives responsible for professional bureaucracies must find ways to preserve professional integrity while pursuing organizational goals.

One final area of importance in developing and implementing strategy is maintaining a creative organization that facilitates the work of physicians (see the box titled "Characteristics of Creative Organizations"). The creative organization embodies the concept of professional autonomy supported by managerial actions—that is, trust in the professional to produce quality work for the organization.

Managerial practices should support this attitude of trust. Most important among these practices are:

- genuine support for risk taking and new ideas;
- willingness to operate outside the usual communication channels;
- provision of resources and recognition for creativity; and
- refraining from argument from a position of authority.

The challenge for managers, again, is to maintain this creative atmosphere while pursuing organizational goals. One way to approach this balancing in terms of strategy formulation and implementation is to negotiate autonomy with the physicians: The more support that a member provides for the organization, the more autonomy that person gains within the organization. Consider the negotiation process as a bank account that increases or decreases according to the willingness of the professional to support organizational goals.

Characteristics of Creative Organizations

- Contact with outside sources is encouraged.
- Nonspecialists are assigned to solve problems.
- Ideas are not argued from a position of authority.
- Experimentation is encouraged and rewarded.
- Decentralization is practiced.
- Participative decision making is the norm.
- Employees have fun.

Sources: Steiner, G.S. *The Creative Organization.* Chicago: University of Chicago Press, 1965; Shapero, A. *Managing Professional People: Understanding Creative Performance.* New York: The Free Press, 1985; Peters, T., and Waterman, R., *In Search of Excellence.* New York: Harper & Row, 1982.

DEVELOPING PHYSICIANS AS MANAGERS

A unique problem exists in professional bureaucracies that does not occur in more traditional organizations. Physicians do not generally view management work to be either essential or a desirable path to career growth or professional success. Thus executives must find ways to attract, train, reward, and maintain physician/managers.[11–13] To accomplish these tasks the executive has several options.

A strong relationship exists between productivity and the number and variety of work-related conversations that an individual has with colleagues, both within and outside the organization. In general, anything that improves the quality and quantity of information to and from the professional will improve the professional's productivity. Liaison devices are important, especially when administrative managers work closely with physicians. To maintain productivity, physicians should be given access to many different channels of communication, including attendance at professional meetings and increased exposure to managers in other organizations—all the more so if they become managers. This variety is important as an incentive for professionals to do work not directly related to their professional training.

To improve productivity and provide incentives for physicians to do management work, observe these simple rules: (1) Don't always give an assignment to the person who has done that kind of work before; (2) deliberately assign some nonprofessional (i.e., administrative) work to physicians; and (3) occasionally make assignments that place an individual into another group, either temporarily or permanently. These new assignments should introduce professionals to management work without requiring them to give up

The executive should develop managers from within, because such persons understand the organizational culture.

their professional duties. For instance, a physician could be asked to evaluate a new piece of equipment to determine whether or not the organization should purchase it.

The executive should develop managers from within, because such persons understand the organizational culture. The most productive physicians should be the first to be considered for managerial positions; however, great care must be taken to avoid sacrificing a good professional in order to gain an incompetent manager.

When selecting permanent managers, choose only those who have a genuine interest in managing. Management work is fundamentally different from technical work. The organization should not criticize those who do not move into management and should provide parachutes for those who do not do well in this type of work. For example, one technique that a medical clinic may use is to guarantee a new manager his or her previous position if the management job is not satisfactory for whatever reason.

Criteria for a successful manager may vary for different organizations, but a common set can be identified. A successful manager should be an excellent individual contributor; and should have high credibility, experience in managing multiple relationships, knowledge of all parts of the organization, good interpersonal skills, and ability to do both management and technical work.

Studies on managerial success, especially with respect to persons in general management positions, have shown that the most important skills are building networks and setting agendas.[14,15] These skills are difficult ones for the physician/manager. Physicians will need to be taught how to build coalitions with organizational members and to set clear direction for subordinates.

The physician is already good at diagnosis—asking questions. This skill should be used extensively. The physician also understands the value of time and of making many contacts in a short period of time. Higher level managers need to develop the skills to analyze the external environment—skills that the average physician does not use often.

One mistake that physicians often make is failing to distinguish between the management of a project and the process of deciding what to work on in the first place. "There does not seem to be a good understanding of how technology-driven opportunities differ from market-driven opportunities. It is one thing to generate an idea for a new device by talking to one's customers. It is quite another to take an entirely new technology and bring from it a new product for which there is no immediate market."[16]

Executives may need to give extra support to a professional who assumes the new role of manager in the organization, and may need to provide new rewards for excellent performance. New managers need training in motivating others and in setting agendas for daily work.

The organization must also continually help managers to address the conflicts that arise between service to patients and the proprietary concerns of the organization. The higher the management position, the more influence the manager has on the organization. The lower the position, the more responsive the manager will be to professional norms and demands. Thus management work will vary according to the manager's level in the organization.

Some organizations use tests or assessment centers to select managers. Tests are useful in that they help interviewers to avoid perceptual bias, their results can be compared easily across individuals, and they can be used as a diagnostic tool to identify areas in which specific skills need to be developed. At the same time, tests for professional managers are generally new, and it may be difficult to find an appropriate test for a clinic or hospital situation.

One of the best ways for physicians to learn about

Recommendations for Developing Physician/Managers

- Provide professionals with diverse work and communication opportunities.
- Develop managers from within, if possible.
- Choose the most productive physicians and those with a genuine interest in managing.
- Train and reward professionals who do managerial tasks.
- Provide extensive performance evaluation.
- Give new managers access to mentors.
- Provide parachutes for those who fail at management.
- Use dual-ladder systems of advancement.
- Use autonomous work groups and other alternatives to traditional management.

management and for executives to select managers is to allow prospective managers to make "successive approximations" to the job by giving them chances to perform on task forces or take on increasingly longer assignments that require management skills. Use autonomous work groups—a practice that is greatly underestimated both as a management technique and as a learning process within professional bureaucracies. Autonomous work groups are small, self-managing groups of physicians that are formed to accomplish certain tasks. The groups are an alternative to traditional task supervision and are often perceived by physicians as more desirable than working alone. In fact, executives should try to develop many alternatives to direct supervision by designing the organization to be as self-managing as possible.

The pluralistic structure that is present in a professional bureaucracy need not have tightly linked and coordinated units. In fact, it works best as a loosely coupled system comprising relatively independent and autonomous units and programs that do not require tight controls and high levels of coordination. The ideal balance of professional and administrative goals is a situation in which physicians spend most of their time on micro issues, such as patient care and quality research, and executives pay attention to macro issues, such as environmental changes and organizational needs.

Use of a dual-ladder system can help to retain physicians who want to be promoted but not into management. Professional lines of progression should be commensurate with administrative ones in a dual-ladder system. Dual career ladders are thus an excellent way to reward professional growth and managerial growth without forcing a professional to choose management in order to get ahead.

Role models and mentors are important. The more contact that physicians have with quality managers, the more capable they will be as managers themselves.

Executives should frequently evaluate new managers' performance. Develop clear, formal monitoring systems that measure the quality and quantity of an individual's contribution to the organization's goals. Here are the critical concepts for performance evaluation:

- Allow participation in the development of performance criteria;
- Treat the formal evaluation as one part of a comprehensive feedback system;
- Use typical incidents, not just goal completion, as the primary basis of feedback; and
- Use an approach to formal evaluation that emphasizes (1) a job description; (2) short-term goal setting; and (3) descriptions of subjective requirements.

The box titled "Recommendations for Developing Physician/Managers" summarizes the ideas discussed in this section.

• • •

The purpose of this article has been to outline the unique features of a professional bureaucracy. The uniqueness derives mostly from the power that member physicians possess and exercise in the service of their profession. Thus the selection of qualified physicians is critical to the success of the organization.

The autonomy of physicians has unique implications for developing and implementing strategy and for developing physicians as managers. The major implication for managing physicians is that their participation in decision making should be encouraged. To develop managers, organizations must provide support and incentives for professionals to do more management work. The professional bureaucracy may well become the model of all organizations in the future. This organizational type has the potential for guiding large numbers of talented people in one direction to accomplish creative and important goals. The challenge for any executive is to manage these talented people in such a way that they will improve their skills and be productive for the organization.

REFERENCES

1. McKinlay, J.B., and Arches, R. "Towards the Proletarianization of Physicians." *International Journal of Health Services* 15 (1985): 161–95.
2. Reed, R.R., and Evans, D. "The Deprofessionalization of Medicine." *JAMA* 258 (1987): 3279–3282.
3. Hillman, A.L., et al. "Managing the Medical-Industrial Complex." *The New England Journal of Medicine* 315 (1986): 511–512.
4. Shapero, A. *Managing Professional People: Understanding Creative Performance*. New York: The Free Press, 1985.
5. Scott, Richard W. "Managing Professional Work: Three Models of Control for Health Organizations." *Health Services Research* 17 (1982): 213–40.
6. Humphrey, W.S. *Managing for Innovation: Leading Technical People*. Englewood Cliffs, N.J.: Prentice Hall, 1987.
7. Kelley, R.E. *The Gold-Collar Worker*. Reading, Mass.: Addison-Wesley, 1987.

8. Shapero, *Managing Professional People.*
9. Scott, "Managing Professional Work."
10. McKinlay and Arches, "Towards the Proletarianization of Physicians," 193.
11. Miller, D.B. *Managing Professionals in Research and Development: A Guide for Improving Productivity and Organizational Effectiveness.* San Francisco, Calif.: Jossey-Bass, 1986.
12. Giblin, E. "Professional Organizations Need Professional Management." *Organization Dynamics* (winter 1978): 41–57.
13. Lorsch, J.W., and Mathias, P.F. "When Professionals Have to Manage." *Harvard Business Review* (July-August 1987): 78–83.
14. Kotter, P. "What Effective General Managers Really Do." *Harvard Business Review* (November-December 1982): 165–67.
15. Peters, T., and Waterman, R. *In Search of Excellence.* New York: Harper & Row, 1982.
16. Kleingartner, A., and Mason, R.H. "Management of Creative Professionals in High Technology Firms." *Labor Law Journal* (1986): 509.

The secret of medical management

James E. Rohrer

A review of the research on group practices punctures the myth of physician autonomy in hospitals and opens the way for administrators to join in controlling the patient care process.

Health Care Manage Rev, 1989, 14(3), 7–13

The nature of work in medical care organizations is determined by the mix of patients who must be treated and the mix of services that the organization chooses to offer. The key management problem is to control the quality of patient care and the resources used to produce it. In short, the secret of medical management lies in the control of the patient care process.

Most administrative effort is misdirected, in that it is aimed at supporting the patient care process without helping to control it. Some organizational benefit can be gained from marketing, financing, community relations, strategic planning, purchasing, risk management, organization design, operations research, leadership, and personnel management. However, these activities are secondary to control of the patient care process, which is necessary if the organization is to be efficient and effective.

The purpose of this article is to suggest that administrative effort should be focused on two key interrelated activities: utilization review and quality assessment. First, the myth of physician autonomy, which has deterred administrators from joining with clinical department heads to manage patient care, is critically examined. Second, the history of utilization review and quality assessment is briefly reviewed. Third, the key technical barrier to efficient administrative monitoring of patient care—that is, controlling case mix severity—is explored. Finally, the article offers a strategy for redirecting administrative effort.

THE MYTH OF PHYSICIAN AUTONOMY

The reasons for the misdirection of administrative activity are obvious. For one, the administrative effort directed at non–patient care functions can, at times, be of enormous benefit to the organization. More importantly, non–patient care functions are arenas of activity that do not encroach on the sacrosanct ground of clinical discretion. All administrators know that they dare not appear to tell physicians how to practice medicine. A myth has arisen that consists of the following argument: Since nonmedical administrators are not able to judge when the use of resources in patient care is unnecessary or when the process of care in individual

James E. Rohrer, *Ph.D., is is an Assistant Professor in the Graduate Program in Hospital and Health Administration at the University of Iowa. He currently teaches medical care organization and health policy.*

cases is appropriate, efforts to control the patient care process would lead to revolt by the medical staff. Medical care cannot be delivered without physicians, and each physician demands professional autonomy.

That this is a myth is shown by the fact that it applies only to nonphysician administrators. Certainly when clinical department heads (who are administrators as well as physicians) are present, they do not hesitate to tell their fellow physicians how to practice medicine. In fact, many of them rule over their medical staffs like absolute monarchs, making despotic decisions capriciously and sometimes badly, but almost always getting away with them.

While only a fraction of U.S. hospitals have such dominant clinical department heads, the fact that they exist and manage patient care proves that individual autonomy is not essential to the practice of medicine. Professional autonomy for organized groups of physicians is sufficient.

There are practical reasons why physicians choose to subordinate themselves to a bureaucracy of their own making, among which is the need to increase productivity, quality, and the appropriateness of services.

An expert in organizational behavior might argue that clinical department heads can behave arbitrarily because they derive their authority from being experts in the relevant subject matter. However, their clinical expertise is largely independent of their administrative behavior; their management decisions may be guided by their clinical knowledge, but they are also drawing from other experience. This is to be expected, as management decisions may be directed at administrative as well as clinical problems. Unfortunately, clinical department heads are experts in the clinical subject matter but may be amateurs in administration, in spite of which they make administrative decisions that impinge on the process of patient care.

Despite their usual lack of formal training in administration, clinical department heads are often effective and efficient managers. They glean administrative expertise from experience in their positions. They are often dynamic leaders. The most important determinant of their success, however, is that subordination of individual clinicians to an organized medical staff often leads to improved performance.[1,2] Analogously, the benefits of organized group practice are real and have been known for some time.

In 1932 the Committee on the Costs of Medical Care (CCMC), chaired by a former president of the American Medical Association, recommended that comprehensive medical services should be provided by hospital-based organized group practices.[3] Although organized medicine repudiated the corporate practice of medicine, the proportion of physicians in group practice increased from 0.9% in 1932 to 46% in 1980.[4] Most group practices are not hospital-based in the sense meant by the CCMC, but they are still more bureaucratized than solo practices. There are practical reasons why physicians choose to subordinate themselves to a bureaucracy of their own making, among which is the need to increase productivity, quality, and the appropriateness of services.

Observing that general practitioners in solo practice operate independently of, and unobserved by their colleagues, Freidson[5] concluded that as physicians band together, they are likely to change the way they practice medicine. The organization of medical practice can be visualized as a continuum ranging from solo practice to "bureaucratic" practice. Bureaucratic practice is group practice in which the characteristics of bureaucracy have emerged. These include the division of labor, systematization of roles and procedures, and hierarchical organization.[6] The advantages of bureaucratization include economies of scale, an increased likelihood of peer review, more frequent consultation, and the substitution of allied health services for physician services.[7] This formulation is analogous to Roemer and Friedman's assertion that the more closely a hospital's medical staff approaches the ideal of the closed staff, where a limited group of physicians has admitting and treatment privileges, the better the performance of the hospital.[8]

Increased bureaucratization can help physicians to be more productive by freeing them from the need to perform tasks other than the exercise of clinical judgment. It may also improve the quality and appropriateness of care,[9] as has been repeatedly demonstrated, both before and after the development of a theory to explain the phenomenon. The following studies, drawn from Donabedian,[10] illustrate the point.

In a 1958 study by Morehead, physicians with hospital appointments were more likely to be judged in Class I (i.e., 76 percent or better compliance with criteria) than were physicians without appointments. Furthermore, the percentage in Class I increased with the number of years of affiliation with the hospital. In the same study, the percentage of physicians in Class I was correlated with the amount of time that physicians devoted to group practice.[11]

In a 1976 study by Payne et al., the percentage of cases that were appropriately admitted to hospitals and had an appropriate length of stay was highest for a prepaid group practice (Kaiser-Permanente), next highest for other multispecialty group practices, and lowest for solo practitioners. Performance index scores were highest for physicians in prepaid group practice, next highest for those in other multispecialty group practices, and lowest for solo practitioners.[12]

In a 1978 study, Payne et al. found that physician performance scores were higher in teaching-hospital outpatient clinics than in primary care office practices for pediatric, adult, and gynecological examinations; for treatment of hypertension, urinary tract infection, heart disease, anemia tonsillitis/pharyngitis, vulvovaginitis; and for appropriate drug use.[13]

In 1979 Riedel and Riedel found that within specialty categories the percentage of criteria adhered to was higher in hospital outpatient departments than in physician offices for the following conditions: hypertension, chest pain, abdominal pain, urinary tract infection, and pharyngitis.[14]

It is clear from these studies that the bureaucratization of medical care is associated with efficiency and quality. In fact, bureaucratization actually causes better performance, because the members of an organized medical practice can jointly offer lower costs and higher quality as well as more specialists and higher levels of medical training, and because administrative procedures exist to control the process of patient care. Fortunately, even ad hoc and ill-considered application of these procedures, in their crudest forms, has some benefit. Even more fortunately, administrative technology exists that can vastly improve management control over patient care. The refinement and judicious use of these mechanisms are the keys to effective medical management.

THE TECHNOLOGY OF UTILIZATION CONTROL

A complete description of the administrative procedures that can be used to control the services offered in the patient care process is beyond the scope of this article. Instead, this section demonstrates that the technology is both well-developed and underused.

In volume III of the Explorations in Quality Assessment and Monitoring Series,[15] Donabedian illustrates the methods and findings of patient care review studies. That workable review methods have existed for many years is perhaps best proven by citing a 1956 study by Lembcke, that is described by Donabedian.[16] Lembcke presented a scientific method for quality assessment. Valid, reproducible judgments were made possible by the following procedures: (1) classification of patients into diagnostic categories; (2) specification of the aspects of care to be judged (e.g., appropriateness of surgery); (3) use of detailed, explicit criteria; (4) verification of basic diagnostic information; and (5) establishment of an acceptable level of compliance in recognition of the fact that no criteria set can fully account for the circumstances of all cases. In the 1956 study Lembcke demonstrated that the number of "criticized" operations on the uterus, ovaries, and fallopian tubes at one hospital declined after the introduction of an auditing process, without affecting the number of justifiable operations.

Much of the quality assurance activity in hospitals is pointless.

The Lembcke study demonstrates what can be accomplished with case review. However, it is also true that case review can be a complete waste of time. If there is no reason to believe that the accepted treatment of a particular condition is suboptimal, then an audit will probably result in no improvement. Indeed, this is what frequently happens. In anticipation of a site visit by the Joint Commission on the Accreditation of Healthcare Organizations (Joint Commission), many hospitals have conducted audits of dubious value. The Joint Commission does not require, or even recommend, the investigation of nonproblems, but when a hospital cannot document the review and correction of genuine quality deficiencies, it may attempt to substitute a pointless audit instead. Thus it creates the semblance of compliance with the Joint Commission's criteria without actually having to tamper with the practice of medicine. Such an audit generates the unpleasant aspects of bureaucracy (i.e., committee meetings and paper shuffling) without achieving any improvement in quality or efficiency.

Much of the quality assurance activity in hospitals is as pointless as that described above. One reason for this, already noted earlier, is that genuine quality assurance

(QA) would interfere with the practice of medicine. A second reason is that meaningful problem identification systems, such as a complete system of continuous monitors, have not been in place. A third reason is that the real quality control activity is done informally, within the medical staff, and without the assistance of nonmedical administrators. This should not be interpreted to mean that informal quality control is not rigorous. On the contrary, clinical department heads constantly review the work of their staffs and are not reluctant to bring heavy pressure to bear on miscreants. However, monitoring and control could be accomplished more efficiently if the QA process were to be formalized.

One way to formalize the review process in the interest of increased efficiency is to transform it into the kind of QA program that the Joint Commission intends. This requires developing a problem identification system, central to which is a set of continuous monitors. The technology for such a system is well understood. Professional standards review organizations (PSROs) have screened aggregate data from their inception, as do their descendants, peer review organizations (PROs). The Commission on Professional and Hospital Activities (CPHA), established in 1955, offers a statistical display and analysis service that originally focused on length of stay and professional activities by type of patient, diagnosis, and the nature of any surgical intervention.[17] Some intermediate or end results could also be monitored: death, nosocomial infections, other complications, removal of diseased or normal tissue, transfers to other hospitals or extended care facilities, and discharges with approval or against advice. Tabulations could be produced that summarize activity by department or physician. Indexes could be constructed that indicate the number of tests performed for a particular case or case type.

When this type of information is purchased from an organization that tabulates data for many hospitals, participating facilities can compare their own performance to that of similar hospitals. Indeed, the information value of aggregated data increases dramatically when administrators can make comparisons, either with peer hospitals or with the performance of their own organizations over time.

In short, examples of systems for tabulating and plotting aggregate data have been published for more than a generation, and such systems could have been used to identify potential problems for case review. In many, if not most, cases they were not used, however, because neither the administrative nor the clinical managers understood or felt compelled to learn how to maximize their benefits. Furthermore, such systems can always be criticized because they do not reveal problems in a definitive fashion. For example, a high readmission rate after a particular surgical procedure does not prove that quality deficiencies exist. The high rate could be due to case mix (software that adjusts hospital data for severity has only recently become available) or bad luck.

Despite these uncertainties, profile monitoring is far more efficient than continuous auditing. Furthermore, administrative control over patient care that is directed at correcting clinical inefficiency has been demonstrated to be effective. If this were not true, then hospital utilization would not have declined as hospitals have come under increased pressure to control costs. Hospitals that could not induce physicians to shorten patient stays and avoid debatable admissions are likely to have experienced serious financial problems in recent years.

THE SEVERITY CONUNDRUM

A system for surveillance of aggregate data can serve as the core of an efficient and effective patient care control system. The value of such a system depends on its screening efficiency—that is, on its ability to detect genuine problems without falsely labelling deviations from the norm as possible problems. Screening efficiency is enhanced by case mix adjustment, because deviations from norms cannot easily be explained away as attributable to the mix of cases. And, as any administrator today knows, aggregate data are far more informative if cases are adjusted for severity.

Severity adjustment is the key technical problem impeding patient care review today. Automated software systems can be purchased that will produce severity-adjusted data for the evaluation of efficiency and effectiveness. However, the decision about which system to buy has baffled many administrators and their clinical advisors. The evaluation of severity adjustment systems is both more complex and, in one sense, less difficult than it first appears.

Unfortunately, the purchasers of the software often do not realize that the construction of a severity index is not just a technical issue, but one that is directly relevant to the objectives of the hospital. What can be obscured by the flashiness of menu-driven report generators are the unstated values that color the assumptions and scaling of the severity-adjusters. This issue is germane to the choice of software products, because it is the patient classification system that converts reams of data into digested or digestible information about quality and efficiency.

The first issue to be confronted is the concept that the severity index will be intended to operationalize. If patient outcomes are being monitored, it is only logical that the severity adjustment be based on factors prior to hospital care that would affect outcomes. However, if utilization rates or other measures of the patient care process are monitored, another basis for severity adjustment may be sought. This point can be illustrated with an example.

To the extent that clinical judgment about the use of hospital resources is open to review, a patient classification system based on the intensity of service use only must be considered to be potentially flawed.

One way to measure severity is to define it as the probability of organ failure, as in the MEDISGRPS system. Each level of severity in MEDISGRPS is, in theory, distinguished from higher and lower levels by the probability that the patient will experience organ failure.[18] Even if the probabilities are accurately assigned, the user should recognize the narrowness of the concept employed by MEDISGRPS. Patients who have a low probability of organ failure but who are handicapped or disfigured would be considered to be successes. Critics might argue that hospitals have a broader sense of responsibility than the prevention of organ failure. In short, any patient classification system must be based on assumptions about organizational purpose as well as on the biological determinants of disease.

Patient standardization systems could also be based on the stage of the disease,[19] the probability of death,[20] ability to function, the intensity of services delivered, or a combination of factors.[21] If a severity index score is based partly on resources used (e.g., placement in intensive care), then the user of the index is implicitly assuming that some decisions about the use of clinical resources are not subject to challenge. While it is true that patients who are admitted to an intensive care unit (ICU) are clinically comparable and that their patterns of resource use are more similar to each other than to those of patients not admitted to the ICU, a resource-based classification system can still be criticized to the extent that admission to the ICU is influenced by factors other than patient needs—for example, practice style. Users of the system can legitimately ignore such criticisms if they have defined the purpose of the hospital to be the provision of support services to clinicians. However, such a system could never be used to evaluate fully the quality of or need for ICU care. To the extent that clinical judgment about the use of hospital resources is open to review, a patient classification system based on the intensity of service use only must be considered to be potentially flawed.

As difficult as these issues are, they represent only one aspect of the value-laden problems with patient classification. Fortunately, administrators need not resolve all of these ethical problems before they implement a severity-adjusted patient care monitoring system. In a perfect world, a specialized severity adjustment system would be used for each indicator that is routinely monitored. Each severity index would be tailored to the mission of the hospital by extending the strategic planning process to include discussion of how the organization measures its own performance. However, such perfection is probably not essential. Most severity adjustment systems rank patients in roughly the same order.

The action-oriented administrator would be justified in selecting a severity adjustment system on the basis of criteria other than validity, with the understanding that it will be necessary to "trade up" every five or ten years. The selection might be made on the basis of price, or of the number of other hospitals that are using the same system and can therefore provide comparable data. On the other hand, perhaps a system should be selected that will operate with the clinical information that is already automated at the purchasing hospital. Any adjustment for severity, after all, will improve the screening efficiency of the monitoring system.

REDIRECTING ADMINISTRATIVE EFFORT

Monitoring and controlling the patient care process are the keys to effective management of medical organizations. The common perception that administrators cannot involve themselves in patient care can be seen to be a myth when it is recognized that the autonomy of individual physicians is routinely subordinated to the organized medical staff. Furthermore, opportunities exist to improve the management of patient care by replacing informal monitoring with existing technology. The most accurate, and politic, way to describe this activity is as the provision of efficient and effective assistance to clinical department heads, and not as administrative interference with professional judgment.

It must be remembered that clinical department heads are also administrators. Management of the patient care process must be accomplished with and through them, just as managing a research organization must be accomplished through senior scientists. Cooperation may not always be achievable; however, the medical staff and hospital administrators have common interests that should serve as the basis of a working relationship.

Not all hospitals are large enough to have clinical department heads. However, this does not imply that they cannot increase control over the patient care process. The medical staff may become organized in the short run, with help from the hospital administrator. Strategic decisions can be made that may increase the degree of medical staff organization in the long run. For example, health maintenance organizations (HMOs) may be established or physicians' practices purchased.

Ways to recruit, train, integrate, empower, provide data to, and reimburse physicians for meaningful participation in the institutional management of patient care—in short, to increase the degree of organization of the medical staff—should be developed and disseminated. However, the analysis of patient care data for management control need not wait. Some benefit can be achieved even at low levels of medical staff organization; indeed, the act of analyzing the data constitutes an increase in medical staff organization. For example, if staff physicians are informed that data analysis suggests that a wide diversity of opinions exists regarding the indications for a common surgical procedure, then the ensuing discussion could lead to consensus on practice standards, or at least to greater uniformity in practice. Feedback on clinical variations has been advocated for several years as a means of changing physician behavior.[22]

The technology for managing patient care is found in utilization review and quality assessment systems. If hospital administrators are to use this technology more effectively than they have in the past, they will have to convince medical staff leaders that these administrative procedures assist rather than impede them. They will have to use efficient systems for screening aggregate data and integrate physician leadership much more meaningfully with hospital management. Such systems will require the automation of as much clinical information as possible.

Truly sophisticated management of the medical care process must await integration of off-site practices with hospital operations, development of a coherent strategy for collection and use of accurate and relevant data, and development of national practice standards that can be applied with all of the authority of medical science. However, smaller steps need not await these developments. Management of medical care can become more effective now if existing techniques are brought into wider use.

Revitalizing quality assurance/utilization review systems will inevitably involve conflict. With finesse, the administrator may be able to contain that conflict within the arena where it can best be managed—that is, among clinical department heads and their staffs. It would, of course, be far easier to avoid the QA issue and concentrate on managing the administrative side of the hospital, such as payroll, purchasing, dietetics, housekeeping, marketing, and other activities that indirectly support patient care, However, the medical care organization that is able to grapple directly with managing patient care will have far more control over its production process. Managed properly, the care process will display examplary efficiency and effectiveness.

REFERENCES

1. Wolinsky, E.D., and Marder, W.D. *The Organization of Medical Practice and the Practice of Medicine.* Ann Arbor: Health Administration Press, 1985.
2. Eisenberg, J. and Kabcenell, A. "Organized Practice and the Quality of Medical Care." *Inquiry* 25, no. 1 (1988): 78–89.
3. Committee on the Costs of Medical Care. *Medical Care for the American People: The Final Report of the Committee.* Chicago: University of Chicago Press, 1932.
4. Roemer, M.I. *An Introduction to the U.S. Health Care System.* 2d ed. New York: Springer Publishing Company, 1986.
5. Freidson, E. *Profession of Medicine: A Study of the Sociology of Applied Knowledge.* New York: Harper & Row, 1970.
6. Ibid.
7. Wolinsky, F. "Why Physicians Choose Different Types of Practice Settings." *Health Services Research* 17 (1982): 399–419.
8. Roemer, M., and Friedman, J.W. *Doctors in Hospitals.* Baltimore: Johns Hopkins Press, 1971.
9. Eisenberg and Kabcenell, "Organized Practice."
10. Donabedian, A. *The Methods and Findings of Quality Assessment and Monitoring.* Explorations in Quality Assessment and Monitoring Series, vol. 3. Ann Arbor: Health Administration Press, 1985.
11. Ibid.

12. Ibid.
13. Ibid.
14. Ibid.
15. Donabedian, *The Methods and Findings of Quality Assessment and Monitoring.*
16. Ibid.
17. Donabedian, A. *A Guide to Medical Care Administration. Volume II: Appraisal.* Washington, D.C.: American Public Health Association, 1969.
18. Brewster, A. Presentation at University of Iowa Hospitals and Clinics, fall 1986.
19. Louis, D.Z., and Gonnella, J.S. "Disease Staging: Applications for Utilization Review and Quality Assurance." *Quality Assurance and Utilization Review* 1 (February 1986): 13–18.
20. Knaus, W.A., et al. "APACHE II: A Severity of Disease Classification System." *Critical Care Medicine* 13(1985):818–829.
21. Horn, S.D. "Measuring Severity: How Sick Is Sick? How Well Is Well?" *Healthcare Financial Management* (October 1986):21–32.
22. Wennberg, J., and Gittelsohn, A. "Health Care Delivery in Maine. I: Patterns of Use in Common Surgical Procedures." *Journal of the Maine Medical Association* 66 (1975):123–139, 149.

Building physician alliances for cost containment

Robert B. Greifinger
and
Maura S. Bluestone

Many cost containment programs are adversarial to physicians and therefore have limited success. Meaningful alliances with physicians hold the promise of cost containment without compromising quality of care.

Health Care Manage Rev, 1986, 11(4), 63–72

Despite many years of effort by both public and private programs to contain the cost of health care, those costs continue to escalate at rates in excess of the overall cost of living. Analysts of the health care economy have been able to describe and often quantify many of the factors that contribute to this cost escalation. These analyses, coupled with political pressure, have led to efforts to control both the supply of services and the amount paid for those services. Continuing cost escalation, however, is evidence that such efforts have had limited success.

Why has it been so difficult to translate our understanding of the health care economy into effective, constructive change? One answer lies in the way many cost containment efforts relate to physicians. Too often, these approaches are perceived by physicians as purely punitive measures intended to interfere with professional judgment, to limit professional income, or in some other way, to penalize physicians for the burden of the health care economy. Such adversarial approaches reflect a failure to understand the attitudes, perspectives, and behavior of physicians and consequently to develop meaningful alliances on which constructive change can be built.

The physician is a key player in generating health care costs. The physician contributes significantly to consumer expectations, creates demand for services directly and through referrals, orders tests, writes prescriptions, and is the only agent entitled to fill a hospital bed. Furthermore, to a large extent, the physician sets the prices for many of these services, thus

Robert B. Greifinger, *M.D., F.A.A.P., is Director, Alternative Delivery Systems at Montefiore Medical Center, and Assistant Professor of Epidemiology and Community Medicine at Albert Einstein College of Medicine, Bronx, New York. Prior to his current position, he was an HMO medical director for eight years.*

Maura S. Bluestone, *M.S., is Director of Project Development at Montefiore Medical Center, including a community health center-based Medicaid prepaid services plan, a geriatric health plan, and a clinical trial program that discharges stroke patients from the hospital to a certified home health agency. She previously spent several years as a health care consultant on cost-containment issues.*

This article was based on a presentation prepared for the Work in America Institute National Advisory Committee on "Improving the Management of Health Care in the Workplace."

The authors thank Reginald Bromeen, F.R.S.; Raymond Fink, Ph.D.; Gilbert Gordon, M.D.; Geoffrey Kane, M.D.; Richard Walker; and Leon Warshaw, M.D., for their suggestions during the preparation of the manuscript.

exercising significant control over both the price and quantity of health care "products."

This is not to say that all physicians are out to soak the system. In fact, most physicians merely behave in a manner that they feel is in the best interest of their patients while fulfilling the expectations of the professional autonomy, prestige, and income that society has bestowed upon them. Broad change in the health care system and its costs can therefore only be achieved if programs for change are based on understanding physicians' attitudes and behavior and accommodating physicians' occupational and social expectations. By definition, this will involve evolutionary change in the culture of health care bred by collaborative efforts of physicians, consumers, and payers.

MAJOR FACTORS THAT SHAPE THE HEALTH CARE ECONOMY

In order to explore opportunities for physician alliances in the battle against excessive health care costs, it is helpful to review some of the major factors that shape the current health care economy.

- The American public has high expectations for technical intervention, cures, and conquest of disease. Individual demands for immediate access to an ever wider array of services are increasing in number and intensity, often fueled by ignorance of the limited efficacy of medical care. Furthermore, changes in the social fabric of this country have resulted in the medicalization of many problems that, historically, did not fall under the umbrella of medical care.
- There has been steady, rapid technological change, some of which has profoundly improved diagnosis and treatment. In many instances, however, such change has outstripped the ability of clinicians to utilize high-technology methods productively.
- Despite recent increases in the proportion of physicians in group practice arrangements,[1] approximately 70 percent of all physicians in the United States continue to work in solo, fee-for-service practices. Opportunities to exercise meaningful review and control of such practices are limited. Furthermore, the fee-for-service payment mechanism itself rewards technical procedures more highly than "thinking" time,[2] and provides incentives for intervention rather than conservative, efficient practice.[3]
- Recent years have witnessed a dramatic increase in professional liability and malpractice activity. In setting their fees, physicians have responded excessively to the realities of malpractice insurance premium increases and lawsuits.
- Largely due to government policy there has been a recent dramatic increase in the number of physicians, resulting in surpluses in many specialities in selected areas of the nation. The forces of supply and demand for medical care services, however, depart from market theory; despite the increased supply of providers, prices have not decreased.
- It is generally recognized that there is an excess of hospital beds that, nevertheless, need to be filled to ensure hospitals' viability; pressures to maintain census lead to inappropriate use and, consequently, unnecessary expense.
- There are profound, unresolved moral issues within American society regarding access and entitlement to health services.[4] Health and health care are generally considered rights rather than privileges. Debates over allocation of scarce and/or costly resources, such as transplantable organs, thus generate moral dilemmas.
- Cost containment efforts by regulation (e.g., professional standards review organization [PSRO]) have often generated large, expensive, questionably effective programs, many of which have been insensitive to the realities of medical care. The recent shift to price controls to contain costs (e.g., diagnosis related groups [DRGs]), however, has generated changes in practice, the results of which are yet to be evaluated.
- Employers, through benefit program design (e.g., preauthorization), and insurers, through negotiated arrangements (e.g., preferred provider organizations), are exerting greater influence on individuals' decisions regarding where and from whom they obtain service. This represents a major new dimension in the medical marketplace.

These and other forces present diverse, formidable obstacles to the exercise of cost control in medical care. Cost containment efforts to date have tended to address only a limited subset of these forces, namely those involving physicians as decision makers. By and large, outside of prepaid group practice, attempts to control health care costs have not directly involved physicians as managers and providers of care. Cost containment measures such as fee limitations, preadmission approvals, length-of-stay limitations, and mandatory second surgical opinions are viewed by physicians as controls imposed by external, often openly adversarial forces. Given the nature of the medical profession, it is not surprising that these cost containment measures have had limited success.

A THUMBNAIL SKETCH OF THE MEDICAL PROFESSION

What, then, are the characteristics of the medical profession and its practitioners, which must be understood in order to build constructive cost containment efforts?

- Physicians, by and large, are solo entrepreneurs, self-righteous, defensive, and fearful of sacrificing the relatively high income, autonomy, and social position that society has historically led them to expect. While there has been recent softening of these traits, the socialization process incorporated in medical education, coupled with the cultural mystique attached to the healer, perpetuates these expectations.

  In order to engage physicians as allies, efforts must be directed toward maintaining high (but not excessive) income, autonomy in clinical decision making, and appropriate social position. Therefore, programs that provide financial reward for cost efficiency will be more attractive than fee limitations; programs that reward creativity (such as options for same-day surgery and early discharge) will enhance the sense of autonomy.
- Medical education and the practice of medicine are overwhelmingly oriented toward individuals, not populations. Broad social issues and the relationship of individual medical practice to the "social good" are therefore not characteristic of the vocabulary or mind set of the average physician. As a result, most physicians sincerely believe that each decision made (except, perhaps, pricing) is in the best interest of each patient, and this, in turn, represents appropriate, highly valued service.
- Despite the often arrogant and occasionally abusive or fraudulent behavior of some physicians, the humanistic tradition in medical care remains relevant for the majority of practitioners. Few physicians are motivated solely by malice and greed.
- Physicians are uneducated for the practice of cost-effective medicine. The sources of physician education—medical school curricula, residency training programs, and the majority of practice arrangements—fail to demonstrate styles of medical care that explicitly address issues of cost-effectiveness. It is therefore not surprising that most physicians are ignorant of the vast potential to reduce unnecessary hospitalization, surgery, diagnostic testing, and therapeutic interventions.

The sources of physician education—medical school curricula, residency training programs, and the majority of practice arrangements—fail to demonstrate styles of medical care that explicitly address issues of cost-effectiveness.

  Although most physicians would claim that they practice by the ancient medical maxim, *primum non nocere* (first, do no harm), they are not sufficiently sensitive to the dangers of misuse and its associated expense. Change will only take place through the gradual process of formal education and the influence of role models.

  The support of programs that develop medical leadership and trained physician managers who are paid to manage the delicate balance of high quality care and cost efficiency will provide role models and leadership. Physicians, like other professionals, take direction only from other physicians. They are reluctant to trust "regulators," "administrators," and other inimical characters. Physicians do respond to other physicians in authority positions, as witnessed in academia, hospitals, medical societies, and group practices.
- The medical profession has a long tradition of self-regulation, ranging from the obligations of the Hippocratic Oath to the authority for credentialing vested in various professional medical societies. Attention to this history provides an optimistic note for cost containment. Physicians have had a modicum of success with utilization review in hospitals; this can be enhanced. Hospital tissue committees, blood bank committees,

and pharmacy committees have also demonstrated success. Programs that support cost containment committees in hospitals and medical societies could build on the manifest ability of physicians to regulate themselves.

In addition to conventional hospital-based activities, the experience of professional medical societies provides examples of effective influence on physician behavior. The American Academy of Pediatrics has been educating physicians and patients on the proper utilization of immunizations for thirty years. Recently, the American College of Physicians, the major society of internists, developed its Clinical Efficacy Assessment Project; the project's mission is to develop consensus on the safety and efficacy of specified clinical practices. It broadly circulates statements aimed to educate physicians to prevent misuse. The American College of Physician Executives, a fledgling organization, is working diligently to train and certify physicians who can take the lead in the management of medical care organizations.

There are also isolated instances of local medical societies working with physician collaboration directed toward reducing misuse. Effectiveness could be improved by compensating participation on the basis of performance, and by recognition that medical societies are the sole organizations for solo practitioners.

- Despite increasing public awareness and interest in health and healthful practices, people still rely on physicians to make medical care decisions on their behalf and still tend to place trust in the physicians' decisions rather than challenge or even question those judgments. It would be helpful to provide patients with lists of the right questions, advice on the timing of the questions, and wisdom on eliciting thoughtful, as opposed to defensive, answers.
- For over 40 years—and, thus, the entire working career of most practicing physicians—public and private health insurance programs have used payment systems that reward those who see patients often and do more to them. Although fee-for-service is still the predominant form of payment, there is increasing recognition by payers of the perversity of this reimbursement method, and some serious efforts are being made to develop rational alternatives.

MODELS WITH SUCCESSFUL COST CONTAINMENT

Physicians working within group practices, including health maintenance organizations (HMOs), have characteristics similar to those of physicians in solo practice. Their behavior, however, is different. Within HMOs, physicians have been able to reduce the cost of medical services without compromising quality by practicing a style of medicine that is markedly less hospital intensive and, consequently, less expensive. HMO physicians use hospitals 25 percent to 40 percent less than fee-for-service physicians, while ambulatory visit rates remain approximately equal.[5] Over 40 studies have documented and confirmed these statements.[6]

While there have been consistent allegations that HMOs achieve their savings by selecting of low-risk individuals,[7] these allegations have been firmly laid to rest by the study conducted by the Rand Corporation on the effect of prepaid group practice on the use of services.[8]

Since the enabling federal legislation of 1973, HMO enrollment has tripled, with particularly large increases in HMO membership during the past twelve months. HMO enrollment nationally now includes more than 19 million people and is growing at a rate of 20 percent per year;[9] this growth has been spurred on by increasing recognition and support of HMO practice by corporate employers, unions, and government agencies at both federal and state levels.

While there is nothing sacrosanct about HMOs, they do provide the best example of successful cost containment without sacrifice of medical quality. Furthermore, their success with cost-effectiveness lies directly in proportion to the type of organizational control exercised over medical services. For example, group practice models that incorporate more direct physician leadership than do independent practice arrangements have demonstrated lower utilization rates, and thus greater cost efficiency. Several features of HMOs have been shown to promote the successful application of cost-effective practice.

- The care in HMOs is organized and supervised. As noted, the most tightly organized are group practice HMOs that have demonstrated greater ability to control costs than individual practice association (IPA) model HMOs, which are more loosely structured.
- Physicians within HMOs have organized peer review of quality of care.

- Successful HMOs have respected physician leadership. This leadership serves as a role model and guide in the development of cost-effective styles of practice. The importance of trained and responsible medical leadership cannot be ignored.
- HMOs have simple but firmly applied utilization control techniques, including the establishment of norms for length of stay, promotion of alternatives to hospitalization for diagnostic testing, and procedures for encouraging the use of ambulatory surgery.
- HMOs deliberately recruit, screen, and select physicians who are eager to learn and practice cost-effective medical care.
- Physicians in group practice share a unified medical record facilitating communication between physicians of diverse specialties.
- HMOs provide timely and organized feedback to physicians on the expenses incurred per patient, by physician and diagnosis. While feedback has been shown to be an important aspect of cost containment, the success of feedback deteriorates over time unless the feedback presentation changes and evolves.
- HMO physicians have clearly defined incentives with rewards for good financial management as well as good clinical management.

It may not be that prepayment is the key to success with physicians. It is possible that there is a coincidence between prepayment and the structure of HMO practices that have demonstrated cost-effectiveness. There are some compelling arguments that it is the fact of group practice, and not prepayment, that encourages more cost-effective practice. Several reputable analysts of health care, including Fink in one report and Scitofsky and McCall in another, present data supporting the argument that the form of practice is more important than the form of reimbursement in the control of unnecessary hospital expenditures.[10,11]

On the surface, this hypothesis seems inconsistent with the recent history of declining IPA hospitalization rates. One might argue however, that office-based physicians, when organized in IPAs, become part of a "group practice without walls." The individual physician now recognizes that he or she is one of many physicians sharing common objectives that go beyond conventional clinical matters to include the cost-effective management of health care resources.

In addition to being able to lower the hospitalization rate and therefore health care costs, it has been suggested that the presence of an HMO in a community may have a sentinel effect, thereby reducing the hospitalization rates and expenses of non-HMO programs.

Whether by the reimbursement mechanism or practice organization, HMOs have been successful. In fact, in addition to being able to lower the hospitalization rate and therefore health care costs, it has been suggested that the presence of an HMO in a community may have a sentinel effect, thereby reducing the hospitalization rates and expenses of non-HMO programs.[12] If this proves to be correct, it would substantiate the supposition that health care competition has a salubrious effect within a community.

Despite their merits and growing popularity, HMOs are unlikely to reach some critical mass within the next several years. In order to achieve broader cost-effectiveness, other organizational forms therefore need to be developed, perhaps transferring and adapting some of the techniques of HMOs.

One emerging trend in organizational form is the physician hospital organization (PHO) or medical staff hospital organization (MeSH). These are collaborative ventures between organized groups of physicians and hospitals; the PHO or MeSH contracts with an HMO for the exclusive right to care for HMO members in a defined geographic area. Both parties share risk, and there are incentives for each to support the other party's interests. This new organizational form reestablishes physician–hospital interdependence; it also shifts risk to the provider.

In developing new organizational forms, it would be helpful to consider various physician factors within and outside of HMOs that appear to affect choice of practice organization. HMO physicians have different attitudes toward medical practice than non-HMO physicians. There is greater acceptability of peer review and external control. HMO physicians, particularly those in group practice, are satisfied with the "trade-offs" that must be made. They accept the structured form of practice in return for reduced working hours and more effective scheduling of patient visits.[13] Physicians in HMO group practice, however, see approximately the same number of patients per week as do physicians unassociated with HMOs, spending more time in the office and less time in the hospital.[14,15]

Physicians who do not work in HMOs have generally negative views of HMOs, which reflect primarily a fear of the unknown. Those who begin to get to know an HMO practice often comment on how surprised they are about the favorable quality of care and the positive work environment. Physicians working in prepaid programs endorse them for their ability to lower expenditures and increase access to care. The most widely perceived benefits are establishment of a practice directly out of residency, structured work time, and income security. These latter factors are increasingly important to physicians coming out of residency programs.

In a report entitled "Medical Practice in the 1980's" prepared for the Henry J. Kaiser Family Foundation, Louis Harris and Associates[16] report that while most physicians believe they are moving into a period of physician surplus, they do not believe that physician fees will be reduced. They attach more importance to personal, nonprofessional concerns than did their predecessors and are fearful of regulatory interference. The authors note a trend toward salaried employment and toward hospital and group-based practice. Physicians agree that their practices will be affected by prepaid plans and acknowledge the effect prepaid payment plans will have on other physicians in the community.

It is interesting to note that Louis Harris and Associates' most recent publication, "A Report Card on HMO's, 1980–1984," reports, "As physician experience with prepaid care has widened so have favorable attitudes to HMO's."[17] By 1984, 43 percent of physicians polled by Harris had signed up for a program that would refer patients to them in exchange for a discounted fee.

FEE-FOR-SERVICE PHYSICIANS' POTENTIAL FOR DECREASING HOSPITAL EXPENDITURES

In addition to the success of prepaid group practice in reducing hospitalization, there is evidence that organizations of fee-for-service physicians have also been able to achieve such success, although to a lesser extent than group practice prepayment models.[18] This too is done by reducing hospitalization as witnessed by the experience of IPA HMOs that, with fee-for-service physicians, reduce hospital days. Since the decision to hospitalize a patient is the most costly decision that a physician makes, it is important to study hospital decision-making practices.

Myers and Schroeder of the Institute for Health Policy Studies at the University of California, San Francisco, School of Medicine, present a thoughtful analysis on influencing physician use of services for hospitalized patients.[19] They reviewed a series of studies on physician ordering behavior in hospitals, consistently showing ignorance of the value of cost-effective styles of practice. Excessive testing is a substantial problem, and teaching proper attention to the cost and outcome of testing appears to be an appropriate area for intervention. Similarly, length of stay can be reduced without harm.[20]

The task of encouraging physicians to reduce testing and to reduce length of stay is frustrating, however, for three reasons. First, physicians perceive that they request services for patients principally to improve the quality of patient care; this perception by the physician is often inappropriate. Second, patients do have influence on physician ordering; patients request and receive treatments that may not be necessary but that increase patient satisfaction.[21] One study revealed that two-thirds of patients polled thought the number of tests done correlates with excellence of the physician.[22] Third, there are financial incentives for physicians to order increasing amounts of services.

TEACHING THE STUDENT

What then are the possibilities for changing incentives and educating physicians to modify their patterns of hospitalization and use of services? There have been poor results from efforts to teach physicians the proper indications for ordering services.[23–27] However, two important conclusions have emerged from various studies of the ability to affect physician decision making during the educational period. First, physicians are totally unaware of the cost of services, particularly diagnostic testing, which are generated by their clinical decision making.[28] Second, physicians have no role models of cost-attentive and cost-effective practice. One of the lessons from HMOs is that periodic, physician-specific, written feedback to physicians on the cost of referrals and diagnostic testing is important in the moderation of ordering behavior. This is done in a nonpunitive and informational manner. It tends to stimulate discussion of methods for further cost reduction, perhaps by improving the efficiency of arriving at diagnostic conclusions. While ordering practices are shared with peers, physicians are not punished; the group collaborates in the development of its own internal role model. This type of peer review is a technique that is transferable to hospital medical staffs. In the absence of other cost containment incentives, however, physician education and feedback are not effective strategies.[29]

While the results of teaching cost containment to medical students and residents thus far have been disappointing, there is no reason not to try. New payment forms, such as DRGs, will teach lessons more quickly to physicians already in practice; consequently, there will be better role models for students.

INFLUENCING THE PRACTICING PHYSICIAN

There have been articles in widely read medical journals during the past several years that attempt to prepare practicing physicians for increasing accountability and responsibility for cost containment.[30–33] Many of the articles in the "throw away" journals have been geared toward encouraging physicians to circle their wagons and prepare for the onslaught of interference in medical practice. Other journals, such as the *New England Journal of Medicine* and the *Journal of the American Medical Association*, have published articles and editorials by physicians that detail physicians' accountability and possible options for intervention. These articles describe the disappointing qualitative results of professional standards review organizations (PSROs). PSROs, however, have had some qualitative success by involving physicians and thus exposing a new cadre of physicians to issues of utilization control.

Proper incentives for physicians are a keystone in successful cost containment. Peer review, which is continuing education in an active mode, is an important component as physicians are much more responsive to review by their own than by outsiders. Practicing physicians are as unaware of the costs of medical services as are medical students and residents. They have not been exposed to cost-effective practice, and, conversely, have had incentives to hospitalize, have experienced ineffective peer review, and have not had a financial stake in cost control. A program combining peer review with potential for reward of cost-efficient practice could thus reap large benefits.

DEMONSTRATION OF COST CONTAINMENT WITHOUT THE BENEFIT OF HMOs

There is little in the medical literature describing interventions that effectively change physician practice patterns without financial or organizational incentives. Some important related work has been published by Wennberg, McPherson, and Caper, and by Wennberg, et al., demonstrating extensive variation in surgical rates as a consequence of physicians' practice styles.[34,35] This variation is shown to be directly related to physician discretion rather than other clinical variables such as case severity. Furthermore, Wennberg, et al. describe success in changing physician behavior by working with local medical societies giving feedback to individual physicians on the variation in their procedure rates as compared to those of physicians in other areas.[36] The increasing involvement of physicians on a local level, analyzing practice pattern variation, could help reduce the individualistic practice styles that are more expensive than other equally effective styles. Implementation of locally managed practice variation monitoring, with practicing physicians developing norms, may also be helpful in preventing increases in hospital admissions secondary to the DRG program. This latter thesis is based on the new opportunity for hospitals to increase admissions in order to fill the void created by DRG-induced reduction in length of stay.

The increasing involvement of physicians on a local level, analyzing practice pattern variation, could help reduce the individualistic practice styles that are more expensive than other equally effective styles.

RECOMMENDATIONS

Physicians control access to medical services. Allied with consumers and payers, they have the potential to enhance the effectiveness of cost containment activities; as adversaries, cost containment efforts will have a rocky course. Any new system, however, must place added responsibility on physicians. These new responsibilities will be accepted slowly and cautiously, only if facilitated by positive reinforcement and financial reward. The major task for those who pay for medical care is to chart a course that will appeal to physicians and consumers without neglecting the quality of care.

The behavior of physicians can be modified by changing reimbursement mechanisms and practice organizations, and by providing information on practice variation and service costs. Specific recommendations for those who manage clinical programs or pay for medical care are offered below.

Clinical practice

Efforts should be made to develop gatekeeper mechanisms, that is, systems in which only primary care physicians (internists, pediatricians, obstetrician/gynecologists, and family physicians) have authority to order diagnostic testing, specialty referrals, and hospitalization. The primary care physician then becomes the financial and clinical manager of care. While capitation is one method to accomplish this, other fixed-payment methods have also been developed. With the primary care physician in control and rewarded, costs should decrease. This role of gatekeeper can be structured so that the function is as personal physician rather than as case manager or routing clerk; the physician is thereby engaged as an ally.[37]

Practical strategies are needed, however, to define the gatekeeper role. The primary care physician has been disenfranchised by movements toward subspecialization and technological intervention, and is ripe for attention, appreciation, and increase in control. Managers should refer to the experience of prepaid group practices for guidance since it is often these organizations in which the primary care physician gatekeeper model functions well.

Three caveats apply, however, in adopting the gatekeeper model. First, the primary care physician is at risk; the system must protect practitioners from so-called adverse selection by patients who have free choice of physicians. Physicians with good reputations, for example, may attract patients with more complex problems who would (and should) generate higher expenses. Establishing a narrow risk corridor for these physicians would reduce their incentive; creating a wide risk corridor would provide a direct financial disincentive. Physicians who are skillful at skimming off the relatively well patients or who are not as well respected for their capability to treat complex problems would be rewarded by having a group of patients who are at lower risk.

Protection against the effects of adverse selection can best be accomplished by pooling the risks, organizing referral resources, and avoiding duplicate diagnostic procedures. This is why capitated prepayment works in multispecialty group practice. The larger this pool, the less risk for any one physician.

Second, why should it be assumed that primary care physicians are prepared and willing to bear the weighty responsibility of acting as gatekeeper for the entire health care system? Are these practitioners adequately trained to fulfill this screening role? Do they have the political, social, and professional status to function effectively as gatekeepers? What major changes in professional behavior must be achieved in order to make possible the conversion to the proposed primary care case-management model? All of these questions must be carefully examined by the clinical program manager before attempting to institute and operate a gatekeeper system.

Third, how would specialty physicians be paid in this system? Whether fee-for-service, capitation, or retainer arrangements are used, who is to set and control the rates? In this highly competitive environment, what is to prevent the primary care physician from looking only for the lowest bid? And what would be the implications for quality of care.[38] Once again, the clinical program manager must carefully explore these issues in order to ensure an effective system.

The development of multispecialty group practice by reimbursement mechanisms, loans, and community pressures would need to be encouraged. Groups using unified medical records and those that provide timely feedback on expenses should be rewarded.

Accurate and timely feedback to medical practitioners on the cost of generated expenses must be provided.[39] At the least, each physician could get a printout of cost generated by patient and have this compared to aggregate data for the region by diagnosis—in other words, practice profiles. However, printing the material and getting physicians to learn from it are different stories. Effective linkage probably lies with medical leadership, financial incentives for cost-efficient practice, and continual stimulation of the feedback mechanism to avoid deterioration of this educational approach.

Financial support for research and training of physicians on cost-effective practice should be made available, to increase the meager amount being invested in this vital area.[40] In addition, responsible medical leaders should be trained in cost-effective styles of practice. Sanctions such as monetary penalties or expulsion from reimbursement panels should be considered for unremitting offenders. The sanctions should be mild enough, however, so that the penalties will be imposed.[41] Finally, systems should be developed that promote the sharing of surpluses among groups of physicians and hospitals to encourage collaboration rather than competition or adversarial relationships.

Consumer programs

Cost-effective alternatives to current health care service practices should be vigorously and aggressively presented to employees; workers should be given a financial incentive for joining an HMO. Corporate medical departments should be developed and strengthened to give them a more strategic role in inducing physicians to practice cost-effective medicine.[42] Finally, effective strategies to educate patients and clinicians that "more is not necessarily better" and that "more may be harmful" need to be instituted.

Public policy

The growth of prepayment mechanisms, particularly those with demonstrated effectiveness such as HMOs, should be encouraged. Everything reasonably possible should be done to shrink the available number of hospital beds in communities where they are excessive, and the number of physicians graduated from medical schools should be reduced. Regulators and legislators should be encouraged to be flexible and responsive to the realities of medical care. In some states, for example, the certificate of need process is so slow and cumbersome that progressive programs, such as ambulatory surgery, are virtually blocked. Finally, the uncertainties of medical care and the diversity of acceptable approaches need to be recognized. Therefore, caution must be exercised with panacea cost containment programs.

REFERENCES

1. Goodman, L.J., and Swartwout, J.E. "Comparative Aspects of Medical Practice." *Medical Care* 22 (1984): 255–67.
2. Almay, T.P. "The Role of the Primary Physician in the Health-Care 'Industry.'" *New England Journal of Medicine* 304 (1981):225–228.
3. McClure, W. "The Competition Strategy for Medical Care." *Employer's Health Benefits Newsletter* 7 (1983): 1–10.
4. Engelhardt, H.T. "Allocating Scarce Medical Resources and the Availability of Organ Transplantation." *New England Journal of Medicine* 311 (1984): 66–71.
5. Manning, W.G. "A Controlled Trial of the Effect of a Prepaid Group Practice on Use of Services." *New England Journal of Medicine* 310 (1984): 1505–10.
6. Luft, H.S. "How Do Health Maintenance Organizations Achieve Their 'Savings'?: Rhetoric and Evidence." *New England Journal of Medicine* 298 (1978): 1336–43.
7. Jackson-Meek, M., and Kleinman, J.H. "Evidence for Self-Selection among Health Maintenance Organizations." *Journal of the American Medical Association* 250 (1983): 2826–29.
8. Enthoven, A.C. "The Rand Experiment and Economical Health Care." *New England Journal of Medicine* 310 (1984): 1528–30.
9. InterStudy. *December 1983 HMO Enrollment in the U.S.* Excelsior, Minn.: InterStudy, 1983.
10. Fink, R. "The Influence of the HMO Experience on Medical Care in the United States." *Bulletin of the New York Academy of Medicine* 60 (1984): 465–78.
11. Scitovsky, A., and McCall, V. "Use of Hospital Services under Two Prepaid Plans." *Medical Care* 18 (1980): 30–41.
12. Aquilina, D., and Appel, G.L. "HMO's Real Competitive Role." *Hospitals* 57 (September 1, 1983) 89–92.
13. Fink, R. "What Does It Mean to be an HMO Physician?" Paper presented to Medical Directors Conference, Group Health Association of America, Washington, DC, January 6, 1984.
14. Goodman and Swartwout, "Comparative Aspects of Medical Practice."
15. Ibid.
16. Louis Harris and Associates. *Medical Practice in the 1980's: Physicians Look at Their Changing Profession.* Menlo Park, Calif.: The Henry J. Kaiser Family Foundation, 1982.
17. Louis Harris and Associates. *A Report Card on HMO's, 1980–1984.* Menlo Park, Calif.: The Henry J. Kaiser Family Foundation, 1985.
18. Egdahl, R.H., et al. "The Potential of Organizations of Fee-for-Service Physicians for Achieving Significant Decreases in Hospitalization." *Annals of Surgery* 186 (1977): 388–99.
19. Myers, L.P., and Schroeder, S.A. "Physician Use of Services for the Hospitalized Patient: A Review, with Implications for Cost Containment." *Milbank Memorial Fund Quarterly* 59 (1981): 481–507.

20. Egdahl, R.H. "Ways for Surgeons to Increase the Efficiency of Their Use of Hospitals." *New England Journal of Medicine* 309 (1983): 1184–87.
21. Myers and Schroeder, "Physician Use of Services for the Hospitalized Patient."
22. Marton, K.T., Sox, H.C., and Wasson, J.H. "The Clinical Utility of the Upper Gastrointestinal Series." *Clinical Research* 26 (1978): 334A.
23. Ingbar, M.L., and Miner, J.C. "Teaching Cost Containment and Health Economics in U.S. Medical Schools, 1980." *Journal of Medical Education* 56 (1981): 851–53.
24. Eastaugh, S.R. "Teaching the Principles of Cost-Effective Clinical Decision-Making to Medical Students." *Inquiry* 18 (1981): 26–36.
25. Williams, S.V., et al. "Teaching Cost-Effective Diagnostic Test Use to Medical Students." *Medical Care* 22 (1984): 535–42.
26. Grossman, R.M. "A Review of Physician Cost-Containment Strategies for Laboratory Testing." *Medical Care* 21 (1983): 783–802.
27. Applegate, W.B., et al. "Impact of a Cost-Containment Educational Program on Housestaff Ambulatory Clinic Charges." *Medical Care* 21 (1983): 486–96.
28. Long, M.J., Cummings, K.M., and Frisof, F.B. "The Role of Perceived Price in Physician's Demand for Diagnostic Tests." *Medical Care* 21 (1983): 243–50.
29. Schroeder, S.A., et al. "The Failure of Physician Education as a Cost Containment Strategy." *Journal of the American Medical Association* 252 (1984): 225–30.
30. Eisenberg, J.M., and Rosoff, A.J. "Physician Responsibility for the Cost of Unnecessary Medical Services." *New England Journal of Medicine* 299 (1978): 76–80.
31. Dresnick, S.J., et al. "The Physician's Role in the Cost-Containment Problem." *Journal of the American Medical Association* 241 (1979): 1606–9.
32. Eisenberg, J.M., and Williams, S.V. "Cost Containment and Changing Physician's Practice Behavior." *Journal of the American Medical Association* 246 (1981): 2195–2201.
33. Egdahl, R.H. "Physicians and the Containment of Health Care Costs." *New England Journal of Medicine* 304 (1981): 900–901.
34. Wennberg, J.E., McPherson, K., and Caper, P. "Will Payment Based on Diagnosis Related Groups Control Hospital Costs?" *New England Journal of Medicine* 311 (1984): 295–300.
35. Wennberg, J.E., et al. "Changes in Tonsillectomy Rates Associated with Feedback and Review." *Pediatrics* 59 (1977): 821–26.
36. Wennberg, et al., "Changes in Tonsillectomy Rates Associated with Feedback and Review."
37. Somers, A.R. "And Who Shall be the Gatekeeper? The Role of the Primary Physician in the Health Care Delivery System." *Inquiry* 20 (1983): 301–13.
38. Greifinger, R.B. "Control of Health Care Costs." *New England Journal of Medicine* 310 (1984): 792.
39. Eisenberg and Williams, "Cost Containment and Changing Physician's Practice Behavior."
40. Hudson, J.I., and Braslow, J.B. "Cost Containment Education Efforts in United States Medical Schools." *Journal of Medical Education* 54 (1979): 835–47.
41. Eisenberg and Rosoff, "Physician Responsibility for the Cost of Unnecessary Medical Services."
42. Walsh, D.C. "Is There a Doctor In-House?" *Harvard Business Review* 62 (July–August 1984): 84–94.

The end of autonomy? Reflections on the postprofessional physician

Stephen J. O'Connor
and
Joyce A. Lanning

Of the many characteristics that classify the practice of medicine as a profession, autonomy plays the most important role. There are currently assaults on the profession's ability to select, train, and license its own practitioners and on the medical knowledge base itself, as well as the standards for applying it. This article examines factors contributing to this reduction in autonomy and reviews potential impacts on the profession, patients, payors, health care organizations, and managers.

Health Care Manage Rev, 1992, 17(1), 63–72

"Now hold on, hold on. You know just as well as I do that a high-priced man has to do exactly as he's told from the morning till night. You have seen this man (the taskmaster) before, haven't you?"

"No, I never saw him."

"Well, if you are a high-priced man, you will do exactly as this man tells you to-morrow, from morning till night. When he tells you to pick up a pig and walk, you pick it up and you walk, and when he tells you to sit down and rest, you sit down. You do that right straight through the day. And what's more, no back talk. Now a high-priced man does just what he's told to do, and no back talk. Do you understand that? When this man tells you to walk, you walk; when he tells you to sit down, you sit down, and you don't talk back at him. Now you come on to work here to-morrow morning and I'll know before night whether you are really a high-priced man or not."

—Frederick W. Taylor, to his pig-iron handler, "Schmidt."[1(pp.45,46)]

Students of health care administration learn early on that the role of physician professionals in health care delivery distinguishes health administration from its more generic business administration counterpart. These students also recognize that the physician presence has major implications for the way in which health care organizations are designed and managed.

In dealing with physician professionals, nonphysician health care managers have faced constraints and limitations to their own organizational power and authority: Justification for this arrangement has typically been based on the premise that management and health care organizations must not interfere with the practice of medicine. Physicians alone may practice medicine; administrators manage the nonmedical bureaucratic structure that supports the physicians' work.

In many health care organizations, especially community hospitals, these distinct domains have resulted in the oft-cited dual line of authority: one medical, the other

---

Stephen J. O'Connor, Ph.D., is an Assistant Professor of Health Care Management in the School of Business Administration at the University of Wisconsin-Milwaukee.

Joyce A. Lanning, Ph.D., is a health care consultant with adjunct faculty positions in the Schools of Public Health and Health-Related Professions at the University of Alabama at Birmingham.

An earlier version of this paper was presented at the 1990 Annual Meeting of the Academy of Management. The authors gratefully acknowledge the helpful comments of Marlene Beggelman, M.D., President, Medical Intelligence (Brookline, MA); B. Kay Snavely, Ph.D., Miami University; and three anonymous reviewers.

administrative.[2] The two domains, like oil and water, do not mix well. Physician professional and bureaucratic management discord is not a new phenomenon, but has occurred in the United States since the time of the Revolutionary War. General George Washington (ostensibly a bureaucratic manager with substantial power and authority), after his first inspection of the Continental Army, lamented in a letter to the early Congress:

> I have made inquiry into the establishment of the hospital, and find it in a very unsettled condition. There is no...subordination among the surgeons; of consequence, disputes have arisen, and must continue until it is reduced to some system. I could wish it was immediately taken into consideration, as the lives and health of both officers and men so much depend on due regulation of this department.[3(p.33)]

Although military surgeons during the Revolutionary War did not have the freedom or professional autonomy later accorded to their 20th century parallels, they nonetheless made it difficult to manage even a highly disciplined bureaucratic military unit. The duality in the structure of authority observed in many modern health care organizations has been a frequent source of frustration, conflict, disagreement, and uncooperativeness for both professional physicians and bureaucratic managers alike. New economic pressures have extended the arena of conflict. As Shortell points out, "No longer is the issue who will control the hospital, but rather who will control the delivery system from the patient's home to the physician's office, to the hospital, to the postacute facility, and back again to the patient's home."[4(pp.11–12)]

This article examines the medical profession, first by analyzing the important role autonomy plays in defining a profession and how it has supported physician professional dominance in both health care organizations and society. The second section discusses the array of macro and micro influences in the health care environment that have contributed to reduced autonomy. The third section explores the consequences of diminished autonomy, and its effect on the medical profession, patients, payors, and on health care organization and management. This article should be of interest to anyone wishing to better understand current directions in the medical profession and how health care organizations are adapting to these altered circumstances.

WHAT IS A PROFESSIONAL? AUTONOMY IS THE KEY!

A profession is often defined primarily in terms of the amount of autonomy and self-direction it maintains.[5–7] One way of establishing and maintaining professional dominance is to obtain autonomy over work.[6,8] Reed and Evans specify 10 major characteristics that bestow professional status on an occupation:

1. The profession is in possession of a circumscribed and socially valuable body of knowledge.
2. The members of the profession determine the profession's standards of knowledge and expertise.
3. The profession attracts high-quality students who undergo an extensive socialization process as they are absorbed into the profession.
4. The profession is given authority to license practitioners by the state, with licensing and admission boards made up largely of members of the profession.
5. There is an ostensible sense of community and mutuality of interest among members of a profession.
6. Social policy and legislation that relate to the profession are heavily influenced by members of the profession through such mechanisms as lobbying and expert testimony.
7. The profession has a code of ethics that governs practice, the tenets of which are more stringent than legal controls.
8. A service orientation supersedes the proprietary interests of the professionals.
9. Professions are terminal occupations (i.e., they are the practitioners' singular and lifelong occupational choice).
10. A profession is largely free of lay control, with its practitioners exercising a high degree of occupational autonomy.[9(p.3279)]

Figure 1 regroups these 10 characteristics in terms of the "who," "what," "why," and "how" of a profession. First is the selection, training, licensure, and cohesiveness of the profession, or who they are; second, their knowledge base and standards, or what they know; third, their service orientation and code of ethics, or why they act as they do; and fourth, their occupational autonomy and impact on social policy, or how they direct their activities. Autonomy is a necessary underpinning for all the other features. To the extent that the public questions physician adherence to the who, what, and why characteristics of professionalism or questions the benefits that society may derive, there is less willingness to allow autonomy—the central component of any profession.

Regardless of their theoretical base, all observers agree that legitimate, organized autonomy is the key feature of a profession. An occupation that is lacking this authentic autonomy may alternatively be given such designations

FIGURE 1

THE MEDICAL PROFESSION: ASPECTS AND ASSAULTS

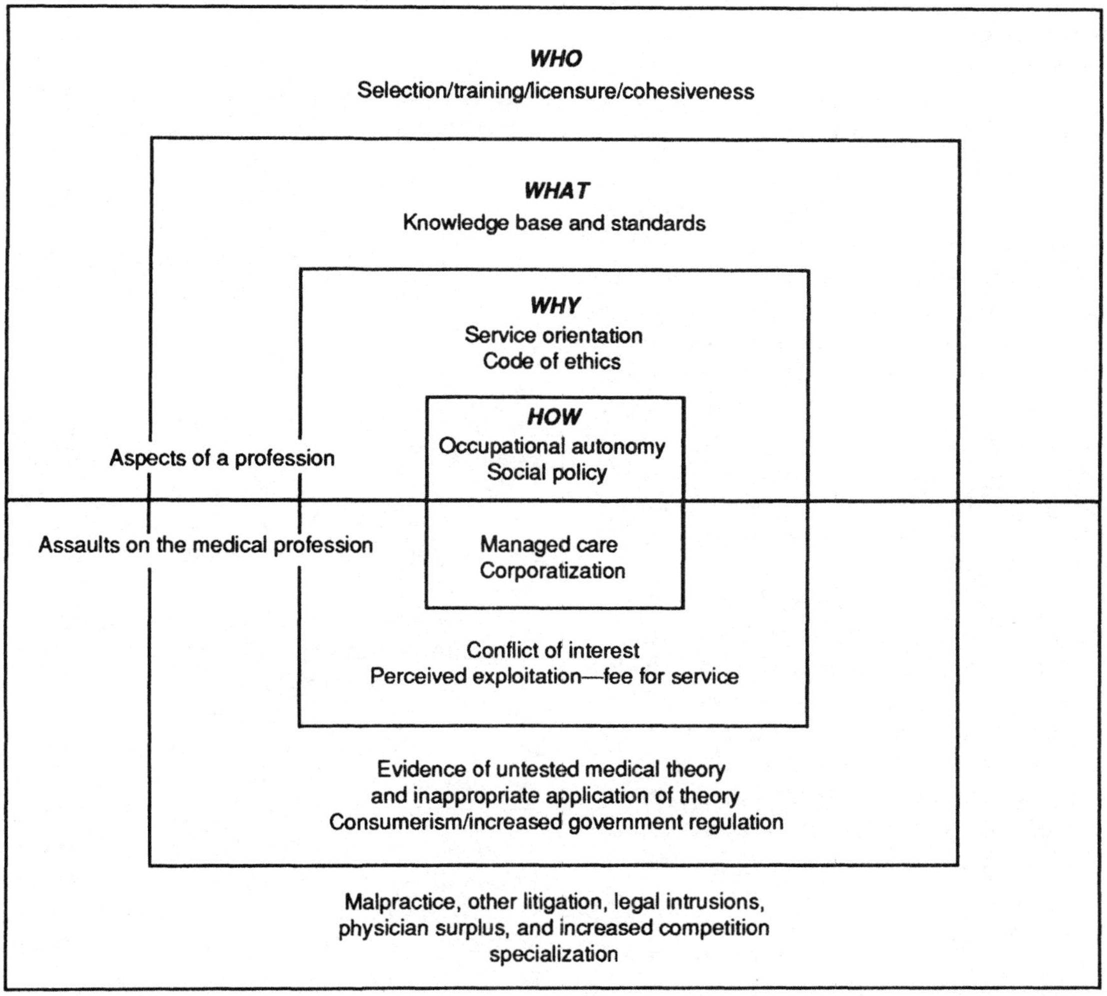

as quasiprofession, paraprofession, semiprofession, subprofession, or a trade. A trade has been defined as a craft in which only skilled workers are employed.[10] Freidson, one of the most prolific writers on the topic of professionalism, places the medical profession squarely at the top of the paramedical hierarchy, primarily as a result of its extraordinary autonomy—"the right to control its own work."[8(p.71)] Others have defined professional autonomy as controlling the content of professional work and the organization of medical practice,[11] or as "freedom from control either by peers or by organizational constraints,"[5(p.53)] or as "the authority and freedom to regulate themselves and act within their spheres of competence."[12(p.146)] In part, this autonomy has been protected in the past by professional physicians' ability to influence legislation and regulation of the profession.

Since 1910, when occupational autonomy was bestowed upon American physicians,[7,13] medicine has been viewed as the quintessence of professionalism. Now, however, assaults on this remarkable autonomy threaten the profession.

ASSAULTS ON PHYSICIAN AUTONOMY

The challenges to physician self-determination are both direct and indirect. In search of value for their health care dollar, third-party payors seek to constrain payments directly for what physicians do and how they do it. Indirect erosion of autonomy is also occurring as the essential components of professionalism (as listed previously) are weakened. The following sections discuss the lower half of Figure 1, which indicates some of the forces that are undermining each of the profession's important components.

WHO: Selecting, training, and licensing a cohesive group

A profession must attract an ample supply of high-quality students who participate in a professionalization process as they are preparing for licensure. Until very recently, trends showed fewer applicants to medical school, and there were concerns that some state-based schools might have to lower admission standards.[14] Fall 1988 was the seventh consecutive year that 127 United States medical schools admitted fewer students than the previous year, and applicants have been decreasing in number since a peak in 1974. With 1.7 applicants in 1987 for each of the approximately 15,850 places, competition has declined substantially.[15]

Some credit the decline in applicants, at least partially, to the report of the Graduate Medical Education National Advisory Committee (GMENAC) in 1980,[16] which predicted a large oversupply of physicians by 1990. Other explanations include the fact that there are fewer people in the age group usually applying, increased tuition, and discouragement from practicing physicians.[15,17] The declining appeal of a medical career may also reflect the loss of social prestige accorded the profession.

The professionalization process for physicians is also under attack. The sharp demarcation between the 4-year undergraduate and 3- to 7-year graduate experience has been called into question, with a suggestion that clinical experience in the last 2 years of graduate medical education should be enough for the general internist, general pediatrician, and family physician.[14] The same authors also question the blurring of roles between teaching, research, and patient care for faculty members in the nation's academic medical centers, suggesting that good teaching be recognized and rewarded as a primary activity.[14] The extended hours and lack of supervision for interns and junior hospital residents have been questioned by the courts in the Libby Zion case, prompting the concern that "the threat of externally imposed controls over how physicians are trained remains very real."[18(p.213)] Libby Zion was a young college student who was admitted to a New York City hospital complaining of headache and fever. Eight hours later she died of coronary arrest. A grand jury investigating the case concluded that overworked residents contributed to Zion's death. Currently, New York is the only state constraining how many hours per week a resident physician may work. However, several other states are contemplating similar measures.[19]

Nor is the licensure process immune from interference. Congress enacted the Health Care Quality Improvement Act of 1986 because of physicians' inability to keep their incompetent members from moving across state lines where their history of incompetence would be unknown. Under the new system, the Department of Health and Human Services assists the licensing and credentialing bodies in each state by operating an independent information clearinghouse on license revocation or suspension, reprimands, and censures or probations for any licensed health professional. The Medicare and Medicaid Patient and Program Protection Act of 1987 expanded the list of information to be collected, as well as the proactive role of the clearinghouse, which presumably will make the information available to a wide variety of organizations and officials rather than merely respond to requests.[20]

Finally, the profession is no longer cohesive. Factors contributing to this condition include increased competition from an oversupply of physicians;[21] increased competition from provider brokers, such as hospitals;[22] fragmentation through specialization and growth of the specialty societies;[7,23,24] extreme disparity in rewards that the different physicians receive;[23] increased malpractice litigation;[25] the burgeoning business of peer review and managed care;[26] or any of a number of other causes. Whether the profession's current status can be attributed to these factors or not, there *is* a lessened sense of collegiality and cohesiveness.

WHAT: Maintaining the knowledge base and upholding standards

As professionals, physicians have a unique responsibility for developing and maintaining a specialized body of knowledge that they hold in trust for the public good. The current fervor over quality of care and outcomes research, however, is a result of the growing realization that physicians often don't know what works and what doesn't, and that they vary widely in the way they apply what they do know.[27] This evidence from the research on small area variations in practice patterns, coupled with a growing consumerism, threatens to undermine the patient's trust and dependency on the physician and further threatens professional autonomy.

With research backing his contention that physicians are guided as much by subjective factors as by science, Wennberg has made a compelling case for the need to evaluate medical practice.[28] Ellwood is among the voices calling for a renewed commitment to outcomes management based on a common national technology to measure the effect of medical care on patient outcomes.[29] The Agency for Health Care Policy and Research (AHCPR), formerly the National Center for Health Services Research, has a major research focus called the Medical Treatment Effectiveness Program. This program is based on the premise that some practice "variations are often the result of inadequate information about treatment effectiveness or differences in the 'practice styles' or preferences of physicians and other providers."[30(p.1)] The American Medical Association (AMA), in partnership with national specialty societies, has been increasingly active in the "development, evaluation and implementation of practice parameters."[31(p.2)]

This lack of certainty among medical professions is not lost on consumers, as the popular press has taken the message to the masses.[32–34] Calling the lack of knowledge about the appropriate test or procedure for a given condition an "intellectual crisis" helps undermine trust. Without this trust, a society will not be willing to accord physicians the professional autonomy they have had in the past.[35] Employers encourage their employees to question the physician about the proposed treatment and its costs, heightening a growing consumerism.[36]

WHY: A service orientation and code of ethics

The concern over the profession's capability to determine the efficacy of medical ministrations is coupled with a growing suspicion that some physician choices are driven by proprietary interests rather than a dedication to service. In some cases, parts of the code of ethics (e.g., the ban on advertising) have been interpreted by the courts to act against the interests of society. As a consequence, self-governance in this area has been replaced by a regulatory decision that overrules the profession's previous prohibition.[37,38]

Several recent *Wall Street Journal* articles reflect what one pundit has called the blood sport of doctor bashing: "Hospitals That Need Patients Pay Bounties for Doctors' Referrals,"[39] "Doctor-Owned Labs Earn Lavish Profits in a Captive Market,"[40] and "How Doctors Boost Bills by Misrepresenting the Work They Do."[41] All reflect a proprietary motivation for physicians rather than the service orientation expected of the profession.

The debate over the entrepreneurial role for physicians has raged in the professional literature. There is disagreement within the profession over the need to limit conflicts of interest by restricting physician financial interest. Some feel that entrepreneurship is essential to stimulating innovation, whereas others feel that the substantial decline in confidence in the medical profession warrants action.[42]

Based on the belief that current law and medical ethics fail to protect consumers from physician greed, Representative Stark introduced a bill that created the Ethics in Patient Referrals Act of 1989.[43] Such legislation, which Congress folded into the Omnibus Budget Reconciliation Act of 1989,[44] is designed to address perceived inadequacies in the profession's own service orientation and ethical standards, further eroding the autonomy of the profession.

HOW: Managed care and corporatization as direct threats to autonomy

Many physicians are beginning to feel their autonomy threatened as they react to individuals and events outside of their profession. This perception is reflected in a letter to the editor of the *New England Journal of Medicine*:

> Slowly but surely the medical profession is allowing itself to be controlled by nonphysicians, who are fast becoming the final authority on medical matters in this country. Lest anyone doubt that this is taking place, the evidence is all around us. Today's physician, instead of being governed by his or her peers, is now subservient to insurance companies or third-party payors and to the business tycoons who run worldwide hospital chains. It is of grave concern that nonphysicians with a smattering of medical knowledge, have deluded themselves into thinking that they can assume most of the functions of physicians.
>
> But the final degradation, the ultimate indicator of just how much we have relinquished our power to nonphysicians and to the marketplace, is to have one's medically correct diagnosis changed to a more lucrative but less accurate one by a clerk recording DRGs. But then DRGs also originated with nonphysicians and were foisted on us by them. Why a once proud and independent profession has permitted this tragic takeover to occur is indeed incomprehensible.[45(p.390)]

However, if the physician is not trusted to know what is best, nor to always choose ethically even if he or she does know, then the social and economic system will step in with alternatives that constrain the physician's ability to define quality of care. The past resistance to such constraints as "cookbook medicine" have been replaced in some quarters with eloquent appeals to fellow physicians to help create practice guidelines as a means of preserving the autonomy of the profession, if not of the individual professional.[27,46] A major guideline developer states, "If the guidelines are developed with the aid of the best methods and if they are applied constructively, then the twin goals of increased health of the American public and physician satisfaction can be achieved."[47(p3027)]

As more physicians assume full-time salaried positions in health care organizations, and as outside threats to their autonomy become intensified, there will be greater incentives for physicians to unionize. Describing the intrinsic objective of physician unions, Sobal and Hepner note that

> [t]he changes currently affecting the health industry represent a threat to the role that physicians have traditionally held in the industry and society in general. Therefore, the physician union often expends significant energy defending the professional integrity of physicians and their status in the medical profession, as opposed to the more traditional union negotiations.[48(pp.334,35)]

In addition, the changing structure and financial arrangements of the health care delivery system have led to the proliferation of payor watchdogs to oversee physician choices.[26] Originally, there were no third parties between the physician and the patient, a situation that the medical profession fought hard to preserve.[13] The advent of traditional insurance did little to change the relationship because the payor simply acted as a pass-through. With increasing concerns over cost, professional autonomy has been directly invaded by payment or service decisions that require preadmission certification, continued-stay review, in-office ambulatory care audits, protocol adherence, and other third-party interventions.

Clearly, changing structural and environmental forces are exerting increasing control over physicians. Deprofessionalization theory suggests that these changes have the effect of moving the profession toward greater rationalization[49] and reduced expectations of work autonomy.[6]

There is little hope of a return to the full autonomy and unhampered patient relationships physicians experienced at the height of their dominance. Brokers or agents will continue to work on behalf of purchasers and providers to buy or sell health care in the most effective and efficient way. The question for the profession and for those who work to administer the facilities in which they practice their art is how will these brokering organizations be structured and who will manage them?

REDUCED PROFESSIONAL AUTONOMY: CHANGING MODELS OF CONTROL

As the professional autonomy of physicians weakens, the health care organizations in which they work will begin to acquire commensurately greater control over them. This control will vary in its extent and intensity depending on the nature of the emerging structural models for the delivery of care.

In an attempt to understand and conceptualize these alternative models, several authors have independently enumerated three related structural categories.[50-52]

Madison and Konrad's alternatives of individual autonomy, administered autonomy, and heteronomous organizations serve as an example of these distinct organizational categories.[50] Individual autonomous and heteronomous structures are at opposite extremes on a continuum of physician self-direction. Heteronomy can be considered the opposite of autonomy.

As the name implies, under an individual autonomous structure, the autonomy of physicians is maintained at both the level of the individual and the physician organization, group, or collegium. At the other extreme, in the heteronomous structure, the individual physician is subordinate to the physician collegium which, in turn, is subordinate to the organization. In between is the administered autonomous organization. In this structural alternative, the physician is subordinate to the collegium or physician governing group; however, the collegium still enjoys professional autonomy at the group level.

Each of these structural categories, characterized by the type of control exerted over physicians—how they do their work—has implications for physician relationships with patients, payors, other physicians, and the organization. In addition, each organizational alternative may also influence who is attracted to a medical career, what they know, and why they act as they do—the other characteristics of a profession. Table 1 provides examples of each of these kinds of organizations and their implications for physician relationships and the profession.

Individual autonomy

In the individual autonomous structure, professional autonomy thrives along with the traditional aspects of the medical profession. As the name implies, autonomy is maintained at both the level of the individual professional and the physician collegium.

Physicians in these organizations control the patient care process without the intrusion of intervening parties. They are also unconstrained in their ability to freely access consults and seek referrals. Decision making is by physician consensus and typically results in a structure that is more reactive than proactive when it comes to the organization's future or external environment. For many professionals, the organizational inertia that often results from extreme individual autonomy is not viewed as a serious problem.[50]

TABLE 1

IMPLICATIONS OF MEDICAL GROUP PRACTICE STRUCTURAL ALTERNATIVES

	Individual autonomy	Administered autonomy (external control)	Heteronomous
Administrative style and accountability	Autonomy of individual physician protected as is autonomy of the group. Consensus by owner-operator physicians.	The physician organization is sovereign, but individual physician subordinate to centralized negotiated policy.	The physician organization is subsidiary to some other entity; physicians are subordinate to the organization. Executive command.
Examples	Traditional private practice or group with fewer than 25 physicians and few managed care payments.	Physician-driven organizations: Mayo, Ochsner, and Menninger Clinics.	Staff model HMO*; military hospital.
Physician relationship to:			
Patient	Direct; no intervening parties except payment constraints like precertification.	Medicated/collegial. Adhere to jointly negotiated protocols.	Mediated by organization that sets standards and protocols.
Client agents	Payors deal directly with each individual physician for constraints on payment.	Payors deal with organization that may negotiate discounts.	Must consider global resources. Organization negotiates with payors; guarantees adherence.
Other physicians	Free access to consults. Referrals unconstrained.	Consults, referrals, and treatment patterns reviewed by peer physician managers.	Consults and referrals out of group discouraged by organization.
Physician organization	Owner-operated with rule by consensus.	Owner-operated or employees; professional staff hierarchy for negotiation and oversight.	Employee subordinate to organizational hierarchy.
Aspects of the profession:			
Who			
Selection	Attracts self-directed entrepreneur; many applicants.	Collaborators, willing to take financial risks.	Fewer risk-takers, less income-oriented, more women, caretakers.
Training	Research-valued; individual decision making stressed.	Managerial, research skills; protocol development.	More emphasis on computer expert systems, decision support.
Licensure	Physician-directed; control most allied health professions, too.	Pressure to allow other health professionals own licensure.	May be some pressure to license alternative systems or providers.
Cohesiveness	Few threats, except RBRVS† fee schedule and income differentials.	Distance between manager and managed, specialty income gaps may decrease cohesiveness.	May increase with development of union-type professional organizations.
What			
Knowledge	Incentives to innovate and use new technology.	Pressure to evaluate medical theory before wide use.	Innovation only if cost-savings required for competitiveness.
Standards	Widely varied in practice, development, and use.	Greater use of guidelines; possibly selling protocols to others.	Strict adherence to cost/quality procedures.
Why			
Service	Continuing disputes over fees and proprietary facility ownership raise questions.	Ties to research and care of underserved could improve service image.	Lack of autonomy may obscure any service orientation of the employed physician.
Ethics	Entrepreneurship seen as conflicting with professional ethics.	Arms-length transactions with patient may limit conflict of interest.	Any capitated arrangement will be required to guard against underservice.
Social policy	"Fewer friends" in D.C.	Greater impact if service role seen to outweigh proprietary.	Ability to influence social policy altered by "union" status.

*HMO, health maintenance organization.
†RBRVS, Resource-Based Relative Value Scale.

Examples of these structures are the traditional solo practice or groups of fewer than 25 physicians. The growth of managed care arrangements coupled with the general reduction in traditional fee-for-service reimbursement, has meant a decline in the number of these arrangements for practicing medicine.

The self-directed individual attracted by this role has very little external guidance, and standards of practice vary widely. When fee-for-service funding systems were commonplace, there were incentives to innovate with new procedures and costly technology. The major threat to physicians still practicing this way is the redistribution of income that is projected to result from Medicare's application of the resource-based relative value scale in 1992. The continued public debate over the appropriateness of physicians as entrepreneurs (e.g., owners of diagnostic and therapeutic facilities) applies in the other alternative structures as well as the traditional one.

Administered autonomous

Individual physicians practicing in an administered autonomous structure lose autonomy by subordinating themselves to a centralized negotiated policy; however, the physician group still maintains autonomy because it is the primary agent directing and controlling the exchanges of health care between patients and member physicians. Reed and Evans term this alternative the physician-driven organization (PDO).[9] Most PDOs are not-for-profit organizations that have a strong legacy of providing high-quality care. Well-known archetypes of PDOs include the Mayo, Ochsner, and Menninger clinics.[9] Numerous less well-known PDOs, primarily smaller group practices, currently exist with new ones regularly forming. The Permanente Medical Group in the Kaiser-Permanente Health Plan is an older example of this structural form.

The administered autonomous structure influences the relationship between individual physicians and patients primarily by requiring adherence to patient care protocols developed jointly by member physicians. The individual physicians' relationship to other physicians is still generally characterized by free access. The major difference in this structure is that consults, referrals, and treatment patterns are reviewed and overseen by peer physician managers. Shortell sees some hospital–physician relationships changing in this direction with the development of parallel structures, such as independent practice arrangements, or eventually the union of separate hospital and physician organizations through contractual arrangements.[4(p.26)] Physicians in such arrangements may be owner–operators or employees; in either case, there is a professional hierarchy for negotiations and oversight. This structure calls for a collaborative approach and requires managerial and research skills for the physician managers. Current communication problems, in the hospital, between the elected or appointed physician leadership and physicians with hospital privileges could also be a threat to this type of organization.

Heteronomous configuration

Another alternative that has distinct ramifications for reduced professional autonomy has been called the heteronomous configuration. *Webster's Third New International Dictionary* defines heteronomy as "subjection to something else: a lack of moral freedom or self-determination."[10(p.1,063)] This structure is characterized by physician subordination to external control by some other entity. For the most part, these controls are developed apart from individual physicians and the physician group; nonetheless, subordination to this control is expected. Although few examples of the pure heteronomous structure exist, staff model health maintenance organizations and military hospitals are health care organizations that come close.

In the heteronomous structure, physician relationships with patients, payors, and other physicians are characterized by substantial intervention on the part of the organization. The organization sets the standards and protocols of patient treatment, conducts negotiations with external third-party payors, and strongly discourages or patently disallows referrals and consultations outside the organization. Finally, the physician's relationship to the organization is one of an employee, subordinate to the hierarchy of the organization.

Physicians in these organizations would be likely to be more risk-averse and less income-oriented. This structure could be more hospitable to the female physician in her child-raising years. More emphasis would be placed on computerized decision support systems and adherence to cost/quality procedures, with emphasis on cost-saving rather than cost-increasing technologies.

A movement away from the traditional individual autonomous organization toward newer forms is underway. It is not yet clear which, if any, of these forms will predominate in the future.

THE END OF AUTONOMY?

We are witnessing the end to the remarkable absolute autonomy that has traditionally been the cornerstone of the American medical profession. The structure of the health care organization, with its separate dual lines of authority and its emphasis on individual and collective autonomy for the medical profession, is giving way to newer structural alternatives. Will the emerging structures that are eroding physician autonomy ultimately reduce the profession of medicine to a trade? This will not happen unless physicians abdicate responsibility for the major task of rationalizing the practice of their art.

Health care managers are exhorted to gain control of the most important component of the organization's mission—the management of the patient care process—[53] while physicians decry the intrusion of lay persons into their realm. The relationship between physicians and health care managers, however, will never resemble that of Frederick Taylor and his pig-iron handlers. Physicians will not become organizational automatons, especially if they actively develop and negotiate acceptable practice criteria and guidelines. As Eddy points out, "The solution is not to remove the decision-making power of physicians, but to improve the capacity of physicians to make better decisions."[27(p.290)] Increasingly, those decisions will acknowledge patient preferences. The challenge incumbent upon managers and physician professionals is to develop a set of mutually responsive solutions to the problems of who physicians are and how they are trained, what they know and how they apply this knowledge, and the service orientation and ethical base for their decisions.

• • •

It is apparent that society will no longer tolerate the inefficiencies and inequities in the current system. The newer management structures that preserve the autonomy of the physician group, while constraining the individual within that group, hold some promise for both sustaining the profession and meeting society's needs. The role of the American Medical Association and the specialty societies in meeting the call for better outcome research and criteria standards for quality patient care may be the salvation of the profession rather than its end. Managers must facilitate the application of these criteria by focusing physician skills on the "gray areas," where they will always be supremely important, rather than assuming that the process of patient care will ever be fully rationalized and routinized.

REFERENCES

1. Taylor, F.W. *The Principles of Scientific Management*. New York, N.Y.: Harper and Brothers Publishers, 1911.
2. Smith, H.L. "Two Lines of Authority Are One Too Many." *Hospitals* 84, (1955): 59–64.
3. Wylie, W.G. *Hospitals: Their History, Organization, and Construction*. New York, N.Y.: D. Appleton & Co., 1877.
4. Shortell, S.M. *Effective Hospital–Physician Relationships*. Ann Arbor, Mich.: Health Administration Press Perspectives, 1991.
5. Haug, M.E. "A Re-examination of the Hypothesis of Physician Deprofessionalization." *The Milbank Quarterly* 66, Supplement 2 (1988): 48–56.
6. Light, D., and Levine, S. "The Changing Character of the Medical Profession: A Theoretical Overview." *The Milbank Quarterly* 66, Supplement 2 (1988): 10–32.
7. Wolinsky, F.D. "The Professional Dominance Perspective Revisited." *The Milbank Quarterly* 66, Supplement 2 (1988): 33–47.
8. Freidson, E. *Profession of Medicine: A Study of the Sociology of Applied Knowledge*. New York, N.Y.: Harper & Row, 1970.
9. Reed, R.R., and Evans, D. "The Deprofessionalization of Medicine: Causes, Effects, and Responses." *Journal of the American Medical Association* 258, no. 22 (1987): 3279–82.
10. Gove, P.B. (ed). *Webster's Third New International Dictionary of the English Language, Unabridged*. Springfield, Mass.: Merriam-Webster, Inc., 1986.
11. Pinealt, R. Contandriopoulos, A.P., and Fournier, M.A. "Physicians' Acceptance of an Alternative to Fee-for-Service Payment: A Possible Source of Change in Quebec Medicine." *International Journal of Health Services* 15, no. 3 (1985): 419–30.
12. Wilensky, H.L. "The Professionalization of Everyone?" *The American Journal of Sociology* 70, no. 2 (1964): 137–58.
13. Starr, P. *The Social Transformation of American Medicine: The Rise of a Sovereign Profession and the Making of a Vast Industry*. New York, N.Y.: Basic Books, 1982.
14. Ebert, R.H., and Ginzberg, E. "The Reform of Medical Education." *Health Affairs* 7, no. 2 (1988): 5–48.
15. Jolly, P. "Datawatch: Medical Education in the United States, 1960–1987." *Health Affairs* 7, no. 2 (1988): 144–57.
16. Graduate Medical Education National Advisory Committee. *Report of the Graduate Medical Education National Advisory Committee to the Secretary*. Washington, D.C.: U.S. Department of Health and Human Services, September 3, 1980.
17. Stimmel, B. "The Study and Practice of Medicine in the Twenty-First Century: Ask Not for Whom the Bell Tolls." *The Mount Sinai Journal of Medicine* 57, no. 1 (1990): 11–24.
18. Hafferty, F.W. "Theories at the Crossroads: A Discussion of Evolving Views on Medicine as a Profession." *The Milbank Quarterly* 66, Supplement 2 (1988): 202–25.
19. Jasperse, P. "It's Training. It's Helping. It's Work. It's the Grind." *Wisconsin—The Milwaukee Journal Magazine* (September 16, 1990): 6–10, 15–16, 19, 30.
20. Kadzieski, M.A. From the *Health Care Law Newsletter*, in *Medical Benefits* (January 15, 1988): 8, 9.
21. McKinlay, J.B., and Stoeckle, J.D. "Corporatization and the Social Transformation of Doctoring." *International Journal of Health Services* 18, no. 2 (1988): 191–206.

22. American Medical Association, Council on Long-Range Planning and Development. "Health Care in Transition: Consequences for Your Physicians." *Journal of the American Medical Association* 256, no. 24 (1986): 3384–90.
23. Benjamin, W.W. "Will Centrifugal Forces Destroy the Medical Profession?" *New England Journal of Medicine* 321, no. 17 (1989): 1191–92.
24. Stoeckle, J.D. "Reflections on Modern Doctoring." *The Milbank Quarterly* 66, Supplement 2 (1988): 76–91.
25. Stuart, S.E., and Maldonado, W.E. "How PPS is Changing Hospital–Physician Relations." *Trustee* (April, 1986): 14–15.
26. Gray, B.H., and Field, M.J. (eds). *Controlling Costs and Changing Patient Care? Role of Utilization Management.* Washington, D.C.: National Academy Press, 1989.
27. Eddy, D.M. "The Challenge." *Journal of the American Medical Association* 263, no. 2 (1990): 287–90.
28. Wennberg, J.E. "Dealing with Medical Practice Variations: A Proposal for Action." *Health Affairs* 3, no. 2 (1984): 6–32.
29. Ellwood, P.M. "Shattuck Lecture—Outcomes Management: A Technology of Patient Experience." *New England Journal of Medicine* 318, no. 23 (1988): 1549–56.
30. Agency for Health Care Policy and Research. *AHCPR Program Note.* Rockville, Md.: Agency for Health Care Policy and Research, U.S. Department of Health and Human Services (March, 1990).
31. Kelly, J.T. "Editor's Report: Practice Parameters Called Key to Effective QA Programs." *QA Review* 2, no. 3 (1990): 1–3.
32. Gibbs, N. "Sick and Tired." *Time* (July 31, 1989): 48–53.
33. Ludtke, M. "Physician Inform Thyself." *Time* (June 26, 1989): 71.
34. Miller, A., Bradburn, E., and Hager, M. "Second-guessing Doctor's Orders." *Newsweek* (May 23, 1988): 44, 45.
35. Winston, R. "Patient Data May Reshape Health Care." *Wall Street Journal* (April 17, 1989): B1.
36. Ricks, T.E. "New Corporate Program Lets Employees Compare Local Doctors' Fees and Training." *Wall Street Journal* (August 4, 1987): 37.
37. Barney, D.R. "Regulation of Health Services Advertising." *Hospital & Health Services Administration* 28, no. 3 (1983): 85–110.
38. Havighurst, C.C. "Antitrust Enforcement in the Medical Services Industry: What Does It All Mean?" *Milbank Memorial Fund Quarterly* 58, no. 1 (1980): 89–124.
39. Waldholz, M., and Bogdonich, W. "Hospital that Need Patients Pay Bounties for Doctors' Referrals." *Wall Street Journal* (March 1, 1989): A1, A6.
40. Bogdonich, W., and Waldholz, M. "Doctor-Owned Labs Earn Lavish Profits in a Captive Market." *Wall Street Journal* (February 27, 1989): A1, A4.
41. Rundle, R.L. "How Doctors Boost Bills by Misrepresenting the Work They Do." *Wall Street Journal* (December 6, 1989): A1, A8.
42. Hyman, D.A., and Williamson, J.V. "Fraud and Abuse: Setting the Limits on Physicians' Entrepreneurship." *New England Journal of Medicine* 320, no. 19 (1989): 1275–78.
43. Iglehart, J.K. "The Debate Over Physician Ownership of Health Care Facilities." *New England Journal of Medicine* 321, no. 3 (1989): 198–204.
44 House of Representatives. *Omnibus Budget Reconciliation Act of 1989. Conference Report to Accompany H.R. 3299.* Washington D.C.: U.S. Government Printing Office (November, 1989).
45. Norstrand, I.F. "Takeover of the Medical Profession by Nonphysicians." *New England Journal of Medicine* 314, no. 6 (1986): 390.
46. Leitner, W.A. "The Third Revolution." *Alabama Medicine* (November, 1988): 7, 8, 11,12.
47. Brook, R.H. "Practice Guidelines and Practicing Medicine: Are They Compatible?" *Journal of the American Medical Association* 262, no. 21 (1989): 3027–30.
48. Sobal, L.V., and Hepner, J.O. "Physicians Unions: Any Doctor Can Join, But Who Can Bargain Effectively?" *Hospital & Health Services Administration* 35, no. 3 (1990): 327–40.
49. Ritzer, G. and Walczak, D. "Rationalization and Deprofessionalization of Physicians." *Social Forces* 67, no. 1 (1988): 1–22.
50. Madison, D.L., and Konrad, T.S. "Large Medical Group-Practice Organizations and Employed Physicians: A Relationship in Transition." *The Milbank Quarterly* 66, no. 2 (1988): 240–81.
51. Scott, W.R. "Managing Professional Work: Three Models of Control for Health Organizations." *Health Services Research* 17, no. 3 (1982): 213–40.
52. Mintzberg, H. *Structure in Fives: Designing Effective Organizations.* Englewood Cliffs, N.J.: Prentice-Hall, 1983.
53. Roher, J.E. "The Secret of Medical Management." *Health Care Management Review* 14, no. 3 (1989): 7–13.

Part III

PRACTICE ISSUES

Physician practice profiles: A case study of the use of audit and feedback in an ambulatory care group practice

Robert L. Braham
and
Hirsch S. Ruchlin

A computerized audit and feedback program has been developed to allocate costs to the provider whose actions generate these costs. Under this program constant dollar charges for ancillary services declined by 23 percent, and program-related savings are substantially above operational costs.

Health Care Manage Rev, 1987, 12(3), 11–16

Management information systems commonly used in hospitals and fee-for-service medical practices delineate the types of expenses incurred but rarely identify the individual physicians whose actions generate these expenses. An information system that is built around the physician as the key generator of resource use has clear management value. Managers must not only control line-item budget categories, but also must be able to affect the actions of care providers.

Greater attention to physician use of resources is long overdue. Studies of physician activity indicate the presence of excessive diagnostic testing,[1,2] great variability in charges generated per patient encounter,[3–7] and a poor correlation between charges per encounter and indices of quality of care or clinical competence.[8,9] Such evidence supports the contention that physician use of resources can be reduced, and that such reductions need not come at the expense of appropriate care.

This article reports on a physician-oriented information system that has been in use since July 1982 at the Cornell Medical Practice, New York, New York, and the reductions in ancillary services that are attributable to this system.

PRACTICE SETTING

The Cornell Medical Practice is a departmental group practice in general internal medicine. It was established in July 1980 when it assumed the patient care responsibilities and all the educational programs of the General Medicine Clinic of The New York Hospital—Cornell Medical Center. Cornell Medical Practice renders care to a caseload of about 5,000 patients who annually generate around 24,000 visits. The

Robert L. Braham, *M.D., is an Associate Professor of Clinical Medicine and Associate Chairman for Clinical Services in the Department of Medicine at The New York Hospital—Cornell Medical Center, New York, New York. He is also Director of the Cornell Medical Practice. His research interests focus on the organization and financing of care.*

Hirsch S. Ruchlin, *Ph.D., is a Professor of Economics in Public Health and Medicine at Cornell University Medical College, New York, New York. His research interests include studies of physician practice patterns and the cost of medical care.*

The project on which this article is based was supported by a grant from the W.K. Kellogg Foundation.

practice's patient mix resembles that at most general medicine teaching group practices of university hospitals.[10] In the period covered by this article, the practice's professional staff consisted of eight full-time faculty physicians, eight general medicine fellows, three nurse practitioners, 90 house officers, and 15 voluntary physicians who were either in private practice or served as medical directors in a corporate setting and attended one session a week. In addition, medical students who elect an ambulatory care rotation spend part of their fourth year in the Cornell Medical Practice. The faculty physicians both see patients and supervise the house staff, nurse practitioners, and medical students.

PHYSICIAN PRACTICE PROFILE PROGRAM

The physician practice profile program consists of two components: audit and feedback. The audit program, which is totally computerized, uses the description and charge for each procedure contained in the practice's computerized billing system. These data are patient specific rather than provider specific. Prior to the inception of this project, the billing file did not contain provider identification and diagnosis codes. These data were added to the billing information at the beginning of the project to create the database for the audit program. A special software program was developed for the audit process by which patient-specific data are allocated to the physician rendering the care. (Copies of this program are available, at cost, from the authors.) At six-month intervals, a series of computerized physician practice profile reports are generated that indicate each provider's average ancillary service charge per visit. The specific structure of audit reports has been described elsewhere.[11] The selection of a six-month interval for each audit was guided by the fact that house staff, who are the largest provider group in the practice, do not see enough patients in a shorter time interval to yield stable profiles. In other settings a shorter audit period can be used.

A simple feedback form was designed for distribution at the end of each audit period. The form lists each provider's average charge per visit for both initial visits and revisits, average charge per visit for that person's peer group (i.e., faculty, nurse practitioners, fellows, senior residents, junior residents, interns, and voluntary attending physicians), and average charge per visit for the entire practice. Comparable data are also provided for the following specific diagnoses that were selected because of their high volume: abdominal pain, anemia, asthma, cerebrovascular disease, diabetes, hypertension, ischemic heart disease, obesity, psychiatric disorders, and thyroid disease. Each feedback form provides data for a current period and, for reference purposes, the previous period. A form cover letter written by Cornell Medical Practice's medical director accompanies each feedback form. It summarizes the practice's overall profile, and where necessary, suggests areas for improvement. In instances where it is deemed appropriate a brief note is added to a provider's feedback form with special comments deemed relevant to that individual. However, in no case is any provider publicly or privately labeled as good or bad. Rather, the thrust of the feedback is to provide individuals with information on their absolute and relative performance, with the expectation that each individual will draw the appropriate conclusions from his or her own feedback report.

In no case is any provider publicly or privately labeled as good or bad.

PROGRAM IMPACT

Methods of evaluation

Pre- and postanalyses were conducted to assess the impact of audit and feedback. A more rigorous evaluation based on random assignment of practitioners to experimental and control groups was not undertaken because it would have been impossible to maintain an effective control group atmosphere within Cornell Medical Practice after the first feedback. The data presented in this article span the program's first three years of operation. The baseline, or preprogram period, was July 1982 to December 1982 when audit was under way but feedback was yet to be initiated. As the audit program was not visible, staff were unaware of the process during these months. This period will be referred to as period 1. The five postintervention periods that follow a feedback cycle covered January 1983 to June 1985, and will be referred to as periods 2 through 6.

All charge data used in the evaluation of the program were kept constant at their July 1982 level. Oneway analysis of variance (*F* test) was used to assess whether the overall trend line of average charges changed over the six time periods. Duncan's multiple-range test was used to assess whether charge differences changed significantly across each of the individual study periods. The Statistical Analysis System (SAS) software package was used for both of the statistical tests. Due to differences in experience levels and type of patients treated it was decided to subdivide all the providers into one of three categories—faculty, house staff (interns, residents, and fellows) and other (voluntary attending physicians and nurse practitioners)—and to analyze each group's performance separately.

Findings

Initial visits

Ancillary service charge profiles for initial visits in the prefeedback and postfeedback periods are presented in Table 1. In the aggregate, a significant decline in average charges occurred over the entire three-year study period. Period to feedback (i.e., in period 1), average ancillary service charges per initial visit were $80.33. After the first feedback cycle, which occurred at the beginning of period 2, average charges rose to $85.03, a level that is not statistically significant from the prior period. However, after the second feedback cycle, which occurred at the beginning of period 3, average charges dropped significantly and dramatically to $66.97, and remained close to that level in the three successive periods.

Within the practice, both the faculty and house staff groups displayed significant and substantial charge profile reductions in the postfeedback periods. However, the pace at which this change occurred differed across these groups. Faculty charge profiles rose significantly after the first feedback ($93.16 versus $80.36) but returned to the prefeedback level in periods 3 through 5. In period 6 they exhibited a significant decline to $61.10. House staff charge profiles did not change significantly after the first feedback ($81.53 versus $84.41). Their charge level did decline significantly after the second feedback ($59.63 versus $81.53) and remained approximately at the $60 level for the remaining study periods.

Revisits

Charge trends associated with patient revisits are presented in Table 2. As in the case of initial visits, a significant decline occurred in charge levels. Prior to feedback average ancillary service charges per revisit for the entire practice were $23.94. After the first feedback, average charges declined significantly to $22.20. Two additional statistically significant declines occurred, the first in period 4 ($19.42 versus $22.39) and the second in period 6 ($18.10 versus $20.32).

TABLE 1

AVERAGE ANCILLARY SERVICE CHARGES FOR INITIAL VISITS

Period	Provider group			
	All providers*	Faculty	House staff*	Other
1 (7/82–12/82)	80.33 (913)†	80.36 (324)	84.41 (493)	60.91 (104)
2 (1/83–6/83)	85.03 (844)	93.16 (381)	81.53 (388)	61.87 (75)
3 (7/83–12/83)	66.97 (1,016)	82.33 (378)	59.63 (625)	51.12 (13)
4 (1/84–6/84)	68.31 (988)	75.04 (297)	65.14 (681)	76.35 (20)
5 (7/84–12/84)	67.96 (1,265)	78.16 (440)	62.62 (724)	61.75 (101)
6 (1/85–6/85)	62.25 (1,070)	61.10 (358)	63.89 (638)	53.61 (74)

* Time period effect based on analysis of variance significant at $p \leq 0.01$.

† Number of visits.

TABLE 2

AVERAGE ANCILLARY SERVICE CHARGES FOR REVISITS

Period	Provider group			
	All providers*	Faculty	House staff*	Other
1 (7/82–12/82)	23.94 (8,993)†	26.87 (3,251)	26.17 (2,730)	18.74 (3,012)
2 (1/83–6/83)	22.20 (9,883)	24.33 (3,202)	23.97 (3,455)	18.18 (3,226)
3 (7/83–12/83)	22.39 (10,189)	22.10 (5,101)	24.22 (3,584)	18.98 (1,504)
4 (1/84–6/84)	19.42 (10,505)	18.63 (5,348)	22.09 (3,958)	14.13 (1,199)
5 (7/84–12/84)	20.32 (10,582)	19.33 (5,623)	23.79 (3,404)	16.33 (1,555)
6 (1/85–6/85)	18.10 (10,896)	15.96 (5,426)	21.09 (3,818)	18.24 (1,652)

* Time period effect based on analysis of variance significant at $p \leq 0.01$.
† Number of visits.

Significant declines in revisit charges occurred for all three provider groups. The largest decline occurred among the faculty physicians. Significant declines in faculty charge profiles occurred after each of the first three feedback cycles ($24.33 versus $26.87, $22.10 versus $24.33, and $18.63 versus $22.10, respectively) and again after the fifth feedback cycle ($15.96 versus $19.33). The slight increase between periods 4 and 5 lacks statistical significance. House staff charge profiles declined significantly after the first feedback cycle ($23.97 versus $26.17) and remained at this general level until period 6 when a second significant decline occurred. Charge levels for the other group (voluntary attending physicians and nurse practitioners) remained constant throughout the first two feedback cycles (periods 1 and 2) and declined significantly by period 4, but rose significantly to the prefeedback level in period 6.

Despite the apparent overall decline in ancillary service utilization per visit (as implied by a reduction in charges), patients were not seen at more frequent intervals in the postfeedback periods. Throughout all the study periods, the number of revisits per patient remained constant at about 2.5 visits per six-month period.

Charges by diagnosis

Charge profiles were also investigated by diagnosis in order to gain insight into the types of cases where charge reductions were effected. No clear pattern emerged for initial visits. The charge reductions achieved were spread over numerous diagnoses, each of which accounted for a small number of visits. For example, in period 1,11 patients presented for initial visits with a primary diagnosis of urinary tract infection for which the average ancillary charge per visit was $89.36. In period 6 the average ancillary charge per visit for the six patients presenting with this diagnosis was $59.08. For revisits, significant reductions occurred for four major diagnoses that jointly account for about 50 percent of the practice's revisits. These diagnoses and the charge reductions over periods 1 through 6 are: abdominal pain ($52.08 versus $22.09), diabetes ($20.35 versus $14.79), hypertension ($20.04 versus $15.37), and ischemic heart disease ($22.55 versus $18.92).

Quartile analysis

Quartile data provide some clues into how the significant charge reductions were achieved. For both types of visits the range between the highest and lowest quartile providers (i.e., the most expensive and least expensive providers in each group) was narrowed. During the initial audit period and prior to feedback (period 1), the range for initial visits between the highest and lowest quartile providers among the faculty physicians was $69.47 (highest quartile = $112.20; lowest quartile = $42.73), and among house staff, $120.49 ($147.15 versus $26.66). By the last study period (period 6) the spreads were $42.45 ($82.26 versus $39.81) and $84.05 ($111.06 versus $27.01). For revisits, the faculty physician range was $17.44 in period 1 ($37.02 versus $19.58) and $7.06 in period 6 ($20.50 versus $13.44). The house staff range narrowed from $29.10 in period 1 ($42.26 versus $13.16) to $24.30 in period 6 ($34.44 versus $10.14). Similarly, the revisit charge range for the nurse practitioner and voluntary attending physician group (i.e., "other") narrowed from $20.29 in period 1 ($26.08 versus $5.79) to $17.02 in period 4 ($22.28 versus $5.26) where the charges for this group were at their lowest level.

Program savings

Although a formal cost-benefit analysis was not undertaken, it appears that the charge reduction achieved exceeds the program's costs by a substantial margin. It is estimated that the marginal cost of operating the program, given the existence of a computerized billing system, is about $15,000 per year (in 1982 dollars). The elements of this estimate are: medical director's time, $3,000; clerical time to ensure the accuracy of the practice's data entry system and generate all audit and feedback reports, $10,000; and computer time costs, $2,000. Savings were estimated, in most cases, by assuming that in the absence of audit and feedback, average ancillary service charges per visit in periods 2 through 6 would have been at the period 1 level. The exception to this assumption is the use of the actual higher initial visit charge for period 2 as the assumed level in the absence of audit and feedback. (The overall assumption used in this calculation is supported by an increasing real charge trend line in the Cornell Medical Practice prior to the inception of this project.) This method yields a total program savings estimate of $242,854. About 25 percent of this saving ($60,443) resulted from reduced ancillary service charges at initial visits, and about 75 percent ($182,411) resulted from lower ancillary service utilization at revisits. The estimated program savings exceed the cost of the program over the three study years ($45,000) by a margin of 5.4 to 1. Even if one assumes that 50 percent of the charges for ancillary services reflect fixed costs that would still be incurred when volume declines, the savings to cost ratio is still a respectable 2.7 to 1.

DISCUSSION

The adoption of a physician-specific information system that utilizes audit and feedback has led to a significant reduction in ancillary service use in a university hospital ambulatory care practice in general internal medicine. To ascertain whether comparable changes occurred in the inpatient area, two typical 30-bed medical units were selected for study, one on the private service and the other on the teaching service. Neither unit had any intensive care beds. The total number of biochemistry tests ordered on these units was converted to College of American Pathologists (CAP) workload units to recognize complexity and resource use. These units displayed a 7.3 percent increase in test use over the July 1982 to June 1985 period.

The adoption of a physician-specific information system that utilizes audit and feedback has led to a significant reduction in ancillary service use.

Physician response to the audit and feedback program was favorable. The program was deliberately low-keyed and provoked no negative responses from any of the providers. Early in the project a staff person was assigned to review the encounter forms and ensure that all tests and procedures ordered were noted on the form, even if this information was not needed for billing. (This function was ultimately reallocated to existing clerical staff.) This process enhanced the credibility of the audit and feedback program. As the data were accepted, the simple transmission of information appeared to be enough to convince the high-cost providers to change their style of practice. As noted in a previous study,[12] feedback information encompassing both individual and practicewide data tells the physician how medicine is practiced rather than how to practice medicine. This may indeed be the best way to get the message across.

Two aspects of the study merit note. First, charge reductions may not occur immediately. Declines in average ancillary service charges for initial visits did not occur until after the second feedback cycle (period 3). Furthermore, one cannot assume that charge reductions will automatically be sustained in subsequent periods. Charge profiles exhibited by the "other" group for revisits rendered during periods 4 through 6 indicate that reductions achieved can disappear. Clearly, vigilance is called for to detect such patterns and attempt to reverse them.

The way the charge reductions occurred is also of interest. Quartile analyses indicated that the charge reductions were achieved, in good part, by compressing the range between the high-cost and low-cost providers. Interestingly, the highest quartile providers exhibited substantial charge reductions while the lowest quartile providers did not exhibit major charge increases. One could have postulated that both types of movement would occur as the highest and lowest groups converged toward the mean. Only the former, however, appeared to occur in our setting. A review of the initial practice patterns among the high-cost and low-cost quartiles indicated that physicians in the high quartile frequently repeated tests that were recently performed either in the emergency department or while the patient was hospitalized. Physicians in the lowest quartile usually photocopied the results of these tests and included them in the patient's medical record maintained by the practice. Furthermore, the high-cost physicians ordered many tests at the patient's initial visit while the low-cost physicians waited for the results of initial testing before continuing a focused workup at revisit.

Audit and feedback programs have been used in other settings and, in the majority of cases, have also had the desired impact.[13–18] However, these efforts were not sustained beyond a demonstration period as they were not integrated into an ongoing information system network. Computerizing the audit process and grafting the audit and feedback program onto an existing billing system facilitates its sustained use.

Two case studies have been reported in the literature where audit and feedback programs have not been successful in reducing utilization or cost.[19,20] In both instances this failure was attributed in part to the absence of both an environment that was conducive to reducing the cost of care and an authority figure who legitimized the need to contain costs. Neither of these conditions prevailed in this case study, nor do they appear to prevail in the industry at large. In today's cost-conscious environment, audit and feedback programs should be an important management aid in ensuring the provision of quality care at reasonable cost.

REFERENCES

1. Griner, P.F., and Liptzin, B. "Use of the Laboratory in a Teaching Hospital: Implications for Patient Care, Education, and Hospital Costs." *Annals of Internal Medicine* 75, no. 2 (1971): 157–63.
2. Griner, P.F., and Glaser, R.J. "Misuse of Laboratory Tests and Diagnostic Procedures." *New England Journal of Medicine* 307 (1982): 1336–39.
3. Griner and Liptzin, "Use of the Laboratory in a Teaching Hospital."
4. Schroeder, S.A., et al. "Use of Laboratory Tests and Pharmaceuticals: Variation among Physicians and Effect of Cost Audit on Subsequent Use." *Journal of the American Medical Association* 225 (1973): 969–73.
5. Lyle, C.B., et al. "Cost of Medical Care in a Practice of Internal Medicine." *Annals of Internal Medicine* 81, no. 1 (1974): 1–6.
6. Lyle, C.B., et al. "Practice Habits in a Group of Eight Internists." *Annals of Internal Medicine* 84, no. 5 (1976): 594–601.
7. Daniels, M., and Schroeder, S.A. "Variation among Physicians in Use of Laboratory Tests: II. Relation to Clinical Productivity and Outcomes of Care." *Medical Care* 15 (1977): 482–87.
8. Griner and Liptzin, "Use of the Laboratory in a Teaching Hospital."
9. Daniels and Schroeder, "Variation among Physicians in Use of Laboratory Tests."
10. Kosecoff, J., et al. "General Medical Care and the Education of Internists in University Hospitals: An Evaluation of the Teaching Hospital General Medicine Group Practice Program." *Annals of Internal Medicine* 102 (1985): 250–57.
11. Braham, R.L., and Ruchlin, H.S. "A Physician Profile System." *Medical Group Management* 32, no. 1 (1985): 58–62.
12. Kincaid, W.H. "Changing Physician Behavior: The Peer Data Method." *Quality Review Bulletin* 10 (1984): 238–42.
13. Ibid.
14. Wennberg, J.E., et al. "Changes in Tonsillectomy Rates Associated with Feedback and Review." *Pediatrics* 59 (1977): 821–26.
15. Myers, L.P., and Schroeder, S.A. "Physician Use of Services for the Hospitalized Patient: A Review with Implications for Cost Containment." *Milbank Memorial Fund Quarterly/Health and Society* 59 (1981): 481–507.
16. Martin, A.R., et al. "A Trial of Two Strategies to Modify the Test-Ordering Behavior of Medical Residents." *New England Journal of Medicine* 303 (1980): 1330–36.
17. Applegate, W.B., et al. "Impact of a Cost-Containment Educational Program on Housestaff Ambulatory Clinic Charges." *Medical Care* 21 (1983): 486–96.
18. Hughes, R.A., et al. "The Ancillary Services Review Program in Massachusetts: Experience of the 1982 Pilot Project." *Journal of the American Medical Association* 252 (1984): 1727–32.
19. Eisenberg, J.M., et al. "Computer-based Audit to Detect and Correct Overutilization of Laboratory Tests." *Medical Care* 15 (1977): 915–21.
20. Schroeder, S.A., et al. "The Failure of Physician Education as a Cost Containment Strategy." *Journal of the American Medical Association* 252 (1984): 225–30.

Using data describing physician inpatient practice patterns: Issues and opportunities

Robert G. Hughes
and
Douglas E. Lee

Information on physicians' inpatient practice patterns is becoming increasingly available through state data systems. This article describes the kind of information that is becoming publicly available, provides illustrations of how these data can be used, and discusses issues and potential problems that may occur in using the data.

Health Care Management Rev, 1991, 16(1), 33–40

Hospitals, managed care systems, payors, and other health care organizations are influenced by the decisions made by physicians. Physicians' decisions affect the allocation of resources that these organizations control. Accordingly, there is great interest in information that accurately describes the behavior of physicians. Information describing the inpatient practice patterns of physicians is becoming increasingly available. In this paper we describe the kind of information that is becoming publicly available, illustrate how that information may be used, and discuss the issues and potential problems that may occur in interpretation of the data.

THE IMPORTANCE OF PHYSICIAN INFORMATION

Physician decisions in the diagnosis and treatment of their patients are at the core of the health care delivery system. They control up to 90 percent of the resources in the system directly or indirectly.[1] Yet despite this central role, systematic information that describes even basic summary descriptions of physician practice patterns has not, until recently, been routinely available. One reason is the complex and loosely coupled structure of hospital and physician relationships in the United States.[2–4] These arrangements inhibit the routine collection of comprehensive information that describes physician use of hospitals. Further, personal medical care has been predominantly private, with the confidentiality of the patient and the private practice of medicine limiting the availability of public information. However, the rising costs of care, geographical variations in utilization, demand for more health care consumer information, and advances in the technical ability to manage data have contributed to increased pressures for information that describes the performance of health care providers, including physicians.[5]

Robert G. Hughes, *Ph.D., is a Research Fellow at the Robert Wood Johnson Foundation, Princeton, New Jersey.*

Douglas E. Lee, *M.H.S.A., is a Partner at Matrix Associates, Phoenix, Arizona.*

The views expressed in this article are solely those of the authors, and official endorsement by The Robert Wood Johnson Foundation is not intended and should not be inferred.

The Health Care Financing Administration's (HCFA) release of hospital mortality rates and data on nursing home quality are the most well known examples of such public data release, but many states also have initiated programs designed to give consumers information on health providers. HCFA's third annual release of hospital mortality data,[6] although still somewhat controversial, has had the effect of shifting the focus of discussion from whether or not such data should be released to the methodological refinements necessary to ensure validity of the information. As review and accrediting organizations, such as the Joint Commission on the Accreditation of Health Care Organizations, increase their emphasis on outcome measures, institutions may become more influenced by external performance assessments, some of which will be publicly available. The acceptance of publicly available information describing provider performance has already been applied to physicians in some states.

By physician information we mean data that link individual physicians with the patients they care for and the hospitals where they work. The usual source of such data is the hospital discharge abstract. Twenty-seven states now have a legislatively mandated system of data collection based on hospital discharge abstracts. While the specific data elements may vary depending on the state and the agency that collects these data, this abstract usually includes patient age, sex, diagnosis related group (DRG) or International Classification of Diseases, 9th Revision, Clinical Modification (ICD9-CM) diagnoses and procedures, zip code, discharge status, and length of stay, as shown in Table 1.[7] In addition, 20 states now collect a physician identifier for each patient's attending physician, and some states collect identifiers for other physicians involved in the patient's care.[8] Additional data elements, such as a measure of patient severity of illness, are being added in some states, such as Pennsylvania and Colorado.

It is important to distinguish between the kind of physician practice pattern information that can be derived from discharge abstracts and the much more detailed clinical information implied in the development of practice guidelines. Practice guidelines suggest the range of acceptable clinical behavior in diagnostic and treatment decisions for patients with a specific condition or diagnosis. They may be used in several ways, from establishing the thresholds for sanctions by payors (boundary guidelines) to positing the preferred clinical standard for physicians to follow (pathway guidelines).[9] Data from hospital discharge abstracts are best suited for identifying broad utilization patterns by type of patient, physician, and institution; they are of insufficient clinical detail to be of use in analysis of specific clinical practice.

TABLE 1

TYPICAL INFORMATION CONTAINED IN HOSPITAL DISCHARGE ABSTRACT

Number	Item
1	Personal identification
2	Date of birth
3	Sex
4	Race and ethnicity
5	Residence
6	Hospital identification
7–8	Admission and discharge date
9–10	Physician identification: attending and operating
11	Diagnoses
12	Procedures and dates
13	Disposition of patient
14	Expected principal source of payment

Source: National Committee on Vital and Health Statistics. Secretary of the Department of Health and Human Services. "Uniform Hospital Discharge Data, Minimum Data Set." Washington, D.C.: Government Printing Office, 1980.

The ability to link individual physicians with patient characteristics and the hospitals they use offers a wide variety of opportunities for applying this information. These data may be used for quality assurance, strategic planning, health services research, marketing, physician recruitment, or analysis of inpatient practice patterns. The data shown in this article are derived from publicly available data in Arizona, which is unique among states because the physician identifier collected by the Department of Health Services includes both the physician's state license number and the physician's name.

USING PHYSICIAN INFORMATION

In discussing the uses of physician information, it is important to note the practical requirements of obtaining and preparing the data for use, the organizations that may prepare and analyze the information, and the purposes of organizing the information in particular ways.

Obtaining and preparing the data

Regardless of the anticipated uses of physician information, obtaining and preparing the data requires resources and specialized skills. The information is often available on computer tape, usually from the agency that collected the information from the hospitals. Therefore, computer facilities and staff capable of handling computerized data are needed to use the data directly. The work of obtaining, cleaning, and preparing the data may be done by an organization's staff or by outside consultants. The advantages of performing this work inhouse are the flexibility in using the information, the ability to answer specific questions of interest to the organization, and the development of internal expertise. On the other hand, many small organizations may find it more expedient to rely on consultants, especially for initial efforts at using the data. When consultants are used, it is important to be as specific as possible about what information is wanted and how it will be used. In many states with publicly available data systems, consultants have developed standardized reports that address many users' needs.

Regardless of the anticipated uses of physician information, obtaining and preparing the data requires resources and specialized skills.

The primary users of physician inpatient information are likely to be hospitals, payors, alternative delivery systems, and physician groups (both group practices and professional organizations). Each type of organization may use the data in a different way or be interested in different components. For example, payors will find the financial information useful, but they also will be attentive to the utilization and quality implications that can be derived from the data. Physician professional organizations may find the data useful as part of a program of study groups exploring the explanations for practice pattern variations.[10]

An important step after obtaining the data is to assess its reliability and quality and then to make adjustments or exclusions to the data in accordance with how the information will be used. Edit checks by the agency that collects the data may catch some mistakes or inconsistencies, but perhaps not all. Users of the data should know what edit checks are routinely carried out by the agency that collects the data and conduct additional checks that ensure confidence in the data for their particular purposes. An important benefit of cleaning the data is becoming familiar with potential pitfalls in interpreting what the data mean. For example, knowing that physician license numbers are assigned in order by the state licensing board, and knowing how many have been issued, can help in reviewing the license numbers in the data for any obvious inconsistencies. In states that have large populations located in border areas, many people may cross into other states for medical care, and this border crossing needs to be accounting for in some types of analyses.

Analyzing the data

Some examples of physician information derived from one state's discharge abstract data system are presented in Tables 2 through 5. They illustrate the kind of physician practice patterns that can be explored. Arizona is unique among states in the public availability of the physician's name with the hospital discharge abstract data. Other states vary in the collection, availability, and accessibility of physician data.[11] Table 2 displays the number of patients attended by Arizona physicians during a six-month period. The 3,267 physi-

TABLE 2

NUMBER OF ARIZONA PHYSICIANS BY NUMBER OF PATIENTS ATTENDED, JANUARY 1–JUNE 30, 1986

Number of patients attended in 6-month period	Physicians: Number	Physicians: Percentage
1–12	616	18.9
13–24	383	11.7
25–36	368	11.3
37–48	359	11.0
49–60	311	9.5
61–72	248	7.6
73–84	207	6.3
85–96	184	5.6
97+	591	18.1
TOTALS	3267	100.0

Source: Arizona Department of Health Services, Office of Health Economics and Facilities Review, Phoenix, Arizona. DRG data tape. Reporting Period 5, 1986.

TABLE 3

NUMBER OF ARIZONA PHYSICIANS BY NUMBER OF HOSPITALS USED FOR AT LEAST ONE PATIENT, JANUARY 1–JUNE 30, 1986

Number of hospitals at which the physician attended at least one patient	Physicians	
	Number	Percentage
1	1302	39.9
2	849	26.0
3	591	18.1
4	272	8.3
5	140	4.3
6	63	1.9
7	30	0.9
8	13	0.4
9	4	0.1
10	3	0.1
TOTALS	3267	100.0

Source: Arizona Department of Health Services, Office of Health Economics and Facilities Review, Phoenix, Arizona. DRG data tape. Reporting Period 5, 1986.

cians who attended on at least one patient represent about 51 percent of licensed active Arizona physicians.

Table 3 shows that over 60 percent of attending physicians used at least two hospitals. This may reflect the open medical staffs of Arizona hospitals and the concentration of hospitals in two urban areas, where a large number of hospitals are close to one another. The data in Tables 2 and 3 may be of interest to physicians, hospitals, or payors. They begin to document the variety of physicians' practices devoted to inpatient care across hospitals. Note that descriptions of physician practice across hospitals, such as in Table 3, require that all hospitals in the state use the same identifier for a particular physician. Having such comprehensive data is often a principal advantage of public data systems over private data systems, such as those from a payor or hospital.

Information can be reported using any of the data elements that are collected, either alone or in combination. For example, Table 4 provides a profile of one physician's inpatients according to hospital and diagnostic category. A physician profile could contain information such as patient ages, lengths of stay, hospital charges, or discharge statuses, including the in-hospital mortality of each physician's patients. A standardized format containing information that a medical staff and a hospital agree is useful could be generated periodically for each physician who attends at the hospital. Many physicians have an intuitive grasp of their patient profile and the impact of their admissions on hospital resources, but a routine report with accurate data may be an informative aid in reflecting on their practice patterns.

Physician professionalization in training and practice fosters a clinical mentality and orients them primarily towards individual patients.[12] The development of physician profiles offers the opportunity to complement this orientation with information describing a panel or population of inpatients cared for by the individual physician. Perhaps the most interesting consequence of such profiles may be the effect on relations among colleagues. Anecdotal responses from physicians in Arizona that were given illustrative profiles of their patients include requests to see similar profiles for other physicians.

Physician data also can be used when focusing on selected procedures[13] or on one DRG. For example, patient mortality by physician was analyzed using Maryland data on patients undergoing cholecystectomy, hernia repair, or prostatectomy.[14] More recently, Maryland data were used to analyze physician rates of caesarian sections.[15] We selected DRG 89, simple pneumonia and pleurisy for patients over age 69, because in Arizona it represents 2.3 percent of hospital revenues, accounts for the fourth largest number of hospital days, and has an in-hospital mortality rate of 9.3 percent. We selected one hospital and 5 of its 24 physicians who attended patients in this DRG for a detailed review of their patients' discharge statuses. The results are presented in Table 5.

The hospital discharged 185 patients in DRG 89, of whom 32 died, 4 left against medical advice, and the

Many physicians have an intuitive grasp of their patient profile and the impact of their admissions on hospital resources, but a routine report with accurate data may be an informative aid in reflecting on their practice patterns.

TABLE 4

SELECTED PHYSICIAN'S PATIENTS BY DRG MEDICAL SPECIALTY GROUP, JANUARY 1–JUNE 30, 1987 (PHYSICIAN 1, 49 PATIENTS IN 34 DRGs)

	Number of patients attended at:		
DRG specialty group	**Hospital A**	**Hospital B**	**Hospital C**
Neurology	2	1	1
Oncology	3	1	0
Pulmonary	0	1	0
Cardiology	3	0	0
General surgery	9	0	1
Gastroenterology	10	8	0
Endocrinology	2	0	0
Nephrology	1	0	0
Obstetrics	1	0	0
Hematology	1	0	0
Psychiatry	0	0	1
Other	3	0	0
Totals	5	11	3

Source: Arizona Department of Health Services, Office of Health Economics and Facilities Review, Phoenix, Arizona. DRG data tape. Reporting Period 7, 1987.

TABLE 5

DISCHARGE STATUS OF PATIENTS IN DRG 89 AT SELECTED HOSPITAL (HOSPITAL A—24 PHYSICIANS)

		Physician				
Discharge status	**All patients in DRG 89**	**1**	**2**	**3**	**4**	**5**
Discharged to home or self-care (routine discharge)	76	8	0	0	4	7
Discharged/transferred to another short-term general hospital	2	1	0	0	0	0
Discharged/transferred to intermediate care facility	61	5	0	0	8	6
Discharged/transferred to another type of institution	10	0	0	0	0	4
Left against medical advice	4	2	0	0	0	0
Expired	32	3	5	2	3	1
TOTAL	185	19	5	2	15	18

Source: Arizona Department of Health Services, Office of Health Economics and Facilities Review, Phoenix, Arizona. DRG data tape. Reporting Period 7, 1987.

remainder were discharged home or to another institution. The pattern of discharge statuses for the five individual physicians' patients may be interpreted in several ways. For example, physicians two and three may receive referrals of terminally ill patients, thus explaining why all of their patients died. Physicians one, four, and five may discharge moribund patients to intermediate care facilities rather than have them die in the hospital. The variety of dispositions may raise questions about treatment alternatives. For example, physicians on the medical staff who treat these patients may want to explore explanations for the differences among physicians in discharges to intermediate care facilities or other institutions.

Caution must be taken in reaching conclusions based on such practice pattern data. The implicit attribution of patient outcomes to a physician is inappropriate without a much more thorough review. Nevertheless, physician information may be quite useful as a stimulus to subsequent, selective evaluation, and as a context for evaluating other, more specific, questions. For example, a state license board could use a physician's practice profile to assess a physician's inpatient experience with patients having a particular diagnosis.

Applying the data

Among the many potential applications of physician inpatient data, some are of obvious relevance to hospitals, payors, alternative delivery systems, and physicians themselves. The data can be used by hospitals to target physicians for marketing. For example, physicians who admit patients to multiple institutions can be asked what factors affect their admitting decisions in an effort to make one hospital more attractive. Data on physician admissions to hospitals also can be seen as a measure of the physician's contribution and allegiance to the institution, and a number of related questions can be addressed using the available information. Does a physician admit patients who live in particular market areas to one hospital rather than another that appears more convenient? Does this vary by the patient's diagnosis or expected source of payment? Are a physician's patients' average lengths of stay different in different hospitals? How does a physician compare to peers in the same specialty in the types of patients admitted, in the average charge per admission, and in average charge per day? Users of the data should be cautioned that the answers to these questions derived from the data are not conclusive; they are really just the starting point to working with physicians to understand what the information means.

It should be noted that users of physician data may be influenced by the policy environment of particular states. The marketing use of physician data, for example, may apply in states that have explicitly adjusted a competitive approach; while such users may not be well received in states with a strong regulatory orientation.

Another use of the data is in physician recruitment. Gaps in services in a particular specialty in a given market area can be identified with these data. Especially in rural areas, the need for a physician in a specialty can be inferred from the extent of out-of-area referral for particular diagnoses. Information from other sources can be used to assist physicians in selecting a practice location.

The availability of physician data offers many opportunities for health services research. One topic that illustrates the potential is the "volume–outcome" relationship, in which higher hospital volumes of patients with certain diagnoses and procedures are associated with better outcomes.[16] When this volume–outcome relationship is found, it raises the following question: To what extent does physician volume, or other physician characteristics, contribute to this relationship? While evidence is not conclusive,[17] results for specific diagnoses have relied on physician data. For example, patients with a principal diagnosis of acute myocardial infarction (AMI) were more likely to survive when their physicians treated high volumes of AMI patients, and patients of board-certified physicians in family practice or internal medicine were less likely to die than AMI patients with non-board-certified physicians.[18] The increasing availability of physician data may stimulate additional research in this area. Note that such research does not depend on the ability to identify individual physicians personally, but on the ability to have a unique number for every physician. Encryption of a physician identifier allows for research while preventing the personal identification of physicians.

Many of the state data systems with physician information were started in the last few years. As these systems become more experienced, not only will the quality of the data undoubtedly improve, the ability to monitor trends will become increasingly important. The practice patterns of physicians over time can be assessed, and a historical dimension can be added to many of the uses noted above. Further, the routine collection of this information provides an in-place mechanism for assessing the effects of actions taken to change physician inpatient practice patterns. These data may also be useful for monitoring a variety of changes in institutional or community health service patterns. They may provide data to evaluate the effects of projects ranging from new financing mechanisms to the introduction of innovative medical technology. Periodic systematic data collection that measures aspects of organization or system performance will be invaluable in evaluating the effects of specific policies designed to influence health services costs or patterns of care.

ISSUES IN USING PHYSICIAN INFORMATION

While the information describing inpatient physician practice patterns has many potential applications, several issues may constrain or inhibit actual use. Perhaps the most important of these is the question of who should interpret the data. Table 5 illustrates the need for careful, informed interpretation of physician data, as well as the caveats that should be observed before reaching conclusions about what the data mean.

For example, a small number of observations may impose statistical limitations,[19] and some data elements may be systematically biased, such as miscoded DRGs more likely to result in higher reimbursement.[20] Knowledge about how the data were produced is necessary for accurate interpretation.

In addition to the question of who should interpret the data is the question of what mechanism will be used. Some preexisting structures, such as quality assurance committees in hospitals or professional review organizations, could be used. However, these mechanisms may bring with them a history and role that may discourage effective, open discussion of physician practice patterns. New mechanisms could be created, but this approach raises the issue of auspice; who has an interest in examining physician practice patterns, and why? If the impetus is generated by a hospital or a payor, it also may raise the sensitive issue of being perceived as encroaching on the legitimate domain of physicians.

A final issue arises from the uncertainty of how best to use the information. Certainly feedback to physicians in one form or another is implicit, but the reactions of physicians may vary considerably and be different than what was anticipated. An analogous activity is the effort of hospitals to establish a group practice from among their medical staff, which may have the unintended consequence of alienating some physicians, rather than cementing their allegiance.

• • •

The public availability of physician information has the potential to benefit physicians and a variety of health care organizations. While appropriate caution must be taken in interpreting these data, the many uses fostered by the public availability of the information appear to be consistent with the public's interest in a high quality, efficient, and accessible health care delivery system.

REFERENCES

1. Eisenberg, J. "Physician Utilization: The State of Research about Physicians' Practice Patterns." *Medical Care* (May 1985): 461–483.
2. Freidson, E. *Professional Dominance: The Social Structure of Medical Care.* New York, N.Y.: Aldine, 1973.
3. Rosenberg, C. "Inward Vision and Outward Glance: The Shaping of the American Hospital, 1880-1914." *In Social History and Social Policy.* New York, N.Y.: Academic Press, 1981.
4. Starr, P. *The Social Transformation of American Medicine.* New York, N.Y.: Basic Books, 1982.
5. U.S. Congress Office of Technology Assessment. *The Quality of Medical Care: Information for Consumers,* OTA-H-386. Washington, D.C., June 1988.
6. Sullivan, L. *Medicare Hospital Mortality Information.* U.S. Department of Health and Human Services/Health Care Financing Administration. Washington, D.C.: Government Printing Office, 1988, 1989.
7. National Center for Health Statistics. "Uniform Hospital Discharge Data: Minimum Data Set." Report of the National Committee on Vital and Health Statistics. Hyattsville, Md.: U.S. Department of Health, Education, and Welfare, Public Health Service, 1980. DHEW Publication no. (PHS) 80–1157.
8. Larks, M. "Access to Health Data by State Health Data Organizations and Quality Assessors." Contractor document. Health Program, Office of Technology Assessment, U.S. Congress. Washington, D.C.: Government Printing Office, December 1987.
9. Lewin, L., and Erickson, J. "Leadership in the Development of Practice Guidelines: The Role of the Federal Government and Others." Paper presented for the Physician Payment Review Commission's Conference on Practice Guidelines, Washington, D.C., October 11, 1988.
10. Wennberg, J.E. "Dealing with Medical Practice Variation: A Proposal for Action. *Health Affairs* 3, no. 2 (Summer 1984): 6–32.
11. Hughes, R.G., and Lee, D.E. "Public Information on Private Practice: The Availability of Physician Inpatient Data." *Hospital and Health Services Administration* 35 (Spring 1990): 55–69.
12. Freidson, E. *Profession of Medicine. A Study of the Sociology of Applied Knowledge.* New York, N.Y.: Dodd, Mead, 1970.
13. Roos, L.L., Roos, N.P., and Sharp, S.M. "Monitoring Adverse Outcomes of Surgery Using Administrative Data." *Health Care Financing Review Annual Supplement* (1987): 5–16.

14. Bargmann, E., and Grove, C. *Surgery in Maryland Hospital 1979 and 1980 Charges and Deaths*. Washington, D.C.: Public Citizen Health Research Group, 1982.
15. Tanio, C., Manley, M., and Wolfe, S.M. "Unnecessary Caesarean Sections: A Rapidly Growing National Epidemic." Washington, D.C.: Public Citizen Health Research Group, 1987.
16. Luft, H.S. "The Relation between Surgical Volume and Mortality: An Exploration of Causal Factors and Alternative Models." *Medical Care* 18 (1980): 940–59.
17. Hughes, R.G., Hunt, S.S., and Luft, H.S. "Effects of Surgeon Volume and Hospital Volume on Quality of Care in Hospitals." *Medical Care* 25 (1987): 489–503.
18. Kelly, J.V., and Hellinger, F.J. "Heart Disease and Hospital Deaths: An Empirical Study." *Health Services Research* 22 (1987): 369–395.
19. Luft, H.S., and Hunt, S.S. "Evaluating Hospital Quality through Outcome Statistics. *Journal of the American Medical Association* 255 (1986): 1780–2784.
20. Hsia, D.C., et al. "Accuracy of Diagnostic Coding for Medicare Patients under the Prospective-Payment System." *New England Journal of Medicine* 318 (1988): 352–355.

Physician satisfaction in a major chain of investor-owned walk-in centers

Suzanne B. Cashman,
Cindy Lou Parks,
Arlene Ash,
David Hemenway,
and
William J. Bicknell

This article describes physicians at a major chain of investor-owned free-standing walk-in centers and reports on their job satisfaction. They derived satisfaction from a sense of autonomy and the corporation's reliable provision of staff and supplies. Their job dissatisfaction results from the corporate emphasis on generating revenue and the lack of opportunity for professional interaction with colleagues.

Health Care Manage Rev, 1990, 15(3), 47-57

Investor-owned free-standing walk-in centers are a recent innovation in organized ambulatory care services in the United States. Since their first appearance in the early 1980s, for-profit, free-standing walk-in centers have proliferated rapidly: In a March 1988 personal communication, the National Association of Freestanding Ambulatory Care Centers, the industry's trade association, put their number at 4,000. Walk-in ambulatory care centers offer extended hours, do not require appointments, and are open seven days a week. Although at first centers sought to attract patients needing acute episodic care, more recently they have begun to present themselves as a viable alternative to the family doctor.

Walk-in centers provide a new choice of practice setting for physicians. But while organized settings add diversity to practice options, they also contribute to the potential for conflict between professional values and job expectations. This can be a source of job dissatisfaction.[1,2] The relationship between quality of care and provider satisfaction,[3–5] coupled with the increasing number of physicians practicing in the organized for-profit ambulatory arena, make these centers ripe for analysis.

Instruments for measuring physician satisfaction are numerous and have been applied in a variety of settings. But none have been targeted to physicians in for-profit walk-in centers. This article discusses results of

Suzanne B. Cashman, *Sc.D, is Assistant Professor of Public Health at Boston University's School of Public Health in Boston, Massachusetts.*

Cindy Lou Parks, *P.A., M.S., is Senior Research Associate at Boston University's Health Policy Institute in Boston, Massachusetts.*

Arlene Ash, *Ph.D., is Assistant Professor of Mathematics and Research Consultant in Health Policy at Boston University's Medical Center and School of Public Health in Boston, Massachusetts.*

David Hemenway, *Ph.D., is Assistant Professor of Health Policy and Management at the Harvard School of Public Health in Boston, Massachusetts.*

William J. Bicknell, *M.D., M.P.H., is Assistant Vice-President for International Health Programs, Boston University, and Professor of Public Health at Boston University's School of Public Health in Boston, Massachusetts.*

This project was supported in part by grant number HS 05501 from the National Center for Health Services Research and Health Care Technology Assessment.

an extensive survey of current and former physicians working full-time at walk-in centers managed or owned by Health Stop Medical Management, Inc. (HSMMI) in Newton Centre, Massachusetts, the corporate body for Health Stop offices. HSMMI is currently the nation's largest chain of investor-owned walk-in centers. The research was designed to answer the following questions:

- Why do physicians choose to practice at walk-in centers?
- How satisfied are they with this setting?
- How do these physicians differ from those practicing in more traditional forms of health care delivery?
- Do the physicians have a commitment to practicing in walk-in centers over the long term or are they transient, filling in time between jobs or training programs?

This study of physicians at Health Stop offices is part of a larger, comprehensive case study encompassing description and analysis of patient and physician populations, measurement of indicators of quality of care, assessment of the centers' impact on traditional modes of health care delivery, examination of financial incentives and practice patterns, assessment of the expectations and influence of investors in the proprietary walk-in industry, and a description of the public policy and regulatory environment.

HEALTH STOP MEDICAL MANAGEMENT, INC.

HSMMI is the nation's largest chain of investor-owned ambulatory care centers. It owns 83 centers in 5 cities, including 31 Health Stop offices in the greater Boston area.

Health Stop offices provide minor emergency and primary care on a walk-in basis, with extended hours for convenience. Each center has at least one full-time physician, nursing staff, and technical staff. Physicians are employed by Ambulatory Health Associates (AHA), a separate but closely affiliated medical professional company that contracts with HSMMI for physicians. Through AHA, HSMMI recruits physicians for specific Health Stop offices. The intent is that the physician view that office as his or her practice. This trend has evolved to the point that, as of 1988, seven physicians had bought their offices from HSMMI. Although self-owned, the offices retain the Health Stop name and hours of operation, and the physicians contract with HSMMI for management services, including technical assistance for practice building. In the corporate-owned centers, HSMMI reimburses physicians either through a volume-based incentive formula (i.e., a predetermined percentage of gross billings) or with an hourly wage of between $28 and $34, whichever is higher.

METHODS

All full-time physicians were surveyed who currently work or have worked at least six months at any of the Boston area Health Stop offices. A questionnaire was developed that combined questions from previous work[5–9] with new questions specific to the present research agenda and setting.

The nine-page survey instrument asked why respondents took jobs at Health Stop; where they might have worked had Health Stop not been an option; what future career plans they had, including intentions to leave Health Stop; and an extensive series of questions regarding satisfaction with their positions.

Satisfaction items on the questionnaire were presented in several forms. The most extensive consisted of six theoretical components of satisfaction for respondents to rank in order of contribution to overall job satisfaction or dissatisfaction. This was accompanied by detailed statements regarding specific aspects of each of the components. The components and their definitions included

- autonomy: job-related independence, initiative, and freedom;
- patient relationships: time with patients and type of problems presented;
- reimbursement: pay and fringe benefits;
- professional relationships: interaction with physicians and other staff at Health Stop;
- resources: availability of appropriate help and supplies; and
- status: perceived prestige from working at Health Stop.

These six factors are similar to those identified by other researchers in their work on health professionals' job satisfaction.[6,7] Results of respondents' rankings permitted gauging of the relative degree of a factor's importance as a contributor to satisfaction or dissatisfaction.

Abstracting from the work of Stamps et al.[10] and Lichtenstein,[6] 26 detailed statements that reflected specific aspects of the satisfaction components were presented. The statements were scored using a Likert-type attitude scale to reflect satisfaction level (e.g., I am satisfied with the responsibilities of my job). For each of the six components of satisfaction identified and defined in the questionnaire, between two and seven statements were given. When the statements were phrased negatively, scores were reversed so that higher scores would denote greater satisfaction. The five-point scales permitted selection of a neutral midpoint. The small sample size ($N = 61$) precluded the use of factor analysis; the detailed statements were grouped with the appropriate component, according to the results of Lichtenstein[6] and Stamps et al.[10] One component, organizational requirements, was not broken out for the physicians to rank. However, specific statements relating to organizational requirements were included in the agree–disagree series. Responses to these items were tallied separately under the heading, organizational requirements.

Also included were three global or overall satisfaction questions similar to those Lichtenstein used in his physician satisfaction work.[6] Finally, physicians were asked through open-ended questions what they thought were the most and least attractive features of the job at Health Stop, and what they viewed as the main goals of the corporation.

Minor modifications were made in the survey instrument so that it would be appropriate for the former full-time physician population. Modifications in the questionnaire consisted of changes in verb tense, omission of questions irrelevant to this population, and addition of a question about the respondents' current job. A policy advisory panel was enlisted to examine the questionnaires. After repeated review by the policy advisory board, pilot testing, and professional editing, both questionnaires were fielded in the summer of 1987. Following the initial mailing, postcard and telephone reminders were used as necessary. With a telephone follow-up, the response rate for the current full-time Health Stop physician population was 93.8% (61 of 65 physicians). The 42 former full-time physicians, however, required multiple mailings and telephone reminders to increase an originally low response rate. It was necessary to obtain recent addresses from the American Medical Association for a subgroup of this population, since many had changed addresses at least twice in the one to three years after leaving Health Stop. Three of the original list of 42 physicians were never located, so the list was reduced to 39. With 26 of 39 completed questionnaires fielded and delivered, the final response rate for the former Health Stop physicians was 66.7%.

Sociodemographic and education and training characteristics of each of the physicians in the survey were abstracted from personnel files at HSMMI. These data items were used in the analysis of nonrespondents to help in assessing nonresponse bias.

SOCIODEMOGRAPHIC PROFILE OF HEALTH STOP PHYSICIANS

Full-time physicians currently practicing at Health Stop in the greater Boston area are typically under 40 years of age, male, American-trained, and board-certified or board-eligible internists who have completed between one and three years of postgraduate training (see Table 1). Approximately one quarter have hospital admitting privileges. Only 26 out of 39 (66.7%) former physicians responded; however, chi-square analyses comparing responding with nonresponding former physicians did not find significant differences on the basis of age, sex, domestic- versus foreign-trained, board certification or eligibility, length of time at the centers, or whether Health Stop had been a first full-time clinical job. Respondents and nonrespondents do seem to differ, by specialty, with nonrespondents less likely to be primary care physicians ($p = .02$, see Table 1).

It has been suggested that investor-owned walk-in centers would bring increased competition and greater numbers of physicians to an area.[11] To determine whether physicians at the offices were practicing in the greater Boston area primarily because of Health Stop, the respondents were asked where they thought they would have located, had this not been an employment option (see Table 2). Nearly two thirds (64%) of the respondents said that they would have practiced in the greater Boston area, and several more (13%) said that they would have settled and practiced somewhere else in Massachusetts. As a group, the physicians find an organized practice setting attractive; only 6% would have considered solo practice if Health Stop had not been an employment option. Forty percent reported that they would have practiced in some other walk-in center, 17% in a health maintenance organization (HMO), and 15% in emergency medicine.

REASONS FOR WORKING AT HEALTH STOP

Physicians work at Health Stop because they want regular hours and because they like primary care. In response to a simple check-off system asking respondents to indicate whether any of 11 reasons had or had not contributed to the decision to work at the walk-in offices, the two most frequently selected responses

TABLE 1

CHARACTERISTICS OF FULL-TIME PHYSICIANS AT HEALTH STOP (PERCENTAGES REPORTED)

	All respondents $n = 87$	All current $n = 63$	All former $n = 40$	All responding former $n = 26$
Age				
30 or younger	14.9	18.0	7.5	7.7
31–40	56.3	49.2	75.0	73.1
41–50	16.1	19.7	10.0	7.7
51–60	4.6	4.9	2.5	3.8
60 or older	8.0	8.2	5.0	7.7
Sex				
Male	64.0	66.7	55	60
Female	36.0	33.3	45	40
Country of education				
United States or Canada	87.2	84.1	92.3	92.0
Europe	3.5	4.8	5.1	4.0
Africa	2.3	3.2		
Asia	2.3	3.2		
Other	4.7	4.8	2.6	4.0
Specialty				
Family or general practice	31.8	32.3	20.5	28.0
Internal medicine	55.3	51.6	64.1	68.0
Surgery	5.9	8.1	15.4	
Pediatrics	3.5	4.8		
Emergency medicine	2.4	3.2		
Other	1.2			4.0
Board certified or eligible				
Certified	34.9	32.3	82.5	38.5
Eligible	40.0	33.9		53.8
Neither	25.6	33.9	17.5	7.7
Time spent in postgraduate training				
None	1.2	1.7		
1 year	14.0	18.3	5.0	3.8
2–3 years	57.0	48.3	70.0	76.9
4 years or more	27.9	31.7	25.0	19.2
Length of time at Health Stop				
12 months or less	62.1	65.1	51.3	53.8
13–24 months	20.7	15.9	33.3	30.8
24 months or more	17.2	19.0	15.4	15.4
Health Stop is first full-time clinical job				
Yes	41.2	38.1	50.0	45.8
No	58.8	61.9	50.0	54.2

TABLE 2

PHYSICIANS' CHOICES IF HEALTH STOP IS NOT AN EMPLOYMENT OPTION ($n = 87$)

Choice	Percentage
Location	
Greater Boston area	65
Massachusetts, outside of Boston area	13
Elsewhere in New England	13
Mid-Atlantic region	2
Elsewhere or do not know where	7
Practice setting	
Other walk-in	40
Health maintenance organization (HMO)	17
Emergency medicine	15
Group practice	11
Solo practice	6
Other or university health center	7
No answer or would not be in practice	4
Specialty	
Internal medicine	51
Family practice	30
Emergency medicine	9
Primary care	3
Other or do not know	7

were "I wanted regular hours" (89%) and "I was interested in primary care" (81%). Current and former physicians differed significantly ($p = .05$) in their likelihood of having been attracted to these offices by the case mix (75% and 54%, respectively). For all the other reasons listed, differences between the two groups were not significant (see Table 3).

The desire for regular hours was identified as one of the two most important reasons for having taken the job at Health Stop by 42% of both physician groups. However, current and former physicians differed in their identification of other important reasons. For respondents who no longer worked at the center, wanting a steady income while deciding on a career path was the only reason identified by a majority as having been one of the two most important reasons for having taken the job at Health Stop. An interest in primary care, avoiding the costs of starting a practice, and limitations due to family or other obligations were each identified as having been important by 23% of this group. Although some of the current physicians also identified the desire for a steady income while deciding on future plans (28%), they also noted the attractiveness of being able to concentrate on practicing medicine while someone else handled staffing and administrative hassles (21%) and the attractiveness of the case mix found at the center (18%).

Most physicians (54%) considered their positions at Health Stop to be relatively short-term interludes in their careers; 48% of current physicians said there was a 0% likelihood that they would be in the same position in five years. For current physicians intending to leave within the next 12 to 18 months, the most commonly stated reason for departure was to pursue further training (23%). This was followed by relocation (18%), starting a private practice (14%), and a desire for increased autonomy (9%). Only 12% said they expected to stay between four and seven years.

Of former physicians, 31% stated that they left Health Stop because they moved out of state or began a fellowship. Close to one half left because of problems with management; 23% resigned because they felt management was too critical of their work or they were dissatisfied with the corporation's monetary emphasis. Another 23% (six physicians) were fired. In explaining the reason for their termination, five of the six said they had been charged with "failure to build a practice." According to management records, a comparable percentage of nonresponding former physicians were fired. While this was not verified through direct query of nonresponding physicians, HSMMI's records are believed to be valid, as they corroborated responding physicians' reasons for having left.

SATISFACTION

Current and former physicians had very different assessments of their overall experiences at Health Stop. Current physicians rated their jobs a mean of 6.5 on a scale of 1 to 10 (10 being best). Former physicians, however, gave it only a mean of 3.9 on the same scale ($p < .0001$). Both groups were satisfied with the time the practice required (87% of current, 96% of former), and with the earnings from their work (75% of current, 65% of former). When asked if, knowing what they know now, they would accept the position at Health Stop again, only 3% of current physicians and 36% of former physicians said they would not. All of the former physicians who were fired said that they would not take the job again. While 78% of current physicians said they

TABLE 3

REASONS FOR WORKING AT HEALTH STOP

Reason[†]	Percentage indicating it was a reason*		
	Current Health Stop physicians (n = 61)	Former Health Stop physicians (n = 26)	Total (n = 87)
Wanted regular hours	86.9	92.3	88.5
Interested in primary care	83.3	76.9	80.5
Need steady income while deciding on future of career	62.3	80.8	67.8
Avoid cost of starting a practice	76.7	76.9	75.9
Comfortable with case mix[‡]	75.4	53.8	70.0
Did not want staffing and administrative hassles	80.3	65.4	75.9
Pleased with income, given level of training and experience	44.3	61.5	49.4
Had limited alternatives because of family or other obligations	41.7	61.5	47.1
Seemed like a relatively low-pressure job	44.3	57.7	48.3
Needed steady income immediately because of medical education debt	19.7	19.2	19.5
Avoid malpractice premiums	32.8	42.3	35.6

* Percentages add to more than 100 because respondent could check multiple reasons.
† Listed in the same order as on the questionnaire.
‡ Differences between current and former physicians significant at $p = .05$.

would recommend the job to a friend, less than a third (30%) of former physicians said they would.

Physicians ranked six theoretical components (i.e., autonomy, patient relationships, reimbursement, professional relationships, resources, and status) in order of importance to their overall satisfaction with the Health Stop job. The two groups of physicians gave similar but not identical rankings (see Table 4), indicating that they have somewhat different priorities for job satisfaction. While 83% of current physicians ranked autonomy as one of the two most important components of satisfaction, only 52% of former physicians did so ($p = .003$). Reimbursement was far more likely to be a high-ranking component for former than for current physicians (48% versus 25%; $p = .038$).

Respondents were asked to indicate how strongly they agreed or disagreed with 26 statements regarding satisfaction with specific aspects of their jobs. Following the factor analysis results of Stamps et al.[10] and Lichtenstein,[6] the statements were grouped by component, and a mean score was calculated for each (see the box, "Components and Statements Comprising Measures of Physician Satisfaction"). The mean score for each component was computed by weighting equally the mean scores of all the questions pertaining to the component. The arithmetic mean of all the components was calculated to determine an average satisfaction score (see Table 5).[1] Overall, physicians currently at Health Stop are more satisfied than physicians who have left ($p = .017$). Three components of satisfaction—organizational policies, professional relationships, and status—contributed most to this difference.

Both groups of physicians agreed that there was too much emphasis on revenue generation, with former physicians more likely than current physicians to note this (58% versus 28%, respectively). Both groups agreed that "administrative requirements did not interfere with patient decisions," and that "HSMMI did not question [their] judgment too much." Three quarters of current and 64% of former physicians stated they were satisfied or very satisfied with their earnings at Health Stop. A majority of current physicians (63%) were sat-

TABLE 4

RANKINGS OF COMPONENTS OF SATISFACTION: PERCENTAGE OF PHYSICIANS RANKING EACH COMPONENT AS FIRST OR SECOND IN IMPORTANCE OF CONTRIBUTION TO THEIR JOB SATISFACTION

Component	Current Health Stop physicians (%)	Former Health Stop physicians (%)
Autonomy**	83	62
Patient relations	76	68
Pay*	25	48
Resources (staffing and supplies	24	28
Professional relations	17	24
Status	14	12

Significance levels of difference between current and former physicians: *$p = .0038$; **$p = .031$

isfied with the volume-based incentives of the practice. By contrast, only 32% of former physicians were. Reasons current physicians gave for dissatisfaction with the incentive payment most often related to the high level of volume needed before the incentive mechanism kicked in; of this dissatisfied group, none were uneasy with the ethical implications of incentives. Of former physicians who were not very satisfied with the payment method, several said that incentives either were too high or were unrealistic (18%) and 27% felt that the volume-based incentives had unethical implications.

Health Stop physicians feel making money is a main goal of HSMMI. Seventy-five percent of current and 88% of former physicians listed making money as at least one of three main corporate goals. In fact, 31% of the former physicians repeated this as the main goal on all three of the blank spaces provided on the questionnaire. (This was far more likely to happen in the case of the former than in the case of the current physicians, $p = .007$.) Forty-four percent of current versus 12% of former physicians listed "provide quality care" ($p = .003$). Other goals mentioned were "run a successful business," "grow," "provide convenient, accessible care," and "fill a need in the community."

Components and Statements Comprising Measures of Physician Satisfaction*

Component 1: Satisfaction with autonomy
- I set the pace of my own work.
- I am satisfied with the responsibilities of my job.
- My professional judgments are questioned too often.

Component 2: Satisfaction with organizational policies
- I have as much opportunity as I want to participate in the administrative decision-making process.
- There is too much emphasis on revenue generation.
- Administrative requirements interfere with how I care for patients.
- I have as much voice as I like in planning policies and procedures.
- Emphasis on revenue generation influences my patient-care decisions in ways that make me uncomfortable.

Component 3: Satisfaction with patient relationships
- I do not have enough time for each patient.
- Patients have problems appropriate for my training and expertise.
- I can get to know my patients to the extent I wish.
- In most of my cases, it is appropriate for the patient to be seeing a physician.

Component 4: Satisfaction with reimbursement
- In light of what other primary-care physicians make, my income is satisfactory.
- Considering what is expected of physicians at Health Stop, my income is reasonable.

Component 5: Satisfaction with professional relationships
- There is sufficient teamwork and cooperation between the various levels of personnel in this office.
- I have as much professional interaction with non-HSMMI physicians as I want.

Component 6: Satisfaction with resources
- I get the help I need from nurses and technicians.
- There is adequate secretarial and receptionist help.
- Administrative tasks like billing, hiring, training, and ordering are handled well.
- Adequate supplies are available.
- Laboratory equipment is usually in good working order.
- Radiographic equipment is usually in good working order.
- There is enough space to see patients.

Component 7: Satisfaction with status
- I feel that what I do in my job is really important.
- HSMMI treats me as if my work is valued.
- My work here is respected by others in the local medical community.

* All statements had a five-point response scale ranging from "agree" to "disagree." Coding of negative statements was reversed for consistency.

TABLE 5

MEAN SCORES FOR LIKERT-TYPE SCALE STATEMENTS, BY SATISFACTION COMPONENTS

Component	Number of statements	Current Health Stop physicians ($n = 61$)	Former Health Stop physicians ($n = 26$)	Significance difference between current and former
Autonomy	3	2.16	2.56	None
Organizational policies	5	3.07	3.55	$p = .02$
Patient relationships	4	1.99	2.13	None
Pay	2	2.84	2.94	None
Professional relationships	2	2.07	2.96	$p < .0001$
Resources	7	1.93	2.13	None
Status	3	2.71	3.28	$p = .01$
Average satisfaction		2.40	2.80	$p = .017$

Score codes: 1, agree; 5, disagree.

Physicians were asked to note the most and the least attractive features of their jobs at the walk-in office. Of the 59 current physicians who answered this open-ended question, an overwhelming majority (59%) listed flexible hours as an attractive feature of their job. Also mentioned as attractive features (in descending order of frequency) were "no night work," "no billing hassles," "no call," "case mix," and "good salary potential." Former physicians agreed, with 58% listing flexible hours. (All former Health Stop physicians responded to this question.) Their second most frequently mentioned feature was "good salary potential."

The least attractive features of the job were similar for the two groups. Current and former physicians alike most frequently identified the financial emphasis of the company as a least attractive feature. Current physicians also listed the length of the days they worked and not feeling valued by HSMMI or other physician colleagues. For former physicians, the second most frequently noted least attractive feature was lack of contact with other physicians.

DISCUSSION

Compared to physicians in Massachusetts and nationally (see Table 6), Health Stop physicians tend to be younger, fewer are board-certified ($p < .0001$), and more are female ($p < .001$). In contrast to the 22% of physicians nationwide who are foreign trained, both Health Stop and Massachusetts physicians are less likely to be foreign medical graduates (16% and 14%, respectively; $p < .001$). That Health Stop physicians are younger, have fewer years of postgraduate training, and are less likely to have hospital admitting privileges is consistent with the Yunker et al. profile of physicians practicing in walk-in centers in Texas.[12]

However, compared to a recent national survey of physicians practicing in walk-in ambulatory care centers,[13] physicians at Health Stop offices were less likely to claim emergency medicine as their specialty and more likely to have trained in internal medicine. The study found that emergency medicine and internal medicine were each identified as the specialty of 24% of physicians surveyed. At Health Stop, 3% of the physicians have specialized in emergency medicine, 52% in internal medicine. This may be a predominantly organizational difference, as HSMMI has never presented its offices as emergicenters and has sought to market its centers as alternatives to the family doctor. Redlinger and Welch's statement that their "results indicate that the [ambulatory care center] market is evolving from one concerned strictly with emergency care to one focused more on traditional primary practice treatment" reflects the orientation that HSMMI has had from its inception.[13]

Numerous studies of job satisfaction of physicians, both in independent practice and in organized settings,

TABLE 6

SOCIODEMOGRAPHIC CHARACTERISTICS OF HEALTH STOP PHYSICIANS COMPARED TO MASSACHUSETTS AND U.S. PRACTICING PHYSICIANS

Characteristic	Health Stop	Massachusetts*	United States†
Mean age	39 years	45 years	47 years
Percentage female‡	33%	18%	15%
Percentage foreign medical graduate‡	16%	14%	22%
Percentage board-certified‡	32%	56%	55%
Years since graduation	15 months	Not available	20 years
Mean income	$72,000	Not available	$80,300§

* Source: *Characteristics of Physicians: Massachusetts (1985).* U.S. DHHS-PHS-HRSA-BHPr. ODAM Report No. 122-87, May 1987.
† Source: Roback, G., et al. *Physician Characteristics and Distribution in the U.S.* Chicago, Ill.: American Medical Association, 1987.
‡ Differences significant at $p < .0001$.
§ Mean net income for family practitioners after expenses, before taxes, 1986. Source: *Physician Marketplace Statistics,* edited by M. Gonzalez. Chicago, Ill.: American Medical Association, 1987.

have been conducted in the past decade.[2] Studies looking at physician satisfaction in relation to organizational setting have categorized organizations as either prepaid groups with salaried physicians or as small or larger group practice settings. Health Stop offices represent a hybrid structure. Physicians practice essentially alone but within the dictates of organizational policy (e.g., hours of operation, charges, staffing patterns). They are salaried but can increase their pay through achieving a high-volume practice.

The literature on physician satisfaction in organized settings has recently been reviewed by Lichtenstein.[2] Although satisfaction differs with the structure of the organization, "it is not working in a group itself that creates dissatisfaction, but certain characteristics of the organization."[2(p.155)] Although most physicians are not opposed to working in groups, the aspect of satisfaction that always appears to be most important in determining overall satisfaction is autonomy.[2,10] This was borne out by the responses of physicians currently working at Health Stop offices who most often ranked autonomy first or second in importance in contributing to job satisfaction or dissatisfaction.

After autonomy, job status was second in importance in the Stamps et al. research of an ambulatory private fee-for-service setting, followed by interaction with other professionals, pay, organizational requirements, and task requirements.[10] Health Stop physicians, both current and former, ranked status as least important in job satisfaction. This may be the result of self-selection. Given the high number of tertiary medical care facilities in the Boston area, physicians practicing primary care in a for-profit walk-in center must accept that they will not be at the status pinnacle of the medical community. However, the small sample sizes, particularly in the Stamps et al. physician population, temper the strength of the conclusions regarding the priorities of Health Stop physicians as compared with others.

According to the series of structured satisfaction questions, physicians at Health Stop offices were very satisfied with the amount and type of resources available. HSMMI presents itself as a skilled management company whose services free physicians to do what they have been trained to do—care for patients—while it sees to the business side of the practice. This includes ensuring adequate supplies and support personnel. It appears that HSMMI performs this aspect of its job well.

The physicians' satisfaction with specific aspects of patient relationships came as a surprise. The image of walk-in centers as "fast medicine," where patients are moved in and out quickly with little time to spend with the physician, was not borne out by survey results. Indeed, the physicians felt that they had adequate time to spend with each patient, and that they could get to know their patients to whatever extent they desired. This may reflect the physician's predisposition and expectations as well as the management company's responsibility for administration and management of the office, which leaves the physician time to concentrate on patient care.

Based on the open-ended questions, Health Stop physicians, like the physicians in the Yunker et al. survey of walk-in center physicians in Texas,[12] found the flexible hours and lack of night work to be the most attractive features of their jobs. But although they liked the work schedule overall, the physicians currently at Health Stop offices most frequently mentioned that the long days dictated by the schedule represented the least attractive feature of their job.

In general, the physicians were most dissatisfied with organizational policies: the perceived lack of opportunity to be involved in administrative decision making, and particularly the corporate emphasis on revenue generation. The issue of revenue generation appeared specifically in the series of satisfaction statements, and it figured prominently in responses to the question regarding perceptions of corporate goals. The effect of financial incentives on physician practice patterns has received much recent attention.[14-20] Central to the debate is the issue of ethics and professionalism, as they may be in conflict with the exigencies of running and managing a business. Physicians in solo practice, of course, manage and run their own volume-based businesses. The difference for Health Stop physicians is that a corporate entity is running and managing the business while they practice medicine exclusively.

Society has been warned of the potential perils of physicians working for overtly for-profit business.[18] Although the physicians surveyed felt that the management company put more emphasis on revenue generation than the physicians would have liked, they did not feel that it influenced their patient care decisions. Apparently the "ethical priorities on which the profession of medicine is based"[18(p.784)] remain in the consciousness of Health Stop physicians. It was not possible to determine through this physician questionnaire whether in fact a perceived corporate emphasis on revenue generation influenced the respondents' patient care decisions, possibly even in ways unapparent to the physicians. A separate section of this study looked at that question by examining the effect of the volume-based payment incentive on physicians' use of ancillary services.[21] However, based on the frequency with which physicians who formerly worked at Health Stop mentioned their dissatisfaction with the company's emphasis on revenue generation, the for-profit environment with its focus on the bottom line creates an atmosphere that many physicians find uncomfortable.

• • •

This study showed that physicians at Health Stop are young and often view their tenure at the centers as an interim position while deciding on a direction for their careers. They are attracted by the regular hours and an interest in primary care. Physicians at Health Stop offices like the patients in the practice, and they place high value on their autonomy and the corporation's managerial services. While somewhat dissatisfied with the lack of opportunity to develop professional relationships with other physicians and the relatively low prestige accorded by the medical community to working at a Health Stop office, the physicians are very unhappy with the emphasis on the need to generate revenue. On the basis of this research, for HSMMI to be successful in retaining its physicians, the corporation will need to reduce its emphasis on revenue generation while developing avenues for professional interaction.

REFERENCES

1. Murray, J.P."Physician Satisfaction with Capitation Patients in an Academic Family Medicine Clinic." *The Journal of Family Practice* 27, no. 1 (1988): 108–13.
2. Lichtenstein, R.L. "The Job Satisfaction and Retention of Physicians in Organized Settings: A Literature Review." *Medical Care Review* 41 (1984): 139–79.
3. Linn, L.S., et al. "Physician and Patient Satisfaction as Factors Related to the Organization of Internal Medicine Group Practices." *Medical Care* 23 (1985): 1171–78.
4. Melville, A. "Job Satisfaction in General Practice: Implications for Prescribing." *Social Science and Medicine* 14 (1980): 495–99.
5. Mechanic, D. "The Organization of Medical Practice and Practice Orientations among Physicians in Prepaid and Nonprepaid Primary Care Settings." *Medical Care* 13, no. 3 (1975): 189–204.
6. Lichtenstein, R. "Measuring the Job Satisfaction of Physicians in Organized Settings." *Medical Care* 22, no. 1 (1984): 56–68.
7. Stamps, P., and Piedmonte, E. *Nurses and Work Satisfaction: An Index for Measurement*. Ann Arbor, Mich.: Health Administration Press, 1986.
8. Linn, L.S., et al. "Work Satisfaction and Career Aspirations of Internists Working in Teaching Hospital Group Practices." *Journal of General Internal Medicine* 1, no. 2 (1986): 104–8.
9. Konrad, T.R. "Organizational Autonomy, Centralization, and Physician Satisfaction in Large Medical Groups." Ph.D. diss., University of North Carolina, Chapel Hill, 1975.

10. Stamps, P.L., et al. "Measurement of Work Satisfaction among Health Professionals." *Medical Care* 16, no. 4 (1978): 337–52.
11. Reinhardt, U.E. "The Health Professions' Collision Course." *Hospitals* 58, no. 16 (1984): 96–97.
12. Yunker, R., Levine, M., and Sajid, A. "Physicians Practicing in Texas' Freestanding Emergency Centers." *Texas Medicine* 82, no. 9 (1986): 22–25.
13. Redlinger, L.J., and Welch, M.G. *Ambulatory Care Centers: Physician and Organizational Profiles.* Dallas, Tex.: Center for Applied Research, University of Texas at Dallas, 1986.
14. Bock, R.S. "Sounding Board: The Pressure to Keep Prices High at a Walk-In Clinic." *New England Journal of Medicine* 319 (1988): 785–87.
15. Bock, R.S. "The Pressure to Keep Prices High at a Walk-In Clinic." *New England Journal of Medicine* 320 (1989): 183–85. Correspondence.
16. Green, L. "The Pressure to Keep Prices High at a Walk-In Clinic." *New England Journal of Medicine* 320 (1989): 183–85. Correspondence.
17. Herold, A.H. "The Pressure to Keep Prices High at a Walk-In Clinic." *New England Journal of Medicine* 320 (1989): 183–85. Correspondence.
18. Relman, A.S. "Salaried Physicians and Economic Incentives." *New England Journal of Medicine* 319 (1988): 784.
19. Scovern, H. "Hired Help: A Physician's Experiences in a For-Profit Staff-Model HMO." *New England Journal of Medicine* 319 (1988): 787–90.
20. Yunker, R., and Sajid, A. "The Pressure to Keep Prices High at a Walk-In Clinic." *New England Journal of Medicine* 320 (1989): 183–85. Correspondence.
21. Hemenway, D., et al. "Physician Responses to Financial Incentives: Evidence from a For-Profit Ambulatory Care Center." *New England Journal of Medicine* 322, no. 15 (1990): 1059–63.

Part IV

TEAM BUILDING

Justice as a prelude to teamwork in medical centers

André L. Delbecq
and
Sandra L. Gill

Concern with teamwork in medical centers has often focused on cohesion and affiliation. Based on data concerning personality propensities and values of physician leaders, it appears that due process is a more realistic leadership aspiration than cohesion.

The need for integration and teamwork in health care organizations seems obvious as the struggle continues to reduce the cost of conflict and inefficiency. Yet recent accounts of teamwork and collaboration efforts in hospitals and medical centers have been noticeably ineffective.[1–3] Since conventional rationales for teambuilding are unlikely motivators in health care settings, it seems prudent to explore the potential of structured decision processes as an alternative route toward cohesive problem solving and organizational justice.

THE TEAMWORK CONTEXT IN MEDICAL CENTERS

In considering teamwork in medical centers, it is helpful to conjure an image of teamwork in another setting: the military. It is not difficult to imagine one's self seated in an audience in which the majority wear military uniforms, or even to imagine one's self as one of the great leadership personages of all time, George Patton, standing in front of that audience. A physician who had been in the military has confessed that this was his fanciful image—that he would be a medical George Patton, with a pearl-handled stethoscope, and that he would stand up in front of the "troops" and lead them onto new and innovative beachheads in medicine.

He said the difference between the Patton image and the reality of his medical leadership could be exemplified by a typical meeting in which: (1) three of the people critical to the meeting and whom he counted on to provide support would arrive late; (2) two other key physicians would argue vigorously against the concept that he was proposing; (3) several other physicians indicated that they would not be at

---

André L. Delbecq, *B.B.A., M.B.A., D.B.A., is Dean of the Leavey School of Business Administration at the University of Santa Clara, Santa Clara, California. Prior to 1979, he spent 12 years at the University of Wisconsin-Madison. Dr. Delbecq is nationally recognized for executive programs delivered to high-technology industries as well as health, human services and government organizations.*

Sandra L. Gill, *B.A., M.A., is a faculty member of the Estes Park Institute and is a doctoral student in organization and management systems at the Fielding Institute, Santa Barbara, California. She has conducted executive and medical staff development programs since 1975. She has been an internal health care consultant in both HMO and community hospital settings.*

all interested in participating in the program; and (4) one physician would indicate that unless he was authorized to expend more money on specialized equipment for traditional programs he would not participate in any new efforts by the organization (but would be willing to head a committee to organize the purchase of the equipment). This limited leadership appears to be a much more realistic image of teambuilding in medical organizations than the command power of Patton.

PHYSICIAN DECISION STYLES

The senior author participated in the Physician-in-Management Seminars (PIMS) funded for the American Academy of Medical Directors (AAMD) by The Robert Wood Johnson Foundation.[4] Kurtz collected data on these physicians.[5] There were 800 physicians in the sample from PIMS. Of these, 94 percent were male; ages ranged from 30 to 60. Instrumentation in the data gathering effort included Fundamental Interpersonal Relations Orientation—Behavior (FIRO-B), Life Orientations Survey (LIFO) and Hall's Style of Leadership Survey. FIRO-B was designed to assess individual's behavior preferences regarding the expression and reception of inclusion, control and affection in general interpersonal interactions.[6,7] LIFO assesses behaviors the individual uses under conditions of stress or conflict, and can be used to identify behavioral reactions to conflict situations.[8] In this way, individuals can assess the circumstances in which their behavior is most productive—or counterproductive, i.e., the "fit" of their behavior with stressful circumstances.

What can be said about these medical leaders with respect to their team interactions? With respect to their attitudes toward interpersonal interaction, these physicians would prefer not to be interactive. The majority would prefer to avoid group involvement. They much prefer solo activity and like to remain detached and distant. This means that a realistic image of teambuilding with physicians has to begin with the realization that many of the key actors will not give it rave reviews.

Needs and values

Kurtz's data suggest that physicians represent a high "need for control" population. They have a very high need for influence, a very high need for dominance and a very high need to be the focal point in decision structures. Under conditions of stress or conflict, i.e., when disagreement occurs (and when other populations of managers would move toward group consensus as a problem-solving strategy), these physicians tend to withdraw support from the group, assert authority, stubbornly fight for suboptimal points of view, and define success as winning and failure as losing, as opposed to defining success as a mutually acceptable compromise. In short, under stress they prefer to impose their point of view on colleagues.

This tendency was manifested over and over in group exercises and case analyses in seminars focusing on problem-solving and negotiation situations in the PIMS series. Graduate students who worked with the senior author described the physicians as "noncollegial" and "primitive battlers."

The anomaly, in light of these personality or behavioral tendencies, is that 84 percent of the physicians do not value authoritarianism. It is a paradoxical situation. Their behavior under conditions of stress reverts to authoritarian behavior, but their expressed value is that authoritarianism is undesirable. Their value preference may reflect what they would prefer from others, but their behavior may reflect (perhaps at a somewhat subconscious level) an action orientation contrary to their value orientation.

Differences by specialty and region

Of course, there are individual and subgroup differences in the data; what are cited here are central tendencies. For example, psychiatrists have lower control needs than physicians in other subspecialties. Internists are much more tolerant of conflict and tend to be more collaborative (as long as they can exercise final control). Pathologists, of all subspecialists, are the most willing to be confronted and the most difficult with whom to deal.

To make matters more stark, all of the "nonteamwork" behaviors tend to increase with age. Managers in other industries are shown to be less affiliative as they get older. Colloquially, it can be said that interaction rates decrease as waistlines increase in most studies of managerial personnel. The right to be moderately obstinate seems to be one of the features of the mid-life evolution. The reason to point this out is that seniority often goes together with either the willingness to volunteer for or the likelihood of election to medical leadership.

There are also some differences by region. The Southeast is the most blatant in terms of need for control by physician leaders. The Northeast is in the middle, and the West is somewhat less control oriented.

STRUCTURAL BARRIERS TO COHESION

Some other barriers to teamwork should be mentioned. Medical organizations are loosely coupled systems.[9,10] That is, physicians see themselves affiliated with but not employees of the organization, so that in their minds income and productivity are often seen as somewhat independent from the administration of the organization. Their focus is on medical technology. Consequently, administration and medical leadership are seldom the "apple of the physician's eye."

There is a strong tendency to view the organization as an institutional support service, which otherwise interferes with what is good for a specialty or practice. This leads to stressing personal needs as opposed to valuing what is good for the organization as a whole. The very physical ecology of the hospital (placing subspecialties in proximity) reinforces this behavior. Physicians can interact much of the time in the medical center only with a small subset of actors within their own medical department who share the same biases.

An additional barrier is "time squeeze."[11] The managerial and organizational decisions that have to be made are processed under conditions that allow only limited time for participation. Physicians who see management as interfering with work (seeing patients) are not going to spend a long afternoon engaged in organizational problem solving. It is often difficult to capture key physicians for 30 minutes. In this respect, physicians do not have shared norms requiring participation in committee work that managers in Xerox, IBM, Intel, Rolm or any other corporation would have.

For organizational development, this reduced focus on cohesion reflects a very different situation than is seen in conventional teambuilding. Interventions focused within a subspecialty (medical department or unit) may indeed approach the preconditions of interdependency and affiliation that are the groundwork for conventional teambuilding. However, when the focus is on the organizational boundaries (between medical units) or on the strategic level of decision making (the medical center as a whole), approaching teamwork from a standpoint of affiliation as opposed to due process is likely to be doomed to failure. To put it another way, when coping with the macrostructure, due process is probably more important.

> *Physicians who see management as interfering with work (seeing patients) are not going to spend a long afternoon engaged in organizational problem solving.*

To a lesser degree, this holds true in industry as well.[12] Approaches to creating cohesion within a marketing department or within a production unit can focus on affiliation. Put production, marketing and finance representatives into a meeting to make a strategic decision, and affiliation is often not the manipulative variable. Due process becomes more important. However, this structural differentiation is reinforced in the medical setting by the unique personality tendencies of physicians. It is then heightened by the loosely coupled structure of medical centers.

JUSTICE VERSUS COHESION

What does this individualist, controlling, combative behavior imply for teamwork in medical centers? What style of leadership does it require? The first premise must be that physician leaders are obviously not individuals who are going to value cohesive harmony in their group as they work through problem solving. Nonetheless, despite these behaviors there is a key value that physicians hold that provides the central approach.

Physicians do express a very strong positive value toward due process. (This is probably the result of the incredible competition in medical school. After medical school, residencies, subspecializations and boards—between 12 and 17 years depending on the specialization—secure, mature physicians often seek an alternative to win–lose combat.) Consequently, they look within the organization for leadership that assures appropriate due process.

Furthermore, physicians believe in majority rule. They recognize that at some point individual expression of strong points of opposing views must cease and a decision must be formulated. Finally, physicians are concerned about maintaining high morale within a professional organization. In short, they are aware of the complex, competitive, individualistic environment and seek to achieve positive morale in the organization by due process and majority rule, realizing that teamwork in the sense of high affiliation is not typically part of the medical culture.

This concern with due process must be the keystone when approaching teamwork among physicians. Responding to this value also provides a positive context for decision making. An organization with key leaders, who believe in due process and majority rule and who seek to come to decisions that create high morale, has to be seen as a positive starting point, even if the interpersonal styles of physicians make achieving this end somewhat more difficult. It is also important to note that if physician leaders do not perceive due process occurring in the organization, and if they do not perceive that there has been sufficient attention to majority rule (if they do not perceive that they have been treated as involved constituents), then they either withdraw from interaction or engage in forms of political fighting that are particularly destructive. As a result, the medical leader has a viable but restricted "zone of tolerance" for leadership.

The conclusion from over 30 collective years of working with physicians is that approaches to teamwork that focus on high norms for affiliation are doomed to failure. Instead, teamwork in medical organizations must acknowledge that medical centers are made up of very independent professionals with high needs for power and control. The mechanisms for enacting leadership must include (1) clearly perceived representative structures, (2) visible processing of decisions and (3) clear decision rules. In a sense, justice is substituted for cohesion. There are prerequisite structures for each of these three necessary elements for morale in medical centers.

ELEMENTS FOR SUCCESS

Clear representative structures

A representative structure is a decision group wherein all relevant factions are represented and have their position voiced by a spokesperson capable of bringing to bear the concerns and values of their particular faction to the political process.[13] In the abstract, this seems to be a viable mechanism. In the concrete, physicians in the PIMS series constantly violated the spirit of such decision groups, confusing three other structures—formal hierarchy, formal standing committee and seniority—with the representative structure.

Formal hierarchy

The most frequent error made by physician administrators (evidenced through critical incident exercises in The Robert Wood Johnson program) was to substitute formal hierarchy for representative groups when engaged in strategic problem solving. Hierarchy is not the "sole source provider" of legitimacy in medical centers. In fact, key opinion leaders for subspecialties or units, standard settlers for professional standards and central communicators to the political networks having to support decisions in health care organizations often include individuals who do not occupy hierarchical positions.

Hierarchy may be included, but composition must be expanded beyond those who hold formal office. Later, these decisions can be ratified and responsibility for enactment turned over to hierarchy. In other words, if the approach is to make decisions only through hierarchy, many key informants will not have input, and much of the diversity of professional opinion implicit in the strong personality profiles cited earlier will be glossed over.

This implies that, in any given planning period for strategic decisions, leaders will have to form special ad hoc problem-solving groups who assemble individuals who both possess unique competencies appropriate for that decision and are representative opinion leaders. Creating representative structures for critical decisions is the manifest enactment of due process. Processing all decisions through hierarchy will inevitably be perceived as decision by power as opposed to decision by due process. To a lesser extent, tendencies to refer matters to standing committees, or to senior staff can, in the same fashion, underrepresent concerned factions who hold strong views and who will be affected by decisions.

Representative structures are not only superior to hierarchy for creating a sense of teamwork, but they are superior to global participation. If participation includes everyone (e.g., all partners in a medical center as opposed to representatives), then it is unlikely that timely decisions will ever be made. Data on multispecialty group practices show that in group practices where all partners have to approve decisions there are low rates of innovation.[14] Where all physician partners participate town meeting style, the diversity of opinion leads to stalemate. Differing points of view cancel each other out. Thus the effective middle ground between hierarchy and global participation is a representative structure composed of seven to nine representatives who bring to bear a cross section of opinion.

Criteria to consider for membership include multiple ages, varied length of service, multiple specialties, differentiated training and experience, clinical as well as research orientations, inside (from within the organization) and outside resource persons. Global participation fails because there are too many diverse opinions and too little time to process the decision. Hierarchy does not work because it is seen as the exercise of arbitrary authority.

In the absence of representative structures, political networks (made up of physicians who major in politics and minor in medicine) will emerge in the attempt to control decision making in an informal but less representative manner. Counterproposals are presented by aggressive physicians. In medical centers where political energy substitutes for reasoned debate, there will be very few who perceive due process.

In summary, it is a bad choice to process strategic decisions only through hierarchy. A second bad choice is engaging everyone in debate. A final bad choice is allowing a random, informal organization to impose politicized decisions on the organization. Thus representative structures are the desired strategy.

Formal committees

Representative structures do not emasculate hierarchy for the majority of day-to-day decisions. Such representative structures are not proposed as a replacement for existing executive or standing committees. Rather, on key issues affecting the welfare of the organization, a representative structure can augment existing hierarchy. And they do not exclude hierarchical participation in representative structures. However, a good behavioral index of enacted due process is the appointment of two or three carefully composed representative structures in any given year inclusive of but not restricted to formal office holders. Issues such as establishment of satellite services, mergers or new services would be examples of topics appropriate for ad hoc task forces.

Visible processing of decisions

Membership composition, which has been the focus of the discussion so far, does not by itself assure due process. The second requirement is that the representative group participate in an open and visible process of strategic decision making.

Decisions arrived at behind closed doors, with no early warning signals regarding the evolving thinking of the committee, and sprung on the larger constituency with the request for immediate ratification, will achieve little endorsement and create as little a sense of teamwork as a decision arrived at behind closed doors by hierarchy. What is required is a visible process in which the evolution of the final decision by the representative structure is understandable and predictable (even if not totally agreeable). How is this achieved?

Information search

Representative groups should always seek information from a broader sample of opinion than their own ranks. The classic error of the average committee is that it does not seek external data. Rather, each person on the committee represents his or her own personal "infinite wisdom." That, of course, destroys any concept of a representative group. Thus, by definition, a representative group must seek additional information at three critical stages of problem solving: (1) identifying the problem, (2) exploring elements that must be included in an adequate solution and (3) reviewing preliminary proposals.

With respect to problem identification, simple surveys, interviews, observational techniques, nominal groups,[16] etc., should be employed by the representative group to be sure that the critical dimensions of the problems are fully understood by the committee, and that relevant concerns of each critical constituency are included in the problem matrix.[15] A briefing by the committee, in a public meeting at the end of the problem-solving phase, to the larger medical center constituency allows professionals at large one last opportunity to be sure that their individual concerns are included in the deliberations of the committee.

Second, a powerful research finding is that solutions based on a committee's talking only to people inside the organization are a lower quality than solutions that include elements identified by talking to informants outside the organization.[17] A sophisticated problem-solving committee always seeks opinions from outside experts, other organizations with prior experience and professionals from other medical centers who have grappled with the problem at hand. Obviously, seeking the input of professionals within the organization but not on the committee is important as well.

The more the preliminary proposal is seen as incorporating conversations with numerous experts and informants, the more the larger constituency in the medical center will see the committee's efforts as well-founded and objective. By contrast, the more the solution is perceived as being developed only by an advocacy committee that engaged in dialogue only with itself, the less likely it will be perceived as arriving at an objective or sophisticated proposal.

The more the proposal is seen as incorporating conversations with experts and informants, the more the larger constituency will see the committee's efforts as well-founded and objective.

Chances for input

The second critical briefing by the committee to the larger constituency (medical center as a whole) should be in the form of an early, unrefined, loosely focused solution concept. This allows the larger constituency to again suggest modifications or solution elements that ultimately increase the acceptability of the proposal.

Only after two public briefings with relevant members of the medical center dealing with problem definition and solution elements should the representative committee refine a proposal for final vote. When the refined proposal emerges, there will be few surprises. The larger constituency will have already been briefed on the committee's perception of the problem, will have had the opportunity through such means as interview and survey to share in this definition, will have been briefed on the preliminary solution concept and will have had a chance to suggest modifications, so that the final refined proposal will be perceived as evolving through a fair and open process.

Such a process requires a certain amount of patience. The process through which such strategic proposals evolve takes a number of weeks (sometimes months). It is not something that occurs after one or two meetings. But it is important to contrast the sense of justice and due process that such a visible and open decision process creates with the alternative. A group's members talk among themselves and mysteriously arrive at a recommendation in closed meetings to which the rest of the medical staff perceives no access or ability to influence. The committee's recommendation is a surprise. Once again an informal organization typically arises to try to bring to bear alternative views that seem to have been neglected in the deliberations of the committee, and decision making gets stalemated.

To summarize, the second requirement, in addition to a representative structure, is an open and visible decision process in which problem definition and solution development encompass opinions beyond those of the formal committee, and the preliminary solution concept is openly discussed with opportunities for modification before bringing the recommendation to final decision.

Clear decision rules

It should not be assumed that such an open and visible process creates consensus among physicians. It is simply part of the due process norm that underlies a fundamentally just approach to arriving at a difficult strategic decision around which divergent points of view have focused. If consensus is not possible, the norm of majority rule is still present. However, the question remains: which majority? Is it the majority of the hierarchical team who reviews the recommendation, the majority of the committee members themselves or the majority of the total relevant professional staff asked to vote in parliamentary style?

An important part of the mandate to any representative committee is to clarify the decision rule ahead of time. Does it make a decision or recommend a decision? If the latter is the case, to whom is the recommendation given? This can differ by character of the decision, size of the organization, time urgency and governance traditions. This final decision authority should be clear to staff as a whole and to the committee before the committee's deliberation. Likewise, the voting statistics of the final decision authority should be honestly reported, even closed votes. Minority opinions will leak out in any case, so accurate ballot reporting is necessary to create a sense of fairness and openness.

BACK TO TEAMWORK

Such a structure, process and final decision rule does relate to conventional concepts of teamwork. Simply mixing constituencies on representative structures creates overlapping networks of interaction that do not occur in the day-to-day communication patterns within the organization. Praise and pride can be lavished on responsible committees who have worked through difficult problem-solving processes. Exhortations for mutual support of fair decisions can be legitimately voiced.

Furthermore, since due process is alive and well, destructive behaviors (rude remarks and neurotic defensiveness) can be confronted and reprimanded. It costs an individual nothing to make rude remarks; the expense to the organization in terms of civility and creative problem solving is very high. Thus a core value is to reinforce rules of civilized and helpful conduct and to sanction hurtful behavior.

In this sense, many of the conventional aspects of teamwork apply and do help. However, more time than is probably warranted is spent in talking about building teamwork in medical centers. Although it is an important task, until medical center personnel become skilled at enacting justice in decision processes, cohesion is a long way off. Administrators are faced with the challenge of testing the due process model as a behavioral enactment of justice on actual issues. Attention to representative structures, open and visible decision processing and clear final decision rules allow relatively independent, non-affiliation-oriented physicians (the real colleagues) to stand at ease and accept cajoling as pleasant. After all, justice is in place in the organization. Why not join the team?

REFERENCES

1. Margulies, N., and Adams, J. *Organizational Development in Health Care Organizations.* Reading, Mass.: Addison-Wesley Publishing, 1982.
2. Lammert, M. "Power, Authority and Status in Health Systems: A Marxian-Based Conflict Analysis." *Journal of Applied Behavioral Science* 14, no. 3 (1978): 321–33.
3. Weisbord, M. "Why Organization Development Hasn't Worked (So Far) in Medical Centers." *Health Care Management Review* 3, no. 1 (Spring 1976): 17–38.
4. Schenke, R., ed. *Physician in Management.* Tampa, Fla.: American Academy of Medical Directors, 1980.
5. Kurtz, M.E. "A Behavioral Profile of Physicians in Management Roles." In *The Physician in Management,* edited by Schenke, pp. 33–44. Fla.:
6. Schutz, W. *FIRO-B.* Palo Alto, Calif.: Consulting Psychologists Press, 1958.
7. Schutz, W. *FIRO: The Interpersonal Underworld.* Palo Alto, Calif.: Consulting Psychologists Press, 1966.
8. Stuart Atkins, Inc. *LIFO.* Beverly Hills, Calif.: Atkins, 1971.
9. Weick, K. *The Social Psychology of Organizing.* Reading, Mass.: Addison-Wesley Publishing Co., 1979.
10. Alderfer, C.P. "Boundary Relations and Organizational Diagnosis." In *Humanizing Organizational Behavior,* edited by L. Meltzer and F. Wickert. Springfield, Ill.: Thomas Publishers, 1976.
11. Merrill, M.J., and Moosbruker, J. "Building an Organizational Development Effort in a Teaching Hospital." In *Organizational Development in Health Care Organizations,* edited by N. Margulies and J. Adams, Mass.: pp. 75–104.
12. Lawrence, P., and Lorsch, J. *Organization and Environment.* Homewood, Ill.: Irwin Publishers, 1967.
13. Delbecq, A. "The Management of Decision Making within the Firm: Three Strategies for Three Types of Decision Making." *Academy of Management Journal* 10, no. 4 (December 1967): 329–39.
14. Delbecq, A., and Pierce, J. "Organization Structure, Individual Attitudes and Innovation." *Academy of Management Journal* 2, no. 1 (January 1977): 27–37.
15. Delbecq, A. "Effective Meeting Leadership." in *The Physician in Management,* edited by R. Schenke. Tampa, Fla.: American Academy of Medical Directors, 1980, pp. 203–27.
16. Van de Ven, A., and Delbecq, A. "The Effectiveness of Nominal Delphi and Interacting Group Decision Making Processes." *Academy of Management Journal* 17, no. 4 (1974): 605–21.
17. Delbecq, A., Van de Ven, A., and Gustofam, D. *Group Techniques for Program Planning: A Guide to Nominal Group and Delphi Processes.* Glenview, Ill.: Scott Foresman, 1974, pp. 124–37.

Clinic management teams: Integrators of professional service and environmental change

Susan Hoefflinger Taft
and
James A. Pelikan

Clinic management teams comprising an administrative director, a head nurse, and a physician manager are interdisciplinary management units in an ambulatory care setting of a large teaching hospital. This article reviews the development of these integrative teams and the factors critical to their success.

Health Care Manage Rev, 1990, 15(2), 67-79

Health care organizations are experiencing unprecedented amounts of change at unprecedented rates, and these forces are of great consequence for patient care and the health care disciplines. Hospitals must be both strong enough to withstand the strains of constant change and supple enough to bend as conditions dictate. They need to be both stable and flexible. One management structure in ambulatory care that responds to both of these imperatives is a collaborative multidisciplinary team called a clinic management team (CMT).

In the typical hospital, stability is maintained through sound fiscal and administrative processes and high-quality, continuous clinical performance by health care providers (physicians, nurses, therapists, and others). Flexibility is reflected in a hospital's responsiveness to its market and environment and through the updating of clinical knowledge by members of all the health professions. An ever-present challenge to the manager of a hospital seeking stability and flexibility is the need to integrate and balance the administrative and clinical components within the organization.[1]

Historically, the clinical component in hospitals (physicians) has taken precedence over the administrative component. However, changes that hospitals are currently undergoing tend to heighten the demands on the administrative component of the organization.[2] For example, one physician recently observed that his primary goal, which was to lower morbidity rates for a certain population of patients, had not received the attention he wanted to give it: "I'm too consumed with organizational and political issues all the time, which is not what I want to be doing."

ADVANTAGES OF CLINIC MANAGEMENT TEAMS

This article reports the results of efforts at Cleveland Metropolitan General Hospital to construct an organization in the ambulatory care area that is both stable and flexible and that promotes integration of clinical and administrative domains (see Figure 1). An ongoing tension between these domains is mediated by clinic

Susan Hoefflinger Taft, *Ph.D., is an Assistant Professor at Case Western Reserve University.*

James A. Pelikan, *M.A., is Associate Vice President of Ambulatory Prepaid Health Service Operations at Cleveland Metropolitan General Hospital.*

FIGURE 1

THE CLINIC MANAGEMENT TEAM (CMT) AS THE INTEGRATOR OF STABILITY AND FLEXIBILITY AND OF CLINICAL AND ADMINISTRATIVE COMPONENTS

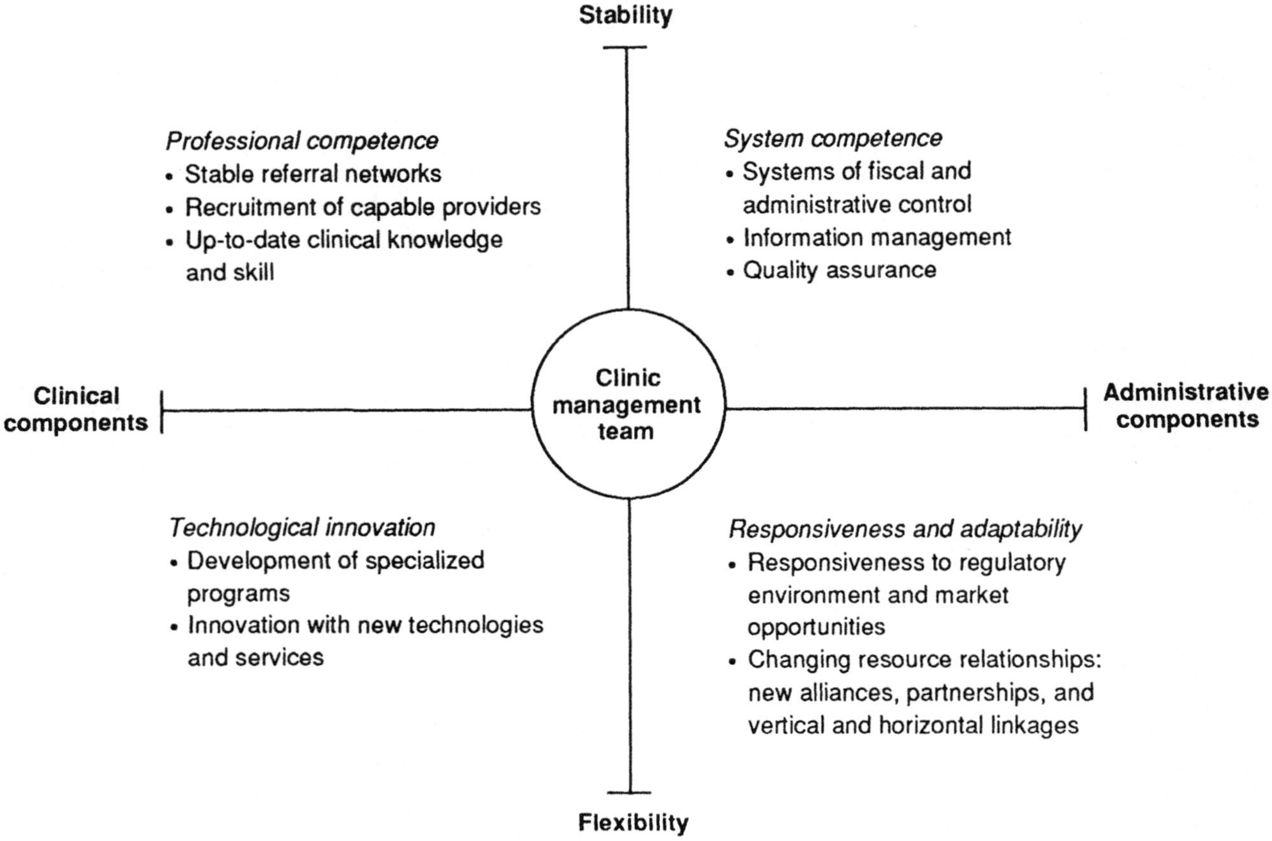

management teams—triadic structures composed of an administrative director, a head nurse, and a physician manager—within each of the specialty clinics. CMTs are critical in stabilizing administrative systems within the clinics (system competence) while modifying procedures to meet the demands of the regulatory environment (responsiveness and adaptability). They also manage programs for new treatments (technological innovation) while using methods to ensure quality in the clinical practice of all providers (professional competence).

In addition to their usefulness in integrating clinical and administrative cores, CMTs are of significance because of their interdisciplinary composition. A long but uneven history exists of interdisciplinary collaboration in the health care industry.[3,4] The ability of professional providers to work together effectively is increasingly important in hospitals. Professionals must provide services for patients with complex care needs, manage in the face of heightened competitive forces and economic constraints, and attend carefully to the quality of care rendered to patients. Yet true interdisciplinary collaboration remains uncommon.

Many organizations have an informal management process that integrates administrative, nursing, and medical perspectives, but few have put in place a formal management team mechanism that governs service delivery. The literature identifies, and the experience at Cleveland Metropolitan General Hospital confirms, that issues of interdisciplinary political parity, team and group development, and disciplinary self-reference—or *professional ethnocentrism*—lie at the heart of team potentials to succeed or fail as truly effective governing units.[3–7] The disciplines usually lack training in or appreciation of others' perspectives, and each discipline has its own professional culture. "The functioning of the group is constantly threatened by the discrepancies in members' expectations of each other and by the tendency for one disciplinary perspective to dominate the others."[3(p.87)] Furthermore, work groups, which go through developmental stages in order to reach high levels of functioning, are challenged by issues of membership turnover and status differences. However, these key issues can be addressed and certain design considerations can be helpful in developing and working with interdisciplinary teams.

CHARACTERISTICS OF CMT SITE

Cleveland Metropolitan General Hospital (Metro), a 721-bed acute care and rehabilitative institution, is a public hospital serving the needs of the Greater Cleveland area, including the medically indigent. Metro is a major teaching hospital affiliated with The Case Western Reserve University (CWRU) Medical School. It also runs its own nursing school and affiliates with a variety of other allied health programs. It employs 322 CWRU faculty members and 253 house staff. The ambulatory clinics receive approximately 398,000 patient visits annually from approximately 115,000 different individuals. The Metro medical center offers a full range of general health care services, but it is particularly known for its rehabilitation services, burn unit, and trauma center.

Managing a large urban teaching center such as Metro is a challenging and complicated undertaking. The size and the numbers of people to be managed are enormous, and inherent contradictions and conflicting pressures are associated with the pluralistic composition of its health workers: Groups, networks, and layers exist by specialties and functional units. There appear to be multiple missions and diverse expectations according to role or position, and there are so many decision-making centers that it is virtually impossible for any person or small group of people—even the top level of the organization—to consistently command the whole. Often, the multiple structures do not integrate fully, and there may be conflicting opinions and perceptions about information that has been circulated, decisions that have been made, or directions that are to be followed.[8] In addition, professional roles have diverse social, legal, and institutional sources of legitimacy, so reference points for professionals may be outside of the organization.

The challenge to Metro was to find ways to create organizational structures and processes that could weave Metro's natural diversity into the fabric of its overall management system.

The diversity inherent in this large, pluralistic setting makes the organization both ruggedly enduring and unwieldy. The challenge to Metro was to find ways to create organizational structures and processes that could weave Metro's natural diversity into the fabric of its overall management system. CMTs were developed to do just that.

Metro's ambulatory care area has 10 CMTs: outpatient surgery, pediatrics, medicine, family practice, obstetrics and gynecology, orthopedics, emergency medicine, psychiatry, dentistry, and the Maternal and Infant Care Project. Several other clinical areas—tuberculosis, dermatology, neurology, gastroenterology, and oral surgery—use an informal triadic structure but do not have formal CMTs.

INCEPTION OF CMTs

The need for clinic management teams arose from an earlier era in Metro's history when ambulatory care was peripheral to the primary focus of the institution, which was care of inpatients. Ambulatory services consistently received less attention. Outpatients were cared for by physicians and their house officers (and generally these professionals, too, valued ambulatory services less than they did care of the inpatient sick). A lack of adequate support systems tended to produce long waits for patients, confusion, inadequate coordination of ancillary services, and widespread frustration for providers and patients alike. Administrators tended to avoid the clinics, since so much needed fixing that some saw involvement in the clinics as a career liability. Accountability for ambulatory care was inadequate, and no one seemed to carry sufficient power to effect needed change. From this chaos a mandate for management approaches eventually emerged that would address clinic coordination, quality, efficiency, accountability, and integration of services.

The CMTs in ambulatory care were developed to address these problems and to fit within the structure and existing authority relationships of the larger organization. They did not stand alone; it was understood at the time CMTs were instituted that management innovations in any one area must have the structural support of the entire institution in order to be effective. CMTs needed to work within the context of an existing, though not entirely satisfactory, ambulatory system.

Structure

CMTs were constructed to follow departmental lines and to form a network of 10 management centers that directed clinic operations. As depicted in Figure 2, the structure instituted was an interdisciplinary matrix design, which gave members of each team equal and shared responsibility for their clinic.[9]

Each clinic team was composed of an administrative director, a head nurse, and a physician manager; several also had representation from key support personnel. The CMT members reported to their functional heads: the physician manager to a clinical department director, the administrative director to an administrative vice-president, and the head nurse to a nursing director. In addition, the CMT as a whole was under the authority of the associate vice-president for ambulatory services and of the physician clinical director for each of the specialty clinics. Members of the CMT carried equal authority and responsibility to manage the day-to-day operations of their respective clinics and to develop the

FIGURE 2

THE CLINIC MATRIX STRUCTURE

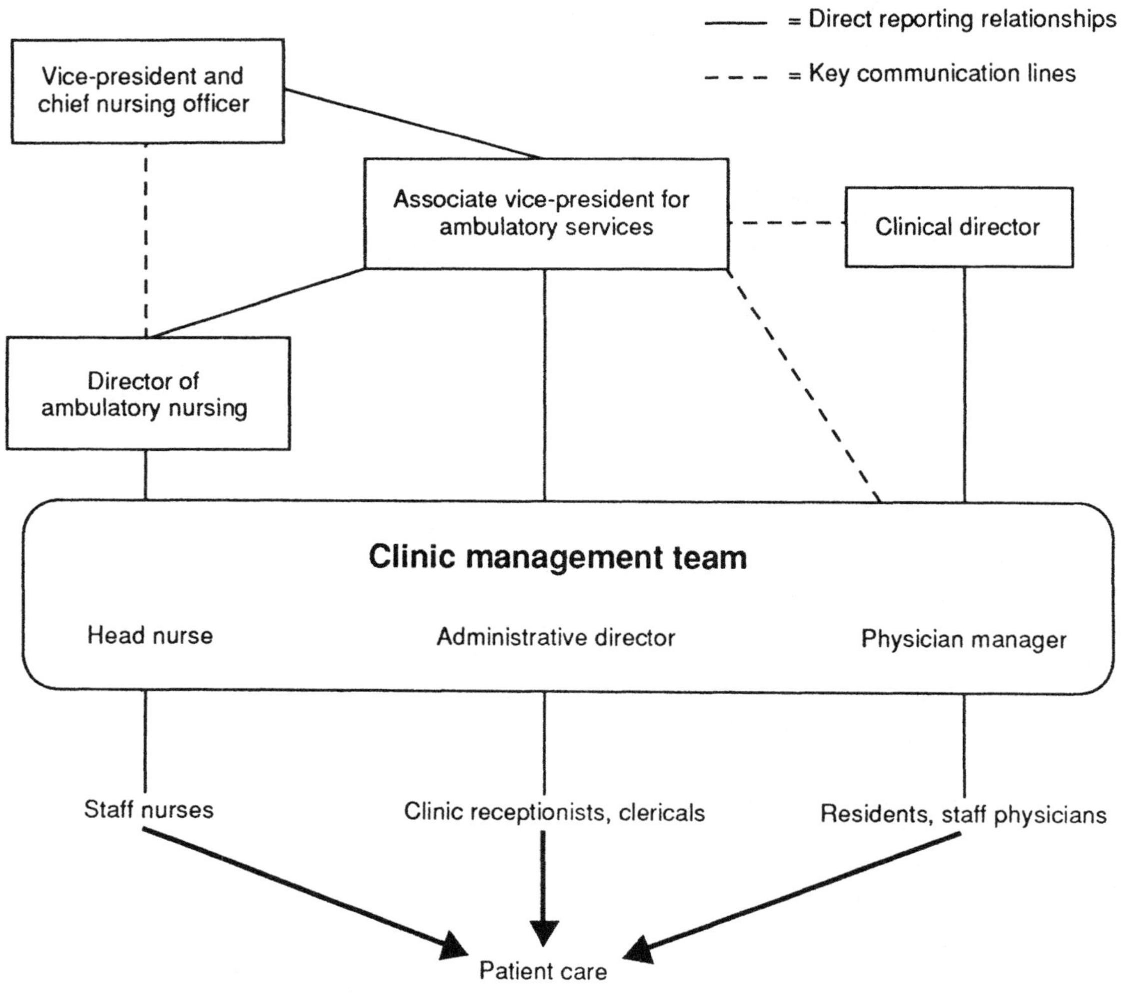

future plans and directions of the clinics.

CMT members were selected by the director of ambulatory nursing, the medical directors, and the associate vice-presidents. Their orientation and training was not formal; supervision, individual contacts, group meetings, and the distribution of information were the principal techniques used to develop the teams. More informal and formal training of these individuals could have been valuable.

Development

The CMTs, established out of necessity, developed and matured over time. At points in CMT history, organizational stakeholders were aware of the teams' development, and these individuals were involved when the situation required their support. The associate vice-president had identified key aspects of the ambulatory function and culture and set forth in concert with others to create a vision of how professionals could work together within a supportive structure. Continuity of vision was essential, since changes of this magnitude could not be mandated or adopted overnight. Natural events in the life cycle of the teaching hospital were used to consolidate support for the project. The endeavor required a hands-on administrator with organizational development skills who maintained the vision and was willing to take risks. Tenacity was needed to carry this champion of change through periods of lack of support and resistance and sustain this leader in managing a highly complex organization. Pockets of significant support developed at all levels of Metro and were critical for success.

The history of the development of the teams at Metro spanned 8 to 10 years and included the following phases:

- *Recognition and creation:* Recognizing a basic need to improve clinic services through an integrative approach to clinic management, the development of authority to make needed changes, and the creation of a framework that broke from traditional approaches.
- *Promotion:* Selling the idea to the clinic providers (the "troops") and a few key stakeholders; asking them to try it and telling them they will like it.
- *First success:* Getting a few small successes, celebrating them, sharing them with others, and continuing to develop the concept design.
- *Formalization:* Reaching out and getting initial formal approvals for the operating principles.
- *Incubation:* Continuing to work with the successes, developing people, getting resources, building systems and ideas, identifying common agendas, working with technical and support staff, and nurturing consensus.
- *Consolidation:* Using external demands (for example, regulations and patient needs) to solidify and institutionalize the innovation; the presence of the administrative directors coalesces the ideas.
- *Routinization:* Incorporating the concept and its operation into the routine management landscape.

These stages did not appear consistently across all clinics at the same time. The development needs varied considerably: One clinic might concentrate on promotion while another clinic pursued incubation and formalization was being addressed at executive levels. The image was of orchestration. All CMTs are now fully operating within the philosophy of CMTs, but their development needs still require regular attention.

Authority

Fully functioning CMTs were key decision-making bodies. Decisions made by the CMTs could result from system demands placed on them or in demands they placed on the system. In both cases, the boundary between the CMT and the larger system needed to be crossed regularly. In the former case, the CMT might address issues of facility design, fee structure, productivity, or information system design, for example. In the latter case, decisions about the appointment system or information processing could alter the approach taken by the entire hospital. Finally, decisions made by the CMTs contributed to the capacity of the specific clinic to function as an integrated whole and to meet external demands.

Much of this internal maintenance activity (decisions concerning staffing and scheduling, performance, modification of service delivery policies, or patient complaints, for example) was enhanced by the blending of three professional perspectives within a common framework. Prior to CMTs, no common framework existed with which to forge the diverse perspectives and objectives into a common unit. These internal maintenance activities made up the often overlooked "bread-and-butter" issues of design and operation in an ambulatory setting. When operations were under control within the clinic, the rest of the system could better respect the boundaries of the unit's operation and reduce the natural interference of the large bureaucracy, a major benefit for practice.

Several coordinating structures were of significance in making CMTs work. One such structure was the Ambulatory Medical Management Committee, which brought physician managers together to solve problems of common concern. Head nurses and administrative directors each met regularly to address discipline-specific issues. Several other ancillary services committees provided coordination and support.

A late addition to the management structure was the Clinic Business Office (CBO). The CBO staff worked with the support departments to develop systems that responded to the needs of the clinic management teams. They pulled together business systems such as registration information or billing, giving common direction and support to the clinic infrastructure.

One other advisory committee important to the CMTs was the Ambulatory Management Group, an interdisciplinary group of six individuals: the administrative vice-president for ambulatory care, two physicians, the director of ambulatory nursing, the director of the CBO, and one administrative director. This group sought to provide coherent direction for ambulatory care.

With the CMTs fully established, efficiency, accountability, sensitivity to patients, and coordination of patient care needs are considered routine at Metro, a significant change from the previous era.

The CMT structure and its various support bodies were designed to provide professionals with the operational focus and authority to generate direction for the clinics. CMTs ran the clinics by integrating the clinical and administrative components of the organization. Because the three professional groups of medicine, nursing, and administration shared the responsibility for clinic operations, all brought their groups' perspectives, values, goals, and technologies to the common task of providing patient services. With the CMTs fully established, efficiency, accountability, sensitivity to patients, and coordination of patient care needs are considered routine at Metro, a significant change from the previous era. When complaints arise, decision making is avoided, or excuses for problems are made, the CMTs are responsible—right at the source of clinic work.

Professional cultures

Members of professional disciplines all view the world around them from their own perspectives, a kind of professional myopia or ethnocentrism. Because of their self-referent view and their close working relationships with other disciplines, professionals have an ongoing need to negotiate and manage their expectations of other groups and those groups' expectations of them.

For example, members of health care disciplines (nurses, physicians, administrators, and therapists) all identify patient care as their overarching goal, but all have different perspectives on what patient care entails. That is, of course, what makes them interdependent: They have different knowledge and approaches to the care of patients. The typical hospital is a role-defined organization: Professional role boundaries are strong, and they are the basis for member identification and affiliation patterns. Each professional discipline has its own culture with its own core mission, technologies, values and norms, language, rituals, and symbols. These cultures have developed over the history of the professions.

Cultural differences by profession are very relevant to the dynamic functioning of clinic management teams. In Metro's CMTs, for example, the physicians, nurses, and administrators had differing perspectives on mission.

- *Physicians* defined their core missions as patient care, medical education, and research: Relative emphases on these activities varied, but usually medical education was stressed the most. When physicians spoke of "patient care," they generally meant diagnosis and treatment of disease. Medical education and research, once seen as a means to patient care, have become ends in themselves.
- *Nurses* defined their mission as patient care; in addition, they devoted significant attention to administrative and organizational activities. When nurses spoke of "patient care," they meant something different from what physicians meant. Nursing care was devoted in part to administering treatments to patients. In addition, their care activities addressed the integration of illness and treatment with the patient's life situation. The latter meant providing supportive services ranging from patient education to home care referrals.
- The *administrators'* mission was tied to organizational continuity. They were responsible for managing organizational stability and change, a highly diverse set of activities ranging from the management of systems

to the maintenance of physical facilities. When they spoke of their mission in "patient care," they meant providing the organizational context in which care could take place.

Differing professional activities, while all contributing to the core organizational mission of patient care, caused members of the CMTs to view clinic functioning from diverse perspectives. The members were, of course, complementary in their roles, but conflict over priorities was common.

Another area in which the professional cultures varied was in the social authority physicians carried relative to administrators or nurses, a result of the prestige of the profession of medicine and the tendency for medicine to attract to its ranks members from the upper and upper-middle social classes. Collectively, physicians were more homogeneous than were the other two professional groups (consider, for example, the great educational diversity among nurses), which further enhanced their influence within the system as a whole.

These and other differences among the professional cultures were manifested implicitly and explicitly in decision making across the institution. Differences in perspective would always be present and would always need to be managed. Because of the potential for differences to create misunderstanding and conflict, a formal structure that addressed clinic issues in an integrative manner was a constructive channel for the professional groups. The CMTs acted as such a vehicle.

Functions

The functions assumed by the CMTs derived jointly from the day-to-day patient care realities experienced by professionals and support personnel and from the management demands imposed by the external environment. Five predominant functions evolved: planning for the delivery of clinic services, ensuring quality, managing operations, maintaining system efficiencies, and directing the business and fiscal functions of ambulatory care.

In planning for the delivery of clinic services, CMT members maintained an understanding of their patient populations and the marketplace affecting their patient referral sources, and they explored new programs. They also conducted program reviews and monitored how service was delivered in their clinics. Quality assurance activities by CMT members were increasingly complex and encompassed a range of activities, such as developing and maintaining standards of care for each of the professional disciplines and ensuring coordination and continuity of patient services.

In managing operations, members developed and implemented policies and protocols, determined role behaviors, maintained communications within the clinic, and effected working relationships with ancillary and support departments. Their most important activities concerned patients: ensuring the delivery of effective and appropriate care, exploring and resolving patient problems or complaints, and matching the supply of services to patient demand.[10] Attention to quality care cut across all professional groups and levels in the organization, and CMTs addressed ways to more efficiently use supplies, equipment, and space, schedule personnel, and facilitate the flow of patients through the system from registration to service delivery.

Finally, CMT members directed certain business and fiscal functions. They provided data on patient demographic, financial, diagnostic, and service characteristics to support information needs and billing. They also monitored patient charges and fee structures. CMTs regularly provided input on institutional policies and procedures regarding these systems.

In all CMT functions, the clinical and administrative perspectives were constantly blended at the level where services were delivered, in the heart of clinic operations. The CMTs thus had the ability to influence the larger system. Teams also provided stability for the clinics by shielding the providers from too much or too rapid change. At the same time, because the degree of change Metro was undergoing required much flexibility, CMTs sorted and instituted change consonant with their clinical operations. The great strength of the CMT was its ability to integrate multiple forces, from the environment and from the organization, with service delivery.

PRINCIPLES OF ORGANIZATION

Several key management principles were used in developing the CMTs. Given the differing perspectives and the powerful status differences among members of the CMT, these principles served to guide the teams in their organization and governance.

A head nurse of one of the clinics described the CMT in her area as a "braid of hair" whose whole was comprised of three distinct parts. The CMT members maintained a sense of ownership for their domain by carrying shared responsibility and authority for the clinic. The decentralized location of the teams in the heart of the clinic activities, where patients were daily seen and cared for, served to pull together the clinical and administrative needs of the organization. The interdisciplinary clinic team blended the professional groups and their functional hierarchies with service delivery through the matrix structure, developing a common frame of reference for task accomplishment.

Early in the development of the CMTs, a few guiding rules were developed to help legitimize the team and to support a team philosophy: teams would meet regularly and conduct business regardless of whether a member was missing; concise minutes were kept and were used to inform all three discipline leaders; responsibility for minute taking was rotated among the members; and an agenda was circulated before members met. Leadership was expected to be a shared responsibility; some CMTs created a rotating facilitator role. Members of all three professional groups were expected to use the CMT as a vehicle for clinic problem solving. Besides aiding the stability and legitimacy of the teams, these rules served to support equality among the members on the team. Promoting interdisciplinary political parity through the design of the CMTs was important for team effectiveness.

Additional dimensions that were considered in the design and development of the CMTs were

- the degree of formal integration of CMT structure into the organizational chart;
- the level of the CMT in the organization [service (local) or policy (system) level];
- the degree of shared or individual control of budgets;
- the degree of congruence of managerial role with existing organizational roles and reward systems;
- the extent to which shared governance or use of a higher authority prevailed; and
- the areas in which CMT authority prevailed over that of a single professional group.

All these dimensions were of critical importance to the success of the CMT at Metro, and all have evolved from their original points on a spectrum. Metro's experience on these dimensions has varied. For example, 10 years after their inception, CMTs were finally reflected in the hospital organizational chart, and this was largely a result of externally imposed demands (from the Joint Commission on Accreditation of Healthcare Organizations or state programs) for clarifying hospital structure.

The CMT's influence in the organization, while largely service-focused, was enhanced through mechanisms that enabled CMT representatives to affect policy. Budgets at Metro were controlled through the individual disciplines, an arrangement rooted in traditional structures but inconsistent with the CMT philosophy. However, support existed for sharing information and decisions across budgets, thereby promoting some measure of integrated budgetary outcomes.

The degree of congruence of managerial role with the established organizational reward systems varied by discipline, but in general the fit was incomplete. More recognition was given to the importance of management in the roles of the head nurse and the administrative director than in the role of the physician manager; the physician manager role was almost totally outside the existing academic medicine reward system, a key factor at Metro in the potential for success with CMTs.

Members of all three professional groups were expected to use the CMT as a vehicle for clinic problem solving.

Finally, Metro's experience with authority systems was largely one of shared governance with CMTs. Higher authority was occasionally appealed to—or at times inserted itself—into CMT activity in an unpredictable or unsolicited manner. However, the team's authority tended to prevail, particularly in areas where overlapping of function occurred, such as with patient flow, scheduling, or information gathering. The organization of teams on these dimensions, evolved over time. The degree of acceptance of CMTs by the medical clinical directors; the strength of commitment by head nurses, physician managers, and administrative directors; and the continuity of membership in CMTs determined how well CMTs fared within the different clinics. The above dimensions have remained as core design considerations in the dynamic management of CMTs.

TRAINING AND DEVELOPMENT

Clinic management teams, once instituted, did not necessarily develop and thrive on their own. Because they were in some ways counternormative (egalitarian and service-driven rather than profession-driven), they needed to be tended. The head of ambulatory care approached the care and development of CMTs like a gardener: He cultivated and encouraged them with a commitment to their long-term growth. The CMTs varied extensively in their stages of development, strengths, problems, and potential. Direction for working with the CMTs flowed from the recognition of differences among them and of their developmental needs and from acceptance of their differences, none of which carried judgments of "good" or "bad." Issues of group development, political parity (supporting equality on the teams), and professional ethnocentrism were in constant play on the CMTs.

Attention to the development of CMTs required an understanding of the normal dynamics of group development. Metro CMTs evidenced a range of developmental stages. New teams (with new members or membership turnover) addressed issues of inclusion and mission and team management role acquisition. In young groups, sensitive power and control dynamics and a jockeying for members' authority positions appeared and then reemerged episodically over the lifetime of the group. An indication of a mature and well-functioning group was the team's ability to recognize, use, and appreciate differences and strengths. The sign of a dying group was the presence of fracturing, dissolution into withdrawal, avoidance, or lack of investment.

Outside support

The support of team development required skillful management attention from the outside. Systems of support were needed from team members' colleagues or supervisors to assist in working out the development needs as they occurred. Power and status concerns and cross-professional cultural understanding frequently indicated the presence of development needs. In addition, while working with individual teams, the vice-president of ambulatory care promoted equity throughout Metro (through team responsibilities, titles, and pay, for example) and the development of a larger sense of teamwork that spanned the organization.

Management training

The physician manager and the head nurse of the clinic teams were unlikely to have had much educational preparation or professional development for management. In all except a few cases, they were not prepared for management but had been practicing as good clinicians when they were asked to move into management responsibilities (a full-time job for nurses but only a part-time activity for physicians).

Physicians and nurses came from work backgrounds in which the identification of illness and treatment of that illness proceeded according to many well-established and relatively delineated protocols.[11] Dealing with high degrees of uncertainty and ambiguity was not typical of the clinical task. However, management activities were a different matter, and the development of a managerial orientation required some investment in training and learning. A common comment from a physician was, "I hate those meetings! We sit around and talk and talk and nothing ever gets done!" In another case, a physician manager commented indignantly that a responsibility he had delegated to another physician had been poorly managed; he focused on the failure of the other physician, unable to see his own responsibility in not having developed that person to assume such responsibilities. Nurses needed to learn ways of approaching problems that used creative thinking and nonhierarchical forms of authority.

The developmental need among physicians and nurses was apparent: learning how to change their frame of reference from completing tasks to managing processes. Therefore, part of the development of CMTs involved the training of physicians and nurses in group, management, and organizational skills. On the other hand, the administrative directors were prepared in these areas, but they needed to enhance their understanding of the basics of clinical care.

Head nurses and management

For the head nurse, the CMT both created a forum for resolution of contradictions in power and highlighted authority dilemmas. No role involved more control of daily clinic operations than that of the head nurse. Yet the head nurse's status as a decision maker and exerciser of power was often ambiguous or indirect. Characteristics of the health care system—such as gender prejudice, weighty bureaucratic hierarchy, and power dynamics among the professions—created the incommensurate relationship between head nurse responsibility and authority.

With the introduction of CMTs, some head nurses saw the formalization of decision making as a threat to the power bases they had informally established. Most others saw it as a tool to develop the effective system they needed for managing the clinic. The CMT structure ensured the participation of administrative and medical personnel in clinic decisions, which served to bolster the authority of resulting decisions; it was the place where communication and accountability met.

The CMT thus provided a credible infrastructure for the head nurse managerial activity. Clinic nurses, when they were able to see that the CMT actually addressed issues affecting practice and service, were also supported through the CMT.

Cross-disciplinary education

A powerful learning opportunity that evolved informally on several CMTs, particularly those mature in their stage of development, was the cross-disciplinary education that members offered each other. In several cases, administrative directors gave informal training on financial management to nurse and physician members, a head nurse reviewed clinic charges with an administrator and described why various diagnostic categories were inappropriately priced, and a physician gave a review of a clinical matter relevant to clinic policy. These episodic sessions allowed for a cross-fertilization of expertise. They enhanced the general management skills of all three members.

Physicians and management

Support for management responsibility was slower to come from the physician group than from the other two groups. Numerous professional culture factors discouraged physician management: Clinical expertise has been and is the core skill from which all professional rewards derive, not management; the physician's professional norm of high autonomy works against the presence of interdependence in traditional management; and clear feedback from work is expected (patients get better or worse), whereas results are rarely immediate in administrative tasks. Also, physicians receive little or no management education, so they are unlikely to seek experiences in which they feel minimally competent; management time is rarely paid at the levels physicians have come to expect; and colleagues are unlikely to see value in management activities.

In addition, organizational factors at Metro made physicians reluctant to take on management responsibility. In this teaching center, management was usually added to the existing demands for clinical care, research, and medical education, so role overload was common. Little or no financial remuneration followed from management effort, and in fact, management time demands were likely to cut into clinical care activities through which income was generated. Middle-level physician managers could receive minimal support from their department chiefs when integrated decisions on a CMT ran against medical interests. Therefore, both the physician culture and the organizational arrangements provided disincentives for physician manager participation, particularly at the middle-management level.

Support for management responsibility was slower to come from the physician group than from the other two groups.

Over time, if physician management proves to be a viable need in the industry, change must occur in how management activity is viewed within the physician ranks and in how structures and role expectations are established within the organization. However, the problematic state of physician management roles was not resolved entirely by the CMT structure. This issue at Metro and at large teaching hospitals represents one of the more significant challenges of health care organization and policy.

What success was realized at Metro with the physician manager role resulted from the associate vice-president's actions. A key aspect of the associate vice-president's role was to maintain solid relations with the medical directors, and the building of these relationships was with design. Resolving the questions of the physician managerial role was recognized to rest outside of the scope of authority of the associate vice-president, yet he had the responsibility to make the ambulatory service system work, and success depended, in part, on consistent physician management. As a result, the associate vice-president's efforts were aimed at incremental actions to create structure, to legitimate the CMTs, to highlight success, to create a sense of continuity and stability, and to encourage participation. To the degree that this was successful, each medical director wanted to see his or her clinics as having a physician manager who participated in the CMT. This was all that was necessary to start the process.

The next steps involved action through the physician manager group, talks between the associate vice-president and physician managers, and most important, the developing interdependence among CMT members. Also, as the physician manager role affected the organization, the role was increasingly legitimated. Attitude change followed the role change.

Commitment and time are required to form such a system. Care must be taken as to the readiness of introducing elements. Eight years passed before a complete CMT organizational chart could be introduced at Metro, but to do so earlier could have pushed the wrong buttons and sounded an alarm. By the time the CMT officially appeared on the organizational chart, it reflected actual experience at getting things done and not a symbolic power maneuver.

The CMT experience helped members of all three professional disciplines to move somewhat beyond a preoccupation with their own discipline and toward a shared responsibility and sense of ownership for the clinical area. While their primary group affiliation remained with their professional specialty, they also expanded their identification with the clinic. In this way, CMT experience enhanced organizational affiliation and loyalty.

CHARACTERISTICS OF HEALTHY CMTs

Clinic management teams that enjoyed a vital, productive esprit de corps tended to be marked by commitment to the team concept from all three of their core members and from the three discipline heads. Lack of involvement from just one member was sufficient to destabilize the three-legged stool. The team members' professional leaders—the administrative head of ambulatory care, the ambulatory nursing director, and the clinical chief—were all background supporters who could either lend stability and flexibility or impede the CMT equation. Several other characteristics marked mature CMT functioning.

Dialogue

The clinic teams were powerful information-processing units, pulling as they did from the information networks of three professional groups and from the specifics of service operations. Regularly scheduled CMT meetings brought the members of the disciplines into face-to-face contact. Dialogue on teams was characterized by mutual, reciprocal, shared inquiry and growth and was central to healthy team functioning.[12] Dialogue also served to mediate the cultural pluralism of the different professional reference groups.

Role suspension

Cross-group dialogue between professional disciplines could either increase understanding or evoke interrole stereotyping. In relatively large gatherings in particular, positional bargaining or political posturing were common between groups. The small CMTs tended to discourage that type of posturing. Members were more free to be themselves rather than solely representatives of large groups, although they did also represent the interests of their colleagues.

The appearance of this greater flexibility was referred to as role suspension, the ability to allow temporary diminution of role identification and strict norms of interrole interaction. Role suspension allowed the prescriptive and sometimes inhibiting norms of the role-bound organization to be temporarily lifted. While roles are central to human organization, form a well-established structure for service delivery, and are essential for safeguarding human life in a hospital, they can also create rigidities and inhibit innovation. Role suspension at Metro allowed new information and new behaviors into relationships, increasing the potential for adaptability and creativity. It was observed to be a catalyst in professional group interrole behavior (for example, among nurse, physician, administrator) and between organizational levels (for example, between leader and subordinates in which the leader let go of the persona of authority). It promoted positive interactions on teams.

Reframing according to multiple perspectives

With the complexity of today's health care environment, a variety of interests constantly compete. Rarely is one point of view or course of action noncontroversial. Therefore, a necessary skill in clinic management at Metro was the ability to hold two or more points of view at the same time and to entertain them equally in one's thinking. The need for this ability was great because the many different groups, goals and subgoals, sources of loyalty, and competing values required members of the professional groups to constantly shift perspective, often experiencing conflict in the process. For example, members of the CMTs needed to maintain their professional perspectives while also directing clinic operations with a multidisciplinary perspective. The ability to think with complexity, to repeatedly reframe their perspective, and to hold multiple points of view enabled CMT members to respond to issues with maximum comprehensiveness and creativity. Beyond the CMT, leadership within the hospital in general required the development of skill in managing complexity.

These characteristic skills of healthy CMTs are not inclusive of all factors associated with their success. The characteristics that were identified above and the influence of systemic factors described earlier were found to be important to the effectiveness of teams. Teams that had developed a high level of maturity tended to successfully resolve issues of major interdisciplinary political parity and professional ethnocentrism.

CMTs AND THE FUTURE IN AMBULATORY CARE

Does the success of clinic management teams at Cleveland Metropolitan General Hospital bear any relevance for other health care organizations? Is this philosophy potentially useful to other ambulatory care—or even inpatient—operations? The answer is both yes and no.

The turbulent environment in which hospitals must function creates continuous inputs for those organizations. Hospital boundaries are increasingly open. Change from the environment is received, interpreted, and translated internally into administrative responses. The rising dependency of hospitals on the skills of their leaders and administrators is altering the traditional power balance between physicians and administrators. It will continue to be essential, and increasingly difficult, for hospitals to balance the role demands, perspectives, and power of the clinical and the administrative components of the organization. CMTs, if given the resources and authority to deliberate, plan, decide, and act, can serve as a fulcrum—a point of equilibrium—between these components.

Resource scarcity, of increasing relevance to the health care environment, demands constant vigilance in moving away from inefficiencies and fragmentation in health services. At the service level of the organization, CMTs can be highly sensitive to the use and abuse of resources, allocation of personnel, and integration of parts necessary to provide responsive service to patients. They can provide some counterbalance to the self-serving actions or parochial views of individual professional groups without undermining a spirit of professionalism and excellence.

Forces for change must be balanced by the twin force of stability. Hospital continuity requires a high degree of stability, for without it change can be destructive. The CMT can buffer the operating core of professionals from the turbulent environment while encouraging and supporting patient care.[13] It is an optimum structure for channeling processes of change while maintaining flexibility and stability.

The traditional hospital has been highly stratified and role-bound and its internal groups have been self-interested. It was also likely to have been highly centralized for all nonphysician employees. The dynamic environment now demands a more flexible structure from hospitals. Clinic management teams are a potential antidote to rigidity and role-boundedness because they do not reinforce rigid hierarchies, they encourage lateral interdisciplinary integration, and they decentralize and share authority. Multidisciplinary involvement is preferred over single-discipline dominance and quality patient services remain the core focus of the CMT.

Ambulatory care must build its own organizational design based on its task, which is fundamentally different from the task of inpatient care. Organizational structure is a key to this design. The characteristics of CMTs make them potentially useful for large, complex, internally differentiated hospitals, but these characteristics may also make CMTs quite unwelcome in settings where traditional norms prevail. Teaching centers in particular, arguably perhaps the best candidates for CMTs, may be so tied to traditional role behaviors that they are not congruent with the CMT philosophy. Philosophical support for the spirit as well as the function of the team must parallel its adoption.

As professionals such as nurses and physicians, in concert with administrators, increasingly take responsibility for management of hospitals, they will focus beyond the boundaries of their clinical domain. A sense of organizational affiliation will be heightened with this responsibility. Clinic teams help to expand system-level involvement across these two groups. Physicians and nurses of the future need opportunities to develop management expertise during their professional education and socialization processes.

CMTs may also serve as important contexts for educating health professionals about interdisciplinary collaboration that moves through clinical work—patient care—and on into management of the structures and processes that create the work context. Models of effective interdisciplinary work at this level are few, and the CMT model may be one source of inspiration for future hospital leaders.

REFERENCES

1. Daft, R.L. "A Dual Core Model of Organizational Innovation." *Academy of Management Journal* 21 (1978): 193–210.
2. Jones, K.R., and Sloate, S.G. "Academic Health Center Hospitals: Alternative Responses to Financial Stress." *Health Care Management Review* 12, no. 3 (1987): 83–89.
3. Kaluzny, A.D. "Design and Management of Discipli-

nary and Interdisciplinary Groups in Health Services: Review and Critique." *Medical Care Review* 42, no. 1 (1985): 77–112.

4. Temkin-Greener, H. "Interprofessional Perspectives on Teamwork in Healthcare: A Case Study." *Milbank Memorial Fund Quarterly: Health and Society* 61, no. 4 (1983): 641–58.
5. Bettner, M. "Physicians and Administrators: Inducing Collaboration." *Hospital and Health Services Administration* 32, no. 2 (1987): 151–69.
6. Mottaz, C.J. "Work Satisfaction among Hospital Nurses." *Hospital and Health Services Administration* 33, no. 1 (1988): 57–74.
7. Simendinger, E.A., and Pasmore, W. "Developing Partnerships between Physicians and Healthcare Executives." *Hospital and Health Services Administration* 29, no. 6 (1984): 21–35.
8. Aluise, J.J., Bogdewic, S.P., and McLaughlin, C.P. "Organizational Development in Academic Medicine: An Educational Approach." *Health Care Management Review* 10, no. 1 (1985): 37–43.
9. Neuhauser, D. "The Hospital as a Matrix Organization." *Hospital Administration* 17 (1972): 8–25.
10. Antle, D.W., and Reid, R.A. "Managing Service Capacity in an Ambulatory Care Clinic." *Hospital and Health Services Administration* 33, no. 2 (1988): 201–11.
11. Gill, S.L. "Can Doctors and Administrators Work Together?" *Physician Executive* 13, no. 5 (1987): 11–16.
12. Hazen, M.A. "Learning How to Learn: An Experiment in Dialogue." *The Organizational Behavior Teaching Review* 12, no. 2 (1987–88): 72–85.
13. Mintzberg, H. *The Structuring of Organizations*. Englewood Cliffs, N.J.: Prentice Hall, 1979.

An integrated inpatient management model

Frederick A. Creighton,
Annette M. Bernard,
and
Laurence F. McMahon, Jr.

The academic health center has emerged as the cornerstone of the American health care system. To assess the vulnerability of the academic medical center to the new competitive forces that exist today, a prototype project has been developed that attempts to address the issue of competition in clinical activity, while at the same time enhancing the academic health center's education and research roles.

Health Care Manage Rev, 1990, 15(1), 61–70

The academic health center, consisting of a medical school and its teaching hospital, has emerged as the cornerstone of the American health care system. This central role has developed due to the academic health center's unique responsibilities and accomplishments. During the same period in which academic health centers emerged as the predominant focus for education, research, and health care delivery, we have witnessed a marked increase in medical care expenditures. Between 1973 and 1983, medical care expenditures increased at an average annual rate of 13.1% in the United States.[1] Additionally, the percentage of the gross national product devoted to medical care increased from 6% in 1965 to 10.7% in 1985.[2] This marked increase in medical care expenditures has altered the health care environment, increasing its competitiveness and placing particular pressure on the academic health center.

To assess the vulnerability of the academic medical center to the new competitive forces, one must evaluate its sources of financial support. In a recent report, Ebert and Brown noted the marked increase in financial support derived from medical service plans. They note, "The most striking change has been the increase in the proportion of funds coming from medical school activities, which in large part represents the increase in medical practice plans on a fee-for-service basis."[3] Given the increased reliance on patient care dollars to meet its diverse goals, society's increased emphasis on cost-effective care, and competition for the patient care dollar, it is clear that the academic health center has entered a new phase in its continuing struggle for survival.

At the University of Michigan Medical Center in Ann Arbor, Michigan, the authors have developed a prototype project that attempts to address the issue of com-

Frederick A. Creighton, *M.H.A., is Chief Operating Officer of the Department of Medicine at Case Western Reserve University in Cleveland, Ohio.*

Annette M. Bernard, *M.D., is Medical Director of the Integrated Inpatient Management Model in the Department of Internal Medicine at the University of Michigan in Ann Arbor, Michigan.*

Laurence F. McMahon, Jr., *M.D., M.P.H., is Chief of the General Medicine Division of the Department of Internal Medicine at the University of Michigan in Ann Arbor, Michigan.*

The study on which this article was based was supported in part by the John A. Hartford Foundation, Inc. The authors thank Patricia Barry, R.N., M.B.A., for her assistance with the research for this study; Wilbur B. Pitinger, M.A., for research and editorial assistance; and Cynthia Kaye, for assistance with manuscript preparation.

petition in clinical activity while at the same time enhancing the academic medical center's education and research roles. The title of this project is the Integrated Inpatient Management Model (IIMM). This title serves to highlight three key features of the project: integration, focus on inpatient care, and management. First, patient care requires the interaction of a diverse group of health care professionals. For academic health centers to remain competitive, the unique expertise of these diverse professionals must be utilized in the care of defined types of patients in an efficient and effective manner. The IIMM integrates the activity of these professionals, with their focus being the care of individual patients. The second feature of this project is its focus on inpatient care. It is clear in reviewing medical care expenditures that the hospital remains the focal point for the treatment of most serious illnesses and, therefore, for most expenditures. The hospital has also been the focus for most of the education of medical students and resident physicians. The IIMM focuses on the central patient care locus of the academic medical center: the inpatient unit or ward. The third key feature in the project's title is management. Whereas the term management is usually restricted to the administrative functions of an institution, in our model the term management has a much broader definition; it refers to not only the organization of ancillary and support services of a hospital (the traditional administrative functions), but also the management of patient care, traditionally the province of physicians and nurses.

Given the integrated nature of this project, its scope and impact cross many traditional professional and administrative boundaries. For example, the model provides the opportunity to test

1. the appropriateness of the medical diagnostic and therapeutic plan and the quality of care delivered by physicians and nurses to defined groups of patients;
2. traditional management practices and organizational relationships; and
3. areas of education traditionally underemphasized in the academic health center, such as quality assurance (QA) and the costs of care.

The IIMM attempts to address a number of important clinical and administrative problems facing academic medical centers.

THE ADMINISTRATIVE COMPONENT

Although this project emphasizes the integration of physicians, nurses and administration in the delivery of patient care, in this article we will concentrate on the administrative component. Throughout the article, reference will be made to some of the unique medical and nursing components of the IIMM as they relate to the administrative component.

Historically, hospitals have been organized in a manner that supported the cost-based reimbursement system. This traditional system of reimbursing hospitals for the allowable cost of the services they provided supported the localization of management responsibility at the level of the hospital's revenue and cost centers (e.g., laboratory and dietary).[4] At the same time, hospitals organized their financial information at the level of these same revenue and cost centers.

Resource utilization information at the cost center level was obscured by the hospital's accounting system, designed to load costs into those centers best reimbursed by third party payers. While this approach to organization and information reporting might have been a reasonable method for measuring the *relative* revenue and expenses associated with the hospital, it did not allow apportionment of true resource utilization to the *individual* patient. As a result, the incentive to identify the locus of professional responsibility for the costs associated with managing a patient did not exist.

As will become clear in this article, the IIMM supports a set of unique organizational relationships and information systems that shift the focus of both clinical and administrative responsibility from the traditional cost center to the patient on the medical inpatient ward.

A HISTORICAL PERSPECTIVE

The problems that have resulted from the traditional approach of hospital organization and information reporting are significant. For example, this approach typically excluded the physician from direct integration into the hospital's organizational structure (see Figure 1). This traditional organization structure resulted in the exclusion of the members of the primary decision-making group (i.e., physicians) from direct responsibility and accountability over their clinical management decisions. As a result, the expenses directly associated with the patient care decisions of physicians became the responsibility of central hospital administration, which had little understanding of the nature of the expenses and limited success in exercising containment or control over them. Furthermore, the exclusion of physicians from the hospital's organizational structure minimized their involvement in many administrative decisions that directly affected many of their patients.

In addition to the absence of direct physician input

FIGURE 1

TRADITIONAL HOSPITAL ORGANIZATIONAL CHART

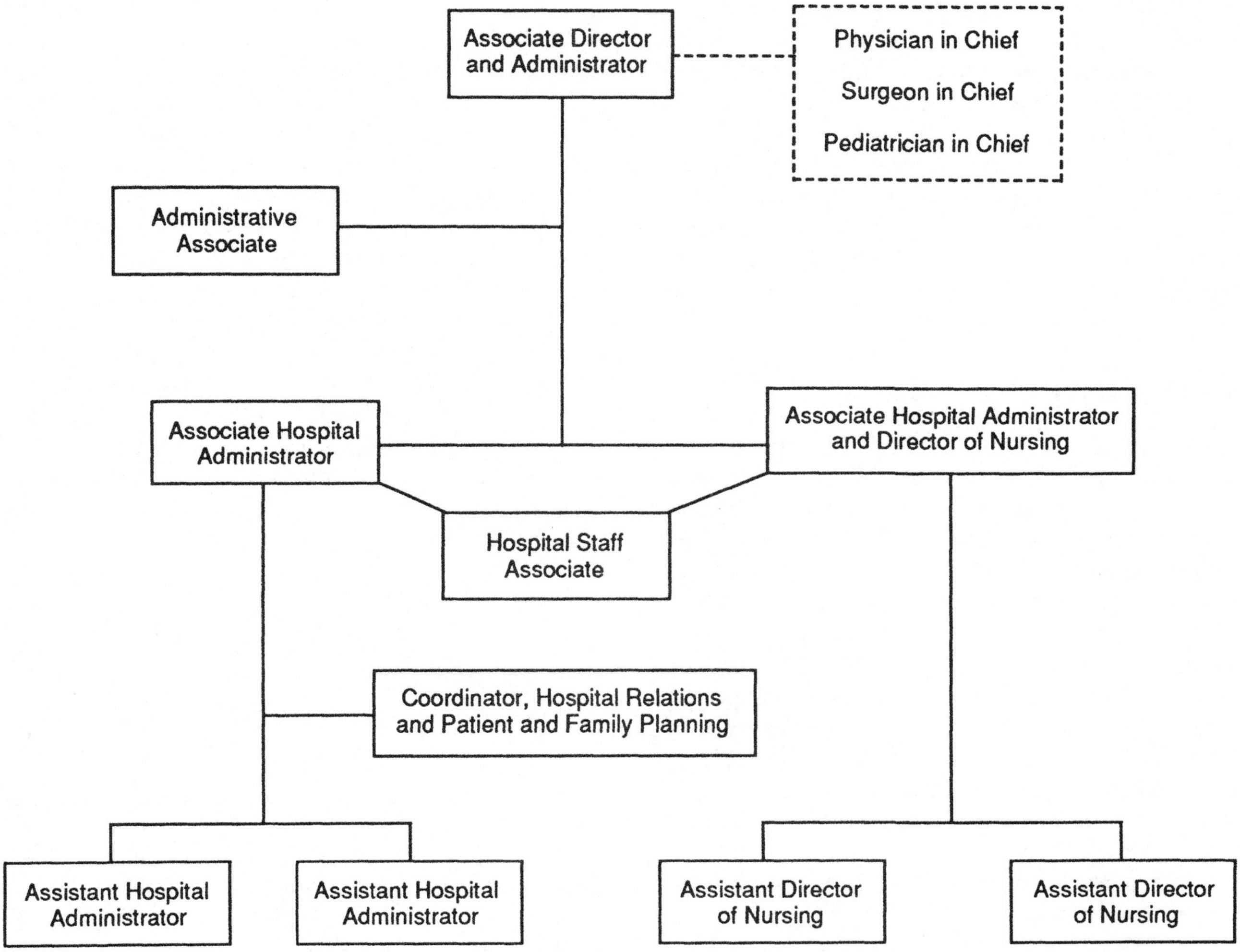

from the traditional model of hospital organization, other patient care providers, such as nurses, were organized as an independent entity, and their services were included in the hospital budget per diem. As the organization of the physicians did, this method of organization compromised the ability for nurses to address patient-specific practice problems, cost control, or financial accountability.

In an effort to decentralize the operating responsibility and financial accountability associated with the management of patient care, Johns Hopkins University Hospital introduced a decentralized management system that shifted this resource responsibility from the corporate to the clinical department level.[5]

This reorganization of the traditional hospital administrative structure at Johns Hopkins disaggregated the hospital into a number of specialty hospitals (i.e., clinical departments) referred to as functional units. Under this approach, a triumvirate of individuals function as the management team for each functional unit. A physician chief (who is also the chairperson of the respective department), a nurse director, and an administrator comprise the team, which is responsible for the direct costs associated with the operation of the unit. Indirect costs are allocated to each functional unit, and ancillary support service levels are maintained under the competitive pressure of an outside-purchase option. While the Hopkins' model was certainly a step toward full decentralization, in practice it appears to have created a number of small hospitals with many of the same organizational constraints as the parent institution.

Our approach to the reorganization of the hospital's administrative functions was to develop a model of hospital organization markedly different from both the traditional hospital organization and the incremental decentralization attempted at institutions like Johns Hopkins. As this article will detail, this is achieved by the further decentralization of operating responsibility from the departmental to the inpatient bed unit level. It will become evident that this fundamental repositioning of clinical and managerial decision making is critical to the practice of efficient and effective health care service delivery.

THE ADMINISTRATIVE APPROACH

The immediate challenge at The University of Michigan Medical Center, as well as at other academic health centers, was to reflect both clinical and managerial information accurately and in a way that would distinctly separate the fiduciary and operational responsibility of administration from those of the physician. A second challenge was to define an organizational structure that would facilitate the identification and assignment of appropriate patient management responsibilities and the associated accountability to both administrators and physicians. A third challenge was to evaluate the decision-making processes of each group; evaluate the clinical, operational, and financial implications of the group's decisions; and use this information appropriately to modify current and future patient management.

To meet these challenges, it was apparent that both types of variation in the patient management process, clinical (effectiveness) and administrative (efficiency), would need to be addressed. The information systems that have been developed for this model provide a level of management report specificity that supports a standards-based review of current patterns of medical practice, case mix, and support service efficiencies very early in the patient care process.

ORGANIZATIONAL STRUCTURE

The organizational framework supporting the IIMM has moved to a clinician manager–based interdisciplinary team that directs clinical and managerial decision making at the inpatient unit level (see Figure 2). Overall, clearly defined reporting lines for all clinical and administrative personnel directly associated with the project's inpatient units terminate with the clinical department chairperson.

The first tier of the organizational structure below that of the department chairperson incorporates positions that oversee the activities of the three disciplines involved in patient care on the clinical units. The administrative, physician, and nursing components are fully integrated at this level of the organization, in direct contrast to the more autonomous approach of the traditional hospital organizational model. This group of supervisors functions as a liaison between the department chairperson and the individuals based at the unit level. Changes in operational policy that may result from the decisions made by the unit-level interdisciplinary team are communicated by the individuals in this liaison group to other affected departments.

The inpatient unit level of the organizational structure represents what functionally is the clinician manager–based interdisciplinary team. It is this interdisciplinary group, comprising individuals representing services directly involved in the care and treatment of the patient, that identifies, analyzes, and decides on patient management options and operational needs. In addition, it is with this unit-level team that the accountability for operational decisions resides. This interdisciplinary team is directed by a clinician manager, who is a faculty physician with clinical expertise applicable to the medical subspecialty units involved in this management effort.

Fundamental repositioning of clinical and managerial decision making is critical to the practice of efficient and effective health care service delivery.

Within this project there exists a clinical manager for both the cardiology and the general medicine specialty units. These individuals, in conjunction with the project's clinical director, review the physician-specific diagnostic workup and therapy of the patients on each unit, making use of the project's clinically-based management information system to identify physician-specific variance in practice styles (see Figure 3). Moreover, the clinician manager interacts directly with the attending staff and house officers three times a week for the purpose of discussing concurrent, patient-specific

FIGURE 2

INTEGRATED INPATIENT MANAGEMENT MODEL (IIMM) ORGANIZATIONAL CHART

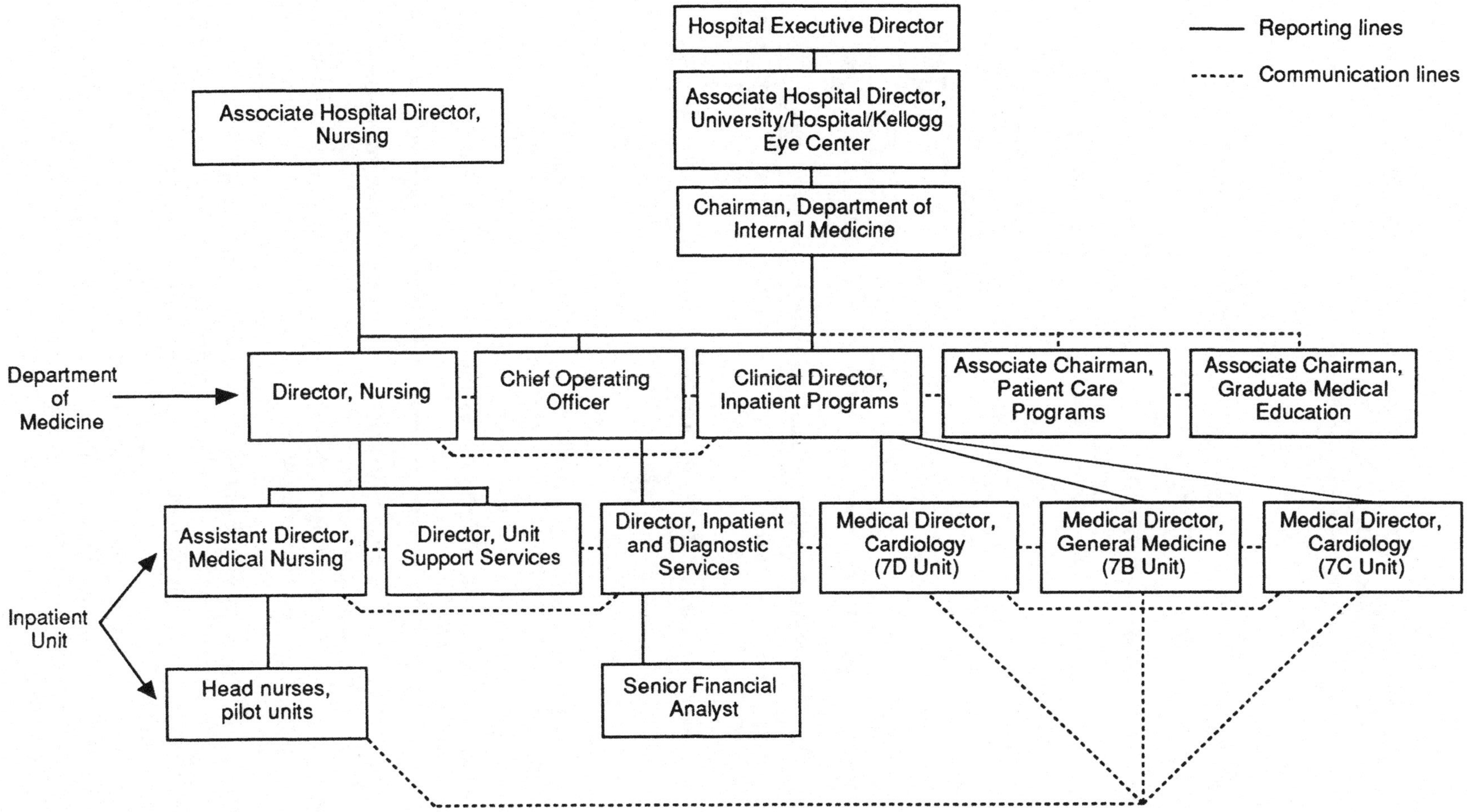

Reprinted with permission from McMahon, L.F., et al. "The Integrated Inpatient Management Model: A New Approach to Clinical Practice." *Annals of Internal Medicine* 3 (1989): 318–26.

FIGURE 3

THE INTEGRATED INPATIENT MANAGEMENT MODEL (IIMM) CONCURRENT EXCEPTION REPORT (DEPARTMENT OF INTERNAL MEDICINE) FOR PATIENT JANE DOE

Service	Attending Physician	Date
Coronary	1466	11Feb89

Admission Date	Patient I.D.	Patient Name
31Jul88	1234	Jane Doe

Action

- ☐ Discuss with Physician
- ☐ Correct the Diagnosis/DRG
- ☐ Patient Clinically Unique
- ☐ Discuss with Discharge Planning
- ☐ Quality Review
- ☐ Other: ______

DRG	Title	DX	Title
138	Cardiac Arrhythmia & Conduction Disorders W CC	4271	Parox Ventric Tachycardia

Los	Radiology	Nuclr Med	Cardiology	Pharmacy	Med/Surg	Blood	Lab
195*	7179*	662*	1895*	277*	3787*	1816*	23299*
5	98	68	129	164	38	3	350

Resptory	Rehab	EEG/EMG	Rad Oncol	Consult	OR/ADSU	Dialysis
24432*	3560*	192*	0	0	3551*	0
96	11	14			53	

* The patient has exceeded the DRG-specific mean plus one standard deviation for this item. The value of the DRG-specific mean plus one standard deviation is indicated below the patient's actual use of the resource at the time of review.

DX = Diagnosis; Los = Length of stay; OR/ADSU = Operating room, ambulatory diagnostic surgical unit.

Adapted with permission from McMahon, L.F., et al. "The Integrated Inpatient Management Model: A New Approach to Clinical Practice." *Annals of Internal Medicine* 3 (1989): 318–26.

resource utilization information. This ongoing interaction between the first-line providers of patient care (the clinician manager and the staff physician) is absolutely critical for the teaching and patient management programs.

The nurse component of this interdisciplinary team is represented by the project units' head nurses and their supervisors. The interaction between the head nurses, who work directly on each unit, and the clinician managers is the predominant interaction with respect to collaborative patient management. Additionally, it is at this level of the organizational structure that the nurse component of the IIMM focuses on two important patient management issues. The first issue is altering the aggregation of nursing resource data from the historical inpatient unit to the more appropriate patient-specific level. This change in focus is increasingly important as the hospital patient population becomes more unstable with increasingly short lengths of stay and an ever-changing case mix. To assign nursing resources to the appropriate types of patients or diagnosis related groups (DRGs) requires the dismantling of the traditional unit-based allocation.

The second issue is enhancing and introducing greater precession in the nursing QA programs on the inpatient units of the IIMM. This will follow a two-step process. First, we will enhance existing QA mechanisms by utilizing QA programs that will be aggregated at the unit level. In order to accomplish this task, we plan to modify the MEDICUS Inpatient Classification System so that information is collected not at the level of the inpatient unit, but rather at the level of the individual patient. This information will then be aggregated across the patient's entire hospitalization to provide a cumulative nursing resource profile for each patient. The nursing resource profile will then be appended to the hospital discharge record for each study patient. The nursing resource profile for each patient will be aggregated at the DRG level to provide a nursing resource profile for each DRG that can be used in the management and allocation of nursing resources, both within and across inpatient units. The linking of nursing resources to specific types of patients is necessary if nursing is to identify the appropriate use of nursing resources for a specific type of patient. Moreover, as the hospital's case mix changes over time, it will be necessary to reallocate nursing resources. Having objective measures of nursing resources at the level of the DRG will facilitate this reallocation process, both at the level of the inpatient unit and across inpatient units.

The administrative component of this interdisciplinary team deals with many of the operational issues that result from the direct integration of the various support services into the operation of the bed units.

In the second step of this process we will extend the postdischarge QA process to evaluate the patient's well-being and discharge outcome after he or she leaves the hospital. Specifically, we plan to construct an interview instrument that will use both open-ended questions and questions structured using a Likert scale to evaluate three components of a patient's care: the patient's overall assessment of his or her well-being, any gaps in the patient's preparation for discharge, and the patient's readiness for discharge. In addition to these three areas, we will also be able to evaluate any intervening hospital admission at facilities other than the University of Michigan Hospitals. The questionnaire will be given to patients via telephone one week after discharge from the hospital.

The compression of the hospital admission is the focus of much concern as prospective payment pushes the staff to discharge patients "quicker and sicker." The assessment of a patient's postdischarge status becomes increasingly important as patient length of stay decreases and patients are discharged sooner. The key question we hope to answer is, Does this compressed hospitalization harm the patient?

The administrative component of this interdisciplinary team deals with many of the operational issues that result from the direct integration of the various support services into the operation of the bed units. As will become clear, this is achieved through a series of formal work agreements between the project's inpatient units and selected ancillary service departments. In addition, the administrative component of the team functions as a resource for decisions relating to, for example, unit-specific operating budgets and capital equipment acquisitions. It is this group of unit-based individuals, supported by the project's decentralized organizational structure, that is responsible for directing patient care at the inpatient level. By inserting the clinician manager into the decision-making processes at a level that is meaningful for this refined approach to cost control, we have vested the responsibility for patient care resource decisions with a group that can control these costs most directly.

WORK AGREEMENTS

Our ancillary service work agreements have proven to be an excellent means of complementing the project's organizational structure by defining expected levels of service for each major ancillary service department. In addition, these agreements serve to identify negotiated operational solutions to long-standing, support-service problems that have historically precluded effective, unit-level resource management. It is important to note that these agreements are different from traditional methods of service contracting. The intent of these agreements is to identify collaboratively, through a series of interviews and negotiation sessions involving the users and providers of the various support services, the necessary service levels that support operationally effective and financially sound management of patient care resources.

Materiel Management Department agreement

Delays in changing quotas for durable medical goods (i.e., medical–surgical supplies) have been a problem historically in inpatient units, especially in areas that experience rather sudden changes in patient case mix. The variations that may occur in patient supply and equipment needs are, for the most part, due to new clinical protocols that support different types of patients, to a rapid change in the mix of patients on an inpatient unit and, to a lesser extent, to changes in physician practice. We have found through experience that the medical–surgical and patient equipment supply needs for cardiogenic shock patients, for example, differ greatly from those of patients with an acute myocardial infarction. As a result, the Materiel Management Department has been unable to respond quickly to case mix–driven changes in product lines, and thus our inpatient units have experienced supply shortages that have required an increasing number of emergency orders. The supply shortages and the emergency orders that follow affect both the management of the patient and medical–surgical commodity expenses.

As part of an agreement developed between the IIMM and the Materiel Management Department, a report was developed that prospectively identified, through the preadmission coding of the patient's diagnoses, planned procedures, and the assignment of the tentative DRG, changes in trends of case mix on the bed units. The information from the monitoring of changes and trends in case mix can be forwarded to the Materiel Management Department and accurately used as a predictor for the modification of disposable supply orders, supply quotas, and patient equipment needs.

Clearly, an important link between the quantification and feedback of this type of clinical information and inpatient unit-level management continues to evolve in each of the areas associated with this project. As with the Materiel Management Department agreement, the results of the IIMM-directed early discharge pilot provide evidence of service improvement within a complex clinical process.

Department of Internal Medicine agreement: Early discharge pilot

In fiscal year 1987–1988, the Department of Internal Medicine at the University of Michigan Medical Center operated within an environment of limited inpatient bed resources, recurring high occupancy rates, and an increasingly complex case mix. This set of conditions prompted an increase in patient days and a leveling off of admissions. This continued high level of activity and changing clinical profile also magnified a problem of relatively few morning discharges (by 11:00 A.M.) from the medical inpatient areas.

To demonstrate the effective of the IIMM's unit-level interdisciplinary approach, two general internal medicine bed units were selected as sites for a review of the discharge planning process. The 32-bed seventh floor unit acted as the study unit with the 32-bed sixth floor unit acting as a clinically suitable (i.e., case mix compatible) control unit.

Recognizing the strong link between the roles of the house staff and discharge planning, the clinician manager and interdisciplinary support group's initial interventions focused on the house officer level. At the beginning of each month's rotation, the clinician manager would reserve the first 30 minutes of attending-physician–directed patient rounds to talk with the attending and the house staffs about the efforts occurring on the seventh floor unit to support the discharging of clinically appropriate patients by 11:00 A.M. Additionally, the clinician manager would emphasize the reciprocal benefit for the house staff of receiving a greater percentage of their admissions on their home unit. (This issue is a strong incentive for the house staff, as more home floor admissions decrease the amount of time spent rounding up and working up admissions accommodated in other areas.) On a weekly basis, the clinician manager provided feedback to the house staff on the

Specific, timely, and recurring feedback to the individuals who have the greatest potential to influence discharge times proved successful in increasing the percentage of discharges occurring by 11:00 A.M.

percentage of patients discharged by 11:00 A.M. and reviewed those cases where an 11:00 A.M. discharge was considered medically inappropriate by the house staff. Finally, to provide the house staff with a second incentive for early-in-the-day discharges, the clinician manager routinely reviewed the time-of-day distribution for elective admissions to the general medicine services. (A systematic movement toward earlier-in-the-day elective admissions is a strong incentive to the house staff because of the potential to receive and work up the patient earlier. This benefits not only the patient, but also the house staff, because it allows them to complete their daily responsibilities earlier in the day and leave the hospital sooner.)

The clinician manager provided monthly feedback to the interdisciplinary team members, also. This group, under the direction of the clinician manager identified unit-based operational and clinical conditions that impeded morning discharges. In a collective manner, corrective actions were discussed, and each approach to reviewing and resolving these impediments to discharge was assigned to the appropriate interdisciplinary team members.

Baseline discharge data were obtained and stratified by time of day and day of week for the seventh floor's home service discharges. Similar data were collected for the sixth floor's home service discharges. These data were aggregated on both a weekly and monthly basis to assess the effectiveness of the management interventions and to provide feedback to both the physician and unit-based support staff on the seventh floor. Each week a posting was placed in an interdisciplinary conference room identifying the time discharge orders were written, the time of discharge, and the percentage of the service's discharges that occurred by 11:00 A.M.

Another tool used to assess the seventh floor discharge activity was the development of an instrument that provided a detailed breakdown of the reasons discharges occurred after 11:00 A.M. (discharge delay factors). Monthly, the interdisciplinary support team reviewed the reasons identified as discharge delay factors as well as the actual time of discharge for these delayed patients. This level of specificity allowed the group to identify environmental (e.g., transportation arrangements), systematic (e.g., discharge prescription orders), and unit-specific (e.g., level of social work support) barriers to morning discharges as well as help set a goal for the maximum percentage of patients (65%) that could be pursued as medically appropriate early discharges.

Lastly, the seventh floor discharge activity performance was presented to the Chairman of the Department of Internal Medicine on a monthly basis. His ongoing review of this information prompted a number of interventions at the departmental level. For example, discussions at departmental meetings and house-officer luncheons as well as direct mailings supporting morning discharge attempts of clinically appropriate patients were sent to each house officer and attending physician within the department.

DISCHARGE STUDY CONCLUSION

Specific, timely, and recurring feedback to the individuals who have the greatest potential to influence discharge times proved successful in increasing the percentage of discharges occurring by 11:00 A.M. on the seventh floor, our study floor. For the six months prior to the initiation of these interventions, the seventh floor and sixth floor (control floor) rates of discharging patients before 11:00 A.M. ranged from 15% to 27% and from 5% to 30% respectively ($p = .77$). During the six months of direct intervention, the seventh floor and sixth floor discharge rates before 11:00 A.M. ranged from 35% to 42% and from 15% to 22%, respectively ($p = .001$). This change was accomplished without demonstrable differences in activity (occupancy rate) or clinical case mix between the two units.

The removal of operational and clinical barriers to the 11:00 A.M. discharge time in areas such as early-morning ambulance and family transportation arrangements, consistent and recurring promotion of the discharge lounge, and expedient processing of discharge orders by ancillary support service personnel occurred through the focused efforts of the interdisciplinary team on the seventh floor. This group, comprised of individuals intimately familiar with unit-specific operations, was able to identify ways to facilitate morning discharges, and more importantly, was in the position to collect and feed back the information necessary to rally the support of other areas that were either directly or indirectly affecting the patient discharge function.

Prior to the initiation of the IIMM, issues such as these were not systematically monitored in a way that made possible a review of the data by the individuals directly involved in the management of patients. As a result of our administrative intervention, ancillary service work agreements, and the interdisciplinary organizational structure on our inpatient units, our ability to test managerial interventions and operational changes in a closed system (i.e., the project's inpatient units) has created a unique opportunity to test approaches to solving administrative problems prior to their general application throughout the hospital operation.

• • •

Over the past year, those in the Department of Internal Medicine at the University of Michigan Hospitals have been working together in an attempt to identify a new approach to the clinical–administrative questions that are fundamental to the care of patients. The success of an undertaking such as this, as well as the potential to transport new management systems and organizational restructuring, is predicated on the following three factors:

1. the perceived severity of the resource utilization problem in our nation's hospitals,
2. the receptivity of institutions to change, and

3. the nature of the IIMM information system's data requirements.

The first question, and perhaps the most important, is What is the perceived need for change in the management of our nation's hospitals?

While much has been written about the crisis in our nation's hospitals, there has been little organizational change to date. Part of the explanation for this is the relatively strong financial position of most of our nation's hospitals. The advent of prospective payment caused many hospitals to lay off workers and make other one-time changes to lower their total operating costs. These short-term changes generally improved the hospital industry's collective operating margin. While the short-term success is to be applauded, it is unlikely that these changes can be repeated over the long term. Furthermore, given the state of most hospital information systems (both clinical and administrative), it is not clear that hospitals could make the next round of cost reductions without causing harm to some of their patients through inability to distinguish clinically necessary resources from superficial ones. The short-term success of hospitals in lowering operating costs has opened a window of opportunity for development and implementation of systems like the IIMM. It is expected that, over the next five years, there will be increased interest in novel management and information systems such as this one.

The question of the receptivity of hospitals to change is one that we cannot explicitly address. Given that the primary responsibility of any organization is to survive, it is likely that, as the competition for patients and their health care dollars becomes more acute, more institutions will welcome organizational innovation of the type outlined in this article.

Finally, the ability to adopt any innovative management information system is directly related to the degree of difficulty an institution faces in changing existing information systems. This concern is explicitly addressed in our development of the IIMM's clinical management information system. We have chosen to reorient all of the hospital's information systems to the level of the individual patient. It is our feeling that by moving away from corporate or departmentally aggregated data, one achieves the level of routine data discreteness that is necessary to effectively manage subtle changes in hospital resource use. In constructing these patient-level management systems, however, we have utilized existing hospital systems (billing and discharge management information systems) for the IIMM that are in general use in our nation's hospitals. This should facilitate the adoption of the IIMM's organizational design and management information systems.

In summary, we are attempting to address one of the principal problems facing our nation's hospitals: the use of hospital resources. The IIMM attempts to shift the focus of all operational management information systems to the level at which daily decisions that affect resource consumption occur, the level of the patient. By using the patient level as the common ground on which information is organized and acted on, hospital-based professionals can provide a coordinated and decisive approach to front-line management in a clinical and operational sense. We feel that the IIMM model addresses the question of the use of hospital resources—both their appropriateness and their role in quality of care—as well as serving as a model for other academic centers and community hospitals that face the same external competition and internal constraints.

REFERENCES

1. Freeland, M.S., and Schendler, C.E. "Health Spending in the 1980's: Integration of Clinical Practice Pattern with Management." *Health Care Financing Review* 5 (1984): 1–68.
2. Waldo, D.R., Levit, K.R., and Lazenby, H. "National Health Expenditures 1985." *Health Care Financing Review* 8 (1986): 1–21.
3. Ebert, R.H., and Brown, S.S. "Academic Health Centers." *New England Journal of Medicine* 308 (1983): 1200–08.
4. Schweiker, R.S. "Report to Congress: Hospital Prospective Payment for Medicare." Washington, D.C.: GPO, 1982.
5. Heyssel, R. "Special Report: Decentralized Management in a Teaching Hospital." *New England Journal of Medicine* 310 (1984): 1477–80.

Building a team on a medical floor

Bernard J. Horak,
Joan H. Guarino,
Carolyn C. Knight,
and
Sandra L. Kweder

The article describes a case in which dysfunctional teamwork was threatening patient care on medical units. Various team-building techniques were used by trained facilitators. Survey results showed that the interventions resulted in improved communication, morale, and working relationships.

Health Care Manage Rev, 1991, 16(2), 65–71

> It is naive to bring together a highly diverse group of people and to expect that, by calling them a team, they will in fact behave as a team. It is ironic, indeed, to realize that a football team spends 40 hours each week practicing teamwork for the 2 hours on Sunday afternoon when their teamwork really counts. Teams in organizations seldom spend 2 hours per year practicing when their ability to function as a team counts 40 hours per week.
>
> I.M. Rubin[1]

Teamwork of hospital staff, particularly among health providers, has been found to be crucial to patient care outcome. For example, Knaus and associates concluded that differences in mortality in intensive care units are directly influenced by the level of involvement and interaction between physicians and nurses.[2] Other authors have pointed out the need for collaboration and team building among health disciplines for organizational effectiveness.[3–5] In addition, physician–nurse relationships have been regarded as important to the job satisfaction and retention of nurses.[6–7]

Although many have stated that the team concept is important, few specific examples discuss how to implement this. There is little about team building in health care literature, particularly with respect to cases on how to build physician–nurse–administrator relationships. No literature could be found to document empirical results of team-building efforts among physicians, nurses, and administrators. This lack of information is somewhat surprising, given the extent and efficacy of team-building interventions in non–health care settings.[8]

Unfortunately, conflict, a lack of cooperation, and poor communication often exist among health disciplines.[9–12] Such was the case on a 140-bed medical floor, consisting of three general medical wards and a hematology–oncology ward, at a tertiary care center.

Bernard J. Horak, *Ph.D., is advisor to the Saudi Arabian National Guard health care system.*

Joan H. Guarino, *M.S., is an organization development consultant in the Federal Aviation Agency.*

Carolyn C. Knight, *R.N., M.S.N., is an oncology clinical nurse specialist at Walter Reed Army Medical Center.*

Sandra L. Kweder, *M.D., is a supervisory medical officer in the Food and Drug Administration.*

The opinions or assertions contained herein are the private views of the authors and are not to be construed as official or as reflecting the views of the Department of the Army or the Department of Defense.

This case study will describe the problems of the medical floor, how these problems were addressed through the use of team-building techniques, the results of these efforts, and the implications for implementation and research by others. In addition, the case challenges previous assessments of the difficulty of successfully implementing organizational development interventions in health care organizations.[13-14]

The case was not part of an experiment or research project, but came about out of the practical necessity of dealing with significant organizational issues. It is thus a description of what happened and why, based on the notes and analysis of the writers.

Although research rigor was not the primary focus of the writers, some pre- and post-study data were collected. The team-building approaches and the variables used for data collection will be presented. This information can serve as a starting point for others to use in the design of team-building interventions or for researchers to build upon as part of a more rigid research or experimental design.

BACKGROUND AND PROBLEM

In the autumn of 1987, the morale on the general medical service was at an all-time low. The medical and nursing staff were fatigued and tempers flared at short notice. Supervisors received clear indications that lack of trust and cooperation among nursing, medical, and administrative personnel threatened to affect patient care. Specifically, it was noted that

- Administrative support of the wards was perceived to be inadequate by the medical and nursing staffs.
- Staff members were sometimes reluctant to perform tasks or help out when needed, often responding to a request with, "It's not my job."
- Considerable confusion existed regarding rules, particularly who to see in order to get a problem resolved.
- Problems would be elevated through nursing or medical channels or be written up through the risk-management program (e.g., unavailability of medical record forms, incomplete 24-hour urines). Minor matters and interdisciplinary conflicts became issues requiring higher-level attention, instead of being dealt with on the unit.
- Stress and fatigue resulting from the difficult on-call schedules of interns and residents led to frequent conflict and harsh words between medical, nursing, and administrative staffs over the preceding four to five months. Although some stress was relieved by a change in the on-call schedule, resentment continued to linger.

Minor matters and interdisciplinary conflicts became issues requiring higher-level attention, instead of being dealt with on the unit.

In addition, considerable disparagement of other groups had become common.

- Nursing supervisors were viewed as CBNs or clipboard nurses by the physicians.
- Nurses and physicians were viewed as disdainful of policies and procedures by the administrative staff.
- Administrative personnel (supply technicians, housekeeping, and medical records technicians) were viewed as lazy, insubordinate, or incompetent by the nurses.
- Interns and residents were viewed by nurses as being hostile and self-serving.

The nursing supervisor of the medical floor recognized that these issues could be better addressed through staff involvement than through mandating change from above. With the concurrence and support of the assistant chief, department of medicine for initiating joint team-building efforts, the floor nursing supervisor contacted two organization development consultants for assistance.

THE TEAM-BUILDING PROCESS AND TECHNIQUES USED

To improve intergroup functioning, collaboration, and communication and to reduce negative stereotypes among groups (such as those among engineering, production, and sales departments), industry has used various team-building approaches. The techniques used in this case were a synthesis of the models described by Beckhard, Dyer, and Schein.[15-17]

The objectives of initiating a team-building process in the case hospital were to improve team and organizational effectiveness. As will be discussed in greater detail, the evaluation of these objectives was facilitated through the use of two surveys (for team and organizational effectiveness, respectively).

To begin the team-building process, the consulting team met with the medical floor nursing supervisor to discuss the problems identified earlier. It was apparent that considerable team and organizational dysfunction existed. Clearly, key team members and leaders had to become involved in team building to resolve these problems. The following four groups were invited to participate in the team-building process: (1) head nurses, (2) nursing paraprofessional supervisors, (3) medical interns and residents selected by the chief resident, and (4) administrative supervisors. These individuals would compose the core group for all team building activities, and then discuss the outcome and issues raised with staff not in attendance.

The medical floor nursing supervisor and the assistant chief of the department of medicine elected not to participate in the team-building activities to ensure that participants could be candid and generate their own solutions.

The role of the team-building consultants was to provide expertise and facilitate the problem-solving process. As a result of the discussions between the medical floor nursing supervisor and the consulting team, the following four team-building activities were planned:

1. a problem-identification meeting to clear the air and clarify existing problems, particularly with respect to team effectiveness;
2. a perception exchange (organizational mirror) session in which each of the four groups would discuss their perceptions of other groups and identify what assistance was needed from each other group as well as what assistance they could provide to the other groups;
3. task force meetings to plan and take action on the major problems identified; and
4. a final team-building meeting in which task forces would report and discuss their recommendations with the remainder of the core group.

The four team-building activities spanned a two-month period with the core group meeting every two weeks for approximately two hours. Task force members met on multiple other occasions to prepare more detailed work. Each of the four team-building activities is discussed in detail below.

Problem Identification Meeting

The nursing supervisor opened the first meeting of the core group by explaining the reason for the meeting and strongly endorsing the team-building effort. She then excused herself.

The consultants presented Dyer's model of the team-building process, consisting sequentially of problem identification, data collection, diagnosis, planning, implementation, and evaluation.[16] It was explained that this model would be the template for team-building activities.

Next, a consultant provided an explanation of four critical elements of team effectiveness—goals, roles, relationships, and work procedures.[18] Each person in attendance evaluated each of these four elements on a survey utilizing a 0 to 5 scale (5 being the highest value). As seen in Table 1, these Time Y scores were all below average. (As will be discussed, the survey was readministered at Time Z to assess the effects of the team-building intervention.)

The scores were posted and the rationale for each was discussed. The consultants then facilitated a 30-minute brainstorming session, recording on flip charts all problems (no matter how trivial) that the participants wished to identify. After discussing these problems and their relationship to the survey, 12 major issues emerged. From this list of 12 items, a consensus emerged that 2 basic problems existed: (1) lack of coordination, communication, and understanding of others' roles, and (2) poor understanding of the organization and how to get things done, particularly with respect to a mechanism for resolving problems.

It was felt that by addressing these two issues, many of the other problems identified would also be resolved. The meeting closed with the expressed desire of the core group to spend the next meeting discussing the first problem.

Perception Exchange (Organization Mirror) Meeting

The same core of participants from the first meeting attended this meeting. As mentioned, its purpose was for participants to discuss their lack of coordination, communication, and understanding of each others' roles. In order to identify each group's perception of the other and to focus on areas of cooperation and communication needed, each group (physicians, head nurse, nursing paraprofessional supervisors, and administrative supervisors) answered three questions:

1. How do we see each of the other groups?
2. What assistance do we need from each of the other groups?
3. How can we be of assistance to each of the other groups?

Each group answered these questions by meeting in separate areas away from the other groups. Each selected a spokesperson who presented the subgroup's responses. The facilitator emphasized that no one was to "shoot the messenger"—that the spokesperson's role was only to report the perceptions of the subgroup; and that these were perceptions to be accepted, not issues to be contested.

What began as a tense, strained, and highly threatening session resulted in laughter as perceptions were honestly (and humorously) shared. The session resulted in the candid articulation of the perceptions listed earlier as well as others (e.g., residents indicated that nurses often have petty complaints and "nit-pick" administrative details; nurses indicated that residents tend to be highly defensive and unsupportive in planning the discharge of patients; etc.).

What began as a tense, strained, and highly threatening session resulted in laughter as perceptions were honestly (and humorously) shared.

Many of the participants commented during the meeting that they had no idea how they were being perceived by others. In addition many stated that it was reassuring to note that others had an understanding of their job pressures and demands (nurses commented that residents often were "stretched to the max"; residents indicated that nurses are unappreciated, and that administrators are often caught in the middle).

Finally, it was noted that the foundation for more effective teamwork was being established by virtue of commitments generated from questions 2 and 3. All groups agreed to achieve greater communication by discussing problems directly with the individuals concerned, by keeping the other groups and individuals informed, by explaining their actions, and by pitching in when possible.

Interdisciplinary Task Force Meetings

At the third meeting, discussion centered around how to further resolve the two major issues: (1) a lack of coordination, communication, and understanding of other's roles; and (2) poor understanding of the organization and how to get things done, particularly with respect to a mechanism for resolving problems.

Task forces for each of the two problems were formed. A third task force was organized to consider the issue of poor morale. Each of the three task forces consisted of at least one representative from each of the four groups. They met at times of their choosing to conduct detailed work and action planning. The assignments given by the core group to the three task forces were:

- Task Force 1—to list all staff titles or positions for all four groups and provide a brief description of the roles and responsibilities of each position;
- Task force 2—to diagram the lines of supervision, identify points of contact for resolving problems, and provide recommendations for mechanisms to ensure continued communication and problem solving; and
- Task Force 3—to explore and initiate means for the health care team members to get to know each other personally in order to improve morale, understanding, and communication.

Final Team-building Meeting

The final meeting consisted of presentations by the task forces to the medical floor core group. The following recommendations were discussed and accepted:

- continued medical floor meetings with the core group on a quarterly basis;
- a weekly meeting between the head nurses, ward residents, and the chief resident to address unit problems and to suggest topics for the core group meetings;
- a more encompassing orientation of new staff, especially interns and residents, to the floor (this orientation would include distribution of an orientation packet and briefings by each of the four groups with respect to roles, responsibilities, and problem solving on the floor); and
- a social activity program that would consist of an annual picnic, potluck lunches, and welcoming coffees for new staff.

RESULTS

Two surveys were used to evaluate the effectiveness of the team-building activities: (1) the 4-item survey of team effectiveness (initially administered to the core group as part of the first team-building meeting), and (2) a 12-item survey of organizational effectiveness in which the variables consisted of the same twelve items of concern identified in the first team-building meeting. Both of these surveys were administered three months after the last team-building meeting.

The four-item survey of team effectiveness showed considerable improvement in comparing pre- and post-team–building evaluations by the core group (see Table 1). Three of the four factors in this survey (role, relationships, and procedures) were statistically significant ($p < .01$). Teamwork is crucial to organizational effectiveness and positive patient care outcome, so far greater potential now exists for improvement in patient care and staff satisfaction.

The 12-item survey of organizational effectiveness was administered to all staff assigned continuously to the medical floor during the intervention period. This survey permitted a more complete evaluation of the effectiveness of the team-building intervention because it included staff at all organizational levels on the floor, not just the core group who attended the team-building meetings. In this survey of organizational effectiveness, participants were asked to evaluate each of the 12 factors for the present (Time Z) as well as retrospectively for the period three months before the commencement of team-building activities (Time X). These evaluations showed that improvement was perceived across all 12 variables (see Table 2). Moreover, the following were found significant ($p < .01$): working conditions, understanding of roles, getting things done, peer morale, staff morale, quality of care, and supervisory support. The results of this survey parallel the gains seen in the survey of team effectiveness.

The survey of organizational effectiveness also asked participants to describe their perceptions of what caused changes from Time X to Time Z evaluations. The respondents indicated that explanations of job descriptions, team-building meetings, and staff discussions resulted in better appreciation of and empathy for the roles and responsibilities of other groups. They indicated that this occurred by opening lines of communication among disciplines. The meetings were also felt to have increased supervisory awareness of problems and commitment to carry out needed changes.

TABLE 1

TEAM EFFECTIVENESS, CHANGE OVER TIME

Factors	Time Y	Time Z
	$N = 17$	$N = 22$
Goals	2.90	3.10
Roles*	2.10	3.32
Relationships*	2.50	3.40
Procedures*	2.20	3.32

*$p < .01$.
1 = very low, 2 = low, 3 = average, 4 = high, and 5 = very high.

TABLE 2

ORGANIZATIONAL EFFECTIVENESS, CHANGE OVER TIME

	$N = 59$	
Factors	**Time X**	**Time Z**
Working conditions†	2.49	3.07
Understanding roles†	2.72	3.35
Chain of command	3.49	3.73
Supervisory support*	3.13	3.69
Admission scheduling	2.70	2.96
Getting things done†	3.22	3.84
Peer morale†	2.35	2.85
Overall staff morale†	2.41	2.92
Administrative support	2.52	2.93
Peer cooperation	3.38	3.68
Quality care†	3.54	3.94
Overall cooperation	2.96	3.33

*$p < .05$.
†$p < .01$.
1 = poor, 2 = fair, 3 = average, 4 = above average, and 5 = excellent.

The respondents indicated that explanations of job descriptions, team-building meetings, and staff discussions resulted in better appreciation of and empathy for the roles and responsibilities of other groups.

RESEARCH LIMITATIONS AND IMPLICATIONS FOR FURTHER STUDY

Although the results show marked improvement, there are several limitations, as this case was not designed as an experiment. These limitations from a research methodological standpoint include

- lack of experimental controls (data on other groups who did not participate in a team-building intervention);
- lack of checks on the validity and reliability of the instruments;
- lack of definitions of the variables used on the survey of organizational effectiveness (these terms were assumed to be understood since they were the 12 issues identified and agreed upon in the initial team-building meeting); and
- potential bias in responses on the survey of organization effectiveness because respondents were asked to simultaneously evaluate the past and present.

Given these limitations and the approaches used, several implications exist for future research, including

- conducting a team-building experiment meeting the limitations identified above;
- evaluations of long-term effectiveness (this was not possible in this case owing to the complete turnover of the resident–intern staff and, approximately a 50 percent turnover in nursing personnel in the one year after the team-building intervention. The 50 percent turnover was largely bad timing—a bolus of transfers of military nurses during the summer. This turnover is not necessarily representative of other parts of the hospital or other similar institutions.);
- comparison studies of different team-building approaches;
- conducting a study in a different unit or hospital (for example on a surgical ward, intensive care unit, or in a nonteaching hospital); and
- conducting study using a different mix of team-building participants.

IMPLICATIONS FOR FUTURE IMPLEMENTATION

Despite the research limitations, the data and our subjective experiences suggest that a team-building intervention has the potential for improving staff satisfaction, as well as team and organizational effectiveness. Based on this case study, we have identified several lessons and implications that facilitate its successful implementation in other hospitals.

1. Trained facilitators are extremely helpful, not only in the design of team-building activities, but also as impartial conflict mediators among different factions. In addition, they may serve as the "conscience" for group meetings, ensuring that difficult issues are confronted.

2. The most powerful technique we used that both broke the ice and resulted in the confrontation of deep-seated issues, was the perception exchange. Before this exercise, communication was extremely constrained among professional groups. We recommend this technique as an initial approach to interdisciplinary conflict management, though it may be very emotionally charged. It requires a skilled facilitator to ensure that issues raised are carefully and sensitively dealt with.

3. Time, seemingly the scarcest resource, must be carefully managed. Premeeting planning sessions, the use of task forces to perform detailed work, and efficient facilitation of the meetings proved highly beneficial. To ensure maximal attendance, meetings should not interfere with morning ward rounds.

4. If no team-building activities have occurred in the past, three or four monthly meetings are initially needed, followed by quarterly meetings thereafter. The frequency and duration of the meetings are dependent on the number and nature of the issues, the existing relationships of staff members, and degree of turnover of staff.

5. A continuous follow-up mechanism must be established, as daily pressures and demands make it difficult for team-building and task force meetings to take place. Minutes of meetings and task lists should be developed as reminders to task force members and core group participants. Continued meetings and documentation of these meetings are crucial in precluding the regression effect—a return to past behavior.[19,20]

6. In view of the frequent turnover of residents and nursing staff, new personnel must acquire a similar level of understanding. This can be accomplished by the new staff's receiving copies of the minutes of meetings and the task lists, and their meeting with supervisors to fully clarify and discuss what has transpired in past team-building sessions.

7. It is particularly important that the agenda of future meetings not only include a review of past problems, but also consider new issues, particularly those generated by new working relationships (and perceptions) as a result of personnel and other organizational changes. Ownership of solutions is enhanced by continued staff participation through all phases of the team-building process (problem identification, data collection, diagnosis, planning, implementation, and evaluation).

8. Finally, it should be noted that benefits were obtained despite the fact that some planned projects such as the orientation packet and the social program were never implemented. It was the process of structured, regular communication among disciplines that proved most valuable in our highly fluid, very busy organization.

The importance of teamwork in patient care cannot be overemphasized. This is particularly true given the ever-increasing complexity of health care. Teams do not just happen; they must be built, nurtured, and supported. Thus, time for team-building activities must be allocated. We believe that the techniques used at our hospital hold promise for other units that wish to strengthen existing teams and manage interdisciplinary conflict.

REFERENCES

1. Rubin, I.M. "Introduction." In *Making Health Teams Work,* edited by H. Wise et al., p. xviii. Cambridge, Mass.: Ballinger, 1974.
2. Knaus, W., et al. "An Evaluation of Outcome from Intensive Care in Major Medical Centers." *Annuals of Internal Medicine* 104 (1986): 410–18.
3. Bender, A.D., Geoghegan, S.S., and Krasnick, C.J. "Planning and Teamwork: Critical Health Delivery Issues." *Medical Group Management Journal* 37, no. 4 (1990): 30–5.
4. Griffith, J.R. *The Well-Managed Community Hospital.* Ann Arbor, Mich.: Health Administration Press, 1987.
5. Rakisch, J.S., Longest, B.B., and Darr, K. *Managing Health Services Organizations.* Philadelphia, Penn.: W.B. Saunders, 1985.
6. Helmer, F.T., and McKnight, P. "Management Strategies to Minimize Nursing Turnover." *Health Care Management Review* 14, no. 1 (1989): 73–80.
7. Bream, T., and Shapiro, A. "Nurse–Physician Networks: A Focus for Retention." *Journal of Nursing Management* 20, no. 5 (1989): 74–7.
8. Golembiewski, R.T., Proehl, C.W., and Sink, D. "Estimating the Success of OD Applications." In *Organizational Development: Theory, Practice, Research,* edited by W.L. French, C.H. Bell, and R.A. Zawacki. Homewood, Ill.: Irwin, 1989.
9. Morgan, A.P., and McCann, J.M. "Nurse–Physician Relationships: The Ongoing Conflict." *Nursing Administration Quarterly* 7, no. 4 (1983): 1–6.
10. Nason, F. "Diagnosing the Hospital Team." *Social Work in Health Care* 9, no. 2 (1983): 25–43.
11. Phillips, R.L., Posner, B.C., and Walker, D.D. "A Strategy for Interunit Problem Solving." *Health Care Management Review* 10, no. 1 (1985): 53–9.
12. Schulz, R., and Johnson, A.C. "Conflict in Hospitals." In *Issues in Health Care Management,* edited by S. Spirn and D.W. Benfer. Gaithersburg, Md.: Aspen Publishers, 1982.
13. Goren, S., and Ottaway, R. "Why Health Care Teams Don't Change." *Journal of Nursing Administration* 15, no. 7/8 (1985): 9–16.
14. Weisbord, M.R. "Why Organization Development Hasn't Worked (So Far) in Medical Centers." *Health Care Management Review* 1, no. 2 (1976): 17–28.
15. Beckhard, R. *Organization Development: Strategies and Models.* Reading, Mass.: Addison-Wesley, 1969.
16. Dyer, W.G. "Basic Programs and Plans." In *Organizational Development: Theory, Practice, Research,* edited by W.L. French, C.H. Bell, and R.A. Zawacki. Homewood, Ill.: Irwin, 1989.
17. Schein, E.J. *Process Consultation: Its Role in Organization Development,* Reading, Mass.: Addison-Wesley, 1969.
18. Beckhard, R. "Optimizing Team-Building Efforts." In *Organizational Development: Theory, Practice, Research,* edited by W.L. French, C.H. Bell, and R.A. Zawacki. Homewood, Ill.: Irwin, 1989.
19. Dyer, W.G. *Team Building: Issues and Alternatives.* Reading, Mass.: Addison-Wesley, 1987.
20. Hardaker, M., and Ward, B.K. "How to Make a Team Work." *Harvard Business Review* 65, no. 6 (1987): 112–19.

Part V

PHYSICIAN EXECUTIVE LEADERSHIP

Physician managers: Personal characteristics versus institutional demands

Hava Tabenkin,
Stephen J. Zyzanski,
and
Sonia A. Alemagno

This article presents results of a survey of 169 physician managers and addresses what influences their task performance—organizational demands or personal characteristics?

Health Care Manage Rev, 1989, 14(2), 7–12

The complex health care system in the United States is changing rapidly.[1-4] Some of the consequences of these changes are the development of large medical industrial complexes; a dramatic shift from hospital to ambulatory care; and an increase in independent practice associations (IPAs), preferred provider organizations (PPOs), health maintenance organizations (HMOs), and large multispecialty group practices. At the same time, competition among health care providers is growing, producing a demand to combine quality of care with cost containment. These situations call for effective management, which can best be served by a combination of knowledge and skills of both management and medicine. The issue today is no longer whether there is a role for physicians in management, but rather how to make physicians more effective as partners in the management of medical resources.[5-7] This challenge is being accepted by organizations searching for better and more effective managers while realizing that very few physicians are formally trained in management.[8]

To date, few studies have addressed the problems related specifically to physician managers.[9,10] Many questions need to be addressed such as the following:

- What are the typical personal and managerial characteristics of physican managers?
- How does the organizational structure or context influence their task performance and input into policy?
- Does the unique structure of each organization influence managerial and personal characteristics?

The study presented here addressed these and other questions. The results provide further insights and guidelines for preparing physicians to be effective managers.

Hava Tabenkin, *M.D., M.S., is Regional Director of Family Medicine, Yisrael Valley, Israel.*

Stephen J. Zyzanski, *Ph.D., is a Professor in the Family Medicine Department of Case Western Reserve University, School of Medicine, Cleveland, Ohio.*

Sonia A. Alemagno, *M.A., is an Instructor in the Family Medicine Department of Case Western Reserve University.*

Research for this article was supported in part by the W.M. Keck Research Scholars Fund of the Health Systems Management Center, Case Western Reserve University, Cleveland, Ohio, and by the Jewish Community Federation of Cleveland.

METHODS

The theoretical premise for this study is based on the Boyatzis model of effective job performance.[11] This model suggests that when the three components of job demands, managerial characteristics, and the organizational environment are in balance, effective action is likely to occur.

To address the research questions within the context of this model, a self-administered, comprehensive mail questionnaire was developed. Questions relating to the nature of tasks and roles performed by physician managers, their personal and managerial characteristics, and the organizational structures in which they work were included.[12] Questionnaire content was derived from the literature on leadership styles and characteristics in the corporate settings and in health care organizations.[13-20] The literature describing the function of executive directors in health care settings also provided insightful material.[21-23] Finally, expert opinion from three senior faculty members of the School of Management, Case Western Reserve University, Cleveland, Ohio, and a pilot study in which twelve physician managers were interviewed also helped to refine the final survey questionnaire.

By means of power analyses for the hypotheses to be tested, a sample of 150 respondents was estimated to be necessary for adequate statistical analysis.[24] Thus, 350 subjects were selected at random from four national sources to obtain the needed sample size based on an expected 50% response rate. These sources were the American Academy of Medical Directors (AAMD), the Primary Care Association of Community Health Centers, the Group Practices Management Association, and the Permanente Medical Group.

RESULTS

Using the Dillman method for survey design and follow-up,[25] a 53% total response rate was achieved. The highest response rate, 64%, was obtained from members of the AAMD while the lowest, 45%, derived from members of the Primary Care Association of Community Health Centers. Previous research by Dillman suggests that one of the factors contributing to the lower response by members of the Primary Care Association of Community Health Centers was the unavailability of physician managers' names. Also, the overall response rate might have been higher had the questionnaire been less time consuming. Still, given the fact that this was a random sample, a 53% response is a reasonable response rate for this type of study group. Furthermore, without the names, it would have been very difficult to get information on nonrespondents. Thus, the extent of bias represented by the respondents is unknown because descriptive data were not available for nonrespondents. Table 1 summarizes these four sources and their response rates. Out of 172 questionnaires received, 169 were sufficiently complete for further data analysis.

TABLE 1

RESPONSE RATE BY SAMPLING SOURCE

Primary Care Association of Community Health Centers (N=170)	45%
American Academy of Medical Directors (N=114)	64%
Medical Group Practices Management Association (N=25)	60%
Permanente Medical Group (N=16)	50%
Total sample size	N=325
Total response rate	53%

Four major ambulatory–primary care organizations were identified: multispecialty group practices (MGPs) (22%); small primary care group practices (17%); community health care centers (HCCs) (39%); and HMOs—IPA, staff, and group models (22%). Group practices are defined here as medical services offered by three or more physicians formally organized to provide medical care consultation, diagnosis, and treatment through the joint use of equipment and personnel. HMOs are legal entities that provide comprehensive medical care directly (staff models) or arrange for care to an enrolled population through a multispecialty medical group (group model) or IPAs. To examine whether or not physician characteristics differed by type of organization, chi square and analysis of variance tests were performed. The physician characteris-

The data reveal significant differences between the various organizations in physician manager characteristics.

tics that differed most by type of practice are presented in Table 2.

The data reveal significant differences between the various organizations in physician manager characteristics. Physician managers in HCCs are significantly younger than those in other organizations. They have also been in practice and in management for significantly fewer years than those in the other groups. Furthermore, physician managers in HCCs are less likely to be board certified.

Physician managers in small primary care practices and HCCs spend significantly more time in patient care and less in management (12 to 15 hours per week versus 20 to 40 hours per week for other physicians). Physician managers in HMOs spend significantly more time in management and less in patient care, with 45% of them not seeing patients at all. A substantial majority of the physician managers in the other organizations continue to see their own patients. Finally, there are significantly more female physician managers in HCCs, 29%, versus only 3% to 8% in the other groups.

TABLE 2

PHYSICIAN CHARACTERISTICS BY TYPE OF ORGANIZATION

	Organization type			
Characteristics	MGP **(36)**	SGP* **(29)**	HCC **(66)**	HMOs **(38)**
Median age†	42	46	35	45
Years in present position‡	2.5	4.2	2	2
Years as physician manager	4.5	5	2.5	5
Years in practice‡	15	19	8.5	17
Hours/week of patient care†	25	30	32	6
Hours/week as physician manager†	20	15	12	40
Male‡ (%)	92	97	71	95
Board certified‡ (%)	92	83	66	92
See their own patients†(%)	89	100	96	55

*SGP = Small Group Practice.
†p = 0.01
‡p = 0.001

TABLE 3

DIFFERENCE IN LEVEL OF TRAINING BY TYPE OF ORGANIZATION

	Type of organization			
Level of training*	MGP **(36)**	SGP **(29)**	HCC **(66)**	HMOs **(38)**
No training	17%	14%	29%	8%
Some/moderate training	69%	72%	51%	42%
Great deal of training	14%	14%	20%	50%
Totals	100.0%	100.0%	100.0%	100.0%

*p = 0.001

Among physician managers in this sample, three levels of training in management were identified. Approximately 19% of the respondents had no training in management; 57% had some to moderate training, which included seminars, informal training, or a graduate course in management. Twenty-four percent had a great deal of training (defined as a graduate degree in management or a degree in progress plus seminars or informal training).

Differences in these three levels of training by type of organization are displayed in Table 3. The results reveal that physician managers in HMOs have significantly more training than physicians in the other three groups. Conversely, those in HCCs reported significantly less training, with 29% reporting no training at all.

Respondents were asked to rate themselves, on a scale of 1 to 10 (low to high), on each of 13 characteristics related to management. These items were subjected to a principal components factor analysis with orthogonal rotation that produced two major factors. The two factors, labeled people- and task-oriented characteristics, along with their respective items and factor loadings, are presented in Table 4. Items are ordered within factors by the strength of their factor loadings. In general, the higher the factor loading, the more important the item is in defining the factor. Factor 1 was interpreted as describing people-oriented characteristics. The two items with the highest factor loadings reflect

TABLE 4

MANAGERIAL CHARACTERISTIC FACTORS

	Loading
People-oriented characteristics	
Ability to delegate	.74
Ability to coordinate	.74
Knowing own limitations	.64
Ability to keep promises	.37
Ability to motivate	.30
Task-oriented characteristics	
Ability to develop new solutions	.81
Ability to take initiative	.73
Ability to deal with uncertain situations	.69
Ability to take risk	.69
Having self-confidence	.59
Ability to work under stress	.52
Having and using intuition	.50
Ability to motivate	.48

the ability of managers to delegate tasks to others and to coordinate, monitor, and follow up the work flow. Factor 1 had an internal consistency reliability (Chronbach's alpha) of 0.85. Factor 2 was interpreted as describing mostly task-oriented characteristics. Key items defining this factor involve the manager's ability to develop new solutions, take initiatives, and deal with uncertain situations. Its alpha reliability was 0.73. These factors reliably describe two important but distinct domains of managerial characteristics. Factor scores were computed by summing the items comprising each factor.

Physician manager self-rating scores on these two factors revealed significant differences between organizations on task-related managerial characteristics. Physician managers in HCCs rated themselves significantly lower on the task-oriented factor in comparison with the other groups. Physician managers in HMOs and primary care practices were found to have the highest task-oriented factor ratings, on the average. Interestingly, there were no significant differences on the people-oriented factor between organizational groups.

Next, 23 specific physician managers' tasks were examined, along with their reported level of involvement in performing the tasks, and their level of input in decision making regarding the tasks. Results revealed that for each of the 23 tasks, a consistently high percent (78% to 100%) of the physician managers in all organizations reported that they were performing these tasks. Between 78% to 98% of the sample also reported having some to a great deal of input in policy making concerning these 23 tasks. Interestingly, the data indicate that only a small percent of physician managers are performing these tasks alone. A factor analysis of the 23 items produced five factors for analysis purposes. Table

TABLE 5

PHYSICIAN MANAGER TASK FACTORS

	Loading
Medical personnel	
Supervising physicians	.80
Advising, motivating physicians	.70
Arbitrating differences between physicians	.50
Recruiting physicians	.45
Negotiating with hospitals on M.D. status	.30
Determining physician salary	.27
Nonmedical personnel	
Recruiting support staff	.86
Monitoring support staff	.73
Budget and planning	
Defining the goals and priorities	.69
Planning new services	.48
Managing the budget	.45
Developing new approaches to health care	.44
Determining number/specialties of physicians	.29
Purchasing medical equipment	.12
Patient and service delivery	
Addressing patient preferences	.64
Assessing needs of population	.59
Contracting with other organizations	.58
Determining physician workloads	.51
QA	
Monitoring patient care quality	.82
Evaluating physicians	.71
Monitoring other services	.66
Organizing educational programs for physicians	.26

5 presents the items and the factor loadings pertaining to medical personnel, nonmedical personnel, and budget and planning, patient and service delivery, and quality assurance (QA). Cronbach alpha reliability coefficients for the factor scores, derived by summing the items comprising each factor, ranged from 0.64 for the medical personnel factor to 0.78 for the budget and planning factor. Patient complaint tasks, although independent of the five factors, were assessed with only one question.

The data reduction value of this factor solution means that a small number of task factor scores can be used to profile a physician manager's involvement in performing tasks within and between organizations. In this sample, physician managers in small group practices and HCCs were found to be significantly more involved in nonmedical personnel tasks and policy decisions at the $p<.001$ level, by analysis of variance. HCC physician managers were significantly less likely to be involved in budgetary and planning activities but significantly more likely to develop and implement policy issues regarding QA than the other group. Overall, managers in MGPs and primary care small group practices were significantly more involved in policy making as found by analysis of variance, $p<.001$.

DISCUSSION

This study reveals that different primary care organizations have major differences in physician manager levels of responsibility, demographics, level of training, and managerial characteristics.

High self-ratings on managerial characteristics and more extensive formal training were the most significant factors descriptive of high levels of involvement in medical personnel, budget and general policy, and QA issues. These results may add further insight to those of previous studies that have found low levels of involvement by managers in the areas of finance. The data from this study indicate that those physicians with additional training and a high-score profile on key management characteristics are more likely to be involved in budgetary and planning activities.

Another contribution of this study is the development of a 23-item task list, similar to a list developed by Betson and Slater.[26,27] The majority of tasks listed in these works was also included in this study and thus provides opportunities to replicate previous findings. The present study also provides some new insights on the input that physician managers have regarding policy-making decisions on specific tasks. No such previous work was found in the literature. Thus, this study gives greater breadth to existing findings.

Physician managers rated their task-oriented characteristics higher than their people-oriented characteristics. Consistently, no differences were noted among organizations for people-oriented characteristics, whereas task-related characteristics were found to be related to age and type of organization.

• • •

These findings suggest the more experience and training in management physicians have, the more competent they feel in management. Thus, organizations need to take formal steps to train young physicians to be better physicians *and* managers. This training needs to recognize that different types of organizational settings will strongly influence the level of involvement and the personal satisfaction of the physician manager. Hence, organizations need to be aware that in addition to required skill levels, creation of the right setting is important for maximizing the personal satisfaction of physician managers and enhancing their ability to contribute significantly to the organization. These data suggest that physician managers would thus have increased confidence in their abilities to perform effectively in multiple areas of health care management, including policy making and finance.

REFERENCES

1. Starr, P. *The Social Transformation of American Medicine.* New York: Basic Books, 1982.
2. Fuchs, V.R. *Who Shall Live.* New York: Basic Books, 1974.
3. Mayer, T.R., and Mayer, G.G. "HMOs: Origins and Development." *New England Journal of Medicine* 312 (1985): 590–94.
4. Kaluzny, A.D., and Shorteu, S.N. *Health Care Management: A Text in Organization, Theory and Behavior.* New York: Wiley, 1983.
5. Ibid.
6. Percy, B.J. "The Role of the Physician Manager." *Health Management Forum* 5, no. 3 (1984): 48–55.
7. Schenke, R. *The Physician in Management.* Falls Church, Va.: American Academy of Medical Directors, 1980.
8. Sayles, L.R. *Leadership: What Effective Managers Really Do...and How They Do It.* New York: McGraw-Hill, 1979.

9. Betson, C.L. *Managing the Medical Enterprise: A Study of Physician Managers.* Ann Arbor, Mich.: U.M.I. Research Press, 1986.
10. Tabenkin, H. "Task and Managerial Characteristics of Physician Managers in Primary and Ambulatory Care Organizations." Master's thesis, Case Western Reserve University, 1987.
11. Boyatzis, R.E. *The Competent Manager: A Model for Executive Performance.* New York: Wiley, 1982.
12. Betson, *Managing the Medical Enterprise.*
13. Boyatzis, *The Competent Manager.*
14. Peters, T.J., and Waterman, R.H. *In Search of Excellence.* New York: Harper & Row, 1982.
15. Hersey, P., and Branchard, K.H. "So You Want to Know Your Leadership Style." *Training and Development Journal* 28, no. 2 (February 1974): 22–37.
16. Zenger, J.H. "Leadership: Management's Better Half." *Training* 22, no. 12 (1985): 44–53.
17. Martin, W.B. "Are You a Manager or a Leader?" *Industry Week* 224, no. 5 (March 1985): 93–97.
18. Aluise, J.J. *The Physician as Manager.* Bowie, Md.: The Charles Press, 1980.
19. Kimberly, J.R. "Managerial Innovation of Health Policy: Theoretical Perceptions and Research Implications." *Journal of Health Politics, Policy and Law* 6 (1982): 637–53.
20. Yanda, R.L. *Doctors as Managers of Health Teams.* New York: Amacom Press, 1977.
21. Kuhl, I.K. *The Executive Role in Health Service Delivery Organizations.* Washington, D.C.: Association of University Programs in Health Administration Press, 1986.
22. Slater, C. "The Physician Manager's Role: Results of a Survey." In *The Physician in Management,* edited by R. Schenke. Falls Church, Va.: American Academy of Medical Directors, 1980.
23. Downs, R.L. "The Role of Physician Managers in Larger Multispecialty Groups." *College Review* 1, no. 2 (1984): 83–95.
24. Cohen, J. *Statistical Power Analysis for the Behavioral Sciences.* New York: Academic Press, 1977.
25. Dillman, D.A. *Mail and Telephone Surveys.* New York: Wiley, 1978.
26. Betson, *Managing the Medical Enterprise.*
27. Slater, "The Physician Manager's Role."

High-performing managers: Leadership attributes for the 1990s

Montague Brown
and
Barbara P. McCool

Entrepreneurial, innovative, energetic, community-oriented leaders are needed for health care enterprises. Successful leaders work on a variety of challenging projects and are able to play multiple roles.

Health Care Manage Rev, 1987, 12(2), 69–75

Wanted: entrepreneurial, innovative, energetic, community-oriented leaders for health care enterprises. If we are to prosper as a profession, the leaders for tomorrow need to be identified and developed today.

What kind of superman or superwoman is needed to tackle successfully the growing complexities of our health care enterprise? Can we find talented people who have the energy, conviction, vision, and attention to detail necessary to get the job done while remaining flexible about the future?

Over the past four years in both informal and in-depth interviews we have talked with today's health care leaders about the attributes and characteristics needed by future leaders. We interviewed people whose accomplishments we had read about, and we received recommendations from members of the *HCMR* Editorial Board, journalists, and people interviewed at earlier stages of the project. In this process many more people were identified than we could include in our project.

Our method of selection and time and energy allotted to each interviewee represents more the methodology of the journalist than of the scientific investigator. Our selection was also biased toward people in their early thirties and forties. We deliberately set out to get as much information as possible from people we thought were the high performers of today and most likely to be the leaders of tomorrow. While we consulted many older leaders in health care our major focus was on those likely to move into top leadership positions in the industry, not those currently there. We also focused heavily on people working in hospitals and hospital systems.

People working in psychiatric care, long-term care,

Montague Brown, *M.B.A., Dr.P.H., J.D., is Chairman & CEO of Strategic Management Services, Shawnee Mission, Kansas, and Editor of* Health Care Management Review.

Barbara P. McCool, *R.N., M.H.A., Ph.D., is President of Strategic Management Services, Shawnee Mission, and Associate Editor of* Health Care Management Review.

This article was distributed to the participants in the roundtable discussion on which the next article is based. They were asked to prepare additional remarks that would expand the discussion beyond the issues presented here.

The authors thank David K. Hamilton, C.P.A., President of Strategic Ventures Group, and Shawnee Mission, Kansas, and Sherry R. Larson, M.T.(ASCP), M.P.A./H.S.A., Consultant for Strategic Management Services, Shawnee Mission, for their assistance in preparing this article.

managed care, and other aspects of health care are underrepresented in our interviews. However, we are confident that excellent leaders are developing there. In fact, they have much in common with the people in more traditional hospital roles with one exception: Because they are often in the new modes of care, these leaders are less likely to defend the status quo of community hospitals in the overall scheme of health care delivery.

Our interviews benefited from years of reading health care and business articles on management as well as recent and classic books on general topics, and, more recently, from working with high-performing people in business, law, engineering, and science.

We set out to address the issue of leadership in health care in a simple yet comprehensive fashion. In this article, we have logically grouped together the key attributes while providing more labels for related attributes. We describe the personal characteristics of high performance and the most likely attributes of tomorrow's health care leaders. While few individuals are likely to possess all of them, most high performers do strive to move in this direction. We have also identified some of the reasons these attributes appear desirable in the context of health care.

TRAITS OF A SUCCESSFUL LEADER

Healthy, energy giving, hard working

The health care environment is constantly bombarded with ideas, issues, and pronouncements of massive change. This can produce inertia and psychological shutdown if administrators do not keep pace with the cognitive overload. It is essential that administrators present themselves to employees, physicians, corporate officials, and others as being in charge and on top of things. Corporate changes, including the development of new major marketing functions, managed care programs, and other innovations add complexities to the job of knowing where to get information, support, and coordination within and outside the system.

All this complexity makes it essential that administrators have sufficient energy to present a strong countenance to all the parties who depend on them for leadership. This is extremely time consuming because of the number of people who need assurance, information, and decisions. It means hard work, often concentrated on separating the important from the trivial. All this must be done amidst the high noise level from numerous information sources including ever higher levels of dissonance within the medical community.

The health care culture should stress good physical conditioning. Like big league athletes, administrators must be fit for action in the ninth inning or the last 30 seconds in the fourth quarter. They cannot expect a fresh substitute in midstream. After the game, they must preside at a department head meeting to go over new changes in strategy. Then they will freshen up before going to dinner to help sell a prospective board member on joining a local group or heading up a new program for the hospital.

At the same time, administrators must be patient like the angler who knows what works and is not tempted to try every new lure offered by an overzealous salesperson. Keeping calm while others panic is helpful and essential.

One might draw on the analogy of the poker player who moves through the game knowing when to bet, when to hold, and when to fold. Health care is not a game of chance, but there are times when it is similarly difficult to sort the good moves from the bad and to know when to hold instead of shifting strategies precipitously in the middle of the game. The energy level has to be high to properly analyze options and sometimes to have the strength to withstand the temptation to jump with every new noise in the dark.

People who have such traits can be recognized and can be developed by health care leaders who possess these traits themselves. These potential leaders will need seasoning in a variety of situations before taking on the big role. This is the true meaning of mentoring.

The successful administrator will be calm in the middle of a stormy environment. This person will be making decisions, working long hours, and seeking the right combination of moves to keep the organization on target.

The successful administrator will be calm in the middle of a stormy environment. This person will be making decisions, working long hours, and seeking the right combination of moves to keep the organization on target.

These traits must be blended with a sense of time and history. The leader may be identified and rewarded in the short term but his or her ultimate success will be a result of working meaningfully in a 3-, 5-, 10-, and 20-year time frames. People with vision, rooted in the future, win many accolades for short-term specific performance because they are prepared to recognize opportunity everyday and they realize the need for changes as the environment shifts.

Creative, intuitive, innovative

The best managers are open to new possibilities, especially in highly complex situations. They engage in scenario-building mental exercises, asking themselves and others many "what if" questions. They have the ability to see many possibilities and the patience to keep their options open until they literally envision the appropriate choice of action. Clearly, these leaders are open to the less obvious, the idea from left field, the "eureka" factor.

They are also calm in the presence of the ambiguous situation before the light clicks on and every piece of the puzzle is clear. Tolerating dissonance is the hallmark of creative managers. They conceptualize well and draw from their previous learning experiences.

Mission oriented, entrepreneurial, visionary

Innovation, creativity, and similar attributes alone can lead to disruptive and even destructive behavior. At times new ideas do come out of the woodwork to energize an organization. But, for the long haul, it is creative thinking within the control of a truly mission-oriented person that moves organizations forward.

This thinking apparently starts from a sense of where the executive wants to go or what he or she wants the organization to be when it is fully mature. This is mission-oriented behavior. It starts with the fundamentals and analyzes alternative futures and actions in terms of how they can contribute to the more general and fundamental concept of the total enterprise. This touchstone in vision guides the successful executive. But it is a sense of the possible linked to a willingness to act, to bet the store, that separates idle dreaming from wholehearted commitment.

In many health care organizations, this often means going with one's gut feeling, telling others about it if it works and burying it when it does not. However, a few buried failures do not diminish the organization's level of energy. The overall batting average is the true test of success, not performance during a single time at the plate.

TYPES OF LEADERS

The successful leader integrates various forms of leadership into an effective style.

Networker, boss leader, resource builder

Hospital administrators operate with less formal authority than almost any managers in the world. Hospital managers are guided by professional norms other than their own. Their biggest customer-worker is the physician who reports to no one and maintains competitive hospital privileges as an ongoing strategy. In voluntary hospitals, the administrator will lead and manage the board. In investor-owned hospitals, where the administrator does not have a local fiduciary board to direct his or her actions, he or she has a corporate body with many centers of power and influence guarding the resources needed to do the job well. Even health professionals who are employees affiliate strongly with their unique professional norms and goals.

Health care, like no other field, rewards the diligent network builder: the man or woman who cultivates relationships and who seeks and provides assistance to multiple consultants. The network builder is one who weighs and balances perspectives to ensure that all relevant stakeholders know he or she cares and will be there for them just as he or she expects they will be there as needed. As the field becomes more complex and as corporate relationships and power shift, the skill of the diligent networker will be essential. He or she understands what is going on and is unlikely to be surprised.

Today's successful hospital leaders excel at networking upward with the boss. They know their bosses' needs and approaches and work to keep their bosses informed about their own needs. Put another way, good subordinates manage their bosses. Bosses must be told, diplomatically perhaps, when something does not fit, but they must be told simultaneously what will achieve the desired end. Since each boss must do this for his or her boss or board or the board's constituents, one can characterize health care as management from the bottom up, while breadth of vision is shared from the top down. The vision leads the manager while the manager leads the visionary. It is hard to specify this situation as a trait or characteristic, but, as Supreme Court Justice Potter Stewart once said about obscenity, "I cannot define it for you, but I know it when I see it." So too, as chief executive officers read this, they will remember those who have worked for them and have managed them well. Those who manage their bosses well will ultimately become the leaders of organizations and will work to manage their various constituencies in a similar fashion.

The ideas, resources, and power to get something done in complex situations come from an increasingly wide variety of sources. The successful leader-administrator is acutely aware of that fact and spends seemingly endless hours cultivating those whose energy and acceptance will be necessary to get the work done. This is not a one-shot task. In fact, many of those interviewed have spent years working to build, maintain, and utilize personal relationships throughout their hospitals and communities, and in the field. This fact underscores the need to develop leadership from within rather than continuously bringing in talent from the outside. On the other hand, new developments in tertiary care centers, marketing, insured products, and other such factors make it essential to bring in outside experts who have new ideas and can bring insiders up to speed more quickly.

The successful manager knows whom he or she needs and has the contacts and networks to bring them in as needed. He or she can orchestrate a mind-boggling array of varied interests in much the same way that a skilled golfer senses the opportunities to make a difficult shot and executes it, while all the spectators wonder how he or she planned such a complex maneuver. The professional executes the shot but only after hard work, study, careful cultivation of interest, and practice. Managers who perform well in networking do so in large part because they are trusted and are expected to be fair in their dealings with other members of the networks.

In talking to leaders, one often gets a sense that what they are talking about is present reality, when in fact it is often a rich imagery of the future. Their constant attention to day-to-day reality reminds us of the work of the sculptor or painter who tinkers, dabs, selects paints, works over, and brings life to a dream. But even as he or she works, the dream shifts and takes on newer realities. Thus we see not a completed master plan but a dream that in its unfolding makes leaders often look like folks just muddling through. In fact, management literature over the years has reflected advice to construct master plans while behavioral studies of reality look like messy muddling through. Master planning may indeed feed dreams but it is dreams that feed these muddling processes and ultimately lead to successful management outcomes.

These skills come from hard work, unceasingly considering alternatives, and having the courage to act when the timing is right. With the market changing dramatically, the dreams of leaders in the field need to be fed from a broader array of ideas and resources than have traditionally fed the hospitals and hospital chains of primary and secondary care hospitals.

Analyzer, synthesizer, evaluator

Not many leading administrators pore endlessly over statistics and number combinations. Still, they are not afraid of numbers: Indeed, those less comfortable with quantitative analysis tend to have quite capable financial and marketing analysts on their team. A number of good administrators have served as controllers in early jobs and retain a keen sense of the value to be derived from analysis of operations and potential returns on investment.

More than numbers, leaders seem to enjoy sampling and testing ideas, using conceptual and analytical constructs of various disciplines. This is a form of play, exploration, and enrichment of one's own thinking. The integration and cross-fertilization of ideas, concepts, and data points lead to more creative approaches to problem solving and to path finding—the direction one takes to serve the organizational mission.

More than numbers, leaders seem to enjoy sampling and testing ideas, using conceptual and analytical constructs of various disciplines.

At times such leaders may seem to be out in left field compared to those wedded to a particular conceptual-analytical perspective. More likely, these leaders have discovered a synthesis that transcends any particular perspective and have incorporated that synthesis into their personal world view. These quantum leaps can likely be explained in a logical, sequential manner only after the fact, and then incompletely.

Implementer

Beautiful thoughts, well formed, seldom finish the job. Action must follow. More thought must follow initial action, planning, organizing, and directing. Management must continually be brought into play with and through other people. Openness to input from others throughout the implementation process contributes heavily to successful accomplishments.

People management, problem solving, and dogged follow-through to ensure correct action remain essential elements of management leadership today. Every successful manager we have met either does these well or has teamed up with someone who complements his or her own lack of skill or time to carry out these functions.

Successful implementers remain optimistic champions of ideas even while appearing to be hopelessly bogged down in transition problems.

People-oriented caregiver

Basically, people seek excellence in service when they use a health care facility. Ultimately, every new service and every change in operations occurs because people can identify with, accept, and believe in what we do because we care about other people, employees, patients, and visitors—the people of the communities we serve. This is implicitly and explicitly on every agenda. It is the touchstone of every action.

As multihospital systems have grown, the key issue raised by opponents has been whether this basic orientation to service will be lost. Leaders of high-performing health care organizations keep sight of this issue, even as they balance the interests of staff, top management, stockholders, regulators, and other important stakeholders. As one leader in the investor-owned sector aptly put it, his firm brought sound business practice to sound clinical practice provided by caring people serving patients. Any component without the others ultimately fails. Integrity and ethical behavior are integral to health care.

Every successful, high-performing manager in every industry knows that delivery of value to customers ultimately separates winners from losers. The high performers in our interviews know it too, and they keep that concept in the forefront of their vision of their firm for the future and for the day-to-day work of the organization.

HIGH-PERFORMING MANAGERS AT WORK

Besides the high-performing characteristics successful managers exhibit, these leaders have definite work tendencies.

Using all opportunities

Innovative, open to change, hard working, moving toward goals driven by an internalized vision of mission and commitment describe the successful manager. This individual probably has a degree in management, and has spent years building a knowledge and experience base working in the health care field and loves it dearly. This person respects the rights and integrity of others and knows how to stimulate people in conflicting situations and bring out the best ideas to fit the inner vision of excellence.

Advancement occurs fairly routinely, but major growth can and does come without any apparent change of place or formal position. Some yearn to travel and do a wide variety of things, while others never cease to grow in the soil of their origin. Growth takes many forms. Understanding this reality will not take the fact of being in one place as a mark against leadership ability and the potential for other things. Given the overall complexity of the field and the necessity for leaders to build the networks or root systems in the soil of their organizations, moving leaders around often can broaden, but it can also lead to an alienation from the deep rooting behavior that seems so much a mark of success of those interviewed in this process.

Not taking no for an answer

Leader-administrators are deeply concerned about the movement of market forces, while at the same time loyal to the traditional customers, the physicians. They have probably tried everything mentioned in the professional literature as well as business and health publications far afield from the more traditional sources. But they continue to scan the possibilities for other skills that will aid them in getting ahead in the marketplace. They have options and probably have exercised many, while holding onto the possibility of more successful moves within their current organizations. They wait while moving ahead. They understand that sometimes one takes one step forward and two steps back while trying to get something right. While leader-administrators may be disappointed that first attempts fail, they help others around them to stay the course and get ready for the next phase or stage of development.

By contrast, the less successful administrators remember the failed attempt but keep wondering when the magic answer will be sent down to resolve their local problems. In the meantime, they sympathize with the principal customers, the physicians, who then wonder if they should not jump ship to stay ahead.

Readying the hospital for all contingencies

Leader-administrators already have a sense of the business community. They build more ties and strive to be visible to this market segment, trying to serve this community's needs while increasing awareness of the potential for more direct dealings with the hospital. These leaders recognize that they are responsible for a major community enterprise and have aggressively inserted themselves into broader community organizations and networks. Again, by contrast, the more pedestrian administrator is not involved in the community, nor is he or she known much outside the hospital's direct areas of operation.

Increasingly, leader-administrators are knowledgeable about managed care systems. They know people who are managing such systems, keep up with their growth, and think about how such systems will eventually be integrated into a more holistic system of services. Moreover, they know that down the road they will have major responsibilities for this element of health care, just as today they have a major leadership role in the hospital sector. Leader-administrators will find ways to bring these components together when their market becomes ready for it.

Less adept administrators do not know much about these things and think either that managed care systems will not develop or that they will develop but will be outside their sphere of influence, perhaps resting in the insurance division of the company or some other arrangement.

Leading vertical integration efforts

Leader administrators are positioning their organizations to play a major role in the coming vertically integrated system of health services. They do not know just how their hospitals will approach all the issues involved, but they see elements of the system coming together and work continuously to bring their teams up to date on possibilities. Furthermore, they build new programs that make their organizations the natural focus of such efforts. They have vision; confidence that they can get things done; working knowledge of the latest movement toward their objectives; and a host of networks conditioned to help make it possible when the time comes.

These people have a far-reaching view. Current acronyms and maneuvers by competitors do not ruffle their feathers so much as they offer grist for scenario-building exercises. From time to time, they add programs, move programs around a bit, or call in some corporate or consulting talent to flesh out the options agenda. When opportunities exist, they act.

Others wonder about whether their hospitals can survive the downward pressures. They want new programs to provide relief from pressures. For example they want a new marketing focus, something directed at women, or a health assessment unit. They shrink from the reality that every new day brings at least ten new challenges.

Leaders dream great dreams. They lose some of their battles, but they can distinguish the battle from the war. Most of all, leaders are courageous. They are not like the weak administrators who become intimidated at the mere sound and fury of marketing rhetoric from competitors.

Welcoming competition

Competition makes leaders work harder, but external competition never seems to be a more powerful driving force than leaders' own dreams and ambitions, which come from an internal sense of mission.

Competition makes leaders work harder, but external competition never seems to be a more powerful driving force than leaders' own dreams and ambitions.

Administrators shaped by competition are not leaders. But administrators with a keen sense of the competition can and do deal effectively to stay ahead most of the time, and even when falling behind know how to regain lost ground. Leaders do not always win the round but they rarely lose the game. Nor are they likely to allow competitors to define the game. Performing well and aspiring toward excellence are uppermost in the thoughts of all high-performing managers.

Being responsible and acting accountably

Leader-executives do not ultimately point the finger at higher authorities. Instinctively and maturely they know and act as though responsibility stops at their desks. Similarly, leader-executives act in an accountable fashion with the many who have a stake in almost every major action of the health care enterprise—patients, employees, physicians, owners of the enterprise, and the community.

• • •

There is no single trait or characteristic that identifies an outstanding leader. However, the presence of several of the characteristics described probably reveal a leader in action.

The composite developed here is imposing. No one person has ever displayed all of these traits. But those who have most of these characteristics are individuals who consistently aspire to do better, and that striving for excellence in performance, perhaps more than all else, is critical in looking for outstanding performers in health administration today.

Lessons learned hiring HMO medical directors

David J. Ottensmeyer,
and
M. K. Key

A medical director has enormous influence on medical cost and quality in managed care organizations. Little empirical work has been done on the attributes of an effective HMO medical director. The survey discussed in this article sought to examine those desirable traits from the perspective of medical directors who have risen in the ranks to become employers of medical directors. Mailed questionnaires asked 30 experts to rate skills and personality qualities based on what they would look for in a prospective hire. The factors that emerged as significant were communication and interpersonal skills, clinical credibility, ego strength, concern about quality, motivation, data orientation, and leadership qualities, along with organizational/systemic variables. Implications for hiring and physician education are drawn.

Health Care Manage Rev, 1991, 16(2), 21–30

Hiring and maintaining competent, effective medical directors for health maintenance organizations (HMOs) is a challenge. Based on our experience and that of colleagues, we see certain HMO medical directors rapidly cycling from job to job, without successful experiences. Why? Is it that they lack the proper background, training, attitude, or motivation? This curiosity led to the present study, in which we sought an answer to the question, "What qualities make a good hire for an HMO medical director?"

The field of managed care is growing, creating more opportunities for medical directors. Trends are toward 76 percent of the insured populace being covered by managed care in 1995, with only 11 percent in straight fee-for-service plans.[1] At the end of 1988, there were 32.6 million persons enrolled in 614 HMOs nationwide.[2] HMOs' market share for large- and medium-sized employer–provided health insurance grew to 19 percent in 1988 from 13 percent in 1986 and 7 percent in 1985.[3] Short of going to national health insurance, America would appear to be banking on managed care as the solution to the rising cost of health care. Managed care is basically an approach that superimposes organizational structure, control, measurement, and accountability upon the health care system to effect a balance in the utilization of health care resources, cost containment, and quality enhancement. It does so by employing three strategies: (1) the alteration of financial incentives for providers, (2) the introduction of management control, and (3) the use of information systems to facilitate operational decisions.[4] To accomplish those strategies, the HMO medical director is expected to understand health care and to have a management orientation in a managed care system.

David J. Ottensmeyer, *M.D., is the President of the Travelers Health Company and Chief Medical Officer of the Managed Care and Employee Benefits Division of The Travelers Companies in Hartford, Connecticut. At the time of this work, he was Executive Vice President and Chief Medical Officer of EQUICOR, Inc. in Nashville, Tennessee.*

M. K. Key, *Ph.D., is a consultant for the Center for Continous Improvement, QUORUM Health Resources, Inc. in Nashville, Tennessee. While this research was conducted, Dr. Key was Director of Administration, Research and Development of EQUICOR, Inc., also in Nashville.*

The authors wish to thank Dr. Howard M. Sandler for his consultation on study design and analysis and Ms. Denise Fenchel for her administrative assistance.

The medical director in an HMO plays the lead role in the management of medical costs. Functions of the HMO medical director were examined in a 1985 survey by Witt Associates.[5] Even though the newly established independent practice associations (IPAs) were underrepresented and larger staff model HMOs were overrepresented in their study, the functions all types held in common were utilization review, quality assurance, and medical staff affairs. Most were active in physician recruitment as well. The HMO medical director has responsibility for the control of medical management costs, which can approximate 85 percent of a plan's budget. The director, in order to be successful, must manage utilization, assure quality standards of care, and influence providers to change the way they practice medicine.

Medical management has become a formalized specialty, owing to the efforts of the American Academy of Medical Directors and the American College of Physician Executives (ACPE). The medical director is one evolving and expanding role of the physician executive.[6] The medical director of the future will have an increasingly important role in speaking the languages of medicine and business and interfacing between the two disciplines.

Permut is one of many authors to note the difference in skills required of managers and clinicians, many of which are contradictory. Others to note manager–clinician role conflict are Doyne,[7] Forkosh,[8] Hartfield,[9] Kurtz,[10] Ottensmeyer and Key,[11] Porter and Royer,[12] and Stearns and Roberts.[13] Many maintain that the crossover from clinician to manager is made more difficult by medical school training. Others point to basic clinician–manager differences in personality and workstyle (autonomous versus teamwork; crisis-oriented versus long-range planner; conflict avoiders versus conflict managers). Others argue that physicians are inadequately prepared to be managers[9] and prescribe programs of managerial training to remedy that deficiency.[12,14,15]

There are many thoughtful pieces about what makes a good physician manager, though not many devoted to the HMO medical director,[6,16] and not many empirical studies about either. One study by Jacobs and Mott[17] surveyed HMO executives with responsibility for physician selection. Two major questions were posed: (1) what emphasis should be given to 21 predefined areas at some time during the medical education process, and (2) what rating should be given to 17 criteria for recruiting or employing physicians. Although the study did not focus on physician managers, it did find that personal attributes and interpersonal skills were nearly equal in weight to items like board certification.

The present study was designed to explore the desirable traits of a prospective HMO medical director. The perspective sought was that of the seasoned medical director, experienced in both managed care and the hiring of HMO medical directors.

METHOD

Instrument

The survey tool was inductively developed through structured interviews with persons who have been medical directors and who are not in management roles, supervising medical directors. These consultants were asked in interviews to define the qualities of the ideal or most effective HMO medical director they could imagine. They produced a list of traits, some of which resembled "Qualifications" for the job (i.e., those items looked for before the hire), while others described an effective medical director by performance on the job—these we entitled "Characteristics." Finally, some traits were more generic personality "Attributes."

Likert-type scales[18] were constructed for the items described as Qualifications and Characteristics. The six-point scales asked for the amount of agreement–disagreement with statements about the hypothetical medical director. A semantic differential scale was created for the Attributes, pairing bipolar opposites. Open-ended questions asked experts to list important traits that had been missed in the questionnaire.

The instructions asked participants to assume that they were hiring a medical director for a 50,000-member metropolitan-area IPA or group model plan that is beyond the initial start-up phase. They were requested to consider the combination of skills and personality characteristics they would look for in a prospective hire. They were asked to keep in mind medical directors they had known who were effective in their roles, as evidenced by such criteria as quality standards and utilization statistics.

The experts were selected because of experience in the field as medical directors, familiarity with the strengths required to perform the job, and their roles in selecting and supervising medical directors.

Questionnaires were delivered by mail or facsimile with a cover letter asking for participation from a group of experts. There were no incentives offered other than feedback on the results of the study. Thirty out of 34 in the sample responded with complete questionnaires.

Panel of Experts

The experts were selected because of experience in the field as medical directors, familiarity with the strengths required to perform the job, and their roles in selecting and supervising medical directors. As portrayed in Table 1, there were 30 people surveyed (29 males, 1 female) with an average age of about 54 years. The ages ranged from 38 to 68. The major positions held by the experts were medical director (13) and vice-president (8), with 2 additional people describing themselves as VP–medical director. These physicians had held their current positions from 2 months to 21 years with a mean of 3.83 years. The mean number of medical directors hired was slightly over 7 (with a range from 0 to 28). Those surveyed had over 13 years of experience in managed health care on the average (M = 13.276, with a range from 5 to 38). Ten had Fellow of the ACPE certification, one had an M.B.A., and another, an M.S. in health care administration. In short, the group was older and experienced both in managed health care and in the hiring of medical directors.

In 1985, Kindig and Lastiri[19] found the average age of physician administrators was 54 years, their tenure in administration was 18 or more years, and HMO administrators spent the highest percentage of time in administration. Nash[20] in 1987 added 3 other studies' data to the Kindig work and found the HMO physician executive to be younger (average age 45) and more likely to possess a management degree (10 percent). Our sample was more like that of Kindig and Lastiri.

Table 2 shows the medical specialty of the respondents. The proportions in each specialty are similar to those of all HMO medical directors, as reported in the Witt survey.[5]

RESULTS

Means and standard deviations were calculated for the Likert scale items. Table 3 presents a rank ordering by means of the Qualifications. A score of five or above reflects moderate or strong agreement with the statement that "It is important that a medical director (have this qualification)." Topmost in the estimation of our experts were *communication skills, a clear philosophy of managed care, a minimum of five years' clinical experience,* and the *willingness to see oneself as different*. Least important were *maintaining a private practice* and *planning to retire in the position*.

Table 4 ranks the means of characteristics of an effective medical director, as described by the experts. Many more Characteristics than Qualifications were strongly rated (meaning more than moderate agreement). These included *concern about quality of care, easy to communicate with,* being *willing to take a stand, able to influence providers to change practice,* having a *medical license,* having the *respect of other providers, using data effectively,* being *skilled at committee work,* having *regular contact with network physicians, working with nurses as peers,* being *flexible in dealing with others, improving utilization statistics,* being *intellectually curious, good at documentation,* and *comfortable in a bureaucracy*.

It is of interest to observe the conformity in opinion; there is very little variance in most of the items. By contrast, a few items earned wide disagreement.

TABLE 1

DESCRIPTION OF THE GROUP*

Attribute	Mean	Range
Age	53.6 yrs.	38–68
Years in current position	3.8 yrs.	2 months–21 yrs.
Number of medical directors hired	7.1	0–28
Total years' experience	12.9 yrs.	4–38

*Gender: 29 males and 1 female.

TABLE 2

MEDICAL SPECIALTY*

		Witt Survey[5]
Internal medicine	11 (36%)	33%
Pediatrics	8 (26%)	19%
Family practice	6 (20%)	18%
Other	5 (16%)	30%

*$N = 30$.

TABLE 3

QUALIFICATIONS

		Mean
Q8	Communication skills	5.93
Q9	Clear philosophy	5.73
Q4	Min. 5 yrs. clinical experience	5.46
Q10	Willing to see self as different	5.00
Q2	UM experience	4.96
Q13	Financial skills	4.93
Q1	QA experience	4.63
Q12	Salesmanship	4.56
Q11	IPA/group model experience	4.53
Q7	Sees self as career administrator	4.53
Q5	Formal management training	3.66
Q3	Is in primary medical specialty	3.23
Q6	Maintains private practice	2.26
Q14	Retire in position	2.26

TABLE 4

CHARACTERISTICS OF AN EFFECTIVE MEDICAL DIRECTOR

		Mean
C14	Is concerned about quality of care	5.96
C1	Is easy to communicate with	5.80
C16	Is willing to take a stand	5.76
C20	Influences providers to change practice	5.70
C21	Licensed physician	5.70
C2	Respected by providers	5.63
C9	Uses data effectively	5.63
C4	Skilled at committee work	5.60
C3	Challenges physicians	1.50 (5.55)*
C13	Has regular contact with network physicians	5.53
C18	Works with nurses as peers	5.50
C10	Flexible in dealing with others	5.50
C17	Can improve utilization statistics	5.43
C6	Intellectually curious	1.66 (5.33)*
C2	Good at documentation	5.13
C11	Comfortable in a bureaucracy	5.06
C22	Regularly phones network physicians	4.96
C12	Entrepreneurial	4.60
C15	Detail-oriented	4.40
C8	Computer literate	3.26 (3.73)*
C19	Needs hospital privileges	2.90
C5	Paperwork is a priority	2.20

*Reflected value (i.e., 7-original value).

Those traits with scores ranging from 1 to 6, with a standard deviation of 1.25 or more, included being in a *primary medical specialty*, having *management training, planning to retire in the position, seeing self as career administrator*, being *intellectually curious, computer literate*, and *maintaining hospital privileges* (the most disagreed-upon item). Our experts disagree with the necessity of these traits. From discussions with the respondents, it seems that *planning to retire* and *career administrator* were misunderstood. Some read these as tongue-in-cheek indices of poor motivation and lack of clinical expertise; other participants probably took them as indicative of commitment to the profession of medical administration, thus the wide disagreement.

Table 5 displays the mean scores on Attributes. It argues that the effective medical director must be *persuasive, people-oriented* (contrasted to *solitary*), *confident, proactive, a team player* and *quality-oriented* (as opposed to *hard dollar–oriented*). There were certain items for which the experts would not commit either way: *patient or physician advocate, intrusive versus retiring, autocrat versus democrat, listener versus talker, peacemaker versus confrontative, product-oriented versus process-oriented, people-oriented versus data-oriented*. This suggests that the effective medical director should possess a combination of these personality dimensions.

The responses were analyzed by the expert's primary HMO experience—staff–group versus IPA (18 versus 10). Staff–group types would be expected to behave more like managers, with more bureaucratic and organizational interests, whereas IPA types would value more political and persuasive aptitudes. After identifying respondents whose backgrounds could be labeled primarily staff–group model or IPA-type, *t*-tests were conducted on differences in each item and overall scores. No differences were found; they did not look at the qualities in materially different ways. Jacobs and Mott[17] also found no difference in a majority of areas across staff, group, IPA, and network HMOs when they were asked about physician training needed.

DISCUSSION

Communication and Interpersonal Skills

Communication skill was rated the most important qualification, not unlike the findings of Cummings,[21]

TABLE 5

ATTRIBUTES OF AN EFFECTIVE MEDICAL DIRECTOR

		Mean
A15	Persuasive (vs. unconvincing)	5.73*
A10	People-oriented (vs. solitary)	5.40*
A1	Confident (vs. hesitant)	5.33*
A2	Proactive (vs. reactive)	5.26
A9	Team-player (vs. autonomous)	5.15*
A11	Quality-oriented (vs. oriented to hard dollars)	5.12*
A4	Flexible (vs. rigid)	4.93
A8	Planner (vs. crisis manager)	4.90*
A12	Generalist (vs. specialist)	4.85
A7	Listener (vs. talker)	4.33
A5	Intrusive (vs. retiring)	4.24*
A3	Patient advocate (vs. physician advocate)	4.02*
A13	Peacemaker (vs. confrontative)	3.96
A16	People-oriented (vs. data-oriented)	3.95
A14	Product-oriented (vs. process-oriented)	3.86
A6	Democratic (vs. autocratic)	3.72*

*Reflected value (i.e., 7—original value).

Fine,[22] Hartfield,[9] and Staley and Staley.[23] Hartfield surveyed nonphysician supervisors of physician executives and found that, next to time and task management, physician executives suffer most from communication problems. An ACPE survey of 185 physician executives asked what they thought about their own communication effectiveness.[23] They agreed that managerial communication skills across the board are vital to the success of the health care organization; of the complex communication skills, managing conflict was rated most important both on the job and in achieving a managerial position; listening and speaking were consistently rated most important and most in need of enhancement; and speaking skills were rated higher than were writing skills. In our own study, writing and oral skills, both one-to-one and with groups, were mentioned in the open-ended questions. On the Attributes, respondents indicated that the medical director must be both a *listener* and a *talker*.

Several of the other highly rated traits cluster with communication skills. *Easy to communicate with, regular contact with physicians, persuasive,* and comments about being a *tough negotiator* all pertain to effective communication for influencing providers. Being a good communicator makes this easier. Even being *skilled at committee work*—a talent physicians lack and an activity few of them relish[8]—is an essential and highly rated communication form.

Interpersonal skills, discussed also by Cummings[21] and Ferguson,[24] describes another cluster of items: *flexible in dealing with others, people-oriented, works with nurses as peers,* and is a *team player*. Flexibility is the key to successful management, according to Doyne.[7] Brown and McCool found that orientation to employees, patients, and visitors is essential to managers in care-giving settings. In dealing with others, networking rather than using formal authority characterizes the successful health care leader of today.[16] The ideas, resources, and power to get something done in complex situations must come from a wide variety of sources, and interpersonal skills are a real advantage.

The ideas, resources, and power to get something done in complex situations must come from a wide variety of sources, and interpersonal skills are a real advantage.

Working with nurses as peers links to the *team player* concept. Open-ended comments made were: "able to have people work with him, not for him", being "group-oriented" and "creating harmonious working relationships", being "nonelitist toward non-physicians," "must be willing to give up the autonomy they had in private practice in order to be an effective team player," and "able to work in a team environment rather than being in control as they were as practitioners." These physicians must not be characterized by the "MDeity syndrome." Doctors have been found to be notoriously poor team players.[7,12] Jacobs and Mott also found that the ability to relate to nonphysician staff members and to work in a team rated high in importance in hiring.[17]

Clear Philosophy

A *clear philosophy of managed care* was the second highest-rated Qualification. As one respondent put it:

> [this is] a belief that health care can be delivered and practiced in a different way—one that is more cost effective; a way that is equitable and acceptable to patients; a way that retains the quality of the present health care system without its excesses and extravagances.

> [It is] a belief that most physicians want to do the right thing for their patients and for society; a belief that physicians can change

their style and practice patterns if shown other effective ways to do it; a belief that physicians will change if given credible information on which to base decisions.

[The philosophy] incorporates an understanding of the role and limitations of the managed care organization as it attempts to organize, staff, and control delivery systems. That results in a belief in the job of the medical manager as a change agent, a coach to the profession and a leader ready to confront the hard issues.

Clinical Credibility

A minimum of five years in clinical practice was the third highest-rated Qualification. Clinical experience is needed for technical competence, to render good clinical decisions for an HMO patient, and for the credibility it carries with other clinicians. Managers need a good knowledge of medicine in order to deal with physician providers effectively (Ailes, R.J.; pers. com.; 1989) as well as a strong understanding and sensitivity to physician problems.[22] For this reason, many of our panel did not want a *career administrator* in this position. Our experts did feel that the HMO medical director should be licensed, but need not be from a *primary medical specialty*, although there was disagreement about this. This is an interesting finding, as three fields still predominate among physician executives: internal medicine, pediatrics, and family practice.[25] There is an old debate about whether physician administrators should keep up their clinical skills,[26] but our sample did not value *maintaining a small private practice*, nor did many see the utility of having *hospital privileges*.

Tied in with the idea of clinical credibility was a set of comments by respondents that pertained to respect and regard. For example, "The medical director must be recognized by others as a highly qualified physician"; and "They should have attained some status as a clinician (board certification, advanced training, reputation)." Furthermore, "if managing in a community where he/she has practiced, their clinical skills should be known to be good." Respected by providers was the sixth highest Characteristic—there is clear value to reputation here. Jacobs and Mott[17] found also that the reputation of a physician's place of residency and his or her training in a U.S. medical school were important hiring criteria.

Ego Strength

Another group of items appears to relate to a phenomenon variously characterized as backbone, security, resilience—a factor we have called ego strength. In other management literature, this has been described as hardiness. In our respondents' words, "being able to take an unpopular position and stand alone," "to take extreme criticism and profit from it," "willing to take flak [sic] and not worry about being popular or loved," "can handle daily crisis, hostility, and anger without...burnout," "can laugh at self and handle constructive criticism." This idea received the most comment in the open-ended inquiry.

Ego strength appears to relate also to the fourth highest Qualification, *willing to see self as different*, and the third highest Characteristic, *willing to take a stand*. As Ailes puts it, "Too many medical doctors have been unable to cut the umbilical cord to clinical practice. Until they make this separation, they generally are not effective in representing the views of their employer in the position of medical director" (Ailes, R.J.; pers. com., 1989). Medical directors must be secure enough to separate their identities from those of the clinical community, to be able to confront others, to take criticism, and to hold differing views.

Many indicated that an effective medical director *challenges physicians* (ninth from highest Characteristic). Physicians as opposed to managers are typically described as conflict avoiders.[9] High-performing managers, on the other hand, respect the rights and integrity of others, while knowing how to stimulate people in conflict situations.[16] The HMO medical director cannot shy away from confrontation and conflict, but our sample rated both *peacemaker* and *confrontative* as required. Confidence was the third highest Attribute, "even to the point of being a risk-taker," said one expert. In the Hartfield[9] study, the author also found that whatever physician executives do, they do with conviction and confidence.

Concern About Quality

The number one Characteristic was *concern about the quality of care*. In the Attributes, the experts valued *quality-orientation* over *hard dollar-orientation*. One of our respondents commented that the medical director needed training, knowledge, and judgment to make proper decisions about appropriateness (of care) without interfering with quality. In a typical HMO, medical review services include those managers qualified to guard quality. As administrators, physicians are unique because they understand the requirements of quality care—they speak the language of patient care, and embody both corporate and clinical cultures.[27]

Motivation

Another group of items pertained to the motivation or ambition to choose the career of medical director and not use it to escape medical practice; to make a "positive move toward management and not away from clinical practice." There were many comments about having a career orientation and desiring to succeed as a medical director and have others do the same. Another commented that the medical director must passionately *want* to change provider behavior and convince others to do the same. Motivation is probably why *planning to retire in this position* was rated so low in this survey and why there was confusion about the value of having a *career administrator* in the position.

This finding agrees with the literature. Cummings[21] mentions desire to become a manager; Doyne[7(p.13)] warns a potential physician executive to not flee to management, but to enter it "...because you want to be there." Ferguson[24(p.1117)] says that "...unless you have a thorough and convincing reason for wanting to become an administrator, don't become one." When Kindig and Lastiri[19] surveyed physician administrators, they found that the reasons for choosing administration had changed over time. The majority these days seek administration for positive reasons—impact on health care delivery, new opportunities and challenges, and managerial enjoyment and talent.

Motivation or drive may link to qualities described by our experts as high energy (4 respondents), optimistic (2), hard-working (2), enthusiastic (1), and having perseverance (1). Brown and McCool[16(p.70)] interviewed health care leaders and found being "...healthy, energy-giving, hard-working" to be an essential trait.

Data Orientation

The proficiency in *using data effectively* rated seventh, and the ability to *improve utilization statistics* ranked number 13 in Characteristics of an effective medical director. Others have cited the value of abilities to interpret data and offer recommendations based on characteristics unique to an organization.[22] Brown and McCool,[16] interviewing primarily high-performing hospital administrators, found that leaders seem to enjoy sampling and testing ideas, using conceptual and analytic constructs, organizing data points and concepts. Our sample reminded us that the medical director must be people-oriented as well as data-oriented.

Formal Management Training

Formal management training was rated very low by the panel, although there was disagreement over this item. In Kindig and Lastiri,[19] 83.6 percent of 2,393 physician administrators said formal graduate coursework in management was required or advisable. Our results are at variance with this. In our evaluation of the study group, it appears that many of this group have grown up in the field and have learned on the job—an apprenticeship system. There were comments about on-the-job training's being superior to formal education; another mentioned that a high-quality clinical background has quality assurance (QA) and utilization review (UR) in it. There were, however, remarks that a medical director "must have a good business sense" and "must be able to understand and work with financial and marketing people." Some felt that management, computers, financial skills, and marketing could all be learned and need not be prerequisites for the job, but acquired through continuing education and on-the-job training.

Leadership Qualities

A constellation of qualities seemed to describe leadership. Cummings'[21(p.7)] "failure to lead" describes one of the reasons managers fail. The panel commented on the importance of being a futurist, having vision and purpose; leadership and management ability; observing the big picture; being mature in judgment, and not capricious. Brown and McCool[16] also describe being mission-oriented, visionary, and entrepreneurial as leadership attributes for the 1990s.

There were two comments about adaptability to change. Brown and McCool[16] wrote that high-performing managers at work are open to change. Our panel rated the effective medical director as proactive, agreeing with Fine.[22] The physician is taught to react and is poor at proactive planning and thinking, whereas a manager must be proactive.[7,12]

The effective medical director *influences providers* (the fourth highest-rated Characteristic). The influence of clinical leadership has been clearly demonstrated in setting practice patterns and determining group norms of practice style. This is particularly prominent in the acceptance of innovations.[28]

The sine qua non's

The survey did not ask about intelligence and integrity, but the panel was quick to point out that these were prerequisites we had not asked about. Comments about intelligence included the need to be smart, able to form concepts as well as put them in operation, analytic, detail and product oriented. The *intellectually curious* Characteristic was rated fairly high by the panel.

Health care professionals are strongly identified with their professional norms and codes of ethics . . . .

Comments about honesty (3); being ethical (2); having the "ability to persist for what is professionally correct regardless of consequences to company" formed a cluster of items having to do with integrity. Health care professionals are strongly identified with their professional norms and codes of ethics; it is not unusual that this would be valued in the present study.

Organizational–Systemic Variables

Most HMOs exist in an organizational environment quite different from the autonomy the clinical practitioner enjoys. Many in fact are owned by large organizations that could be characterized as bureaucracies. Our sample agreed with the supposition that effective medical directors need to be *comfortable in a bureaucracy*. This factor describes a special set of skills—for meetings, paperwork documentation, adherence to policy and procedure, multitiered management, and political influence tactics—that are typical of a bureaucracy. The *good at documentation* Characteristic ranked one place above the *bureaucracy* item. This form of communication is critical for continuity of care, audit trails, and legal liability. In our experience, medical directors take a keen interest in the documentation of medical practice; yet our panel seemed to feel that paperwork is a low priority. Paperwork may have a negative connotation not borne by documentation (e.g., insignificant memos as opposed to patient records).

Comments were made that the medical director must have an organizational sense of purpose; must strongly identify with and understand the provider community; and, at the same time, have strong organizational skills that facilitate the use of the managed health care system.

We were reminded that the *organization* is also responsible in some part for the success of its medical directors. Managers often fail because of poorly defined institutional goals, poorly defined criteria by which the results of their efforts will be measured, and inadequate resources, according to Cummings.[21] Ailes[25] asserted that maintaining competent, effective medical directors is a function of the employer (Ailes, R.J.; pers. com.; 1989). It is the organization's responsibility to define what it wants the medical director to accomplish (be specific about job descriptions, too often written like "walk on water") and provide on-the-job training.

COMPARISON WITH NON-M.D. EXECUTIVES

In a survey subsequent to the one described above, the authors presented the same questions to non-M.D. HMO executives with experience hiring medical directors. The instructions asked the respondents to make the same assumptions about a prospective hire as posed in the physician survey, and to keep in mind effective medical directors they had known. Of the 20 people surveyed (19 men, 1 woman), the average age was 41.9 years—considerably younger than the physicians surveyed earlier. They had hired about 8 medical directors each (M=8.1) and, as a group possessed almost 12 years experience in managed health care (M=11.7). Most described themselves as vice presidents (N=11); some cited the job title of president/CEO (N=6). Eight held master's degrees, three held J.D. degrees, with the rest described as holding B.A. or B.S. degrees or none. Although their years of managed care experience were comparable to the physicians', the extent of their formal education was less—thus their ability to start their careers earlier.

When compared to the physician responses, the non-M.D. results were essentially similar. For the most part, they agreed with the M.D.s on which Qualifications, Characteristics, and Attributes were important in the person they hire. On the Qualifications scale, for example, they gave *communication* and *clear philosophy* (in that order) their highest ratings. On the Characteristics scale, the non-M.D.s rated *quality of patient care* (M=5.95) second only to *licensed physician* (M=6.0), while the M.D. group rated *quality of care* the highest (M=5.976). Both groups included *confident*, *persuasive*, *people-oriented*, *a team player*, and *proactive* in their top five most-desired Attributes.

There were a few minor, but interesting, differences between the two groups on the Characteristics scale. The M.D.s rated both *easy to communicate with* (5.8 vs. 5.45, $t(48)=2.117$, $p<.05$) and *skilled with committees* (5.6

vs. 4.9, $t(48=3.36$, $p<.005)$ higher than the non-M.D.s, perhaps indicating that these were areas of difficulty for the M.D.s. This is somewhat supported by the larger difference on *feeling comfortable in a bureaucracy* (5.067 vs. 3.100, $t=6.837$, $p<.001$), with the M.D.s' apparent discomfort being reflected in the importance they placed on this item. The only other difference was found on *low priority for paperwork*, where the M.D.s rated this slightly lower than did the non-M.D.s (2.2 vs. 2.9, $t(48)=-2.158$, $p<.05$).

On the whole, both groups were in substantial agreement about which Qualifications, Characteristics, and Attributes were important in choosing a medical director. The small differences may be reflective of uneasiness with some aspects of the management role, as expressed by the physicians. If this is the case, hiring processes might best be directed to an exploration of factors like comfort with bureaucracy, paperwork, and committees as well as ease of communication.

For a more complete summary of the non-physician survey findings, write to Dr. M.K. Key, 1857 Laurel Ridge, Nashville, TN 37215.

CONCLUSIONS

Most of these areas of managerial competence can be classified as Edgar Schein[29] described them: analytical, interpersonal, and emotional. They are personal traits rather than formal credentials. Communication, interpersonal skills, ethics, intelligence, clear philosophy, data orientation, motivation, and ego strength all surfaced in this exploration. Technical competence was also identified in the form of clinical and managerial skill, but not as achieved through formal management training. This reflects how the panel acquired their training, for the most part. The panel seemed to feel that most of the requisite management skills could be learned on the job and that the employer should be, in large part, responsible for that training. The majority of this group developed the field of medical management over many (13) years, with on-the-job training and experience plus continuing education. To meet the high demand for medical directors today, there now may be a need to standardize, formalize, and abbreviate the length of time spent acquiring the prerequisite skills.

Most of these factors cannot be determined by resume-type qualifications, but must be teased out and verified during interviews and by checking references. One obvious predictor of future success is past behavior, as one respondent reminded us. An understanding of local market or local community experience is useful for an IPA medical director, another panelist maintained. But for the longer haul, the experience needed comes from being on the job, and that outweighs local knowledge of the community or medical politics.

Based on the results of this study, licensed physicians with more than five years of clinical practice, sound clinical skills, and good reputations should be sought to fill HMO medical director positions. They need not be in a primary medical specialty, have a degree in management, maintain hospital privileges, or plan to keep up a private practice. They need data skills as well as people skills, and should have demonstrated ability to control utilization and influence providers. Their motivation is important: they must have chosen management and not fled medicine, and have status among physicians but be secure enough to separate their identities from those of physicians. They must demonstrate concern for quality of care over hard dollars. Their communication skills are of utmost importance, from being a team player to being persuasive to being willing to confront. They must understand and believe in managed care, have leadership skills, be able to work within organizations, and possess a certain hardiness to perform in this role.

This is just an exploratory study, much akin to anthropological inquiry, so the next steps could include tightening and refining of criteria into factors and validation of these traits in the hiring process. Future efforts might also include prospective research on their relationship to medical director success criteria. Studies could then examine the relative predictive power of each factor to performance on the job, and this information be used to modify hiring criteria.

Medical directors could have enormous influence on the future success of managed care organizations. In their management of utilization, they are concerned with approximately 85 percent of the expenditures of the organization, that is, medical benefits. Because they blend clinical knowledge with managerial acumen, they are uniquely positioned to influence providers to change their patterns of practicing medicine, as one peer to another. One panelist remarked that medical directors must passionately *want* to change provider behavior and convince others to do the same; as another said, they must have the ability to move and change other physicians.

No single trait or characteristic identifies an outstanding medical director, yet the composite painted here is imposing. There will clearly be trade-offs for any one candidate. But look keenly for communicators with clinical credibility, leadership ability, the proper personality, character, and motivation, and all the rest will follow—provided they are adept at working within large organizations, and those organizations support the medical director with clear direction and training.

REFERENCES

1. Ward, B. "Medical Meetings: Wilkerson Group Symposium." *In Vivo: The Business and Medicine Report* 25, no. 12 (1987): 11–13.
2. Group Health Association of America. *National Directory of HMOs 1989*. Washington, D.C.: GHAA, 1989.
3. Bureau of Labor Statistics. *Employee Benefits in Medium and Large Firms*. Bulletin 2236, 36. Washington, D.C.: U.S. Department of Labor, 1989.
4. Key, M.K., and Ottensmeyer, D.J. "Managed Health Care: The Benefits Approach to Cost and Quality." *Personnel* (1990): 67(9): 29–30, 32.
5. Belton, D.G., and Baron, C.R. "Profile of the HMO Medical Director." *Medical Group Management* 34, no. 2 (1987): 17–22.
6. Permut, R. "Medical Director, and Evolving and Expanding Role of the Physician Executive." *Group Practice Journal* 38 (1989): 52, 54, 59–60.
7. Doyne, M. "Physicians as Managers." *Healthcare Forum Journal* 30, no. 5 (1987): 11–13.
8. Forkosh, D.S. "Good Doctors Aren't Always Good Managers." *The Hospital Medical Staff* 11, no. 5 (1982): 2–5.
9. Hartfield, J.E. "Physicians in Management: The Costs, Challenges, and Rewards." In *The Physician Executive*. Tampa, Fla.: American Academy of Medical Directors, 1988.
10. Kurtz, M.E. "The Dual Role Dilemma." In *The Physician Executive*. Tampa, Fla.: American Academy of Medical Directors, 1988.
11. Ottensmeyer, D.J., and Key, M.K. 'The Unique Contribution of the Physician Executive to Health Care Management." In *The Physician Executive*. Tampa, Fla.: American Academy of Medical Directors, 1988.
12. Porter, R.D., and Royer, T. "Physician Managers—A Challenge for Training and Teamwork." *Medical Group Management Association Journal* 35 (1987): 42–47.
13. Stearns, N.S., and Roberts, E.B. "Why Do Occupational Physicians Need to be Better Managers?" *Journal of Occupational Medicine* 24 (1982): 219–24.
14. Fink, D.J., and Goldhar, J.D. "Management for Physicians: An Annotated Bibliography of Recent Literature." *Annals of Internal Medicine* 92 (1980): 269–75.
15. Hillman, A.L., et al. "Managing the Medical Industrial Complex." *The New England Journal of Medicine* 315 (1986): 511–13.
16. Brown, M. and McCool, B.P. "High-Performing Managers: Leadership Attributes for the 1990s." *Health Care Management Review* 12, no. 2 (1987): 69–75.
17. Jacobs, M.O., and Mott, P.D. "Physician Characteristics and Training Emphasis Considered Desirable by Leaders of HMOs." *Journal of Medical Education* 62 (1987): 725–31.
18. Nunnally, J.C. *Psychometric Theory*. New York, N.Y.: McGraw Hill, 1967.
19. Kindig, D.A., and Lastiri, S. "Administrative Medicine: A New Medical Specialty?" *Health Affairs* 5 (1986): 146–56.
20. Nash, D.B. "Growing Demand for an Emerging Subspecialty." *Consultant* 27, no. 11 (1987): 97–108.
21. Cummings, K.C. "Why Some Managers Fail." *Physician Executive* 14, no. 4 (1989): 6–8.
22. Fine, A. "New Challenges for Medical Directors." *Physician Executive* 16, no. 2 (1990): 36–7.
23. Staley, S.S., and Staley, C.S. "Physician Executives and Communication." *Physician Executive* 15, no. 2 (1989): 15–17.
24. Ferguson, G. "Advice for Physicians Considering Careers as Administrators." *Canadian Medical Association Journal* 134 (1986): 1177–8.
25 Ailes, R.J. Qualities of an Effective Medical Director. Written communication. October 9, 1989.
26. Nelson, S. "The Rising Incomes—and Numbers—of MD Execs." *Hospitals* 61, no. 18 (1987): 63.
27. Friedman, E. "Physician-Administrators Making a Comeback." *Medical World News* 1 (1986): 34–43.
28. Nash, D.B., and Hillman, A.L. "Physician-Executives Can Be Mediators." *Modern Healthcare* 16, no. 24 (1986): 49.
29. Eisenberg, J.M. *Doctor's Decisions and the Cost of Medical Care*. Ann Arbor, Mich.: Health Administration Press, 1986.
30. Schien, E. *Career dynamics: Matching Individual and Organizational Needs*. Reading, Mass.: Addison-Wesley, 1978.

Commitment and discipline in hospitals: Leadership protocols and legal precedents

Sandra L. Gill,
Eric W. Springer,
and
André L. Delbecq

Leadership protocols may be used to develop commitment to organizational goals and norms, and to maintain disciplinary policies and procedures in health care organizations. Recent legal decisions and research from management and social psychology support these protocols.

Health Care Manage Rev, 1987, 12(3), 75–82

It is becoming clear that hospital management is liable for all professional activity that takes place under its jurisdiction. Yet, few hospitals can afford the time and resources needed to gain commitment and compliance from the disruptive professional or egregious coalition. In this era of rapid change and competitive forces hospital leaders need to make timely decisions establishing protocols based on recent legal decisions[1] as well as sound management principles.

The focus of this article is on the development of organizational commitment to norms and the application of disciplinary policies and procedures in hospitals and medical centers, consistent with recent legal decisions and social psychological research. In this article the term hospital management will be used to denote not only the chief executive officer and the administrative staff but also the medical staff leadership consisting of officers, department or service chiefs, and chairpersons of committees. The term, of course, also includes hospital boards of trustees and directors.

The emphasis of this article is on physicians and dentists. However, the term health care professional is more accurate because nurse practitioners, psychologists, podiatrists, and similar health care professionals other than physicians are subject to the same stresses and pressures and act out in the hospital environment; moreover, medical staff appointments and clinical privileges are being opened to a variety of health care professionals.

Sandra L. Gill, *M.A., is President, Performance Management Resources, Inc., a health care leadership development firm. She is a doctoral candidate at the Fielding Institute, Santa Barbara, California.*

Eric W. Springer, *Esq., is Principal in Horty, Springer and Mattern, P.C., a law firm in Pittsburgh, Pennsylvania, specializing in hospital and health care law.*

André L. Delbecq, *D.B.A., is Dean, Leavey School of Business and Administration, Santa Clara University, Santa Clara, California. Each of the authors is also a faculty member at the Estes Park Institute for Medical Staff Leadership.*

The authors thank Henry Casale, J.D., for his extensive and insightful legal research and editorial assistance on this article, and David Caldwell, Ph.D. and Kay Currey, M.A., for the helpful comments on an earlier version of this manuscript.

LEGAL AND MANAGERIAL PERSPECTIVES

No longer is professional conduct considered separate from the impact of one's behavior on others in the hospital environment. As Skillicorn has stated, "Behavioral incompetence can be as detrimental to patient care as professional incompetence."[2] Legal decisions have clearly established

> . . . that the hospital's legal responsibility for the quality of patient care embraces the quality of medical care as well, and that the hospital, therefore, has not only the right but the duty to establish and enforce standards of competence in physicians who practice in the hospital. The quality of care cannot be divorced from the hospital's environment in which it is provided and therefore the hospital must require that physicians, no less than hospital employees and visitors, meet reasonable standards of personal behavior in the hospital.[3]

Managerial and social psychological studies have also established the link between individual behavior and organizational circumstances and events.[4–6] Organizations are known to be powerful influences upon the behavior of new members, just as individual behavior of one member may impact on others in the same setting.[7] This article examines a series of managerial interventions that could precede if not preclude formal legal actions regarding the behavioral competence of health care practitioners. After summarizing some of the relevant research on such interventions, disciplinary guidelines in four hypothetical circumstances will be presented. While the guidelines are consistent with recent court decisions, it is recommended that hospital management develop and review with legal counsel its bylaws, policies, and procedures regarding the expected and approved behavior of health care practitioners. Indeed, the legal climate toward hospitals has shifted from total immunity from liability to one of almost strict liability for all tortious acts committed in hospitals.

DEVELOPING COMMITMENT

From a management perspective, health care organizations, like universities and law firms, have been identified as a special kind of entity, i.e., a "loosely-coupled" system.[8] The hospital is more often treated like a workshop rather than one's primary organization,[9] a view that weakens the influence of the hospital on health care practitioners.

Under these circumstances, the contemporary hospital leader needs to establish and employ the three key factors that build commitment to organizational goals and norms: volition, visibility, and irrevocability.[10]

First, opportunities for voluntary choice regarding organizational entry must be provided, i.e., once credentials and character have been determined to meet standards, the individual must perceive a sense of free choice to join the organization and behave in a compatible way.[11,12] Second, visible leadership and mentoring are important to provide ongoing reinforcement and illustration of voluntary, constructive organizational behavior.[13] Symbolic rewarding of individuals who meet the hospital's standards of excellence is one visible and dynamic way to increase others' sense of commitment to the organization.[14] Third, a system of conformance must be established to provide restraint against disruptive, noncompliant acts. The irrevocable consequences of failing to observe the established behavioral norms should be delineated in a clear code of conduct.[15] That this is a useful, even powerful, mechanism for hospital leadership is strongly supported by a growing body of legal decisions. Springer and Casale conclude that "the clear trend of the legal cases supports the view that a hospital may deny initial appointment, terminate an appointed practitioner or deny reappointment, solely on the basis that the practitioner's behavior is disruptive."[16] In this regard, a record of disruptive conduct is not different from a record of substandard clinical performance.[17]

Considering that commitment to the organization may be gained by allowing its members voluntary choice, by offering visible leadership, and by having a clear code of expected behavior, what can hospital management do if faced with instances of noncompliant behavior, evidencing lack of commitment to the organization's protocols and practices?

THE PSYCHOLOGY OF REWARDS AND PUNISHMENT

One of the consistent findings in social psychology over the past 20 years is that punishment, i.e., negative sanctions, compared to rewards and incentives as a primary mode of changing individual behavior, is rarely effective in the long run.[18] Individuals who perceive their leaders to be rewarding and capable of recognizing constructive behavior and commitment show a willingness to be influenced by the leader, express higher rates of attraction and commitment to the organization, engage in more self-motivated problem solving and constructive behavior, become more self-disciplined, and have less need for formal control because informal norms maintain the high rates of performance.[19] Contrast the findings regarding positive leadership with those that result when leaders take a problem-oriented focus, often the prevailing modus operandi in the clinical domain. At best, negative sanctions tend to cause a temporary lull in the punished behavior and may simply result in more covert acts, or in more egregious behavior that challenges the authority of the leader. The leader who uses recognition and incentives for the desired behavior will less often need to resort to negative sanctions, though such secondary intervention may sometimes be necessary.[20]

DIAGNOSTICS FOR DISCIPLINARY INTERVENTIONS

The leader who uses a positive incentive style of leadership may still need to consider disciplinary intervention and will need to be able to diagnose the appropriate response to the undesirable behavior.

Delbecq proposed a matrix for the analysis of appropriate managerial interventions in health care circumstances, along with specific intervention guidelines.[21] His model is augmented here to incorporate recent court decisions regarding disruptive health care practitioners (see Figure 1).

In the work place, individual behavior is a function of perceived role(s) and individual style or preference. Managerial intervention must consider not only the behavior but also the rights of the individual who may exhibit stylistic or idiosyncratic behaviors that do not affect his or her professional competence.[22] Thus, two diagnostic questions may be used to help select an appropriate intervention: (1) Is the (alleged) behavior role related, or is it a matter of personal style that does not inhibit the individual's professional competence; and (2) is the behavior observable, that is, can it be corroborated? In the Delbecq model, a corroborated behavior is deemed public and an allegation of behavior is called private, e.g., suggested through rumor or hearsay.

FIGURE 1

DELBECQ MATRIX FOR DISCIPLINARY INTERVENTIONS

Task Outcomes

Observability	Instrumental	Stylistic
Public	1 **Sanction** Discipline Steps	2 **Give Information**
Private	3 **Cite Norms** Obtain Data	4 **Avoid**

A second leadership act to promote the development of commitment and "fit" between individual values and organizational philosophy is the demonstration of visible, symbolic communication.[23] As symbolic communicators, health care leaders need to provide at every opportunity an articulation of the philosophy, vision, long- and short-term goals, and examples of desirable conduct and standards of excellence. This combination of explicit statements and symbolic action provides a benchmark for emerging leaders and other members to reinforce desired behavior patterns. Some examples of such hospital efforts include the clarification of organizational values; identification and reward of individuals who manifest these in their daily actions; and role clarification to develop a consistent management behavior pattern with the stated hospital philosophy.[24]

Finally, the leadership acts of solving problems, establishing priorities, adjusting to new circumstances around key projects, and linking priorities to organizational goals and norms remain effective strategies for developing organizational commitment to philosophy, inasmuch as they are used as arenas for discussion and clarification.

IRREVOCABILITY: THE LEGAL IMPERATIVE FOR ORGANIZATIONAL BEHAVIORAL COMPETENCE

While social psychological studies have demonstrated the importance of volition to organizational commitment, legal decisions have sounded a much greater note in the orchestration of behavioral competence among health care practitioners. Most of these cases have dealt with the disruptive person, i.e., the individual whose behavior interferes with what may

While social psychological studies have demonstrated the importance of volition to organizational commitment, legal decisions have sounded a much greater note in the orchestration of behavioral competence among health care practitioners.

otherwise be acceptable—if not superior—clinical competence. As noted by Springer and Casale, action may be taken against a practitioner solely on the basis that the practitioner's behavior is disruptive.[25] In this regard, a record of disruptive conduct is not different from a record of substandard clinical performance.[26] Thus, legal precedents support the managerial need for a clear code of professional conduct, for example, bylaws that include the specification of consequences for noncompliant behavior. Protocols for intervening in disciplinary circumstances are detailed in the second section of this article.

Three elements have been discussed as they relate to developing a leadership strategy for organizational commitment. First, opportunities for voluntary choice regarding organizational entry must be provided, that is, once credentials and character have been determined to meet standards, the individual must perceive a sense of free choice to join the organization and behave in a compatible way. Second, visible leadership and mentoring are important to provide ongoing reinforcement and illustration of voluntary, constructive, organizational behavior. Third, a system of compliance must be established to provide restraint against disruptive, noncompliant acts. Commitment to the organization depends on the presence of all three.

In the following section four specific protocols are presented for intervening in hypothetical yet conceptually distinct behavioral events. These guidelines are consistent with both social psychology and legal findings.

CASE STUDIES

Case number 1: "public" role-related behavioral infractions

When infractions of clearly role-related expectations are corroborated, the imposition of negative sanctions is a managerial imperative. Social psychological studies have demonstrated that a laissez faire style of leadership, in which normative and overt deviance is tolerated, contributes to an unproductive, neurotic organizational climate. When there is clear evidence that misconduct has occurred, sanctions are recommended as soon as possible after the event to optimize the corrective impact. Such interventions should be decisive, specific, and clear in terms of the consequences for the present misconduct and future consequences for any additional misconduct.

One approach is offered through the managerial method of "progressive discipline,"[27] which suggests that a verbal reprimand be followed by progressively more severe disciplinary actions (see boxed material).

Traditional Progressive Discipline Sequence

Assumptions

Review of organizational norms (formal, informal), policies, and procedures:

- upon interview
- upon employment
- after employment interim period

Actions taken upon "violation" of job-related behavior

1. Verbal reprimand, followed by
2. Written reprimand, followed by
3. Temporary discharge/pay penalty, followed by
4. Permanent discharge

This is not an easy decision to make, because the hospital is at risk whatever action it takes. If the hospital does nothing in the face of disruptive behavior, it contributes to a laissez faire atmosphere. If managerial action is taken, legal counteraction may be threatened or pursued. However, the courts have dealt with and upheld hospital intervention regarding a variety of disruptive behaviors in hospitals. Some are selected here to help illustrate this cell of the matrix in Figure 1, including: impertinent and inappropriate comments written (or "cute" illustrations drawn) in patient medical records or other official documents that impugn the quality of care in the hospital or attack particular practitioners, nurses, or hospital policy; sexual harassment of nurses, other hospital employees, or patients; refusal to accept medical staff assignment, or to participate in committee or departmental affairs on anything but one's own terms, or to do so in a disruptive manner; rude or abusive conduct to nurses or other hospital employees; threats and/or physical assaults on physicians, employees, or others on hospital property.[28]

It may be noted that the courts have upheld hospital decisions to act in three points in the cases of disruptive practitioners. First, a series of cases have established the right of the hospital to deny initial appointment to the medical staff on evidence of or reasonable doubts about an applicant's prior conduct. However, bylaw language should be clear on the issue of behavioral competence to defend against the inevitable suits that will emerge from denied applicants. Second, courts have upheld denial of reappointment of disruptive health care practitioners: "Every court which has reviewed a hospital's denial of reappointment due to the physician's disruptive behavior has found such misconduct to be a sufficient basis for the decision not to reappoint."[29]

When disruptive behavior occurs during the term of appointment, both wisdom and decisive action are required. A single episode of disruptive behavior, which taken alone might not appear to be sufficiently serious to warrant revocation of privileges, may actually be one in a series of similar episodes that render the practitioner's continued presence in the hospital intolerable. In fact, practitioners may well claim that the absence of previous intervention precludes the consideration of their history in current decisions. However, "no court has yet held, that by failing to take action at some particular point in a continuing course of disruptive conduct the hospital has, in effect, waived earlier incidents and is therefore foreclosed from considering them in revoking an appointment."[30]

What about the single episode of disruptive behavior—can summary suspension be invoked? The courts have held in support of suspension in single episodes of clinical misbehavior, but decisions are split regarding disruptive behavior. Presumably, disruptive behavior would have to be shown to impose a severe threat to patient safety or directly impair the orderly operation and management of the institution.

In summary, individual disruptive behavior that impairs the competence of the health care practitioner or burdens the effectiveness of others requires decisive disciplinary action. Such protocols should be clearly stated in the bylaws of the hospital and medical staff. Hospital management and medical staff leaders should be thoroughly coached and provided legal counsel in such events. While protocols may not, in fact, curb the disruptive behavior of the individual, they do protect the rights and responsibilities of the hospital to provide quality medical care free from either clinical or behavioral incompetence.

Case number 2: "private" role-related behavioral infractions

As noted, the hospital is at risk for all professional activity that takes place under its jurisdiction. While this risk may support hospital management's efforts to rid itself of disruptive practitioners, the nature of legal proceedings requires a full, often tedious and redundant development of evidence to support facts in the adversarial format of law. Thus, the managerial imperative to intervene on rumors of misconduct may be outweighed by the potential of a court battle for injunctive relief and money damages for wrongful charges. One result is a kind of institutional paralysis in all but the most exceptional cases. Maintaining fundamental due process considerations and a full and fair opportunity for allegedly disruptive practitioners to avoid onerous discrimination is as important in the management of discipline and sanctions as the appropriate imposition of disciplinary action.[31] Perhaps nowhere does the dilemma become as challenging as in this second circumstance, where a role-related allegation of misconduct is made, but not immediately corroborated. What protocol can hospital management follow in this risky circumstance?

Where an allegation of role-related behavior is made, but defies immediate corroboration, the leader is advised to take the earliest possible opportunity to restate institutional bylaws and policies that have allegedly been violated, along with the penalties for such behavior. In this fashion, information is communicated and the opportunity for volitional self-correction is provided. Of equal importance, restatement of policies reinforces the grounds for the work group to intervene with corrective action, in the event such an infraction is inadvertent.

If the severity of the allegation is great, such as a threat to patient safety or to other hospital practitioners and employees, an immediate investigation may be appropriate. If a reasonable doubt exists regarding an individual's competence, further actions may be taken, such as suspension. Of particular importance here is that no individual be subjected to unreasonable treatment or castigation, lest it create a witch-hunt atmosphere and consequent threat of wrongful charge litigation.

Case number 3: individual style versus conformance—respecting rights

Respecting the practitioner's due process rights is perhaps most clearly illustrated in this third circumstance, where the behavior at question is a matter of individual style that does not interfere with clinical or behavioral competence. However, what happens if it creates an irritation or wake of public interest with which hospital management would rather not have to deal?

Hospital management must respect the rights of practitioners who are "different" to the same extent that they invoke action in the midst of disruptive individuals.

Hospital management must respect the rights of practitioners who are "different" to the same extent that they invoke action in the midst of disruptive individuals. Expressing unorthodox opinions, displaying unusual tastes, or manifesting alternative life styles are often seductive areas of inappropriate—and risky—management intervention. While the board, medical staff, or hospital management may be in a majority whose preferences run counter to the life style in question, the hospital has a positive obligation to treat such practitioners with the same degree of tolerance and acceptance it affords others. So long as personal idiosyncrasies as expressed in word or deed do not affect the ability of others to do their jobs, nor impinge on others' rights to complete their business free of burdensome harassment, and the practitioner continues to perform well professionally, negative sanctions should not be involved.[32] What course of action is appropriate?

Such a circumstance requires a combination of mentoring and constructive feedback for the purpose of providing information and support to solicit the voluntary cooperation of the individual at issue. Delbecq and Ladbrooke have developed the theoretical rationale for this protocol elsewhere, so only the action steps will be summarized here.

First, in meeting with an individual whose preferences are different, a clear statement of the issue is required. This includes what is not at issue, that is to say, the individual's clinical or professional competence. In fact, a statement of his or her value to the organization is recommended to provide a testament to the true context of the meeting. Second, a specific behavioral description of the event should be made, for example, seemingly impatient or curt telephone manner, a pattern of interrupting coworkers or subordinates in meetings, a manner of making comments that seem cynical or particularly harsh. Along with this specific description of behaviors should follow a description of the impact of such conduct, for example, apparent anger, embarrassment, or pain, on the immediate and indirect participants in the situation. The unintended consequences of such conduct should be discussed, such as alienation and lack of cooperation from other members or groups in the organization. Finally, an opportunity for problem solving and follow-up support or coaching should be provided, should the individual express the desire for such assistance.

The purpose of such feedback is not to change behavior through coercive action; rather, it is to provide accurate, unambiguous information about the consequences such behavior has on the organization, and to provide an opportunity for the health care practitioners to engage in more compatible behaviors if the individual so chooses. Of utmost importance is the element of volition in this event, since the person at issue may well decide that the price of conformity is too great. At least he or she has an accurate account of the apparent impact the behavior in question has on others, and vice versa.

Case number 4: "private" behaviors—avoid interventions

Organizational leaders may well be tempted to intervene when coworkers and subordinates appear to be experiencing personal problems or when rumors imply that someone ought to be concerned. Common examples include marital difficulties, family distress, and age-related life transitions. Organizational leaders can ill afford the role confusion or ambiguity that may accompany such concerns.[34] As leadership interventions, such acts often contribute to the recipient's confusion about management's intent, credibility, or capacity to provide appropriate help. Furthermore, management assistance in such personal matters may confuse the role relationship should subsequent events require disciplinary action due to work-related problems resulting from these matters. While management may intend to be helpful and friendly, the cost to subsequent credibility and capacity to maintain appropriate role authority is often quite high. Instead, many hospitals provide professional staff, special programs, and counseling services that are usually better equipped to manage such potentially complex situations.

• • •

Court decisions have established that a hospital is at risk for all its professional acts, whether clinical or behavioral. Inappropriate action and failure to take appropriate action are both part of the complex context of risk affecting contemporary hospitals and medical centers.

This article has provided a brief review of social psychological research and legal precedents for an integrated managerial strategy that enhances organizational commitment and maintains appropriate standards for behavioral competence. Commitment derives from free choice and volition; visible examples of constructive role-related behaviors; and irrevocable parameters to competence, such as a compliance system of bylaws, policies, and procedures for the maintenance of quality care and an orderly institutional environment.

Four circumstances for managerial interventions were described, along with protocols for leadership actions that are consistent with recent court decisions. Beyond these guidelines, the development and review of corporate bylaws with adequate legal counsel are advocated to provide a bulwark against continuing legal involvement in health care organizational management.

Finally, it should be noted that a variety of leadership development strategies have already been established to augment these recommendations. Training in role clarification and negotiation; appraisal interviews; feedback and effective communications; and problem-solving techniques are already available for leaders.[35-39] Because turnover of departmental and medical staff officers, board members, and chief executive officers in hospitals and medical centers attenuates leadership and disciplinary continuity, it is suggested that these guidelines be supplemented with annual leadership development programs, which include a review of current and emerging legal and disciplinary issues affecting the hospital.

REFERENCES

1. Springer, E., and Casale, H. "Hospitals and the Disruptive Health Care Practitioner—Is Inability to Work With Others Enough to Warrant Exclusion?" *Duquesne Law Review* 24, no. 2 (1985): 377–423.
2. Skillicorn, S. "Peer Group Committee Tackles Physician Behavior Problems." *The Hospital Medical Staff* 10, no. 7 (1981): 2.
3. Horty, J. "The Disruptive Physician." *Hospital Law* 2 (December 1984): 1.
4. Reis, M. "Surprise and Sense Making: What Newcomers Experience in Entering Unfamiliar Organizational Settings." *Administrative Science Quarterly* 25, no. 2 (1980): 226–51.
5. Van Maanen, J., and Schein, E. "Toward a Theory of Organizational Socialization." In *Research in Organizational Behavior,* edited by B. Staw. Vol. 1. Greenwich, Conn.: Jai Press, 1979, pp. 209–64.
6. Van Maanen, J. "Breaking In: Socialization to Work." In *Handbook of Work, Organization and Society,* edited by R. Dubin. Chicago: Rand McNally, 1976, pp. 67–138.
7. Springer and Casale, "Hospitals and the Disruptive Health Care Practitioner."
8. Weick, K. "Management of Organizational Change among Loosely Coupled Elements." In *Change in Organizations,* edited by P. Goodman. San Francisco: Jossey-Bass, 1982, pp. 375–408.
9. Gallagher, T. "The Hospital: Is It a Place or a Thing?" *Health Care Management Review* 9, no. 1 (1984): 71–76.
10. Angle, J., and Perry, J. "An Empirical Assessment of Organizational Commitment and Organizational Effectiveness." *Administrative Science Quarterly* 26 (March 1981): 1–14.
11. Calder, B., and Staw, B. "Self-Perception of Intrinsic and Extrinsic Motivation." *Journal of Personality and Social Psychology* 31 (1975): 599–605.
12. Ross, M. "Salience of Reward and Intrinsic Motivation." *Journal of Personality and Social Psychology* 32 (1975): 245–54.
13. O'Reilly, C. "The Creation of Corporate Culture: Lessons from Cults and High Technology Firms." Paper presented at Santa Clara University Executive Seminar in Corporate Excellence, Santa Clara, California, February 1985.
14. Brozovich, J., and Shortell, S. "How to Create More

Humane and Productive Health Care Environments." *Health Care Management Review* 9, no. 4 (1984): 43–44.
15. Delbecq, A. "Influence of Professional Behavior: The Management of Norms and Behavior." In *The Physician in Management*, edited by R. Schenke. Tampa, Fla.: American Academy of Medical Directors, 1980, pp. 179–92.
16. Springer and Casale, "Hospitals and the Disruptive Health Care Practitioner."
17. Horty, "The Disruptive Physician."
18. Luthans, F., and Kreitner, R. *Organizational Behavior Modification*. Glenview, Ill.: Scott, Foresman, 1975.
19. Delbecq, "Influence of Professional Behavior."
20. Ibid.
21. Ibid.
22. Springer and Casale, "Hospitals and the Disruptive Health Care Practitioner."
23. O'Reilly, C., "The Creation of Corporate Culture."
24. Delbecq, "Influence of Professional Behavior."
25. Springer and Casale, "Hospitals and the Disruptive Health Care Practitioner."
26. Delbecq, "Influence of Professional Behavior."
27. Sartain, A., and Baker, A. *The Supervisor and the Job*. New York: McGraw-Hill, 1978.
28. Springer and Casale, "Hospitals and the Disruptive Health Care Practitioner."
29. Ibid.
30. Ibid.
31. Ibid.
32. Ibid.
33. Delbecq, A., and Ladbrooke, D."Administrative Feedback on Behavior of Subordinates." *Administration in Social Work* 3 (Summer 1979): 153–66.
34. Katz, D., and Kahn, R. *The Social Psychology of Organizations*. 2nd ed. New York: Wiley, 1966.
35. Harrison, R. "Role Negotiation: A Tough-Minded Approach to Team Development." In *The Social Technology of Organization Development*, edited by W. Burke and A. Hornstein. La Jolla, Calif.: University Associates, 1972, pp. 84–96.
36. Koontz, H. "Making Managerial Appraisal Effective." *California Management Review*, 15 (Winter 1972): 46–55.
37. Gordon, T. *Leader Effectiveness Training*. New York: Wyden Books, 1980.
38. Delbecq, A., Van de Ven, A., and Gustafson, D. *Group Techniques for Program Planning: A Guide to Nominal Group and Delphi Processes*. Middleton, Wis.: Green Briar Press, 1986.
39. Ulschak, R., Nathanson, L., and Gillan, P. *Small Group Problem Solving*. Reading, Mass.: Addison-Wesley, 1981.

The entrepreneurial physician

Richard L. Johnson

This article draws on the experience of interviews of hundreds of physicians in the last few years. Those at mid-career have deep concerns about what lies ahead for them. A character, Dr. Charles Evans, has been created to describe some of the major possibilities being thought about and explored by physicians who believe their profession is now changing in ways they never had anticipated.

Health Care Manage Rev, 1992, 17(1), 73–79

The last patient for the day had just left the office of Dr. Charlie Evans (a pseudonym), an internist with a primary care practice. Charlie sat back and glanced at the clock. It was 6:13 P.M. Thinking back over his afternoon in the office and the patients he had seen, he had a sense of satisfaction about their visits, with the exception of Mrs. Jones who had not had her lab work done that he previously ordered. Quickly, he jotted down a note to have Mrs. Taylor, his office manager, call to remind Mrs. Jones in the morning.

Looking down at his desk, he noticed the financial summary, a document routinely prepared each month, indicating the number of office visits, divided into new patients and return visits. Hospital visits were detailed separately. Each category had total dollars billed and a grand total of revenues for the month. In addition, the report listed the outstanding accounts receivable, as well as the cash received during the month. Glancing over the summary, he noted that the accounts receivable had lengthened by another two days and were now at 73 days. The receivables totaled $89,000, which he ruefully reminded himself were the highest they have ever been in his 23 years of practice. Picking up the calculator on his desk, he punched in $89,000 times 8 percent and then divided the result by 12 months. The number $593.33 popped up. He discovered he was losing in interest each month an amount nearly equal to his monthly rent.

Turning to the neatly piled stack of forms in his in-box, he began signing all of the insurance forms for patients who had been seen that afternoon. When completed, it was 6:35 P.M., and he considered whether or not to go by the hospital and check on Mr. Atwater before going home. Deciding this was not necessary, Charlie slouched down in his chair, stared out of the window, and decided to think about the future of his practice.

He realized that he did not like what was happening to medicine. Thinking back to when he was completing his residency training, he recalled he had not gone into medicine to deal with all of the side issues that now seem to require more and more of his time. Smiling to himself, he remembered when he had started into practice he had followed a simple rule—always do what is best for the patient. How unlike the way one has to practice today. This brought Mrs. Jones to mind and her failure in not

Richard L. Johnson is President and co-founder of TriBrook Group, Inc. He has served in various capacities during his health care career; Assistant Superintendent of The University of Chicago Hospitals, Associate Director of the Graduate Program in Hospital Administration, and Assistant Professor of the Graduate School of Business at the University of Chicago.

getting the necessary lab work. He appreciated that, while the lab report was desirable and might be useful, he was also motivated by a desire to develop a totally defensible medical record. Sadly, he recounted the time he had been sued six years ago. It had forever changed the way he practiced. Even though he had successfully defended himself in court, he now appreciated that he had to practice defensive medicine. He had learned this lesson the hard way. He wondered to himself what a waste it was to have to practice defensively, ordering more tests than medically necessary just to be able to justify objectively all clinical decisions. From experience, he knew he was ordering tests that were overkill, but he also knew it was the only way to protect himself in the event of a lawsuit.

Flipping through the pages of the *New England Journal of Medicine*, he skipped over an article on "Therapy For Epithelial Ovarian Cancer" and decided to read the one describing the coming implementation of the relative value scales by the Health Care Financing Administration. Finishing the article, he shook his head in anger. Not only was the paperwork increasing each year, but malpractice premiums had gone out of sight. Now, the federal government was going to redistribute physician payments for Medicare patients, which was nearing 55 percent of his patients. The Feds were claiming that family practitioners and internists would be winners even though the total dollars would not be reduced, merely reallocated from the surgeons. He recalled the bitter statement made by Ev Wesbury, the president of Memorial Hospital, who last month had commented that Medicare had never lived up to its commitments. Ev said that, each year, the Health Care Financing Administration had come up with a different reason for not doing what it was legislatively obligated to do. Charlie knew he would soon be facing the same problem, in spite of the statements to the contrary by federal officials. He concluded that medicine was no longer any fun, not like it had been when he had first entered practice. But what does the future hold in store?

Mentally, he reviewed his personal obligations that lay ahead. One son was in college and his daughter would be graduating from high school in two years and looking forward to attending an out-of-state private university where her boyfriend was now a freshman. These would be major outlays for the next several years. His house payments had reached the point where, in another 2 years, he could burn the mortgage, or if he had an exceptional year, he might even be able to pay it off at the end of this year. Looking around the office, he visualized only minimal expenditures that would be needed for office equipment. The computer on order might require additional software in the next couple of years, but that would not be a major cost.

But what would happen to his income? Walking over to the file cabinet, he opened the drawer marked "Financial Statements" and pulled out the last 10 years. Reaching into the top drawer of his desk, he took out a pad of paper and set up five columns and filled in the numbers for the last 10 years in practice (see Table 1).

Scanning the figures, he recognized that while the annual practice revenue had increased every year, the rate

TABLE 1

RESULTS OF LAST TEN YEARS IN PRACTICE

Year end	Annual practice revenue ($)	Office expenses ($)	Income ($)	Ratio of income to gross (%)
10	173.9	81.9	92.0	52.9
9	186.0	88.3	97.7	52.5
8	202.7	98.1	104.6	51.6
7	219.2	107.0	112.2	51.2
6	235.6	116.1	119.5	50.7
5	253.0	126.7	126.2	49.9
4	269.5	137.2	132.3	49.1
3	278.8	140.5	138.3	49.6
2	281.3	144.4	136.9	48.7
1	290.6	150.2	140.4	48.3

Looking ahead, he concluded that if he continued to practice in the same way in the years ahead, there would be only minimal increases in his income.

of increase had slowed down dramatically in the last three years, while at the same time, office expenses had continued to rise at about the same rate each year. As a result, his income, for all practical purposes, had leveled off. Looking ahead, he concluded that if he continued to practice in the same way in the years ahead, there would be only minimal increases in his income. This prospect was not appealing, yet he was unsure of his alternatives.

Picking up a copy of *Medical Economics* that was lying on his desk, he quickly thumbed the pages until his eye caught an advertisement for a Medical Director of a large eastern hospital. Perhaps this type of position was an alternative to his 70-hour work weeks; the never-ending telephone calls; and having to worry constantly about bringing in enough revenue to pay salaries, rent, utilities, and supplies each month. The treadmill never seemed to end. Nor was seeing patients providing the same sense of satisfaction that he had once felt. He realized he was making the same kinds of decisions and ordering tests he had done a thousand times before. Certainly, a medical directorship in a hospital would be a welcome relief—or would it?

His thoughts turned to Bob Long, the Medical Director at Memorial Hospital. He had known Bob for the last 10 years. The first 3 years, Bob had been in private practice in the next office before moving into the hospital position. Thinking about his role since joining the administrative staff, Charlie concluded that most of the members of the medical staff now saw Bob in a different perspective. Before becoming Medical Director, physicians held a high regard for Bob's clinical skills. He seemed to have an uncanny knack for diagnosing patients with puzzling symptoms. But since becoming Medical Director, fewer and fewer medical staff members sought out his opinion. Instead, they now viewed him as an honest, hard-working person, likeable to deal with, but one who seemed preoccupied with matters that are only of peripheral interest to attending physicians. As a result, he was no longer a member of the informal inner circle of physicians at the hospital. While this did not appear to bother him, Charlie realized that with his own personality he would find it difficult to accept this role. Furthermore, being his own boss and not having to march to someone else's drum beat was important to him. He doubted that after 23 years, he would be able to take his marching orders from anyone else, let alone someone in management at the hospital.

Having decided he was probably not cut out to be a Medical Director, he turned to wondering what he would do if he ever left medicine as a career. For starters, he knew he would not want to be employed, rather he would want his own business. However, his dedication to medicine left him feeling inadequately prepared for the business world. If he was serious, should he obtain an M.B.A. and, if he decided to follow this course, should he do it on a full-time or part-time basis? If he elected full-time, he knew he could complete the program in one year and nine months, but if part-time, it would probably take four years and by then he would be 56 years of age, hardly a time to be taking a risk-filled leap into the business world. If he failed, he would wipe out the savings he had accumulated for his retirement at a time when he would have relatively few years to recoup the losses.

On the other hand, if he decided to forego an M.B.A., how should he proceed? As a physician, he was accustomed to long hours and responsibility, but was this enough for what was required? If so, what type of business should he buy? A retail store? A franchise of a fast food chain? An automobile dealership? Start up a real estate firm? Buy a seat on an exchange? Farming? Own and operate a resort motel? A bed and breakfast? None of these seemed out of the question, but all would require hands-on management, dealing with employees and all of their problems, plus customers who from time to time could be quite unreasonable. Did he really want to trade his existing problems for new problems, which might turn out to be old problems with new faces?

Or perhaps none of these were viable. He did not even know how to find out about investment opportunities for buying a business. Mentally, he made a note to talk with his next door neighbor, Elliot Root (a pseudonym). As a stockbroker, he always seemed to have a wealth of information about the business world.

Having decided that being a Medical Director or buying a business were not high on his list, he began thinking about joint ventures. He had overheard some of his friends on the medical staff discuss this subject in the doctors' lounge at the hospital. Just three weeks ago, he overheard three of the busiest surgeons and an ophthalmologist talking about building an ambulatory surgery center across the street from the hospital. They had been saying that they were sure they could get 90 percent financing at the local bank on very favorable terms. The ophthalmologist had been urging the others to get at least 10 surgeons to put up $25,000 each. One of the surgeons had commented that it would be easy to convince the bank officers that the project was solid, because previously he had informal discussions with the president of the bank. Another surgeon indicated that he had been looking over Memorial Hospital's operating room schedule and had figured they could shift between 35 percent and 45 percent of the hospital cases to this proposed facility. He further commented that, if they could shift at least 40 percent of all outpatient cases, the center would be profitable in the first year. The 10 investors would have their original investments returned in two years, and from that point on the center would provide positive cash flow to each of them.

Charlie, upon overhearing the conversation, had begun to wonder about the types of joint ventures that internists like himself might be able to undertake. Staring at the sheet of paper with the last 10 years' financial results on it, he concluded that this was an avenue worthy of exploration. Pulling out another piece of paper, he began a list:

Possible Joint Ventures

- Stress Lab
- Executive Physical Exam Program
- Industrial Medicine Program
- G.I. Lab (Hospital as a Partner)
- Pharmacy
- Cath Lab
- Medical Office Building

Looking for other possibilities, he began to appreciate the limited opportunities that really exist for family practitioners or internists. While he might establish an Executive Physical Program or an Industrial Medicine Program, the chances of either of them becoming a self-sustaining activity were slim to none, at best. The Cath Lab, G.I. Lab, and Stress Lab all required making deals with other physicians for their technical skills. By the time the excess revenues were split, the remainder would lead him to question whether or not it was worth the effort. As for a pharmacy, the larger supermarket chains all have pharmacies that dispense their drugs at prices a local, free-standing pharmacy has difficult in meeting. As for the Medical Office Building, Charlie asked himself if he really wanted to be a landlord. Erecting and operating a Medical Office Building would be a tremendous financial risk in the beginning, followed forever by complaints from the physician tenants. None of these ideas had much appeal. Were there other opportunities?

Getting up from his desk, he poured himself a cup of coffee. Sitting back down at his desk, it occurred to him that he might sell his practice. In the future, if his income was going to level, or even be reduced, then it might be wise to sell out now and work for a salary, or a percentage of the billings he would generate.

Picking up his financial statement, he saw that the figure for the last year's gross revenue was $290,600. Using his calculator, he punched in 8.0 percent. The result was $23,248. Obviously, he could not sell a practice for one year's billings and live off of the interest it would produce. However, if he sold the practice for three years' billings, the result would be a sale of $871,800. Taking out 33 percent for capital gains, the net amount would be $584,106. At 8 percent, the annual interest would be $46,728. By working for a corporation or hospital at $100,000 per year, together with the fringe benefits that would come with the position, a comfortable living would be possible while still having $584,000 in the bank. In addition, the financial worries would be on someone else's shoulders. With any kind of appropriate schedule, Charlie thought that he might be able to have a more normal work day, like 9 to 5, and no weekend duty, or only one weekend of duty each month. Such a position might be very attractive, he thought.

Tying both events together, he began to think about a plan for selling his practice and finding a position. While he did not know much about it, he had heard that some hospitals were purchasing the practices of some physicians, particularly those in primary care specialties. On the bottom of the page with the financial information on it, he wrote—"Talk to Ev Wesbury about buying my practice." He thought to himself that he could spend the next several years seeing patients for the hospital and not be too unhappy about it as long as he could concentrate on seeing patients and not be concerned with the business aspects of practice.

Taking another look at his watch, he realized that he should be on his way home but decided he still had an unresolved issue that he wanted to mull over. From time to time during the past year, he had been concerned about managed care. In some respects, he resented the public's growing acceptance of the concept. On other occasions, he recognized why it was so attractive to the public. In his own practice, he had signed up two years ago with two managed care plans, but lately had been flirting with the idea of terminating the contracts. He thought it would be a good idea to have some firsthand experience with managed care but now came to the conclusion that it was time to evaluate what had transpired over the last two years and how he will now choose to deal with managed care in the future.

Looking back on those past two years, Charlie knew he resented a third party being in a position of second-guessing his clinical decisions, even though it had not actually interfered with any aspect of his practice. What bothered him most was that he had to consider not only what should be done clinically, but also at the same time he had to think about the cost of his clinical decisions. In a way, he regarded managed care as compromising his professional judgment as a physician. It bothered him that someone could look over his clinical shoulder as if he lacked a real concern about his patients' welfare. He knew he cared about his patients—that's what being a physician is all about. He had to admit, however, that for a typical office visit from a managed care patient, the paperwork was no problem; no insurance forms to complete, no coinsurance or deductibles to figure out, just record the visit in the patient's medical record and have it logged in at the front desk.

In a way, he regarded managed care as compromising his professional judgment as a physician.

Being curious about the number of managed care patients he had seen in his office, he went back to the file cabinet and pulled out the monthly summary report on patient visits by third-party payors (see Table 2).

These numbers surprised him, particularly the totals for years one and two. When compared, they indicated he had over three times as many patient visits in the second year as in the first. He had not realized this growth had occurred because he could not recall ever seeing more than two or three managed care patients on any one day in the office.

Spotting a report on his desk dealing with managed care, he noted that the number of enrollees had grown steadily over the past decade and now stood at about 40 million people, or 16 percent of the population. This report forecasted an enrollment of 85 million people, or 32 percent of the population by 2000, slightly more than double the present enrollment. Whereas it was still only a minor part of his own practice, he appreciated that it could very well represent half of his patients at some point in the future.

Another table in that same managed care publication reported on the number of member enrollments in each of the three major carriers in the local area. As of last month the report showed:

Plan A	46,550
Plan B	72,641
Plan C	69,743
Total	188,934

The total enrollment was almost 20 percent of the metropolitan area, up from 10 percent just three years ago. Making a quick calculation, he saw that enrollment was likely to be over 300,000 by the late 1990s, clearly a trend that cannot be ignored. As an internist, Charlie recognized this trend as a growth market, which means that fee-for-service will decline. From what he could tell, the growth in managed care would have to be at the expense of fee-for-service. He had discovered another reason for concern about the future of his practice.

He then pondered the ethics of being a physician under the managed care umbrella. To be a participating physician, he had to make economic decisions that must be balanced against the clinical interests of each patient. While this would continue to bother him, he concluded that he probably could learn to live with this reality, pro-

TABLE 2

MANAGED CARE OFFICE VISITS FOR LAST TWO YEARS

	Months												
	J	F	M	A	M	J	J	A	S	O	N	D	Total
Year 1	2	5	4	7	6	8	0	11	6	15	7	10	81
Year 2	16	13	19	24	18	17	26	21	29	33	28	31	275

vided he never had to put a patient in jeopardy—an unlikely occurrence. On the other hand, it was true that fee-for-service had its problems. In his years in practice, he had seen some of his colleagues take economic advantage of patients under fee-for-service. Each system of payment had its drawbacks; what was fundamentally important was the integrity of the individuals using either system.

Aware that he might have to modify some of his attitudes toward managed care, he wondered if he should just let that aspect of his practice grow naturally, or whether he should actively seek more managed care patients. To date, he had not sought managed care contracts and had signed two of them only because their representatives had made appointments, come to his office, and explained their programs. He had been interested in what they had to say, but he remembered thinking at the time that these plans would not be around for very long. Well, he certainly had been wrong on that score. Not only were they around, but they were also growing.

If he had to get more involved with managed care, Charlie thought he should visit the three plan offices and talk to them in greater detail. Based on his present understanding, he considered a managed care case load of 900 to 1,000 patients would not be too much of a strain on him or his staff. Depending upon the average number of office visits for each patient, 1,000 patients would make up between 30 percent to 40 percent of his practice. By using his office nurse to a greater extent, he believed he could hold his average time with each patient to 15 minutes. On a capitated basis, 1,000 patients would produce a monthly revenue of $12,500, at $12.50 per member, or an annual revenue of $150,000. This amount would be assured. In addition, another $12.50 per member month would go into the specialist pool for his referrals to them. He could receive a bonus if he was judicious in referring his managed care patients to specialists.

Thinking about referrals, he went to Mrs. Taylor's desk and found the lists of approved specialists for the two managed care programs with which he was affiliated. Running down the lists, he noted that several of his friends, to whom he typically referred patients, were on the approved list, but some others were not. Recalling the way the two plans were supposed to work, he realized that he had never received a bonus check from the specialist pool. Frankly, he had never taken the trouble to find out what specialists were permitted to charge by their contracts with the plans; he had just assumed it was none of his business. He made a note to ask about the specialist fee schedule when he visited the managed care plan offices. If he could control specialist referrals more closely, he might be able to get an additional 10 percent bonus, adding an additional $15,000 to his revenues.

Likewise, he suddenly realized that he had never received a bonus check from either of the managed care plans for making judicious use of hospital days for his patients. Once again, he knew he had not paid attention to the per diem rates called for in the managed care contracts with hospitals. While he routinely used Memorial Hospital because of its convenient location to both home and office, he also had privileges at St. Joseph's Hospital. He seldom used St. Joseph's because it was more distant, even though it was only 10 minutes extra in driving time. Looking at the per diem rates in the manual for the two hospitals, he noted that St. Joseph's per diem rate was $575 per day, while Memorial's rate was $712 per day. No wonder he had never been paid a bonus from the hospital pool. He was going to have to be more careful in the future. If he had 1,000 managed care patients, he might be able to earn a bonus of $15,000 to $20,000 per year from the hospital pool. From all three sources—capitation, specialist pool, and hospital pool—he could realize annual practice revenues of $180,000 to $185,000 per year, of which $150,000 would be assured. Each month, he would receive a check for $12,500. One check for that amount each month would make him breathe more easily financially. It would take a lot of worry off his mind about what the future held.

All of these ideas made Charlie wonder about managed care. Clearly, if he were to work closely with the plans, he would not be well regarded by his peers. But since his practice was in a primary field, as a general internist, he could not be hurt by referrals being cut off. Of course, there might be social pressure, but luckily many of his friends were non-M.D.'s. His wife insisted on having a wide assortment of friends that crossed many career fields.

If he was really serious about managed care, what could he make happen over the next three or four years?

Then, the thought crossed his mind: if he was really serious about managed care, what could he make happen over the next three or four years? Immediately, he could see some possibilities that would never occur in his present practice. "Suppose I visit the largest managed care plan in the community, the one that is rapidly enrolling new subscribers, and ask them to see if I can be assigned 5,000 new enrollees who do not have a physician.

In the meantime, I can line up four primary care physicians, probably just completing their residencies, but interested in remaining in the community to practice. By offering them 1,000 patients each at a capitated rate of $9 per month per member, they immediately have guaranteed annual practice revenue of $108,000. Because I will have negotiated with the managed care plan for my present $12.50 rate per month, this will provide me with an additional revenue of $3.50 per month per member, or $54,000 per year. As an experienced clinician, I can then act as a resource for these physicians, provide quality assurance to the managed care plan, and carefully control the use of resources, preparing any reports that are required in my office. With four physicians, my annual revenue for providing my services to the managed care plan and to the four physicians will generate an additional $216,000, in addition to the $180,000 to $185,000 for the managed care patients I take care of in my own practice."

Turning to the specialist component, Charlie appreciated that, with 5,000 additional managed care patients, he could probably negotiate lower fees than were now being paid to specialists by the plan and might even be able to generate a year-end amount of 15 percent from the specialist pool through lower fees and controlled referrals to these specialists. Rather than the $15,000 he had previously thought might be generated by a 10 percent bonus, with the kind of leverage of having 5,000 patients under his wing, he might be able to realize a 15 percent bonus that would generate $22,500 per physician. For the four physicians, this would total $90,000 annually. If he split the amount 50/50 with the four, each would receive an additional $11,250, and he would have an additional revenue of $45,000 in his practice.

He then turned his attention to the possibilities for a bonus from the hospital pool. By careful screening, he might be able to generate a bonus that would average $20,000 per primary care physician. For four physicians, the total bonus from this source could easily reach $80,000. If he split the amount 50/50 with the other four physicians, his share would be $40,000.

In order to keep up with all of the reports and quality control monitoring activities that would have to be in place, it might require an additional two persons at a cost of about $80,000, annually. Adding up the pieces, Charlie wrote:

My Practice	
Managed Care Patients	$150,000
Specialist Pool Bonus	15,000
Hospital Pool Bonus	15,000
Management of Network Physicians	
Regular Care	216,000
Specialist Care Bonus	90,000
Hospital Bonus @$20,000	80,000
Subtotal	$566,000
Less Network Specialist Split	45,000
Less Network Hospital Split	40,000
Less Administrative Costs	80,000
Net Revenues	$401,000

Charlie whistled softly when he completed the written computation. Under such an arrangement, he would do far better than he had imagined possible. Furthermore, each of the four associated physicians would have annual practice revenues of

Managed Care Patients Capitation	$108,000
From Specialist Pool	11,250
From Hospital Pool	10,000
Total	$129,250

Deep in thought, Charlie got up slowly from his chair and methodically went through the office turning off lights. As he returned to his desk, he made a list:

- Continue Practice as Is
- Seek Medical Director Position
- Buy an Unrelated Business
- Develop Joint Venture
- Sell My Practice
- Become a Managed Care Entrepreneur

Glancing at his watch, he realized it was 7:45 P.M. He was not only late for dinner once again, but he was going to have to hurry because the Breightons (a pseudonym) were due at 8:30 P.M. for the monthly bridge game.

As he started up his car to go home, Charlie appreciated that the years ahead were going to be very different from the past ones. He had changed, the economics of medicine had changed, and he was going to have to adapt to the changing times. The question in his mind was not that he had to change, but what should be the direction of change he should choose. There were advantages and disadvantages to each of the six possible courses. Tomorrow, he would have to begin the process of sorting them out.

Pulling in the driveway, he braked to a stop at the garage, turned off the ignition, ran up the stairway to the back door, walked in, and said, "Sorry I'm late, but I've been thinking about our future. At breakfast tomorrow, I'll lay out my ideas and we can start evaluating them. We probably should make a decision within the next several weeks. Now, what's for dinner?"

Index

A

Academic medical centers, economic pressures on, 165-166
Access to care, in for-profit settings, 28
Acquisitions process
  case study methodology, 39-40
  and hospital-physician relations, 47-48
  implications for physicians, 37-38
  physician participation in, 40-42, 47-48
  physician satisfaction after, 44-47
  staff structure after, 42-44
  stages in, 38-39
  variations by hospital type, 41-42
Admissions
  data, and marketing to physicians, 126
  identifying physicians by percentage of, 49-51, 54
  related to physician appraisal of hospital, 50-55
  scheduling, and hospital-physician relations, 7
Audit and feedback program, physician-specific, 116-120
Autonomy/control issues
  in alternative care settings, 107-108
  challenges to medical profession, 105-108
  and cost of care, 95
  in defining professional status, 104-105
  in managing physicians, 76-79, 81, 83
  in medical teams, 144-145
  myths of, 85-87
  organizational models, 108-110
  physician concerns during acquisition, 41
  in physician job satisfaction, 137
  and physician training, 106
  and professional ethics, 107
  and state of medical science, 106-107

B

Board of directors. *See* Governing boards

C

Capitation, to reduce cost of care, 100
Case review, efficacy of, 87
Clinic management teams
  advantages of, 151-153
  development of, 155, 158-161
  future of, 162
  good qualities in, 161-162
  role in large teaching hospital, 153-154, 157
  structure of, 154-158, 162, 168-171
  See also Medical teams
Clinical Efficacy Assessment Project, 96

Compensation
  in HMOs, 97
  physician incentive programs, 22
  salaried physicians, 5, 9
Competition
  and antitrust implications, 6
  barriers to, 29
  and hospital-physician relations, 5-6, 8
  leadership response to, 196-197
  market conditions affecting, 4-5, 97
Consumers
  declining trust in medical profession, 106-107
  demographic changes in, 4
  hospital selection by, 49
  role in cost containment, 101
  role in professional bureaucracy, 78
Contracted/salaried physicians, 5, 9
Corporate culture
  conceptual evolution, 21-22
  physicians in, 21-22
Cost of care
  audit/feedback program to reduce, 117-120
  audited by diagnosis, 118
  computerized system for allocating, 116
  consumer role in, 101
  containment strategies in managed care settings, 96-98
  factors affecting, 94-96
  in for-profit settings, 28
  initial visit, 117
  organizational structure related to, 166-171
  as percentage of GNP, 165
  physician monitoring of, 7-8, 10, 20, 93-94, 95, 98-101, 115
  professional societies' efforts in containing, 96, 99
  public policy in containing, 101

D

Discharge abstracts, 122, 124-126
Discharge planning
  management review of, 172-173
  physician responsibility in, 7-8

E

Entrepreneurship in medicine, ethical issues, 107
Ethical issues
  in hospital-physician relations, 6-7
  in medical entrepreneurship, 107
  prospective payment and quality of care, 6
Ethics in Patient Referrals Act, 107

F

For-profit settings
  Institute of Medicine study on, 27-28
  physicians in, facing acquisition, 41
  theoretical modeling of, 31-34
  See also Freestanding ambulatory care centers; Managed care programs
Freestanding ambulatory care centers
  development of, 129, 136
  physican profile in, 131-133, 136
  physician satisfaction in, 133-138
  research in, 129-131

G

Governing boards, physicians on, 22, 45-46

H

Health Corporation of America, study of acquisitions process, 37-48
Health maintenance organizations (HMOs). *See* Managed care programs
Health Stop Medical Management, Inc., 130-138
Hospital-physician relations
  in acquisitions process, 38, 40-42, 44-48
  admissions scheduling in, 7
  autonomy/control models in, 108-110
  compensation issues, 22
  and competition, 5-6, 69
  establishing behavioral norms in, 210-212
  ethical issues in, 6-7
  exchange model in, 7
  factors in, ranked by physicians, 50-55
  hospital needs in, 7-8
  influencing physician cost containment, 98-101
  as joint venture, 10-11, 19, 71-73
  legal issues related to physician behavior, 211-215
  medical privileges in, 20
  and medical staff corporations, 71-73, 72
  myths of physician autonomy in, 85-87
  and organizational structure, 166-171
  physician expectations in, 8-10, 145
  in professional bureaucracy, 76-80, 86
  and reimbursement issues, 5
  strategy formulation in, 80-81
  suggestions for improving, 10-12, 19-20, 69-70
  traditional forms of, 3-4, 69, 70, 103-104
  trends affecting, 15-16, 69
  See also Freestanding ambulatory care centers; Joint ventures; Medical teams

I

Information management
  in decentralizing academic center, 168, 174
  of discharge abstracts, 122
  effect of reimbursement policy on, 166
  interpretation of data, 127
  manager skills in, 205
  physician practice patterns, 122-127
  physician-specific records, and cost of care, 116-120
  and public release, 122
Institute of Medicine, report on hospital economic structures, 27-28
Integrated Inpatient Management Model, 166-174

J

Job satisfaction, physician's
  autonomy and, 137
  method of assessing, 130-131
  in walk-in centers surveyed, 131-133
Joint ventures
  current state of, 70-71, 72
  future of, 72-73
  hospital-physician, 10-11, 19, 71-73
  new forms of, 97-98

L

Legal issues
  competition and hospital-physician relations, 6
  in data management, 122
  hospital liability for practitioner behavior, 210, 211-215
  hospital malpractice liability, 3-4
  minimizing hospital liability, 210
  and professional code of ethics, 107
  in residency schedules, 106
Licensing issues, 106

M

Managed care programs
  career opportunities in, 199
  director's responsibilities in, 199-200, 207-208
  future of hospitals in, 70
  growth of, 96, 199
  hospital-based, 86
  and hospital utilization, 96
  medical director qualifications, survey on, 200-208
  physician attitudes toward, 97-98
  and physician autonomy, 107-109
  physician status in, 96-97
  and successful cost containment, 96-98
Management issues
  allocating costs, 115, 189
  autonomous work groups concept, 83
  clinic management team authority, 155-156
  clinic management team structure, 168-171
  communication skills of leaders, 202-203
  cost containment in managed care settings, 96-98
  decision-making within economic model, 29-31, 33, 34
  developing physicians as managers, 81-83, 159, 185-189
  dysfunctional medical team, 176
  high-performance work habits, 195-197
  HMO director's skills, survey on, 200-208
  in hospital-physician joint ventures, 71-72
  in hospital-physician relations, 23, 89-90
  identifying skills, 82
  improving materiels management, 171-172
  interdepartmental work agreements, 171-173
  interpersonal skills of physicians, 144-145, 202-203
  in large teaching hospital, 153
  leadership styles, 193-195
  leadership traits, 192-193
  in managing professional bureaucracies, 76-80, 86, 206
  and myths of physician autonomy, 85-87
  needs in resource planning, 173-174
  physician manager characteristics, 187-188
  physician manager responsibilities, 188-189
  physicians on governing boards, 22
  progressive discipline method, 212-213
  rewards vs. punishments in behavior modification, 210-211
  role of HMO medical director, 199-200
  selecting a patient classification system, 88-89
  setting a code of conduct, 210
  training nurses as managers, 159-160
  training physicians as managers, 159-161, 187, 189
  utilization control, 87-88, 90
Marketing
  hospital help to physician in, 11-12
  physician role in, 3, 5-6, 79
  to physicians, and data management, 126
Materiel management, and inpatient unit-level management, 171-172
Medical equipment
  evaluating expenditures for, 23
  and hospital-physician relations, 8, 22-23, 45
  importance to physicians surveyed, 51-54
Medical staff corporations, 70-71, 72, 97

Medical staff hospital organization (MeSH). *See* Joint Ventures, new forms of
Medical teams
assessing effectiveness of, 178-179
decision-making in, 147-149
due process in, 145-146
organizational barriers to, 145
performance and outcome, 175
physician interaction in, 144-145
signs of poor functioning in, 176
structure of, 146-147, 168-171
team-building process for, 176-178, 180-181
See also Clinic management teams
Medical Treatment Effectiveness Program, 107
MEDISGRPS system, 89
Mortality data, 122
Multihospital systems, growth of, 37

N

Not-for-profit settings
physicians in, facing acquisition, 41-42
theoretical modeling of, 29-31, 34-35
vs. investor-owned hospitals, 34
Nurses
in clinic management teams, 156, 159-160, 170-171
in organizational structure, 167
relations with physicians, 4, 50, 51, 55, 203
resource management, 170-171

O

Organizational structure
autonomy/control models, 108-110
barriers to teamwork, 145
clinic management team in, 157-158, 162
of clinic management teams, 154-155, 159-161
following acquisition, 42-44
Health Corporation of America policy on physicians in, 45-46
for hospital-physician joint ventures, 71-72
inpatient management model, 166-171
Institute of Medicine report on, 27-28
interdepartmental work agreements in, 171-173
of large teaching hospital, 152
of medical teams, 146-148
performance in not-for-profit vs. investor-owned hospitals, 27-34
physician expectations of hospital's, 8
and physician satisfaction, 136-137, 138
physicians in, 75-76, 166-167
physicians in group practice, 96-97
in professional bureaucracy, 75-76, 86, 206
related to managerial success, 206
and staff commitment, 210
type of, and physician characteristics, 186-187

P

Patient classification systems
resource-based, 89
severity adjustment in, 88-89
Peer review, 77-78
in cost-containment efforts, 99
and physician autonomy, 109
Performance appraisal
of institutions, 122
of physicians as managers, 83, 186-189
and prospective payment, 5, 20
Physician hospital organization (PHO). *See* Joint Ventures, new forms of
Physician practice patterns, 122-127
Physician practice profile program, 116
Practice valuation
acquisition value in, 58
asset accumulation approach to, 59-60
discounted net flow approach to, 58-59
example of, 60-64
fair market value in, 57-58
market data comparable approach to, 59
objectives of, 57
Productivity
improving physician's, 81-82, 86
in managed care settings, 96-98
Program reduction, 7
Prospective payment programs
and equipment acquisition, 22-23
ethical considerations in, 6
and hospital-physician relations, 17-23
hospital responses to, 16-23
and medical staff privileges, 20
physicians and, 5
See also Reimbursement issues
Public relations
hospital goals in, 21
physicians role in, 4, 21

Q

Quality assurance, 87-88, 90
and severity adjustment systems, 88-89
Quality of care
in for-profit settings, 28
manager's concerns for, 204

and medical knowledge base, 106-107
physician views during acquisition process, 46-47
and prospective payment implications, 6
in transition to prospective payment system, 17-19
volume-outcome relationship, 126

R

Recruitment of medical staff, 43, 79-80, 126
Reimbursement issues
and capital equipment expenditures, 22-23
in cost of care, 96, 100
and duty to serve, 6
and hospital-physician relations, 5
and information management, 166
and physician autonomy, 108
in success of HMOs, 97
See also Prospective payment programs
Research
based on physician practice patterns, 126
investments, in for-profit settings, 28

S

Severity adjustment systems, 88-89

T

Tax Equity and Fiscal Responsibility Act of 1982, 5
Training
management skills, to nurses, 159-160
for managers, 205
of physicians, problems in, 106
of physicians as managers, 159-161, 187, 189
Turnover of staff, after acquisition, 42

U

Unions, physician, 108
Utilization review, 87-88, 90
provider specific system of, 116
and severity adjustment, 88-89

V

Valuation. *See* Practice valuation
Volume-outcome relationship, 126

W

Walk-in centers. *See* Freestanding ambulatory care centers

About the Editor

Montague Brown is a consultant and Director of Strategic Management Services, Inc. a national management consulting firm, with offices in Shawnee Mission, Kansas and Washington, D.C. Brown is Of Counsel with the law firm of Calligaro and Mutryn, Washington, D.C. and is also Editor of *Health Care Management Review.*

Dr. Brown's practice focuses on strategic issues and policies including mergers, vision and strategy, active aging, and building comprehensive vertically integrated systems of health service.

He has served as a hospital trustee and is currently on the boards of the Johnson County Foundation on Aging, the Consumer Health Information and Research Institute, and the Forum for Health Care Planning. He also serves as founding director of the Florida Foundation on Active Aging.

Dr. Brown's work in health care includes service with the New Jersey Hospital Association, Director of the Program and Associate Professor in the W.K. Kellogg School of Management, Northwestern University, and Professor, Department of Health Administration, Duke University. Dr. Brown also serves as adjunct professor, University of Kansas. He has held numerous voluntary positions over the years and has written many books, articles, and reports on issues dealing with the profession of health administration and ways of improving organizational performance.

Dr. Brown holds an AB and a MBA from the University of Chicago, a Doctor of Public Health (Dr PH) and a Juris Doctor (JD) from the University of North Carolina. He has lectured at dozens of universities and participated in international workshops in Canada, Austria, Germany, and England. He continues to lecture, write and participate actively in ongoing research and education programs.

9 780834 203006

Printed in Dunstable, United Kingdom

82623345R00141